A Brief Introduction to Psychology

McGraw-Hill Book Company

New York
St. Louis
San Francisco
Düsseldorf
Johannesburg
Kuala Lumpur
London
Mexico
Montreal
New Delhi
Panama
Rio de Janeiro
Singapore
Sydney
Toronto

Clifford T. Morgan

University of Texas, Austin

A Brief Introduction to Psychology

A Brief Introduction to Psychology

1 2 3 4 5 6 7 8 9 0   K P K P   7 9 8 7 6 5 4 3

This book was set in Baskerville by Black Dot, Inc. The editors were Walter Maytham, John Hendry, and David Dunham; the designer was Merrill Haber; and the production supervisor was Joe Campanella. The drawings were done by Vantage Art, Inc. The printer and binder was Kingsport Press, Inc.

Library of Congress Cataloging in Publication Data

Morgan, Clifford Thomas.
    A brief introduction to psychology.

    Includes bibliographies.
    1. Psychology. I. Title. [DNLM: 1. Psychology.
BF121 M847b 1973]
BF121.M588   150   73-14642
ISBN 0-07-043116-7

Contents

Part II
Individual Differences

Part III
Group Processes

Part IV
Biology of Behavior

Preface

This book, as its title indicates, is a short text for the first course in psychology. A short textbook can serve two purposes. It can provide all or most of the printed material for a course that is truly intended to be a survey and not go into the details covered in longer psychology texts. A short textbook can also be used to make room in a more intensive course for other study materials, such as a book of readings, which can give students a perspective that even the lengthiest textbook cannot provide.

Decisions about what to include are more difficult in a brief book than in a longer one. My main aim, however, has been to present an accurate picture of what psychologists know, as distinguished from what they think or how they work. Secondly, I have kept in mind the fact that most students who take the first course in psychology will not major in it. So I have tried to cover information that students can apply to their varying fields of interest and in their own lives. At the same time, the book contains enough material to provide a good foundation for students who take further courses in psychology.

To keep the study materials truly brief, no study guide or workbook accompanies this text (although an instructor's manual is available to teachers of the course). Instead, I have tried very hard to make the text as clear and as easy to study as possible. A glossary has also been included as a study aid, and learning objectives have been provided at the beginning of each chapter. These objectives should help the student shape his or her goals in studying each chapter.

Instructors who are familiar with behavioral objectives in education will see that these learning objectives are not, for the most part, stated formally in behavioral terms. I have used a more informal mode for several reasons.

Not all instructors are familiar with or committed to the behavioral-objectives approach. Nor are any two instructors likely to have the same criteria of what constitutes an adequate performance by the learner. Well-constructed behavioral objectives often take up a lot of space, and this is a short book. Finally, these learning objectives are intended to be suggestive only. That is, they are meant to help the reader's study, not to specify in detail what he should be able to do on a test or what he is "responsible for." If these informally stated learning objectives give the student some useful guidance in studying and reviewing the material, then they will have achieved their intended purpose. No grander claims are made for them.

As might be expected, this book resembles in outline and content the longer book by Richard A. King and myself. However, all the writing, with minor exceptions, is new. I felt that a brief book, to do the best possible job, should be expressly planned and written to present psychology clearly and succinctly. But since I have drawn on the work that Dr. King and I had previously done, Dr. King has also contributed to this book.

Others have contributed, too. Several reviewers went over my first drafts, and I have profited from their criticisms and suggestions. I am also grateful to the staff of the McGraw-Hill Book Company and in particular to John Hendry, Basic Book Editor. Credit to the many individuals and publishers who kindly permitted the use of their material is given on the pages where the material appears and in the References and Acknowledgments.

Clifford T. Morgan

1

Psychology as Science

LEARNING OBJECTIVES

Main objective

After studying this chapter, you should be able to distinguish between psychology, the natural sciences, the social sciences, and the behavioral sciences.

Other major objectives

You should also be able to

Name seven subfields of psychology and describe what they are concerned with.

Trace the origins of psychology from prescientific times to the modern period.

Describe the conditions for performing an experiment.

Other objectives

State three controversial issues that were debated during the period of the schools and "isms."

State the characteristics of modern psychology.

Explain how natural observation leads through systematic observation to the development of tests.

Describe clinical methods.

Define independent variable and dependent variable.

Define the significance of a difference and a correlation.

Distinguish between reliability and validity.

This book has two purposes. One is to give you a better understanding of people and of why they do what they do. A person cannot become an expert by taking a short course in psychology, but he can learn some of its rudiments and apply them in his own dealings with people in day-to-day life. The second purpose is to provide a better understanding of what psychology is and what it is not.

But first a word of warning. Because we have all been dealing with people from the day we were born, we are all amateur psychologists. We develop our conceptions of people and what makes them tick long before we take our first course in psychology. Some of these conceptions are wrong. Therefore you will probably have to do some unlearning as well as some learning. To help you, this book will sometimes point out common misconceptions. You can also help yourself by comparing what is said here with the ideas and opinions you have already formed about psychology and psychologists.

THE FIELD OF PSYCHOLOGY

Let us begin by looking at psychology as a field of study. First we will see how it is usually defined; then we will examine its major subfields and specialties.

Definition of Psychology

The definition that most psychologists accept is this: *Psychology is the science of human and animal behavior.* You may be surprised at the words science, animal, and behavior. Is psychology really a science? Why is it the study of behavior rather than the study of mind, thoughts, or feelings? What has animal behavior to do with psychology?

Let us see why each of these words is essential. We call psychology a *science* rather than an art because a science is a body of systematized knowledge, and modern psychology clearly possesses such a body of knowledge. This knowledge has been gained in the same way that other sciences develop their knowledge—by carefully observing and measuring events, often with the aid of specially designed experiments.

In contrast, an art is a skill or knack for doing something which is acquired by study, practice, and special experience. Skilled psychologists are certainly artists in that they learn for themselves how to do certain things well. But art in psychology, as in medicine or engineering, is best learned after the underlying science has been mastered. Besides that, the psychological arts, as they are practiced in such fields as salesmanship, psychotherapy, and politics, are still not very effective in solving our most serious human problems. On the other hand, the efforts of many research workers over the last century have given us a body of scientific knowledge which helps us understand behavior. That is why we say psychology is a science.

The word *behavior* is in our definition because we have learned in the course of psychological research that behavior is the only thing we can study. By behavior we mean generally the responses of a person or animal in a situation. These consist of any movements he makes that can be observed or recorded, including spoken or written verbal responses. On the physiological side, such responses include changes in heart rate, breathing rate, electrical conduction of the skin, and even blood composition. All these we can study objectively. But we cannot observe a mind, a thought, or a feeling. Although we do not doubt that they exist, we cannot get at them directly. All we know for sure is what a person does—that is, how he behaves. From his behavior we certainly infer a great deal about what goes on inside him. But all we can really study is that behavior.

Finally, consider the word *animal* in the definition. Strictly speaking, human beings are animals, but here we mean animals other than human beings. Psychology includes the study of animals in this sense for two reasons. One is that animal behavior is a legitimate field of inquiry, just as zoology is. A second and more important reason is that we really need to study animal behavior in order to understand human behavior. We cannot, for example, rear children in the dark to see how early visual experiences affect their perception of objects. Experimenters are quite limited in how they can use people as "guinea pigs." Hence much of what is known about people has actually come from studying animals.

This, of course, implies that men and animals are similar; and indeed they are in many respects. For example, psychologists are sure that the basic principles of learning apply rather well to both. Hence the frequent references to animals in this book are not "irrelevant." On the other hand, the capacity to talk or even to think like a human being is beyond the reach of animals. So there is a point at which the similarity breaks down. Psychologists are therefore cautious in applying their findings from animal studies to humans.

Behavioral Sciences

How does psychology, this science of human and animal behavior, relate to other sciences in the curriculum? The sciences are commonly divided into two groups: natural sciences and social sciences. Psychology does not fit neatly into either. Many aspects of psychology are concerned with social behavior and thus belong to the social sciences; yet much of the experimental work done by pscyhologists on animals is essentially biological and therefore a part of natural science.

Another way of grouping sciences that has become popular in recent years is to distinguish the natural sciences from the *behavioral sciences.* In the second category are all the fields that deal with human and animal behavior. Each behavioral science does this in a somewhat different way. Sociology and social anthropology are concerned with the behavior of organized groups of people. The sociologist typically studies modern, literate cultures, and the social anthropologist more primitive cultures. History may be classed as a behavioral science because it reconstructs the behavior of people in making history. Economics and political science are also included as behavioral sciences because they deal with men's economic and political behavior.

Thus the behavioral sciences include what are often called the social sciences. But they also cross over into the natural sciences. Zoologists, for example, have long been interested in the behavior as well as the structure of animals. In fact, ethology—a specialized branch of zoology—is concerned exclusively with the forms of behavior that characterize different species of animals. Many physiologists and physicists also become involved in the study of behavior. Some of the most distinguished work in vision and hearing, for example, has been done by physicists. Similarly, physiologists often study the senses or the brain in much the same way that some psychologists do.

It is difficult, then, to draw clear lines between the sciences that study behavior. Each of the modern behavioral sciences is quite diverse, overlapping one or more others. But psychology is one of the most diverse; it is a meeting ground for natural sciences such as physics and biology and for social sciences such as sociology, economics, and political science.

Subfields of Psychology

The diversity of psychology becomes apparent when one looks at its subfields or specialties. At least eleven can be distinguished. They are given in Table 1.1, which also shows the percentage of psychologists in each specialty and indicates the way they work—their primary activity.

Clinical psychology   Clinical psychology is the largest specialty. Of the 30,000-odd members of the American Psychological Association, about 29 percent were clinical psychologists in 1970. These specialists come closest to the layman's idea of the psychologist. They are "doctors" who diagnose emotional disorders and treat them by means of psychotherapy.

Many people are confused about the difference between a psychologist and a psychiatrist. Their confusion is understandable, because the two often do exactly the same thing—treat people with psychological problems. The only clear distinction between them is that the practicing clinical psychologist normally holds a Ph.D., whereas the psychiatrist is an M.D. This difference means that the psychologist lacks medical training and therefore is unable to prescribe medical treatment (drugs, surgery, and other forms of physical therapy). It also means that wherever there is the possibility of a medical disorder, a patient should be examined by a psychiatrist. On the other hand, when

TABLE 1.1
The major subfields, or specialties, of psychology and primary jobs of psychologists.

		% of total
Subfield:	Clinical	29
	Experimental	10
	Counseling	10
	Educational	10
	Industrial and personnel	7
	School	9
	Social	3
	Developmental	3
	Personality	2
	Psychometric	2
	Engineering	2
	Miscellaneous	11
Primary activity:	Teaching	23
	Clinical practice	15
	Administration	19
	Basic research	7
	Psychological testing	10
	Counseling practice	6
	Applied research	5
	Industrial consulting	2
	Clinical research	2
	Miscellaneous	10

Source: Based on Cates, 1970.

properly trained, the two are equally competent to provide psychotherapy. Another distinction, though a far from clear one, is that psychologists are usually better trained in doing research, and more psychologists are actively involved in research.

The layman also frequently confuses the psychologist and the psychoanalyst. Again the confusion is understandable, for both may practice psychotherapy according to the same principles. Most psychoanalysts and many psychoanalytically oriented psychologists rely heavily on free association and dream analysis (described in Chapter 11). These techniques, though somewhat modified in recent years, originated with Sigmund Freud. Freud was an M.D., and his ideas were first taken up by the medical profession. For that reason most practitioners who call themselves psychoanalysts hold the M.D., while those who go by the name "psychologist" have the Ph.D. There are also some people holding neither degree who have been trained in, and practice, psychoanalysis. These practitioners are called "lay analysts."

Relatively few clinical psychologists are in private practice. If, for example, you consult the yellow pages in any community, you will probably find that the number of psychiatrists listed far exceeds the number of psychologists. But the reverse is true in institutions such as state hospitals, veterans' hospitals, and community mental health centers. There, while psychiatrists are often in charge or available for prescribing medical treatment where necessary, the bulk of the professional work is done by clinical psychologists. In these institutions clinical psychologists also do most of the research.

Counseling psychology The counseling psychologist is a close cousin of the clinical psychologist. The difference between them is that the counseling psychologist works with milder emotional and personal problems. In this respect he often serves as a screen to separate people who need no more than wise counseling from those who need intensive attention. He also counsels people with vocational and academic problems, and in doing so may put a person through a battery of tests to assess his aptitudes, interests, and personality characteristics. But the counseling psychologist often practices psychotherapy as well.

Just because a person is called a counselor, it does not mean that he is a counseling psychologist. In fact, many of the people who work as counselors in schools and other institutions have had little or no training in counseling psychology. But if you go to the counseling center at your college or university, the chances are that you will be counseled by a person who has had formal training—including a Ph.D. and a year's internship—in counseling psychology.

School and educational psychology Counseling psychologists who test and guide individual students are generally called school psychologists. By using some combination of tests and interviews, they try to find out what the trouble is when a student seems to be having difficulty in school. After studying a case the school psychologist may recommend that a student with reading difficulties be assigned to a remedial reading class. On the other hand, a student with mild adjustment problems may be counseled by the school psychologist in a way that amounts to psychotherapy.

Educational psychology may include school psychology, but educational psychologists usually have other concerns. They are more interested in increasing the efficiency of learning in school through the application of psychological knowledge about learning and motivation. In this role, they are most often found as teachers and research workers in schools of education.

Personality and social psychology A relatively small specialty in psychology is personality psychology. Like the clinical psychologist, the personality psychologist is concerned with individual people, and both use tests extensively. But there the similarity ends. The clinical psychologist is interested in applications—in the *treatment* of *deviant* individuals; the personality psychologist is interested in *understanding* the *nondeviant*, or normal, case. As such he is most often found in teaching and research rather than in a clinic.

In a sense, every clinical psychologist is also a personality psychologist, for he cannot function without a *theory* of personality. In order to find a strategy for working with a patient, he must have a notion of how personalities are formed and how they can be altered. Hence different methods of psychotherapy have almost always been accompanied by a different theory of personality. An outstanding example is the work of Sigmund Freud, who is just as famous for his theory of personality as for his particular method of treatment, psychoanalysis.

Personality psychology is closely linked with another specialty, social psychology. This is because we are social animals, and our personalities develop through social influences. Social psychologists are especially interested in these social influences and how they work. They analyze the social interactions of people in various kinds of groups, large and small. They often make experimental studies, and in this role they are really a variety of experimental psychologist (a specialty that is discussed below). On the other hand, they often make practical measurements—say, of attitudes. For example, the Survey Research Center of the University of Michigan regularly turns out statistics on the buying intentions of consumers—statistics watched carefully by businessmen and politicians.

Developmental psychology   Developmental psychologists study changes in behavior that accompany changes in age, from conception to death. Since behavior and abilities change most rapidly during the early years, child psychology has traditionally received the most attention from developmental psychologists. But there is a growing interest in behavior changes at the other end of life—old age—and in the periods in between.

Developmental psychology has both pure and applied aspects. On the pure side, a great deal of research has been done on the development of thinking in children. Are systematic changes taking place in the nature of thought as a child grows older? In applied work, developmental psychologists are often concerned with disturbed children. The kinds of deviant behavior found in children are frequently quite different from those found in adults, and different methods are used to treat them.

Psychometric psychology   Table 1.1 indicates that psychometric psychology is one of the minor specialties, accounting for only 2 percent of all psychologists. But it is a pivotal specialty, for it serves many other fields.

The term *metric* comes from a Greek word that means "measure," and psychometric psychology is the science of psychological measurement. The psychometric psychologist develops new tests (measurements), evaluates the usefulness of existing tests, and devises statistical techniques for handling the data obtained from tests. Thus the psychometric psychologist provides the tools used by other psychologists in the applied fields of clinical, counseling, school, social, and industrial psychology.

Industrial applications   The world of work—industry, business, government—is the most recent field in which psychology has been applied. The first psychological instruments used in this setting were intelligence and aptitude tests, for they were the first kinds of measurements to do an effective job of selecting and placing personnel. They were initially developed on a major scale during World War I for the selection and placement of soldiers. At almost the same time, they were introduced into public schools for evaluating the learning ability of students. Shortly afterward, in the 1920s, they were adopted by industry to screen people for jobs.

Today, psychological applications to the world of work range far beyond the intelligence or aptitude test. Psychologists are involved in such things as vocational training, the supervision of personnel, the improvement of communications, counseling employees, and alleviating industrial strife. Usually they are employed as consultants and research workers who explore the best way to do these things. Then they train managers and labor leaders to do them.

The most recent application of psychology to industry, which began during World War II, is sometimes called human factors engineering or engineering psychology. Psychologists in this subfield try to design equipment, or instruct engineers to design equipment, that is as easy as possible for people to operate. Closely related is the design of *tasks* to help people perform them more easily, more efficiently, and more accurately. This kind of work was first done with military equipment—gun controls, airplane cockpits, information centers—but today it extends to a wide range of products such as stoves, refrigerators, cranes, printing presses, computer controls, and spacecraft interiors.

Experimental psychology   A sizable number of psychologists (about 10 percent) are engaged in work that has no direct practical application. They are interested in experimental psychology. This field is concerned with understanding the fundamental principles of behavior. The topics most often dealt with are sensation and perception, learning and memory, motivation and emotion, and the physiological basis of behavior. In recent years some experimental psychologists have also been working with social behavior, personality, and behavior disorders. But whatever their particular interests, experimental psychologists study the "fundamentals," not applications.

Although the work of experimental psychologists may appear to have little practical application at the time they do it, they are convinced, as most scientists are, that their work is useful in the long run. In fact, applied problems often cannot be solved without information previously developed by basic science (often called basic research). For example, the *Human Engineering Guide to Equipment Design* (1963), a book much used by engineers in designing equipment for human use, provides hundreds of tables and graphs about human perception and performance. Many if not most of these data were originally obtained in the laboratory with no practical application in mind.

THE ORIGINS OF PSYCHOLOGY

Here is a brief sketch of the history of psychology to broaden your understanding of what psychology is, what problems it grapples with, and what it does and does not know. The sketch will be divided into four historical periods that are fairly distinct even though they sometimes overlap.

Prescientific Psychology

Almost from the time man became man, he has been trying to be a psychologist. At least, he has had some kind of theory of human behavior. For centuries this theory took the form of a *dualism* or *spiritism.* He regarded the mind or soul—the distinction was never very clear—as something immaterial that usually inhabits the body in the waking state but can leave it in dreams or the afterlife. He believed that in cases of "possession," the body is inhabited by demons or evil spirits. This notion of an immaterial mind inhabiting a material body gave little hope of understanding man, for it begged the question. It simply explained behavior by blaming it on the unpredictable actions of a "man within a man."

This notion, of course, was just one part of man's prescientific conception of his universe. Not only was human behavior caused by spirits, but so were events in nature. Storms, fires, earthquakes, and the like were whipped up by the wrath of the gods or the devil. Good weather for growing crops, on the other hand, was the work of "happy" gods—often made happy by sacrifices or other offerings. Such a view of the universe could never produce any kind of science, psychology or otherwise.

What was needed for a science to emerge was a completely different view of things based on two related beliefs. One was the belief that the events of nature are orderly or lawful—that one event leads predictably to another. The second was that lawfulness can be discovered by some kind of observation. Thus careful observation of events can uncover orderly relations between them. This is the essence of all science.

Some progress in this direction was made by the ancient Greeks, but it was limited to physical things. The Greeks worked at developing mathematics, and also weights and measures. Putting the two together, they sometimes did what might be called an experiment—for example, Archimedes' experiment on the displacement of water—but mostly they depended on *natural observation* (discussed on page 19). This, the first and crudest of scientific methods, consists of observing events in a natural setting, without any manipulation of the events, while being careful to distinguish one's own feelings from purely objective details.

For centuries after the Greeks, as most students know, little happened in science until the Renaissance. Then the method of natural observation was rediscovered and put to work with profit. From it came such advances as Galileo's conception of the solar system, Newton's law of gravitation, and Leonardo da Vinci's principles of space perception. But great as these advances were, they were limited because the method of natural observation is limited. It only permits the scientist to observe the events and things that nature has provided for him. He may have to wait a long time for something to happen, and even when it does, it may be mixed up with unrelated events that make analysis of cause and effect difficult. Although natural observation had, and still does have, its place—astronomy, a science par excellence, is largely observational—what was needed for science to bloom on many fronts was a more powerful method.

Experimental Psychology
The more powerful method that was eventually discovered was the experimental method. It was a long time coming, however—to science in general and to psychology in particular. In the meantime the business of collecting natural observations and interpreting them was in the hands of philosophers. This may come as a surprise to students who do not think of the modern philosopher as a scientist. In the early days, philosophers were the custodians of science, or what there was of it. They distinguished three kinds of philosophy: (1) natural philosophy, which included what we call physics, chemistry, and the natural

sciences, (2) mental philosophy, which covered what is now psychology, and (3) moral philosophy, which considered many of the social problems that today are handled by the social sciences. Thus philosophy was the parent of our modern sciences—a fact still reflected in the awarding of the Ph.D. (Doctor of Philosophy) degree to advanced students in such diverse subjects as chemistry, psychology, and economics.

It was the discovery of the experimental method that caused the breakaway of science from philosophy. The important thing about this method is that it permits the scientist to make events happen when he needs them to happen and in a way that lets him see which ones are related and which are not. It is more productive than natural observation, for the scientist can work as fast as his time and facilities allow instead of waiting for things to happen on their own. It is also more efficient, because it selects just those things he wants to look at rather than those that nature may jumble together.

Roughly speaking, the experimental method took hold first in physics (1600s), then in chemistry (1700s), and much later in psychology (1800s). Its entry into psychology was heralded by a book written by Gustav Fechner (1801–1897) entitled *Elemente der Psychophysik* (1860). The book recounted many experiments in which sensory experience was measured. It also offered a law, still known as Fechner's law, that relates stimulus intensity to the intensity of experience. Several other books and treatises describing the results of experiments appeared in the following years. Then came the formal founding of a laboratory of experimental psychology at the University of Leipzig in 1879. Close on that, the first laboratory in the United States got under way at Johns Hopkins University in 1883. By 1900, psychology laboratories were flourishing at universities in both Europe and the United States.

Schools and "isms"

The experimental method in psychology will be taken up again later in this chapter. To continue with our brief history of psychology as science, the next period has sometimes been called the era of schools and "isms" because it was marked by sharply differing views of what experimental psychology should be. Mainly, they differed on three issues: (1) mind versus behavior, (2) field theory versus "atomism," and (3) nativism versus empiricism.

Mind versus behavior   The issue here was, What is the proper study of psychology? Wilhelm Wundt (1832–1920), the founder of the first laboratory of psychology (1879), led a school that came to be called *structuralism.* His answer to this question was "mind," probably because the structuralists, being the first to experiment rather than just to

Figure 1.1 *Some influential men in the development of psychology: Wilhelm Wundt, William James, Sigmund Freud, J. B. Watson. (Bettmann Archive, Photo World, Bettmann Archive, Underwood & Underwood.)*

observe, were still tainted with dualistic or spiritist thinking. They were also clearly influenced by the new chemistry, which had recently discovered that all chemical substances reduce to atoms. Drawing a parallel between mind and chemistry, they hoped to analyze mind into elements called sensations. Ultimately, they thought, a mental event could be broken down into sensations such as red, cold, sweet, or putrid.

In the hope of accomplishing this, they used a special method called *introspection.* A subject was trained to report his experience with a particular stimulus as objectively as possible, disregarding the meanings he had come to associate with it. He might, for example, be presented with a colored light, a tone, or an odor and be asked to describe it minutely. In this way, it was hoped, complex mental experiences could be constructed from elementary sensations.

In the early 1900s two groups of psychologists in the United States arose to dispute the structural approach. The first group, headed by William James (1842–1910) and John Dewey (1859–1952), called themselves *functionalists.* They were moderate in their claims. They said the proper study of psychology is *both* mind and behavior. More important, they said, it is not content that should be studied, but function: they wanted to know how mind and behavior function, not how these things are constructed. Beyond that, they wanted to know how mind and behavior function to *adapt* a person to live effectively in his environment.

The addition of "behavior" to the proper study of psychology was taken a step further by the *behaviorists* under John B. Watson (1878–1958). Watson said nobody can study mind because we cannot see it, feel it, or measure it. The only thing we can observe is behavior; hence behavior is the *only* legitimate subject of study. In taking this position he had a good point, and one which persuaded the majority of psychologists. Although no one today is as extreme as Watson, and we all would agree that mental events exist, most psychologists feel that behavior itself is important and that the only approach to mental events is through behavior.

Field theory versus atomism   Although structuralism and behaviorism were opposed on the issue of *what* to study, both schools assumed that the *way* to study psychological events was to break them down into elements or units. For structuralists, the unit was a sensation. For behaviorists, the unit was a conditioned reflex (Watson believed that man's behavior is a complex set of habits, in effect a "bundle of reflexes," which can be analyzed separately). The notion held by both structuralists and behaviorists that psychological events can be reduced to units was called elementalism or *atomism.*

Opposing this notion was another school of psychology known as gestalt psychology. The school flowered in Germany around 1912, but later in the twenties, largely because of the Nazi tyranny, its leaders migrated to the United States. Here it had considerable influence. Those who adopted the basic viewpoint of gestalt psychology without subscribing to all its early tenets have called themselves *field theorists.*

The difference between a field theorist and an atomist is this: the field theorist believes that the whole is more than the sum of its parts—a house is more than the building materials which went into it. Hence the whole cannot be dissected into its parts. The idea is conveyed by the German word *Gestalt,* which has no exact translation but means something like form, organization, or configuration. Thus gestaltists or field theorists argue that our experiences are patterns or organizations, somewhat analogous to a magnetic field, in which events in one part of the field influence events in another part. A gray piece of paper, for example, is gray only in relation to its background or to something with which it is compared. On a black background, it appears light; against a light background, it appears dark. A series of dots in an orderly arrangement is perceived as a pattern. When, for instance, you view a series of dots arranged in a circle, you perceive a circle, not merely some isolated dots. The dots are somehow organized in perception. This is what the field theorist means by organization.

They had a good point. Their argument holds pretty well for perception, especially visual perception, as we shall see in Chapter 8. Yet when the theory is carried over, say, to the learning of verbal materials, things are not so clear. Sometimes field theory best explains the data, but sometimes atomistic theory does. We are still in the process of finding out when each approach is best.

Nature versus nurture   A third issue that has been with us for a long time is the question of nature versus nurture. A century ago the terms used were nativism and empiricism. In any case, the problem is,

How much do inheritance and learning, respectively, contribute to human abilities and behavior?

The structuralists took no strong position on this issue, although they implied that the basic sensations are native (that is, are natural properties of a person's brain) and that complex mental events are put together from these through learning. The functionalists did not stress the issue either, but they were certainly more interested in what a person can learn than in what he inherits.

The field theorists and the behaviorists, however, staunchly opposed each other on the question of nature versus nurture. The gestaltists and field theorists felt that the organization of perception, and the rules governing it, are inherited properties of the brain. Moreover, they believed that little can be done to alter them by training. The behaviorists, on the other hand, left practically nothing to inheritance except some basic reflexes to be conditioned. They denied the existence of instinct or of inborn tendencies. To Watson, the archbehaviorist, almost all that a man becomes is a matter of conditioning his reflexes. One of Watson's most famous statements, in fact, was that he could take almost any infant and through training make him into a beggar, a lawyer, or any other kind of person.

American psychologists have been strongly attracted to Watson's point of view. Undoubtedly they have been influenced by the American dream of "rags to riches," the idea that anyone can "succeed" if he really tries. Today we know, however, that the scientific truth lies somewhere between the extremes of nature versus nurture. The question is not, Are any tendencies in behavior inherited? but, How do inherited tendencies interact with learned behavior? Similarly, there is a limit to what some individuals can learn, as can be seen in any case of mental retardation. Again, the question is not whether there is a limit, but what it is and what sets it in any particular case. Chapter 2 goes into this question in detail.

Psychoanalysis Standing apart from these controversies among the schools of psychology was a movement which many laymen think is part of psychology. This was psychoanalysis. It was not involved in the disputes because it did not belong to experimental psychology, nor indeed to psychology at all. Psychoanalysis developed in the medical profession, and it was based on clinical rather than experimental evidence. For this reason psychology and psychoanalysis were long separated by a gulf which only began to close in the late 1930s, after the controversies within psychology had largely died down. Since then, psychoanalysis has strongly influenced psychology, especially clinical psychology. So it now belongs in an account of the schools of psychology.

Psychoanalysis was founded and developed during the years 1885 to 1939 by Sigmund Freud (1856–1939). Before that, psychiatry as a medical specialty had an elaborate system of classification, but little in the way of treatment for patients. What treatment there was, Freud quickly found out when he entered psychiatric practice, usually did not work. So he started from scratch to try to understand, not to classify, his patients and to find an effective treatment for their troubles. His attempts to understand, based on years of observing patients, became a theory of personality; his efforts at treatment evolved the technique known as psychoanalysis, or more specifically, free association.

Both attempts by now have had a great impact on psychology. Freud's theory of personality was strongly nativistic: it attributed the basic motivations of people to inherited instinctual tendencies. Only by understanding humanity's instinctual strivings, he felt, can we start to comprehend a patient's trouble. On the other hand, he recognized the powerful role of social learning. Such learning, he observed, often represses or distorts the instinctual strivings, producing frustration and conflicts within a person. His descriptions of these conflicts and the habits people learn to deal with them are still about the best that are available. (This book relies on them heavily in Chapter 11 on adjustment and psychotherapy.) Freud's techniques of free association and dream analysis were designed to uncover the repressed conflicts as a step in getting the person to adopt better ways of dealing with them. His methods have strongly influenced psychologists—so much so that many clinical psychologists go through a "training analysis" in preparation for their practice, and many use psychoanalytic techniques in therapy. Since Freud's day other techniques of psychotherapy have been developed, some of them based directly on experimental psychology, others on non-Freudian theories of personality. But as we shall see, Freud's theories of both personality and treatment are still prominent in this field.

The Modern Period

By 1940 schools and "isms" in psychology were beginning to disappear, and today they are practically dead. Behaviorism had the greatest impact, for modern psychology is quite behavioristic. Yet many of the ideas of gestalt psychology and psychoanalysis have been absorbed into our way of thinking. We now recognize, for example, that gestalt-like principles of organization apply to complex perceptions (Chapter 8) and to memory for "meaningful" materials (Chapter 6). We have also found ways of fitting behavioristic learning theory to many of Freud's notions of personality and psychoanalysis (Dollard and Miller, 1950). Moreover, modern techniques of psychotherapy are blending Freudian methods with principles of behavior modification that have been taken over from the experimental psychology of learning (Bergin and Garfield, 1971).

The three issues discussed above—mind versus behavior, field theory versus atomism, and nature versus nurture—are no longer major issues, if they are issues at all. Our behavioristic thinking makes us agree that behavior is the proper subject of psychology. At the same time, we recognize that when we study behavior, we are getting at mental events. On the issue of field theory versus atomism, we conceive of simple conditioned responses in an atomistic way, but apply more complex principles of organization to many kinds of learning and perception. On the issue of nature versus nurture, psychologists generally lean toward nurture—that is, they tend to explain behavior largely in terms of learning. They recognize, however, that learning interacts with inherited potentials. Thus they see perception, intelligence, personality, and mental disorders as the result of an interaction of learning and inherited predispositions.

In short, psychology has become more or less unified. It does not have a "grand theory" of the sort found in physics and chemistry. It does, however, have a set of principles on which psychologists are largely agreed. Disagreements are more often at the level of minitheory than on the larger issues so prominent in the past. A minitheory is a theory to account for a very restricted set of events. For example, there are different theories for explaining how people learn nonsense syllables or how rats learn a maze. Such differences always exist in science. In fact, they often help researchers devise experiments through which science progresses.

THE METHODS OF PSYCHOLOGY

To round out your introduction to psychology, let us consider how psychologists do what they do, both in conducting research and in making practical applications of their knowledge. The methods used in psychology can be put into three categories: descriptive, experimental, and statistical. Of these, experimental methods are used mainly by the research worker whose purpose is generally to discover new knowledge. (Sometimes they can also be of help, however, in arriving at practical decisions.) Descriptive and statistical methods are used by either the research worker or the practitioner.

Descriptive Methods
Descriptive methods, as the term implies, provide a description of the thing being studied. In the case of psychology the "thing" is the behavior of a person or animal. The description may be a crude one,

perhaps just a few words that distinguish one bit of behavior from another; or it may be numerical, as when we assign an IQ score to a person; or it may be some combination of words and numbers. Following are a few examples.

Natural observation People have always been able to learn a great deal by natural observation. As we have seen, the ancient Greeks first employed it, and in doing so, they laid the groundwork for the various sciences. Although more precise methods have largely superseded the method of natural observation, it still has its uses in psychology and other sciences.

Some years ago, for example, a group of child psychologists wanted to make an intensive study of the behavior of a 7-year-old boy (Barker and Wright, 1951). Eight observers, working in shifts, watched and recorded everything the boy did in one day, from the time he got up at 7 o'clock in the morning until he went to bed at 8:30 that night. Their purpose was to obtain a detailed description of how a boy behaves at this age. The description was indeed detailed; it made a book of 435 pages. From this bit of naturalistic observation come ideas for further, more systematic research. (Of course, the boy knew he was being observed, and that knowledge may have changed his behavior somewhat, making it less "natural" than it would have been otherwise.)

Another example, this time from social psychology, is the study of a group of religious fanatics who believed that the world would come to an end on a certain day (Festinger et al., 1956). Two psychologists joined the group to see how the members would react when they found it had not. Their observations give some insight into the way people alter their beliefs to fit the facts—an insight that we shall consider in more detail later (page 291).

Systematic observation The method of natural observation is unsystematic in the sense that the observer simply records what he sees and hears without consciously selecting some events and ignoring others. That kind of observation is time consuming, as illustrated by the 435-page record of one day in the life of the 7-year-old. Often natural observation does not yield enough *useful* information to be worthwhile. Most of the time the psychologist is interested in the answer to some specific question, and he can answer the question by going about it in some systematic way. This method is known as systematic observation. Here is an example (Bennett and Cohen, 1959).

Two psychologists were interested in the question of whether men and women look at themselves differently, and if so, how. In psychological terminology, this is the question of how the self-concepts of men and women differ. To answer it, they gave a long list of adjectives to large groups of men and women, ranging in age from 15 to 64, and asked them to pick the words that they felt best described themselves. (This is a variety of the so-called adjective-checklist technique of self-rating.) The experimenters then grouped the adjectives into clusters of closely related characteristics. For instance, the adjectives "loving," "affectionate," and "tender" formed a cluster called *social warmth.* Next they looked at their data to see which clusters distinguished men and women. The results are shown in Table 1.2. There you will find many ways in which women and men see themselves differently.

The method of systematic observation is applicable to many practical problems: for example, the problems of studying public opinion and the factors influencing it, analyzing the effects of advertising on consumer purchases, predicting success in college, and even investigating such basic questions as the role of heredity and environment in the growth of intelligence.

Developing tests Systematic observation can be made more precise and even more systematic with *tests* and *scales.* These two words are used almost interchangeably by psychologists. Terms like *inventory,*

TABLE 1.2
An example of the method of systematic observation. The results of adjective self-ratings by the male and female subjects of this study indicate that there are marked differences between the sexes in self-concepts.

More characteristic of women	More characteristic of men
Social empathy (sympathetic understanding of others)	Social coarseness
	Social iniquity
Social warmth	Overt aggressiveness
Social unselfishness	Personal maturity
Social morality	Technological feelings
Social honesty	
Negligence	
Imprecision	
Impetuousness	
Personal fear	
Personal weakness	
Happiness	
Euphoria	
Covert (hidden) hostility	
Democratic feelings	
Domestic feelings	

Source: Based on data from Bennett and Cohen, 1959.

record, and *questionnaire* are also used. Whatever the word, they are talking about some instrument for measuring some aspect of a person's behavior: his abilities, aptitudes, interests, traits, opinions, or attitudes. They devise such an instrument—and thousands have been constructed—by going through some fairly standardized steps (more on these in Chapter 10). Once the final form of a test is decided on, norms are obtained by giving the test to a large, representative group of the kind of people for whom the test is intended. The Scholastic Aptitude Test, for example, has norms obtained from high school seniors. Thus a psychologist can tell how any particular score compares with those of high school seniors in general.

Clinical methods   As shown earlier in Table 1.1, clinical psychology is the largest specialty in psychology. It is called clinical psychology because it uses clinical methods. These combine all the descriptive methods mentioned above and use them for the purpose of solving someone's personal problem.

Perhaps little Alice is doing badly in school, and her parents bring her to the psychologist to find out why. Or little Basil is throwing temper tantrums, not eating his meals, crying all night, and generally making life miserable for his parents. Chumly, a high school boy with a fine record, is caught stealing nickels from the Sunday school collection plate. John, a strapping young man of 20, is depressed because he does not make the grades or have the friends his brother does. Or young Mr. Squabble, married for 5 years, is worried because he and his wife just cannot get along. The examples could go on endlessly. All are people with problems who come to the clinical psychologist for help.

Not all clinical problems require detailed study, but when they do, the psychologist does a number of things. He usually begins by getting a detailed account of the person's history and his family relations, commonly from interviews with the person and his associates—a sort of natural observation. Sometimes he has a social worker investigate the person's social background and environment—more natural observation.

Besides these observations, the psychologist may use tests of various kinds—an intelligence test, a reading test, an interest test, a test of emotional maturity, and so on—methods of systematic observation. From these tests and the biographical information, he tries to make a diagnosis of the problem—that is, tries to decide what specifically is wrong—and then takes steps to remedy it. The tests, the diagnosis, and the remedy vary with each individual. (Later, in Chapters 10 and 11, we will see in more detail just how they are used.)

Clinical methods are most valuable in the treatment of individual cases. But sometimes they also contribute indirectly to our basic knowledge when a clinician, working with individual cases, *observes* some factor that seems to be especially important. By observing patients, for example, Sigmund Freud discovered a number of devices that people use in attempting to cope with anxiety. His observations by themselves did not prove much, but they gave him "hunches" or hypotheses which other researchers later tested in experiments. It is in this way that clinical observations contribute the most to science. Although our knowledge would progress very slowly with them alone, without them we would never get the idea to do certain experiments. So, backed up by the experimental method, clinical observations are a great help to science.

Experimental Methods

As already pointed out, the experimental method has enabled science to take many giant leaps. The essence of the method is simple: The experimenter (1) changes or varies something, (2) keeps other conditions as constant as possible, and (3) looks for some effect of the changes or variations on the thing he is trying to study. Let us examine these features more closely.

Variables   The crux of an experiment is the use of two or more variables. A variable, as the name implies, is something that varies. Ideally it is something that can be quantitatively measured—that is, we can obtain precise scores for performance on each variable. The graph in Figure 1.2, for example, shows two variables. One is the average number of errors made by a blindfolded subject learning a finger maze. The other variable is the number of trials. You can see that the

Figure 1.2   A finger maze used for studying human learning, and a motor learning curve that plots the subject's average number of errors (dependent variable) against his number of trials (independent variable).

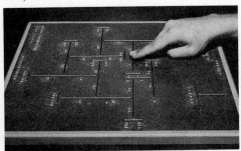
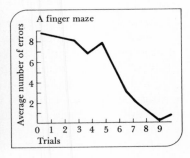

subject made fewer errors as the number of trials increased—forming a typical learning curve.

In another kind of experiment, the behavior of subjects was tested before and after they smoked marijuana (Weil et al., 1968). Two groups of subjects were employed: "naïve," or inexperienced, users, and experienced users. The experimenters compared the difference between subjects on their "before" and "after" behavior in certain tasks.

One of the tasks was a digit-symbol substitution test, a simple process of pairing numbers and symbols, as illustrated in Figure 1.3. Table 1.3 shows the average changes in the various groups' performance on that test 15 minutes after smoking the marijuana and 90 minutes after smoking it. As you can see in the table, subjects in a third group (called the control group) were not given the drug; they smoked cigarettes containing no marijuana. These no-drug subjects did slightly better on the test after smoking than they did before, probably because they were improving with practice.

The table shows that naïve subjects, on the other hand, did slightly worse after a low dose of marijuana, and much worse after a high dose. In contrast, chronic users (who were not given a low dose) did somewhat better after smoking than before.

In this experiment there were three variables. One was the measurement of performance in the digit-symbol test, a fairly precise variable. The second was a drug variable, which was fairly crude, consisting of three conditions: no drug, low dose, high dose. The third variable was also crude; it was a simple division of subjects into naïve and chronic users.

Variables fall into two classes: independent and dependent. An experiment must have at least on independent and one dependent variable. An *independent variable* is a variable that the experimenter selects and manipulates—for example, a drug (marijuana, in this case)

TABLE 1.3
Performance on the digit-symbol substitution test after smoking marijuana.

Dose	Naïve subjects, after smoking		Chronic users, after smoking	
	15 min.	90 min.	15 min.	90 min.
No drug	+0.9	+0.4	—	—
Low dose	−1.2	−2.6	—	—
High dose	−5.1	−3.9	+0.25	+2.8

Note: Scores are the average increase or decrease over the before-marijuana test scores on the digit-symbol test.
Source: Based on Weil et al., 1968.

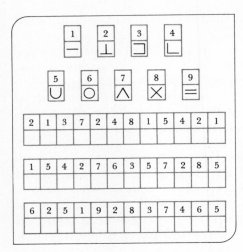

Figure 1.3 *A portion of the digit-symbol substitution test used in the experiment that studied the effects of marijuana on behavior. Subjects were allowed 90 seconds to fill in as many blanks as possible with the appropriate symbols from the key. Their performance on this task is shown in Table 1.2 (Weil et al., 1968, from* Psychopharmacologia, *1964.)*

that he administers. A *dependent variable* is the subject's behavior or report of his reactions—in the marijuana experiment, it was his scores on the digit-symbol test. An experimenter always selects the dependent variables he is interested in, but he does not set their values (for instance, he does not set the test scores). That is why the measurement of what the subject does is called the dependent variable.

An experiment may, and often does, employ more than one independent and more than one dependent variable. In the marijuana experiment, a second *independent* variable was the experience of the subject: whether he was naïve or a chronic user. In that experiment too, other tests were used to measure performance besides the digit-symbol test. These were additional *dependent* variables. Research workers usually employ several variables in order to get the fullest possible understanding of the roles played by the different variables.

When we put the results of an experiment into a graph, we must follow a rule: the horizontal axis (abscissa) depicts the independent variable, and the vertical axis (ordinate) the dependent variable. In Figure 1.2, for example, the horizontal axis (trials) is the independent variable, and the vertical axis (number of errors made) is the dependent variable. If you keep that rule in mind in looking at any of the graphs of experiments in this book or elsewhere, you can tell without further reading which is the independent and which the dependent variable.

Controls

An experiment, then, is not an experiment unless it has at least one independent and one dependent variable. But it is not a *good* experiment unless it has something else—controls. In fact, the main point of doing an experiment, rather than a descriptive study, is to control factors that otherwise would make it difficult to tell what is going on. Not only *can* we control these factors but we *must,* if we are to draw valid conclusions from the experiment. In deciding what to control, we try to anticipate anything that is even suspected of altering the effects of our independent variable. In general, three sorts of variables need to be controlled: conditions, groups, and experimenter effects.

To control conditions, we make the circumstances of an experiment the same for all subjects. Take the marijuana experiment, where the researchers wanted to measure the effects of a drug on a task. To control for conditions, they asked themselves what factors other than the drug could conceivably affect a person's performance on a task. Of course a long list immediately comes to mind: whether a person is rested or tired, whether he has previous experience with the task, how much time is allowed, whether the person is distracted by noise or is in a quiet environment, and so on. To control for such conditions, the experimenters made sure that all conditions were the same for all groups of subjects.

Another set of variables to control for is the characteristics of the groups. Age, for example, is a factor influencing drug effects. Size and weight of a subject also determine the effectiveness of a drug. Intelligence mightily affects performance on a digit-symbol substitution task—in fact, such a test is part of one of the major intelligence tests. And so on. To control for these factors, the experimenters might have carefully matched their groups in all respects—age, size, weight, intelligence—that could affect performance on the dependent variable, memory span. Another way of controlling for differences in groups is to use the *same* group for both conditions. And this is what the marijuana experimenters did, by giving each group the digit-symbol test before and after smoking marijuana.

Another general factor that must be controlled concerns the experimental situation itself. The attitude of the subjects toward the experiment may affect the results obtained from it. In one famous study, conducted in the Hawthorne plant of Western Electric, the company attempted to assess the effects of different working conditions, chiefly lighting, on the productivity of female employees (Roethlisberger and Dickson, 1939). At first it looked as though better lighting increased productivity; but when the lighting was made worse, production still went up. Something else had to be at work, and it turned out that the morale of the girls had improved when they realized that the company "cared." Their higher morale had then increased their production.

Another aspect of the experimental situation is the experimenter himself. The way he acts, the way he is perceived by the subject, and what he expects to happen in the experiment are all factors that can bias the outcome. If one of them does, it is called *experimenter effect* (Rosenthal, 1964). If an experimenter knows, say, that he is testing a drugged subject, and if he hopes to measure positive effects of the drug, he can influence the results he obtains. An honest experimenter will try not to, and honesty in experimentation is a must of science—but he may give cues *unintentionally.* The expression on his face or the tone of his voice may give away his disappointment or his satisfaction with how the subject is performing. Many subjects, wanting to please, or feeling rewarded or punished by the experimenter's actions, will perform accordingly.

To control for such cueing by the experimenter, we often have someone other than the experimenter assign subjects to groups. In this way the experimenter does not know which group the subject is in—for example, whether the subject has been given a drug or not. This is called a *blind* procedure. It is also desirable, if possible, for a subject not to know which group he is in—whether he received a drug or not. If neither the subject nor the experimenter knows which group he is in, the procedure is called *double blind.*

Experimental design   At this point it should be plain that doing a psychological experiment is no simple matter. It must be planned with great care to control for the various factors just mentioned. It must also be planned so that the scores or numbers obtained in the experiment can be statistically analyzed. This kind of planning is called *experimental design.* In itself it is a subject so large and complex that graduate students in psychology normally devote an entire course to it.

Statistical Methods

Most of the results we obtain in psychological research, whatever method is used, are in the form of numbers. But simply obtaining numbers does not make a science. We need to know what they mean and how to draw valid conclusions from them. For this purpose psychologists, often working with mathematical statisticians, have developed a number of statistical methods. These fall into two general categories: significance of differences and correlation.

Significance of differences   In the experiment on marijuana we saw that there were some differences between each of the groups and conditions. As shown in Table 1.3, the chronic users of the drug differed in their performance on the digit-symbol test from the naïve subjects. There were also differences between the conditions of no drug, low dose, and high dose. The differences make a certain amount of sense and thus seem believable. However, the fact that we obtain differences does not necessarily mean that there really *are* differences. To determine whether there are, we need to run a test on the significance of the differences.

The need for such a test stems from the fact that there are chance differences in scores—called sampling error. Our tests are never completely reliable; hence scores made by the same person on the same test can vary from time to time. Our controls are never perfect, so that two matched groups are never matched well enough to expect that they will give exactly the same scores. The net result is that we can expect chance variations in scores and therefore chance differences in the mean scores of the groups employed in experiments.

For any given experiment, however, the statistician can compute the amount of difference between groups that can be expected by chance. First he computes the variability of the scores in the different groups and then determines how likely it would be for the differences obtained to occur by chance. His result is stated as a probability (p) that the difference obtained is a chance difference. For a particular comparison between groups, he might compute a probability (say, a $p =$ .01) that the difference is a matter of chance. This means there is 1 chance in 100 that the difference is only a chance difference. Those are pretty good odds, so the experimenter concludes that the difference is *significant.* In practice, p values as poor as .05 (that is, 5 in 100) are usually accepted as significant. Differences with odds higher than that are said to be nonsignificant.

Correlation   Another statistical measure often computed from experimental data is a correlation coefficient. To obtain this, we must have two sets of scores on the same subjects (animals or people). As the term correlation implies, it refers to a co-relationship between two sets of scores. Does little Johnny, who has a high IQ, also score high in reading ability? Does little Jimmy, who is not so high in IQ, score lower on a test of reading ability? If so, there is a correlation (and in fact there is) between IQ and reading ability.

To obtain a correlation, we follow a statistical procedure that makes this kind of comparison for each pair of scores. We see how the standing of one score among its set of scores compares with its mate in the other set. If the correlation is perfect—that is, if the standing of one score is exactly the same as its mate, and this is true for all pairs of scores in the two sets—the correlation is 1. That is as high as a correlation can get. (Note that a correlation of -1 is also a perfect correlation, only it is negative. In a negative correlation, a high score in one set is accompanied by a low score in the other set, and vice versa.)

If, on the other hand, there is no correlation, the correlation is said to be 0. In this case the standing of a score in one set of scores tells us nothing about the standing of the other member of the pair. It can be anywhere in the set. Various degrees of correlation are expressed by numbers between 0 and 1 (see Figure 1.4). Hence a correlation of .8 or .9 is high, one of .4 to .6 moderate, and one of .2 or .3 low. However, exactly what is considered high, moderate, or low depends on what we are accustomed to obtain for a particular kind of experiment.

Correlations, like differences in averages, can occur by chance, for chance variations in scores can yield chance correlations. But statisticians have ways of computing what size of correlation can be expected to arise by chance in a given set of data. From this they can compute the significance of the correlation (a p value) in much the same way that they can tell the significance of a difference in averages.

If a correlation is not significant, it does not matter how large it is. In fact, if the number of scores we are dealing with is small, we can have a fairly large correlation, say of .50, arising by chance. Hence it is not significant. And if the p value is only .05, we have some certainty that the correlation is "for real," but little idea of how large it really is. When the significance level gets below .01, not only does our certainty go up, but we can start to say that a high correlation means that the two variables are highly related.

Reliability and validity   Correlations are used in another important way in psychology: to assess the usefulness of our measuring

Figure 1.4   A correlation plot showing different degrees of correlation. Each dot shows where a score stands on one measure (vertical axis) and where its corresponding score places on another measure (horizontal axis). As the plot comes closer to a straight line, the correlation approaches 1. The more the plot resembles a circle, the closer the correlation is to zero.

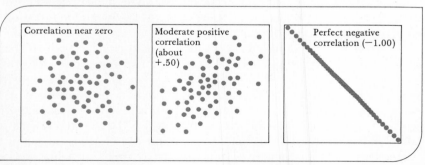

Correlation near zero

Moderate positive correlation (about +.50)

Perfect negative correlation (−1.00)

devices. Such an assessment involves first determining the reliability, then the validity of the device. Usually the device we are talking about is a test, but it can be any kind of measurement that psychologists make.

Reliability refers essentially to "repeatability." Leaving aside sampling error, if we gave the same test twice (or gave two different forms of it) to the same set of subjects, would we obtain the same scores? To get an answer to this, we do not in fact have to give the test twice. We merely need to split the test into two parts, obtain a score for each part, and correlate the two sets of scores. The resulting correlation coefficient is know as *split-half reliability.* If the correlation is high, we say that the test was high reliability. That is, it measures rather accurately whatever it is measuring. For tests of intelligence, for example, we obtain reliabilities in the neighborhood of .90, which means they are rather accurate as psychological tests go.

Validity refers to what the test is supposed to be measuring. We establish validity by correlating a test with some criterion that represents what we would like it to measure. The Scholastic Aptitude Test, for example, is supposed to measure aptitude for college-level study. Hence to obtain the validity of that test, it is correlated with how students actually perform in college.

The important point here is that tests are not necessarily valid just because we think they are, or think they ought to be. We must prove validity. And we do that by establishing a criterion or standard against which we correlate the test. Only when this correlation turns out to be significant and reasonably high can we say that it is valid.

SUMMARY

Psychology is the study of human and animal behavior. As such it is both a natural and a social science. It includes seven major subfields: clinical psychology, counseling psychology, school and educational psychology, personality and social psychology, psychometric psychology, and experimental psychology.

Psychology first began to be a science with the founding of experimental psychology in the 1880s. In the period that followed, three major issues were debated: (1) whether psychology should study mind or behavior, (2) whether field theory or an "atomic" theory was best for understanding behavior, and (3) the relative importance of nature and nurture—heredity versus environment. Psychoanalysis developed independently as a branch of psychiatry and only began to influence psychology in the 1930s.

Psychologists use three general methods. One is natural observation, which is made as systematic as possible by the development of psychological tests. Another is the experimental method, which permits independent and dependent variables to be controlled. The third uses statistical methods to state the central tendency and the variability of scores or test results. Statistical methods are also used to test the significance of differences obtained and to compute correlations between variables.

SUGGESTIONS FOR FURTHER READING

American Psychological Association. *A career in psychology.* Washington: American Psychological Association, 1972. (Paperback.) *A description of the major activities of psychologists and the training needed for psychology as a career.*

Baker, R. A. (Ed.) *Psychology in the wry.* New York: Van Nostrand, 1963. (Paperback.) *A collection of amusing and satirical articles about psychologists.*

Gardiner, W. L. *Psychology: A story of a search.* Monterey: Brooks/Cole, 1970. *A brief, interesting primer of psychology.*

King, R. A. (Ed.) *Readings for an introduction to psychology.* (3d ed.) New York: McGraw-Hill, 1971. (Paperback.) *A book of readings designed for the first course in psychology.*

Psychology Today. A monthly magazine containing popularly written articles on psychology.

Webb, W. E. B. (Ed.) *The profession of psychology.* New York: Holt, 1962. *Descriptions of the jobs psychologists do in various subfields.*

PART I

Basic Principles

Chapter 1 was a general introduction to the subject of psychology. Its various subfields were described, along with some of its history and its methods of gaining knowledge. The rest of the book is divided into four parts: I, Basic Principles; II, Individual Differences; III, Social Behavior; and IV, Physiological Background.

Part I, Basic Principles, describes the general principles and concepts necessary to understanding the behavior of people. The first chapter in this part, Chapter 2, deals with the problem of nature versus nurture introduced in Chapter 1. It shows that behavior is the result of an interaction between genetic and environmental influences. The other chapters in this part fall into three groups of two each. Chapters 3 and 4, the first pair, deal with the mainsprings of behavior, motivation, and emotion. Chapters 5 and 6 describe the ways in which behavior is learned. The last pair, Chapters 7 and 8, cover what some psychologists call "cognitive processes"—processes of thinking and of perceiving the world.

The principles described in this part apply generally to all people. Then, in Part II, we shall see how and why people differ from one another.

2

Behavioral Inheritance

LEARNING OBJECTIVES

Main objective

After studying this chapter, you should be able to explain how heredity and environment interact in producing behavioral abilities.

Other major objectives

You should also be able to

Distinguish species-specific inheritance from individual inheritance.

Indicate the relative contribution of heredity and learning in acquiring skills such as standing, walking, and climbing.

Describe the interaction of heredity and environment in the development of intelligence.

Other objectives

Describe how heredity and environment set limits for psychological development.

Define instinctive behavior and distinguish it from reflex behavior and learned behavior.

Indicate the role of the home and the rest of one's educational environment in the development of abilities.

Describe the effects of impoverished and enriched environments on behavioral abilities.

To what extent is our behavior—the things we do or can do—the outcome of our heredity, and to what extent is it the result of the environment in which we learn and develop? We know, of course, that both heredity and environment shape human skills and capacities; the problem is to find out how much each contributes.

The question is not just academic—it has been, and will continue to be, a practical one. How we answer it affects what we can expect of a retarded child, for example. It affects our view of the educational capacities of individuals. And it even affects our social decisions on such policies as head start programs or free lunches for school children.

INTERACTION OF HEREDITY AND ENVIRONMENT

To take an extreme position on the heredity-environment issue is clearly naïve and wrong. To say, as Watson did in 1925, that any child can be made into anything through conditioning is simply not so. To say that everything is heredity, as racists imply, is not true either. The correct view, as psychologists have now learned through much research, is to say that both heredity and environment shape an individual. And the relation between the two is one of *interaction.* The simplest way to comprehend such an interaction is to think of the two as multipliers. Heredity *times* environment produces an individual, both physically and psychologically. In this equation, zero heredity would not produce an individual, and neither would zero environment.

Setting Limits
A more precise way of understanding the interaction of heredity and environment is to think of each as setting a limit to what an individual can become. Without a good heredity, no environment, however ideal, can develop the individual beyond a certain mediocre point.

This fact is illustrated by familial mental retardation (page 225), which runs in families and has a genetic basis. Mentally retarded individuals can never reach a mental capacity that is normal, let alone superior. On the other hand, the same individuals also illustrate the role of environment. When they are committed to institutions and given little attention, they learn few skills. But when they are given special training designed to develop them to their hereditary limit, they are *educable* and can perform useful roles in society (Telford and Sawrey, 1967).

Both heredity and environment, then, set limits on the development of human capacities. Let us see more precisely how these limits are established. First we need to distinguish two kinds of environment: the physiological environment and the sensory environment.

Physiological Environment
The effect of environment does not begin just at the moment of birth; it starts influencing a person's development the moment he is conceived. From this point on through the period of pregnancy, he is in a fairly uniform *sensory* environment. The temperature is quite constant, and so are certain other features of the environment, including light

and sound. On the other hand, his *physiological* environment may or may not be uniform. And even if it is, it may not be normal. The new individual's blood, though not directly connected with his mother's blood, receives all its nutrients, as well as drugs and hormones, from the mother's blood. If the materials he receives from his mother are not normal, he will not be normal.

This physiological environment may be abnormal in several ways; two are known to be particularly important. One is nutrition. The body, especially the brain, needs normal nutrition in order to develop properly. If the mother's blood is deficient because of malnutrition, particularly because of lack of protein, the blood of the fetus will be similarly deficient. And this deficiency will retard the growth of the brain and limit later mental capacity. We know this from animal experiments in which mothers are kept on deficient diets and their offspring later tested for such abilities as maze learning. Exactly how *human* individuals are affected, and how many are, we do not yet know. But we certainly cannot consider individuals to have had an "equal chance" until such malnutrition is controlled.

Drugs in the blood of the mother may provide another kind of abnormal environment for the fetus. Many drug effects are subtle and not precisely known, but one very dramatic instance has made news in recent years. This is the drug thalidomide, a mild tranquilizer. When taken by the mother during pregnancy, it frequently causes badly deformed children. The drug's physiological effect on the fetus is sometimes so profound that it interferes with the genetic mechanisms which normally determine the shape of the body. Thus the physiological environment provided by the mother can be critical in the development of the fetus.

The effect of the physiological environment does not end at birth. It is important throughout the growth of the child, particularly during the first two or three years. The newborn infant, especially its brain, is far from mature. In fact, its cerebral cortex, which is crucial to its eventual mental capacity, is undeveloped. During the baby's growth following birth, nutrition continues to be important (Cabak and Najdanvic, 1965). Again, a sufficient supply of the proper proteins is essential. We know this from animal research, which has shown that protein deficiency in infancy retards learning ability. So an infant has not had an equal chance until it has had a normal diet through this period.

Sensory Environment

At birth the baby leaves a relatively constant sensory environment and emerges into an ever-changing one. William James has said that it must seem like a "blooming, buzzing, confusion" to the infant. But the amount and kind of sensory stimulation he receives varies a lot from one environment to another. In a large, poor family, a baby may be left in a dark corner with little sensory input. In a well-to-do family, he may be immediately showered with all sorts of attention and stimulation during his waking hours. In an environment that is "impoverished" in sensory stimulation, only his bodily needs may be attended to, and those not very well. But in an "enriched" environment, he may enjoy much attention from other people, be given many toys to play with, and be offered every chance to learn the differences between various objects as rapidly as possible.

Later this chapter will show how the improverishment or enrichment of the sensory environment makes a difference in the ability to learn and develop. For now, just remember the general point that physiological and sensory environments are important early in life, and that they interact with heredity.

Heredity

Heredity, as nearly everybody knows today, is controlled by the chromosomes and genes (page 42). It determines such simple physical characteristics as eye and hair color. In more complicated ways, it governs height and weight. And in still more subtle and complicated ways, it sets limits for many psychological characteristics. Heredity does its job by controlling the way bodily structures are formed. It determines not only the gross structure of the brain, but also biochemical events in the brain and elsewhere in the body.

Maturation

Heredity often takes a long time to work. Its role does not stop at birth; the effects of heredity keep appearing at various stages in life. For example, even eye color, which is surely hereditary, is not fixed at birth. Most infants are born with blue eyes, although some will become brown-eyed a few weeks later. And though the external sexual organs of a male may mark him as a boy at birth, the hormones that provide such adult male characteristics as a beard and a low voice do not begin to flow until puberty 12 or so years later. Even the person's life expectancy, and the likelihood of his dying of certain diseases, is partly inherited, as insurance actuaries know. These effects of heredity do not show themselves until many years later. The results of heredity, then, appear at different times throughout a person's life, from birth to death.

The physiological process through which heredity works after birth is know as *maturation.* During maturation changes take place in bodily structure, the glands, and the nervous system. But since the emergence of certain kinds of behavior hinges on this process, we can also think of the *maturation of behavior* which depends on, and reflects, physiological maturation.

Psychologists usually distinguish between innate and learned patterns of behavior. *Innate* means inborn, but it does not necessarily mean "present at birth." It merely means that the potentiality is present at birth and that the behavior will almost surely appear, given normal conditions, at some time in life. Thus the term innate covers both patterns present at birth and those that will appear under the influence of heredity at some time in the course of maturation.

To sum up, heredity and environment each sets a limit on the other for the making of an individual. The rest of this chapter goes into the details of the interaction. The next two sections put the emphasis on heredity, the last section on environment.

SPECIES INHERITANCE

Broadly speaking, there are two kinds of inheritance. One is *species-specific*; it characterizes all members of a species. Species-specific inheritance is what makes one species—horse, dog, cat, man—look and act differently from any other species. It is also what makes one species unable to interbreed with another. The other kind of inheritance is *individual* inheritance. This is what makes individuals within a species differ from each other in both appearance and behavior, leaving aside the influence of the environment. First let us consider the kinds of behavior that are typical of a particular species and are therefore part of the species-specific inheritance.

Instinctive Behavior
Probably no psychological terms have been so abused—especially by laymen—as the words *instinct* and *instinctive.* Used loosely and improperly they refer to any automatic reaction, that is, any reaction which is fairly predictable and is made without thinking. The trouble with this usage is that many kinds of automatic reactions are *learned* reactions. In fact, almost anything that a human being does automatically is learned. The father who "instinctively" leaps into the water to save his drowning child does it because he has learned many reactions for protecting his child from danger. Such loose references to the term instinctive mix up what is innate and what is learned.

Actually, "instinctive" should be applied only to inherited or innate behavior. Even here, it is easy to confuse different kinds of behavior that might better be separately labeled. One is the *reflex.* A reflex is a specific response elicited by a stimulus—the blink of an eye to a bright flash of light, or the kicking of the leg when the knee tendon is struck. A reflex is species-specific; we find different reflexes in different species, and all members of a species have the same reflexes. But a reflex is over soon after the stimulus stops. Not so with an instinctive reaction.

Instinctive behavior, in contrast to reflexes, involves the whole body, not just one part of it. In addition, in order to qualify as instinctive, a pattern of behavior should meet three criteria. (1) It should be so prevalent in a species that it is characteristic of the species. (2) The pattern should emerge full-blown without previous training, even if it is first seen some time after birth, as it often is. (3) It should be relatively constant in form, occurring in much the same way each time.

The most common examples of instinctive patterns meeting these criteria are found in sexual and maternal behavior. Just before a house cat has kittens, she finds an appropriate nesting place. She carefully cleans up the kittens as they are born, and lies in a position for easy nursing. If a kitten squirms its way out of the nest, the mother quickly grabs it by the neck and puts it back. All this constitutes an instinctive pattern of behavior. So too are the sexual activities of, say, cats and dogs. These begin with a period of courtship and end in copulation, the whole sequence being about the same from one time to another and occurring without previous training.

Evolutionary Changes
If we look at various species of animals, keeping in mind our definition of instinctive behavior, we can see marked evolutionary patterns. Instinctive patterns are much more prominent in animals representing early stages of evolution than in animals higher on the evolutionary scale.

From insects to mammals   Instinctive behavior seems to play its largest role among the invertebrates, especially the insects. Watch cut-ants marching from their foraging area to their nest, or a spider build a nest, or caterpillars making cocoons, and you will see extremely stereotyped behaviors that are truly instinctive. Among the vertebrates, instinctive responses are not so pervasive as they are in insects, but they are still prominent from fishes through birds. The male stickleback fish attacks other males; careful laboratory studies show that the "triggering" mechanism which releases this attack is the sight of another male stickleback's red belly (Figure 2.1). The mating and nesting reactions of birds, which have also been intensively studied, are largely instinctive. In mammals (animals that nurse their young with the milk of their breasts) instinctive behavior plays a smaller role. But many mammals

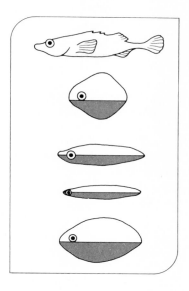

Figure 2.1 *Models of the male stickleback fish used in an experiment to isolate the stimulus which triggers fighting behavior in the male of that species. The top model, accurate except for its lack of a red belly, was not attacked by the male fish. The other three models, much less accurate but with red bellies, were fiercely attacked. The stimulus, a red belly, is said to be an innate releasing mechanism: it triggers instinctive behavior. (From Tinbergen, 1951.)*

such as dogs and rats, display instinctive patterns in their mating, and their patterns of maternal behavior—giving birth to young, feeding them, and retrieving them when they wander from the nest—are instinctive.

On the whole, though, in the higher mammals the extent of instinctive patterns is limited. We see those patterns only under certain circumstances; much more of the higher mammal's life appears to be spent in doing things that are learned. We have to use the word "appears," however, because there are other species traits besides instinctive fixed action patterns that are inherited. These are (1) an orderly maturation of skills, and (2) readinesses to learn.

Maturation of Skills

Maturation, we have seen, is a physiological process through which patterns of behavior emerge. They do this with little or no practice. The maturation of basic motor skills such as walking or flying is an example. Such maturation is species-specific: it occurs in the same order and roughly along the same time scale for each species. In relation to the time of birth, it may be rapid in some species (walking in monkeys) and slow in others (walking in humans).

Take motor maturation in human infants. The fact that its order is innate and species-specific is shown in a number of ways. One can observe, for example, a practice of the Hopi Indians, who bind their babies tightly to a board. Hopi infants are let out of their bindings only for an hour or two while they are being cleaned. Hence they have little opportunity to move, let alone practice the movements involved in standing and walking. Yet later, when these infants are freed from the board, they develop the ability to sit, creep, and walk just as rapidly as unbound infants. Motor maturation, then, seems inborn—apparently it does not hinge on practice or training.

A classic study of human motor maturation (Gesell and Thompson, 1929) employed the method of co-twin control in human subjects. A pair of identical twins was treated quite differently for the first year or more after birth. One was given special training in activities such as climbing, while the other was prevented from practicing. After the practiced twin became proficient, say, at climbing stairs, the unpracticed twin was given a chance to do the same thing. On her first attempt, she was not quite as good as the practiced twin; she took 45 seconds to climb the stairs as compared with the practiced twin's 26 seconds. Within two weeks, however, one was as good as the other. Thus training made a little difference at first, but the main factor in the development of the ability was the innate rate of maturation.

Other evidence for maturation comes simply from observing the age and order in which babies acquire different skills (Figure 2.2). With minor exceptions, different babies acquire the basic skills—lying on the stomach, sitting, creeping, pulling to a stand, standing alone, and walking—in the same order. The whole sequence is just too orderly to be explained any other way than by an innate "time clock" of maturation. Of course, there are differences among children: some are

Figure 2.2 Norms for the development of some important motor skills in the human infant. Although some babies develop such skills earlier than others, they appear in a definite order. (Based on data from Shirley, 1931.)

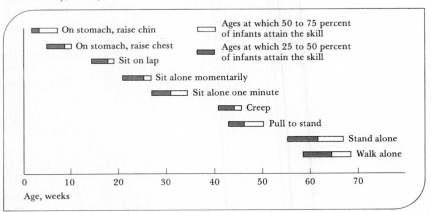

slow, some fast. This reflects differences in individual heredity (discussed later), but the remarkable thing is the "preprogrammed" order of events.

Motor skills is only one example. Other capacities besides motor skills also mature in an orderly way: for instance, the ability to perceive the world (that is, to make certain discriminations), and the ability to learn and use language. But these skills demand more learning than the motor maturation involved in sitting and walking. Even so, the ability or readiness to acquire these more complicated skills is a species-specific heritage.

Readiness for Learning

It is fairly obvious that there are some things which members of a species cannot learn to do. Man cannot learn to fly like a bird, nor can a dog learn to typewrite. This would probably be the case even if they had the same brains, because their bodies are built differently.

Learning symbols   There are two species, however, whose bodies are very much alike: man and the chimpanzee. Monkeys and chimpanzees have actually been taught to punch typewriters, but what they typed has never made any sense. That, we may suppose, is because they did not learn the language needed to type sense. A better question would be whether, given the same opportunity as a man, a chimpanzee could learn to speak in our language or to develop other human skills, such as eating with utensils.

There have been several studies in which a young chimpanzee was raised practically from birth in a human home. In one, the chimp was compared with a boy born at about the same time (Kellogg and Kellogg, 1933). In another, a childless couple devoted much of their time to bringing the chimp up like a human child (Hayes and Hayes, 1951). In these two experiments the chimp's motor maturation in basic skills compared well with that of human children and was often more rapid than theirs. And it was not hard to teach the chimp such skills as eating with utensils or throwing a ball.

But when it came to spoken language, the gulf between the chimp and the human child opened up. With three years of intensive training, about the most that the chimp could learn was to say "mama," "papa," or "cup" meaningfully—that is, to communicate some particular want. From these studies it appears that there is a species-specific difference in ability to speak language. Humans almost universally have the ability; chimps have very little of it.

Spoken or written language, however, is only a special case of the ability to use symbols. Although the chimp's brain may not be constructed to learn spoken words, is it capable of using other kinds of symbols, or signs, that stand for other things? Recent studies have taken this tack with some success. Since the chimp is nimble with its hands and makes all sorts of natural gestures, one chimp was systematically taught to use gestures as symbols (Gardner and Gardner, 1969). After a couple of years of training, the animal had learned 30 different gestures that it could use to make simple, meaningful sentences. One such gesture was putting its thumb in its mouth to show that it was thirsty. In other experiments, chimps have learned to push buttons and levers in complicated ways to symbolize things (Premack, 1970). So, although the chimp is far inferior to man in capacity to learn symbols, it does not rate a zero. It has a species-specific capacity to learn and use a limited number of them.

Learning to speak and read   What seems clear from research so far is that the ability to learn written and spoken speech is a species-specific characteristic of man. Like motor skills, it is on a maturational schedule. The skill does not develop without training, but the capacity for learning it does. Here are two examples, one of learning to speak, the other of learning to read.

Nearly every child in the world has a chance to learn speech from his parents and other children as soon as he is capable of it. But once in a great while there is a child who has been deprived of this opportunity, as in the case of the daughter of a deaf-mute (Davis, 1947). Hidden away because the mother was ashamed that the baby was illegitimate, and deprived of experience with language because the mother was a deaf-mute, this child lived six years with no language training. When she was eventually discovered by neighbors, she could utter only incomprehensible sounds. Yet after two months of training she learned many words, and soon she was putting sentences together as fast as a 3-year-old. Her ability to learn language had clearly matured, and all that was necessary was an opportunity to learn.

For our example of learning to read, we must introduce the concept of mental age (MA), a measure derived from an intelligence test. This is an overall index of mental development which compares any given child's score with that of the average child. Thus, an MA of 6, which a bright child might score at age 5 or a dull one at age 7, means that he has the mental development of the average 6-year-old child.

In a now classic study (Morphett and Washburn, 1931), a large number of children were scored on MA when they started the first grade. About halfway through the year, teachers who did not know these test results rated each child on his progress in learning to read by marking him satisfactory or unsatisfactory. Then this rating was compared with the

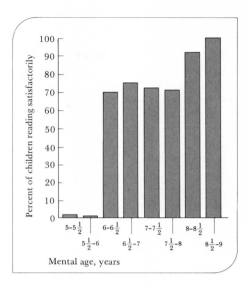

Figure 2.3 *The relationship of reading readiness to mental age (MA). As the graph shows, the number of children making satisfactory progress in learning to read jumps rapidly between the mental ages of 6 and 6.5 years. (Based on Morphett and Washburn, 1931.)*

children's MAs. The dramatic result was that progress in reading depended on MA (Figure 2.3). From nearly zero at an MA of 5$^{1}/_{2}$ to 6, it jumped to 70 percent at an MA of 6 to 6$^{1}/_{2}$. We would have seen nothing of this kind of jump, however, had we used the actual ages of children. They were all so near 6 that the differences were inconsequential.

This outcome has both a general and a practical meaning. Its general meaning is that learning to read is a readiness which matures with the mental development of the child. Before the child has matured to the proper point, he cannot learn; afterwards, he can. The practical meaning is that it is a mistake to group children according to their actual age, as is so often done in U.S. public education. Rather, mental age is much more closely related to reading readiness.

As we shall see, individual differences in maturation depend largely on a person's individual inheritance. But this study of first-grade children shows that our species heritage of being able to learn to read has a maturational schedule which brings the average child to "reading readiness" when he is about 6 years old.

INDIVIDUAL INHERITANCE

All the members of a single species share a certain common heredity that endows them with their species characteristics. Within a species, however, there are variations in heredity that make individuals different. Thus each of us has our species heredity and his individual heredity. And there are so many possible variations in individual heredity that, except for identical twins, no two individuals in the world are exactly alike. Occasionally, out of millions of people, two nontwins may look enough alike to pass for one another, but even then they can be distinguished by a number of biological characteristics, including their fingerprints. What do these individual differences in heredity mean for behavior?

Mechanisms of Heredity

The mechanisms of heredity—that is, the methods by which heredity is passed on to a person—begin with conception, when the ovum of the mother unites with the sperm of the father to form a zygote. Ovum and sperm merge into a cell consisting of a nucleus surrounded by cytoplasm, the whole being enclosed in an external membrane. The nucleus contains the genetic material that transmits hereditary characteristics from the parents to the new individual.

Chromosomes and genes　Chromosomes inside a cell are visible under the ordinary microscope. The number of chromosomes a cell has varies with the species of animal; in man the number is 23 pairs. The genes—the parts of these chromosomes that determine heredity—are visible only under the much more powerful electron microscope. The way genes govern heredity is now getting to be well understood. Basically, genes work in pairs, each member coming from one of the parents. When two genes are identical, the genetic outcome is a sure thing. For example, in the pair of genes that govern eye color, if each is a "blue-eyed" gene, the offspring will be blue-eyed. If each represents brown eyes, the child will be brown-eyed.

It is when the genes of each pair are not identical that things become more complicated. Usually one member of the pair is dominant over the other (Table 2.1). In the case of eye color, brown-eyed genes are dominant. But eye color is a very simple trait controlled by one pair of genes. (A trait is any specified characteristic of an organism.) Other physical traits, as well as most psychological traits that are heritable, frequently involve more than one pair of genes. When they do, we speak of *polygenic determination* of a trait. This means that a particular trait in the offspring is the outcome of more than one pair of genes, each one of which many have a dominant and a recessive member.

Polygenic traits　When traits are polygenic, it becomes difficult to figure out their genetic rules. In most cases we cannot say that the presence of a trait requires a dominant gene A, a recessive gene B, etc. Geneticists are sometimes able to make such identifications for some

TABLE 2.1
Some dominant and recessive characteristics in the genes of human beings.

Dominant gene	Recessive gene
Brown eyes	Blue eyes
Dark or brunette hair	Light, blond, or red hair
Curly hair	Straight hair
Normal hair	Baldness
Normal color vision	Color blindness
Normal sight	Night blindness
Normal hearing	Congenital deafness
Normal coloring	Albinism (lack of pigment)
Immunity to poison ivy	Susceptibility to poison ivy
Normal blood	Hemophilia (lack of blood clotting)

Source: Modified from Krech et al., 1969.

traits in rather simple organisms, such as the fruit fly. These insects breed so rapidly—sometimes in a few days—that geneticists can study trait inheritance through many generations in a relatively short time. But complexly determined traits in complex animals—for instance, intelligence in human beings—cannot be so easily studied.

Fortunately we do not need to know the detailed genetic rules in order to tell what is inherited and roughly how it is inherited. We know something about the way genes are distributed in human families, and we can also inbreed animals for particular traits. If, in studying human families, we are able to correlate variations in the trait with genetic differences, we have established a connection. And if, in breeding animals, we are able to produce quite different amounts of a trait in two strains of animals by inbreeding, we can be sure of a hereditary component in that trait. The examples in the following sections show how scientists make these studies.

Family Inheritance

The combination of genes an individual receives from his two parents is a matter of chance. Since the number of genes is very large, the number of possible combinations is astronomical. This is why no two unrelated individuals can be exactly alike.

Individuals of the same family, on the other hand, have similar genes and traits. The reason is that each parent contributes half of his genes to his child, and the child in turn contributes half of his genes to his children. Some of the genes of a brother and sister are sometimes identical. So too are some of the genes of parent and child. Thus a child tends to resemble his parent and his brother or sister in some degree.

He also resembles his grandparent or his uncle, but to a lesser degree, for a child on the average receives only one-quarter (one-half of one-half) of the genes of a particular grandparent. In other words, we know, on the average, the degree of genetic relationship between two individuals if we know their blood relationships. This is helpful in determining the genetic component in some psychological traits such as intelligence.

The genetic difference between identical and fraternal twins has been especially useful to psychologists. *Identical twins* develop from one zygote; thus they have identical heredities. (For this reason they must also be the same sex.) Therefore any differences we find between identical twins must be caused by environmental differences. *Fraternal twins* develop from two different zygotes that happen to be formed at the same time. Since each zygote has a chance combination of the parents' genes, these nonidentical twins are no more alike than brothers and sisters born at different times. On the other hand, the environments of fraternal twins who are raised together are often more similar than those of brothers and sisters. If these environments were exactly alike, we would know that any differences between the fraternal twins must be hereditary. In reality, no two individuals can ever have exactly the same environment. But the environments of fraternal twins are sometimes similar enough to help psychologists understand more about the interaction of heredity and environment.

Inheritance of Intelligence

The human psychological trait that was first thoroughly studied for heritability was intelligence. Intelligence may be defined as a person's entire repertoire of intellectual skills—all the things he has learned and has the present ability to learn (Humphreys, 1971). An intelligence test contains items that measure a sample of these skills and abilities. A person's score on the test is thus an estimate of his total repertoire. This is why we say that an intelligence score is a measure of the overall intellectual ability of a person. Stating that score as an intelligence quotient (IQ) is a way of comparing his ability with that of other people of the same age.

Studies of lower animals   A human intelligence test is an elaborate affair, consisting of many subtests, because human children can and do learn many different things. The tests we can give animals are much more limited, but they serve the same general purpose—they measure the ability of an animal to solve problems. One such problem (Thompson, 1954), the Hebb-Williams maze, is a kind of "intelligence test" for rats. Two sample mazes with different sets of barriers are shown at the bottom of Figure 2.4. They are square enclosures with a starting box in one corner and a goal box (containing food, in this experiment) in the opposite corner. To get from one corner to the other, a hungry rat must make detours around the barriers. The problem can be changed in many ways by repositioning the barriers. The number of errors made by a rat in a series of problems is its "intelligence score" in this particular maze.

To use the maze test to find out about the inheritance of intelligence, psychologists employ *selective breeding,* or inbreeding. They breed rats that are bright with other bright rats, dull rats with dull, for several generations, testing the rats of each generation in the maze to pick out bright ones and dull ones. If during the course of inbreeding, the offspring of bright rats turn out to be brighter still while dull rats' offspring are even duller, this is evidence that rat intelligence is inherited. And as Figure 2.4 shows, that is in fact exactly what happens.

Genetics of human intelligence   Moral and legal constraints prevent us from inbreeding human beings. Psychologists can, however, study differences in heredity and environment within families and ask how intelligence varies with these differences. To do this they use the measure known as the *correlation coefficient,* which was explained in Chapter 1.

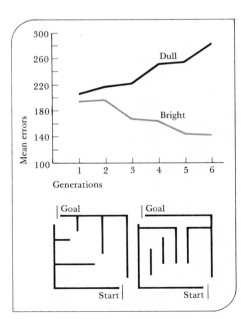

Figure 2.4 *Results of selective breeding for rat "intelligence." The performance of several generations of "dull" and "bright" rats in a Hebb-Williams maze, where a rat must find its way around a set of barriers to reach a food box. A series of problems with the barriers in different positions is presented. (Two sample problems are shown at bottom.) The total number of errors a rat makes is the measure of its maze-learning ability, or "intelligence." (Graph based on Thompson, 1954; sample mazes redrawn from Rabinovitch and Rosvold, 1951.)*

To summarize what has been found, the results of several studies are shown in Table 2.2. On the left, indicated by brackets, are different degrees of *hereditary* similarity for different family relationships. On the right, also shown by brackets, are different degrees of *environmental* similarity for these relationships. Now look at the column labeled "correlation of intelligence." At the top, note that the correlation coefficient for identical twins, who have identical heredity, is .88. That for fraternal twins (same sex), with no more hereditary similarity than siblings, drops to .63—a substantial drop. Yet the table classifies the environments for both kinds of twins as "very similar." This indicates that *heredity* has an important influence in determining intelligence.

Next note that the correlation of .63 for fraternal twins (same sex) drops to around .52 for siblings, although the table classifies the heredity of fraternal twins and siblings as "similar." They differ when it comes to environment; as shown in the right-hand column, the environment of fraternal twins is classified "very similar" while that of

TABLE 2.2
Correlations of intelligence scores (IQs) and heights for pairs of individuals with different degrees of relationship.

Heredity	Relationships	Correlation of intelligence	Correlation of height	Environments
Same	Identical twins*	.88	.93 ⎫	Very similar
	Fraternal twins (same sex)*	.63	.64 ⎭	
Similar	Siblings † ‡	.51–.53	.54–.60 ⎫	Similar
	Parents and children‡	.49	.51 ⎭	
Somewhat similar	Grandparents and grandchild‡	.34	.32 ⎫	Slightly similar
	Uncles (aunts) and nephews (nieces)‡	.35	.29	
Slightly similar	Cousins	.29	.24 ⎭	

Newman et al., 1937.
†*McNemar, 1942.*
‡*Burt and Howard, 1956.*

siblings drops to "similar." This shows that *environment* has a substantial effect on intelligence.

In running your eye down the table, you can see similar drops for both inheritance and environment. Conclusion: *Both heredity and environment play a role in a person's score on an intelligence test.*

Another fascinating point about these studies can be seen in the column "correlation of height." All along the line, there are drops in this relationship that parallel those in intelligence. But the correlation coefficient of height is higher than that of intelligence for identical twins, and lower for distantly related people. Height, of course, is not free of environmental influences—for example, consider the role of a good (or poor) diet. It is interesting, however, that height seems to be as strongly controlled by heredity (or environment) as intelligence. We can conclude that intelligence and height are influenced by both heredity and environment.

Inheritance of Emotionality

Emotional responses must also have a hereditary basis, since wolves, lions, and gray rats are savagely emotional, while their domesticated counterparts—dogs, cats, and white rats—are relatively tame. Can the difference be due to taming experiences? Perhaps in part, but these wild animals have seldom been domesticated. Certainly the major factor in their emotionality seems to be inheritance. This was first made clear in the laboratory by comparisons of the wild gray rat and the white rat (Stone, 1932).

> The wild rat, although it responds somewhat to taming, always remains a tense animal, ready to attack. When gray rats and white rats are crossed, some clearly inherit the tame disposition of the white rat, others the savageness of the wild gray. Savageness, moreover, turns out to be related to hair color. The wild gray looks "gray" because its coat is a mixture of dark brown and light tan hairs. These two hair factors separate genetically in the crossing of the gray and white so that some offspring are either brown or tan. Along with tan goes the savageness of the parental gray; the brown is practically as docile as the white. Hence savage emotional responses are linked by inheritance to the tan pigment. No one has ever bred tame tan rats! (Incidentally, this relationship of hair color and emotionality is not, so far as we know, a causal link. The tan color does not "cause" savageness or vice versa.)

Another experiment on the inheritance of emotionality made use of the inbreeding procedure and of a so-called "open-field test" of emotionality (Hall, 1938). Rats placed in a relatively large open space are at first afraid. They show their fear by profuse urination and defecation as well as by "freezing" to one spot instead of running around to explore. The test measured the amount of exploration as an index of emotionality: the more emotional the animal was, the less it explored. When the most emotional rats and the least emotional rats were interbred separately for several generations, two strains developed. One strain was more emotional than the most emotional rats of the first generation; the other was less emotional than at the start of inbreeding. Here, too, is a clear demonstration of the heritability of emotional reactions.

Extending this finding to human beings has not proved easy. Emotional reactions are harder to identify precisely, and harder to measure, than intellectual performances. Measures of such bodily states as pulse, respiration, salivation, and skin resistance have been made in individuals related in different degrees by blood (Jost and Sontag, 1944). As in the case of intelligence, correlations of these bodily states are much higher for identical twins than they are for brothers and sisters, and higher for brothers and sisters than for unrelated individuals. Hence, though the proof is not so striking as in the case of intelligence, it is nevertheless clear enough to show a hereditary component in the emotional behavior of people.

ENVIRONMENTAL INFLUENCES

The studies we have been looking at all show that heredity plays an important part in the development of various responses and capacities. In fact, there is hardly any genetic study of anything that has not turned up a genetic factor in behavior—sometimes strong, sometimes weak, yet always there. But heredity never accounts for all the variation we find in human and animal behavior. Some part of this behavior is always caused by the effects of the environment. The environment, as we have said from the beginning, sets some limits on what an individual may become. Let us examine a few of the environmental influences that fix these limits.

Rearing Conditions
Psychologists can get some idea of the effect of environment on intelligence by studying cases in which children of the same parents have been reared apart. The studies use the familiar technique of correlating IQ scores of individuals who are related in various degrees —siblings, fraternal or DZ twins, and identical or MZ twins. (DZ and MZ are shorthand for dizygotic and monozygotic. Dizygotic, or fraternal, twins each develop from a separate fertilized egg, or zygote. Monozygotic, or identical, twins both develop from a single zygote that

divides into two cells. Since these two cells have exactly the same genes as the zygote, the heredity of the two twins is identical.) The difference between these studies in Table 2.2 is that these compare the coefficients for children reared *together* and those reared *apart.*

Rearing apart   The results of one large survey are shown in Figure 2.5. Too few cases of nonidentical (DZ) twins reared apart were available to make a comparison, so all we learn from this part of the study is what we already know—that the correlations for nonidentical twins reared together fall between those for identical (MZ) twins and those for siblings. But the rest of the data are interesting because in every case, the correlations for individuals reared together in the same home is higher than it is for similar pairs of individuals brought up in different homes. The correlation for identical twins brought up together was about .90, but it dropped below .80 when they were reared apart. This, to a psychologist, is a sizable drop. The difference was not so great for brothers and sisters, yet it was there.

The bars on the left, labeled "unrelated," compare data for foster children reared in the same home and in different homes. The correlation for unrelated children brought up in different homes was, as we would expect, practically zero. But it was above .20 when they were brought up in the same home. Although that is not very high, for the psychologist it is significant: it largely reflects the influence of the home environment on intelligence.

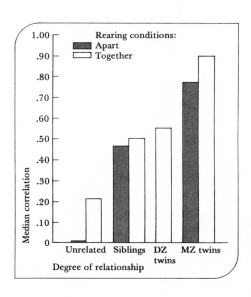

Figure 2.5 *This bar graph indicates that both nature and nurture determine a person's IQ. It shows median IQ correlations of pairs of individuals with several degrees of relationship. The correlations were obtained from many studies in which family members were brought up apart or together; both rearing conditions are shown for all but the DZ twins. (Too few studies have been made of DZ twins reared apart.) Note that in both conditions, IQ correlations increase with increasing degree of genetic similarity. (Based on Erlenmeyer-Kimling and Jarvik, 1963.)*

Educational advantages   Another way of determining the effect of environment on intellegence is to find identical twins who were reared apart and see how their IQs were affected by the different educational advantages of their homes. Such a study is summarized in Table 2.3. Most of these twins were separated before they were two years old, although one pair was parted as late as six. All the twins were tested years later, when they ranged in age from 11 to 59. Judges independently rated the educational advantages of the homes in which each twin was raised, giving each home (that is, each environment) a score from 1 to 10. Then the data for the twins were grouped into three classes: (1) twin pairs with very unequal advantages, (2) pairs with somewhat unequal advantages, and (3) pairs with relatively similar advantages.

As can be seen in Table 2.3, differences in homes made quite a difference in the subjects' IQ scores, especially in the first case, where the educational advantages were very unequal. Subjects who had superior homes averaged 15 points more than their twins who were reared in disadvantaged homes. This amount is about one-sixth of the entire spread of IQ scores. It could make the difference between finishing or not finishing a certain level of school—for instance, high school or college. Such a result leaves little doubt about the importance of the environment.

Environmental Impoverishment

When there is a difference in the effects of environments on intelligence, it could be because one environment is especially poor, another especially rich, or both. In other words, one does not know whether the effect shown in Table 2.3 was due to enrichment or to impoverishment of the environment. This question has to be studied by separately comparing the effects of environments that are poorer or richer than most.

There are many human studies on this point. Mostly they were done in orphanages, where children are frequently crowded together with few facilities for play or learning and with too small a staff to give them much attention. (Not all orphanages are like that, but too many are.) Such children are then compared with a group reared in normal homes. These studies are often flawed; they are usually too subjective, and one does not know whether the groups were matched in hereditary potential. But the results generally show that children in the impoverished environments are retarded in mental and social development compared with normal children (Hunt and Kirk, 1971).

The problem can, of course, be studied in animals, and has been many times. Baby monkeys have been reared in isolation from birth,

TABLE 2.3
Comparison of IQs of identical twins reared apart. The data
indicate that the environment (here, the home environment)
has a major influence on intelligence.

Number of twin pairs	Educational advantage	Age at separation (in months)	Average difference in IQ between twins	Superiority in IQ points of twins with greater advantages
6	Very unequal (5.1 on 10-point scale)	15	15.2	15.2
7	Somewhat unequal (2.4 on 10-point scale)	9	5.4	4.6
6	Relatively similar (1.6 on 10-point scale)	24	4.5	1.0

Source: Based on Newman et al., 1937.

and later their behavior has been compared with that of normally reared monkeys (Harlow, 1962). All sorts of tests show that the monkeys which have been isolated are deficient in a number of respects: rate of learning, sexual behavior, and social behavior. Dogs that have been similarly raised in near-isolation, receiving little experience with objects or other dogs, also show markedly inferior traits (Thompson and Melzack, 1956). They are naïve and immature, easily excited by strange objects. In learning tests they are significantly retarded, which may be due to their increased emotionality. Thus animal experiments, which have been conducted with much more rigor than the human studies, also uniformly show that an impoverished environment markedly retards mental, emotional, and social development.

Environmental Enrichment
The other side of the environmental coin is enrichment. Does an environment super-rich in stimulation and opportunities for learning about the world speed up development? The question is difficult to answer, and in fact there is no clear answer at present. The trouble in animal studies is that the normal environment of the laboratory animal is not very rich. For economy, animals are housed in plain cages without many stimuli besides the conditions required to take care of their basic physiological needs. Hence when the psychologist enriches

their environment and finds, as he usually does, that they are helped by it (King, 1958), he does not know whether it was because of the enrichment itself, or because the "normal" animal was impoverished.

Whatever the explanation, these experiments do regularly confirm the superiority of the so-called "enriched environment." Almost anything we do makes the animals in the enriched group superior in social and learning performance to the "normal" group. Simply getting them out of the cage and handling them every day makes them superior in learning ability and in resistance to all sorts of stress—like surviving in a swimming tank. If they are provided with a "Coney Island" cage, in which they have various paths they can explore and various objects to play with, they are later superior in learning discriminations and maze problems. These general statements apply to various experiments with rats and dogs. The question still remains, though, whether it is impoverishment of the "normal" animals or enrichment of the others that makes the difference.

Implications of Environmental Differences

The question of environmental effects is not simply academic: It affects major areas of social policy. In trying to provide every child with an equal chance in education, we need to know whether his early environment makes a difference in his ability to progress in public school. We also need to know as precisely as possible *what* differences in the early environment make a difference, so that we can plan the appropriate "enrichment."

Head Start, the ambitious federally funded project for preschool children, is an attempt at such enrichment. In this project preschool children from impoverished homes are placed in nursery schools designed to provide them with a learning environment similar to that of middle-class children. Unfortunately, the results are not impressive (Jensen, 1969; Kagan, 1969). Gains in IQ, which are a standard measure of environmental effects in children, are rather small, ranging from 1 to 10 points. Often even these gains are not permanent. This fact, however, does not prove that environmental enrichment has no value. Head Start probably provides too little enrichment (one summer or one year of schooling) and comes too late, since the children are 4 years old (Hunt, 1969). If started earlier and continued longer, it might make a substantial difference.

Fortunately, IQ is not the only measure of the success of an enrichment program. IQ is only a general measure of academic ability, whereas a number of specific aptitudes are important in educational success at all levels: motivation, attention span, verbal skill, and number ability, to name a few. And large gains have been made in enrichment programs focusing on these skills (Glaser and Resnic, 1972). Consequently, there is hope that enrichment programs will succeed when we find out exactly what kinds of enrichment are required to improve academic skills.

SUMMARY

Heredity and environment interact in producing both psychological and physical traits. Each sets limits on the effects of the other. The physiological environment during pregnancy and the early sensory environment of the infant are important in psychological development. The effects of heredity are seen partly at birth and partly throughout a person's life.

Each animal or person has two kinds of inheritance: a species-specific inheritance of traits inherited by all members of the species, and an individual inheritance of traits that differ from one individual to another. Both reflexes and instinctive patterns of behavior are species-specific. Instinctive behavior is much more prominent in lower animals than it is in man. The maturation of skills, such as walking or flying, is also species-specific. Through maturation, skills appear in about the same order in each member of the species. In addition, the readiness for learning various skills, such as reading, is inherited and unfolds on a timetable of maturation.

Individuals related by blood have some inherited traits and abilities in common. The more closely related they are, the more similar their inheritance. Many psychological traits, such as intelligence and emotionality, are strongly influenced by inheritance.

Intelligence is also greatly affected by a person or an animal's early environment. If the environment is rich in psychological stimulation, intelligence is improved.

SUGGESTIONS FOR FURTHER READING

Bonner, D. M. *Heredity.* Englewood Cliffs, N.J.: Prentice-Hall, 1961. (Paperback.) *An introduction to modern genetics.*

Fuller, J. L., and Thompson, W. R. *Behavior genetics.* New York: Wiley, 1960. *A treatment of the genetic bases of behavioral characteristics such as intelligence, personality, temperament, and behavior disorders.*

Hirsch, J. *Behavior-genetic analysis.* New York: McGraw-Hill, 1967. *A summary of the genetic aspects of psychological characteristics.*

Sluckin, W. (Ed.) *Early learning and early experience.* Baltimore: Penguin, 1971. (Paperback.) *A collection of readings on the effects of early experience.*

Thorpe, W. H. *Learning and instinct in animals.* (2d ed.) London: Methuen, 1963. *A source book on animal behavior, with interesting examples of innate behavior in lower animals.*

3

Drives and Motivation

LEARNING OBJECTIVES

Main objective
After studying this chapter, you should be able to name and describe the primary and social motives.

Other major objectives
You should also be able to
Explain how negative and positive goals are learned.
Outline three general ways of measuring motivation.
Indicate the role of fear in the affiliation and achievement motives.

Other objectives
Outline the steps in the motivational cycle.
Explain, using an example of your choice, how motives converge in maintaining learned behavior.
Indicate the physiological basis of hunger, thirst, and sex.
Describe the need for sensory stimulation and the role of curiosity as motives in learning.
Explain how activity and manipulation function as motives.
Describe the origin of affectional motivation.
Explain how achievement need and fear of failure are connected in risk-taking situations.
Outline the causes of aggressive behavior.

Motivation is both a fascinating and a frustrating subject. It is fascinating because it lies behind everything a person does. A child goes to school each morning, a college student studies to be a doctor, a politician runs for election, a boy asks a girl for a date, a robber holds up a bank, and a deranged man goes around strangling people. All

nd any others we can name, are motivated. And we spend a
of time trying to figure out what each person's motive is in
way he does. It makes a fascinating game in which we are
's right and sometimes wrong.

precisely this reason, motivation is also frustrating. We never
iotive. We only see what a person does, and sometimes we
tand how it is connected with a goal. But the motive that impels
, hidden within. The best we can do, at least in everyday life, is
, what motive lies behind what he is doing. How often we say
something like, "I wish I knew why Johnny does that!" Often, too, we
think we know why Johnny does something, and later we find out we
were dead wrong.

Psychologists have made some headway in uncovering motives and
in measuring them. They are still far, however, from a complete
understanding of this interesting and difficult subject. What we cover
here and in the next chapter on emotion is just the best we can do at
this time.

THE NATURE OF MOTIVATION

Several hundred words in our vocabulary refer to motivation: wants,
striving, desire, need, motive, goal, aspiration, drive, wish, aim, ambition, hunger, thirst, love, revenge to name a few. Each can be defined
somewhat differently from the other, but their meanings overlap so
much that there is no uniformly accepted terminology.

Motivational Cycles

Motivation is the all-inclusive term covering just about anything that
psychologists want to say about the subject. It has three distinct aspects:
(1) some motivating state within the person impelling him toward some
goal, (2) the behavior he displays in striving for the goal, and (3)
achievement of the goal. These three aspects of motivation normally
occur in a cycle (see Figure 3.1). The motivating state leads to behavior,
behavior leads to the goal, and when the goal is reached the motive
subsides—at least temporarily.

The general term used for the first phase of the cycle is *motive*. It
comes from the Latin word meaning *to move,* and we can think of
motivation as the mover of behavior. Many motivational terms refer to
this part of the cycle: drive, need, wish, want, striving, aim, ambition,
hunger, thirst, for example. The two terms most often used by
psychologists are drive and need. *Drive* appears more often in discus-
sions of physiological urges such as hunger, thirst, and sex. *Need* is
more often applied to more complex motives for achievement, love,
social approval, status, and the like.

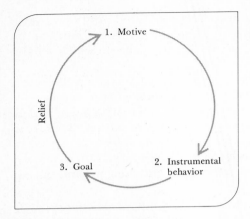

Figure 3.1 *The motivational cycle.*

Although all motives are regarded as internal states—that is, something within the organism causing it to strive toward a goal—motives are often aroused by external stimuli. A painful shock, for example, arouses a motive to get away from the shock. Through learning, all sorts of problems in the environment may come to be motivating; they arouse a motive to solve them. Thus motives arise not only from within the person but also from stimuli in the environment.

The second phase of a motivational cycle is some kind of *behavior* evoked by the drive or need. This behavior—in a later chapter it will be called *operant behavior*—is usually instrumental in arriving at the goal and thus satisfying the underlying motive. If a person is thirsty, for example, he moves about looking for water.

The third phase is, as we have said, achievement of the *goal.* When the thirsty person finds water (the goal), he drinks and satisfies his thirst, ending the motivational cycle for the time being.

Positive and Negative Goals
The thirst drive is an example of a motive with a *positive goal*—a goal we search for or approach. But a motive can also have a *negative goal*—something we try to avoid or escape.

Illustrating positive goals is the story of a 3-year-old boy admitted to a hospital because he did not seem to be growing properly (Wilkins and Richter, 1940). While undergoing a series of tests, the boy died after 7 days in the hospital. An autopsy performed to find out why revealed a tumor on the child's adrenal glands. The pathologist immediately guessed what the trouble was. The secretion of one part of the adrenal gland normally keeps salt from being excreted in the urine, and the tumor had blocked this function. The child had died of salt deficiency.

Questioning the parents, the physician learned that the boy had never eaten properly. He seemed to crave salty things, eagerly licking salt from bacon or crackers. When he got a chance, he would even eat straight salt from the shaker. Eating all this salt had compensated for the great salt loss due to the faulty adrenal gland. In the hospital, however, the regulated hospital diet did not supply enough salt for his needs.

To retell the story in terms of a motivational cycle, the boy (1) had an unusually strong need for salt, (2) looked for salt at every opportunity, and (3) ate salt to satisfy his need for it.

As an example of a negative goal, suppose a child is afraid of dogs—which is usually a learned fear. When approached by a dog, the child runs to his mother or some other safe place. Then he is no longer afraid. In this instance, the motive comes from the environment; it is the sight of the dog that arouses a state of fear (stage 1). The fear causes him to run (stage 2) to a safe place (stage 3), which makes his fear subside.

In comparing these examples of positive and negative goals, note that they play somewhat different roles. A positive goal is the *result* of a motive; we eat (positive goal) because we are hungry (motive). In the case of negative goals, the goal *causes* the motive; the dog caused the child to be afraid, and he ran to escape the negative goal. In both cases, however, achieving the positive goal or escaping from the negative goal ends the motivational cycle by weakening the motive: in one case, hunger; in the other, fear.

Learned Goals

The goals encountered in motivational cycles may be innate or learned. Innate or unlearned goals, like other aspects of behavior already covered in Chapter 2, may be present at birth, or they may emerge through maturation with little or no learning involved. On the other hand, goals may be acquired through the process of learning. For example, most of us have come to value money; we want to win friends; we desire achievement in some phases of life; and we like social approval. All these motives involve learned goals.

Learning goals is basically a simple process. It occurs when some neutral stimulus which is not yet a goal is paired with an unlearned goal. Money by itself is worthless paper or metal, but it comes to have value because it is paired with or associated with the satisfaction of primary goals. It buys food, drink, and other things that are primary goals.

The examples of learned goals just mentioned are *positive learned goals.* Like other goals, learned goals may be either positive or negative. Here are two examples.

Learned negative goals The learning of a negative goal is illustrated by an experiment in which rats were given electric shock (Miller, 1948):

> Rats were used because it is not feasible to do this experiment with people. White rats, one at a time, were placed in a white box separated by a door from a black box. In the floor of the white compartment was a grid through which mild shock could be applied. The rats were given brief shocks every 5 seconds. Then the door to the box was opened and the shock was turned on steadily. The rat could escape, however, by running into the adjacent black box. The sequence was repeated on 10 different occasions. These were enough to arouse fear in the rat at the sight of the white box. After that, the shock was never used again.
>
> On five subsequent occasions, rats were placed in the white box with the door open. Their learned fear was strong enough to make them run quickly into the black box every time. The white box had become a *learned negative goal.* The learned fear was so strong, in fact, that when the experimenter closed the door but made it possible for the rat to open the door by turning a wheel or pushing a bar, the rat quickly learned that response too.

This experiment illustrates how pairing of shock with the white walls of a box causes "white" to become a learned negative goal. The animal learns to avoid white because it was associated with painful shock.

It is important to note that this process of learning a negative goal is typical of human fears. Most of the things we now fear as adults we did not fear as infants (see page 87). We came to fear them through a learning process. These learned fears in turn motivate us to learn other habits to escape or avoid learned negative goals.

Learned positive goals The learning of positive goals is illustrated by another animal experiment, this one with chimpanzees (Wolfe, 1936). The animals were taught to obtain a grape or raisin by putting a poker chip into a small vending machine called a Chimpomat (Figure 3.2). The experimenter merely showed a chimp how to insert the chip into the slot and collect its reward. The chimps caught on quickly, and in doing so they learned to value the poker chip itself as a positive goal. This was proved by giving a chimp a task in which it had to work for poker chips; the animal would pull heavily weighted boxes in order to obtain chips. Moreover, it would do this much as a person works for money: to collect chips that it could use only *later*, when the Chimpomat was again wheeled up to its cage. Still later, the experimenter taught a chimp to discriminate among learned positive goals by having the animal use a red chip to obtain food, a blue one for water, and a white one to get out of its cage and run around.

Figure 3.2 *A chimpanzee using tokens (secondary positive goals) to obtain food (primary positive goal). The animal has learned to place poker chips in the machine to get fruit. Chimps in this experiment would "work" to obtain chips and would hoard them when they could not spend them immediately. (Yerkes Laboratories of Primate Biology, Inc., Henry W. Nissen, photographer.)*

Note that in this series of experiments with the chimpanzees two things were learned. First, the animals learned a new goal (poker chip) because it was associated with a primary goal (food). Second, they learned to work at something (pulling boxes)—that is, they learned an instrumental act—in order to achieve the goal (chips). Hence in learning new goals we usually learn new ways of doing things. In learning to value money, for example, we learn all sorts of skills that are rewarded with money in our society. In acquiring goals for such things as achievement and social approval, we learn to do the things for which these goals are rewards.

Survival of learned goals How long does this kind of learning usually last? Human beings acquire a bundle of learned goals and keep these goals through most of their lives. Can we explain the fact that people continue to work hard and long at achieving some goals just by saying that these goals were once associated with primary goals? It seems hard to believe. For this reason it was thought for some years that learned goals, once acquired, need little additional pairing with primary goals to be fairly permanent. In psychological terms, it was thought that learned goals become functionally autonomous (Allport, 1937). This, we now think, is not the case either. There is another answer—but a different one for learned negative goals than for learned positive goals.

As discussed in Chapter 6, the learning of negative goals associated with shock or pain lasts a lot longer than learning associated with positive goals like food. Fears, for example, are quickly learned, and usually stay learned unless we go to some trouble to unlearn them (page 117). The learning of positive goals, however, is not so hardy. For them to last, they must occasionally be reinforced by the achievement of primary goals. Chimpanzees, for example, soon learn to work no harder than necessary for poker chips; that is, they acquire only about the number they need to obtain their food. Similarly, people who work only to eat and to secure the simple comforts of life work no harder than necessary. To explain the fact that most people work harder than this requires something more than the notion that they learn isolated positive goals.

Convergence of motives   The "something more" is a convergence of motives. This means that several motives become involved in a single activity. Put another way, one kind of work may lead to the satisfaction of different motives at different times. Take the case of a penniless boy who becomes a millionaire. He, like the rest of us, has a bundle of motives. At first the motive that gets him working for money may be the need to survive. But in the working situation he finds the satisfaction of other motives. Work keeps him active, thus satisfying an activity drive; it may present problems which challenge his curiosity motive; and it brings him into contact with other people who become his friends. Thus working for the original learned goal of money also satisfies other motives such as activity, curiosity, and companionship. So he goes on to make much more money than he needs. Out of habit, he may say that he is working for money; he may be unaware of the fact that his goals have shifted—that he is now satisfying a different set of motives from those he started with.

Learned positive goals, then, remain goals only so long as they continue to be paired with the satisfaction of primary goals. But these can shift as the activity becomes the means of satisfying new goals.

Generalization   Both positive and negative goals are subject to *generalization*, which is the *tendency to respond in the same manner to objects and events that are similar* (see page 120). This definition is a bit circular, because in practice we must infer that situations are similar when a person reacts to them in the same way. In any case, when a subject has learned a new goal, he will regard other situations similar to that goal in the same way. Generalization of goals applies especially to fear. For example, a person who tries too hard to please people, whether they are teachers, strangers, or anyone else, may very well be moved (motivated) by fear. Perhaps his father was difficult to please and used punishment freely when displeased. In this case, fear of the father's displeasure generalized to other adults.

Cooperation and conflict of motives   In most people most of the time, several motives are operating at once. The motives may work either in cooperation or in conflict. As an example of the cooperation of motives, a man may work to make money partly for what it will buy (a learned positive goal) and partly out of fear of being poor (a learned negative goal). As an example of a conflict of motives, a person's desire for achievement (positive goal) may conflict with his fear of failure (negative goal). A person who wants to get a college education, go all out for sports, or start his own business is frequently caught in this kind of conflict. Indeed, few situations in life do not arouse some conflict of motives. The topic is so important that Chapter 4 devotes a section to it.

Unconscious Motivation

Another important point about motivation is that *human motives are often unconscious.* Frequently a person does not know what his real motive is or what his goal is. He may try to give some good reasons for his behavior, but many times these are not the right reasons.

One explanation of unconscious motivation is based on the principle that motives and goals are often intertwined. Thus it can be difficult for anyone—the individual himself or even a skilled observer who knows that person's life history—to correctly identify the motive or motives behind an act.

Another possibility in unconscious motivation is suggested by the fact that a person acquires habits of which he is largely unaware. A teacher, for example, may bite his nails, pull on his ears, tap on a table, or pace back and forth in front of the class and not be conscious of any of these habits until they are called to his attention. Complex motives may function in the same way. Moreover, motives are not as easily observed as habits, so that the person is less likely to be reminded of them.

A third factor in unconscious motivation may be *repression,* a concept contributed by Freud. In repression a person does not want to recognize a motive because it is undesirable. He may dislike his mother, covet the success of his brother, or be sexually attracted to his brother's wife. These are unacceptable motives. He therefore refuses to think about them—he represses them, meaning that he pushes them out of his mind. (More about unconscious motivation and repression in Chapter 10.)

Measurement of Motivation

How do we know whether a motive is present or not? And if it is, how do we measure its strength? Because motives are never directly seen, questions of how best to measure them have not been easily settled.

Considering both animals and people, however, we can list five methods of measuring motivation: (1) consummatory behavior, (2) deprivation, (3) performance, (4) learning, and (5) personality tests.

Consummatory behavior Consummatory behavior is the specific behavior that satisfies a motive. For a thirsty organism, drinking water is the consummatory behavior; for a hungry animal, eating food is. The thirstier a subject is, the more water he drinks; the hungrier he is, the more food he eats. Thus the amount of consummatory behavior can be used as a measure of the strength of motivation.

Deprivation In experimental work, a related method of measurement is to vary the length of deprivation. Food or water can be withheld for a specified period of time: say, 12 or 24 hours. The length of the period of deprivation is then used as a measure of the strength of motivation. Since this method is convenient to use, it is often employed in animal experiments where strength of motivation is a variable.

Performance Another method of measuring motivation is to determine what a subject will do to reach a primary goal. The scientist can, for example, impose a barrier to the goal of a motive, then measure the number of times the animal will overcome the barrier. In some pioneering work of this kind (Warden, 1931), the barrier was an electrified grill. The number of times a rat would cross the grill in a given period was the measure of the strength of the motive. (This experimenter found, incidentally, that the maternal drive in female rats is as strong or stronger than drives like hunger and thirst. Also, the exploratory drive is almost as strong as physiological drives.) A variant of this method is to make it necessary for the animal to push a lever or haul a box in order to secure some goal object.

Learning A very similar method of measuring motivation is to find out what a subject will learn to do to reach a goal. As Chapter 5 will show, achieving a goal acts as a reinforcement in learning the behavior that is necessary to get to the goal. (A corollary is that anything which acts as a reinforcement in such learning is motivating.) In the experiment described earlier, where rats in a white box were given electric shock, we concluded that the white box had become motivating because rats would learn to push a lever or turn a wheel to get out of the box. How fast they learn in such a situation can then be used as a measure of motivation. Similarly, children are motivated by social approval, and a teacher or parent can use social approval as a reward in getting them to learn things.

Personality tests The four tests just described are most suitable for animal subjects. In working with people, we are more likely to be interested in motives for such things as achievement, affiliation, or aggression. One kind of test that has been devised to measure motives like these is called a *projective test* (discussed in more detail in Chapter 9). The projective test most often used in motivation research is the Thematic Apperception Test, or TAT. In it subjects are shown a series of ambiguous pictures and asked to tell a story about what is going on in each picture. The assumption is that in telling his stories, the subject projects his own needs into the behavior of the characters. The skilled tester then identifies the needs being projected and judges from the number of related items in the story how strong each need is.

Other personality tests used to measure motivation come under the heading of *personality inventories.* These are pencil-and-paper questionnaires made up of true-false or multiple-choice questions about a person's habits, likes, and ambitions. One such test, The Edwards Personal Preference Schedule, is designed to measure human social needs. Another, Taylor's Manifest Anxiety Scale, is a good general measure of anxiety level. There is even a personality inventory, the Mandler-Sarason Test Anxiety Questionnaire, that measures anxiety in taking achievement tests.

Unfortunately, measures of motivation obtained with inventories seldom correlate highly with those derived from projective tests. Yet both kinds have been helpful in research on social motivation (Cofer and Appley, 1964).

Occasionally a *situational test* can be used to get some idea of the strength of human motives. In this test a person is put into a real situation, and an observer sees what he does. A child's aggressiveness, for instance, can be measured by letting him play with dolls and observing the number of times he does something aggressive or destructive with them. Or aggression may be studied by insulting a person and observing what angry things he says in reply.

PRIMARY MOTIVES

The rest of the chapter will treat one by one the motives found in man and animals. These can be divided according to whether they are learned or unlearned. Unlearned motives are those with primary goals and can be called *primary motives.*

Some of the primary motives have their origin in known physiological changes in the body—for instance, hunger and thirst. They are often called physiological drives, and this section will discuss them first.

Then there are unlearned motives for such things as sensory stimulation and affection, and these have no physiological basis that we know of.

Hunger and Thirst
The physiological drives of hunger and thirst are closely related, because water is required in the body to handle digestion and other biochemical steps in the body's use of food. In fact, about 90 percent of an organism's water intake has this physiological purpose. Put another way, people or animals that are fasting or deprived of food drink only about 10 percent of the water that they do when they are eating regularly.

General hunger The experience of hunger seems to vary from person to person and from time to time. Sometimes it is associated with hunger pangs (contractions of the stomach), but not always. These are certainly not necessary in order to feel hungry (Morgan, 1965). Sometimes a feeling of lightheadedness is reported, but again, people can be ravenously hungry without such a feeling. So there is no experience that regularly accompanies hunger, other than a strong desire to eat.

Several parts of the brain are involved in the regulation of hunger and eating. The most important is the hypothalamus, located at the base of the brain. Here are two centers, one called a feeding center and the other a satiety center, that are affected by conditions in the blood circulated to them (Teitelbaum and Epstein, 1962). The feeding center, when activated, causes a person to be hungry and to eat. The satiety center brings eating to a halt when enough food has been consumed.

Preferences and aversions Children and animals, if left to their preferences, tend to select what they eat so that they consume a balanced diet over a period of time (Rozin, 1967). We used to think they did so because they could distinguish among their "specific hungers" and eat the particular materials they needed to satisfy these hungers. Now we know that this belief is not generally true. It does seem to apply to things like salt and certain minerals (as in the case of the salt-starved boy described earlier), but it is not true of all elements of the diet.

Rather, we maintain a balanced diet, if given a chance to, because we tire of one kind of food and turn to another. In other words, we like novelty in food and tend to eat something different from what we have been eating. Besides, if we eat a diet that lacks something like vitamin B, the diet is not satisfying. We develop an aversion to it and will choose a novel food if we can. In this way we stand a very good chance of eating food that contains the elements we need for health.

Thirst Water is constantly being lost through the lungs, the sweat glands of the skin, and the kidneys. But the body needs to maintain a certain amount of water in the blood and tissues, and this need is reflected in the thirst drive.

The physiological mechanism of thirst is now well understood (Corbit, 1969). Like hunger, thirst is controlled by several parts of the brain, principally by the hypothalamus. In this center lie nerve cells that are especially sensitive to loss of water—to mild dehydration. When activated by a lowered water supply in the blood, they cause the organism to search for water and to drink it.

Psychological factors Hunger and thirst are primarily controlled by internal physiological factors. But external psychological factors also have an influence on them. We sometimes drink water when we do not need it physiologically because it "tastes good"—maybe because it has been flavored, as it is in popular soft drinks. Such psychogenic drinking can be induced in rats when they are made to work for food but obtain the food intermittently. While waiting for the next pellet, they drink much more water than their bodies need.

External psychological cues can also be very important in hunger. They seem to have an especially strong influence in cases of human obesity (Schachter, 1971). Normal, nonobese people regulate their food intake almost entirely by their internal hunger stages. If they are not "internally" hungry, they pay little attention to food. But an obese person walking by a window of pastries is likely to find it an overwhelming temptation. Similarly, he cannot resist appetizing foods in the refrigerator and keeps nibbling away at them. Just why this happens we are not sure; we only know that obese people get that way because they overrespond to external food cues.

Sex and Maternal Drives

We think of the sex and maternal drives as physiological drives because in animals *below man* they depend on hormones in the blood. The *androgens*, secreted by the testes of the male, cause the male to be sexually active. *Estrogens*, secreted by the ovaries of the female, cause her to come into estrus ("heat") so that she readily accepts the male. Normally, this period of heat comes at the same time that an ovum in the ovary is ready to descend, or has descended, to the uterus. Consequently pregnancy regularly follows sexual activity in animals.

Toward the end of pregnancy, other hormones come into play. The presence of the fetus in the uterus stimulates the production of *prolactin* by the pituitary gland. Prolactin in turn stimulates the mammary glands, which supply milk for nursing the young. Prolactin also produces maternal behavior in the mothers. When it is injected into a virgin female rat and the animal is placed with foster infants, it acts just like the natural mother of the young. There is good reason to believe that in animals such as the rat, cat, and dog, this hormone evokes maternal behavior, and other hormones produce sexual behavior, by acting directly on nerve cells in the hypothalamus.

Does the hormonal explanation of the sex and maternal drives apply to people? The answer is a qualified "No." We do know that hormones spark sexual motivation in humans as well as in lower animals. The secretion of hormones is correlated with the emergence of sexual drive. On the other hand, they are not necessary for sexual drive to be maintained. The drive continues in many women, for example, after the menopause, when their ovaries have stopped secreting estrogens. Similarly, men (as well as some other male animals) continue to be sexually active even if they are castrated and thereby lose the source of male hormones. Moreover, there is no evidence that treatment with sex hormones restores sexual drive when it is weak. So, although hormones play a part in the development of sexual drive, once the drive is present it continues without them. This is an example of psychological motivation persisting after its physiological basis has ceased.

In the case of maternal behavior, we are fairly sure that hormones are not essential in either humans or animals (Rosenblatt, 1967). In animals, experience with young is about as important as hormones. Virgin female rats and hamsters, for example, display fairly typical maternal behavior *without* prolactin injections just by being exposed to young for a couple of weeks. Thus this instance experience with young does about the same thing as the hormone. The function of the hormone is to have the maternal motive operating at the moment of birth rather than after a period of experience with young.

Curiosity and Sensory Stimulation

If we look at the everyday behavior of both people and animals, we can see that some of it stems from the physiological drives we have just discussed. On the other hand, we can hardly escape the conclusion that all, or even most, of it is not caused by physiological drives. Think of the amount of time people spend just looking at things—newspapers, books, television, sports events, mountains, busy construction sites, and "points of interest." And think of the amount of activity they put into playing games, skiing, boating, hiking, hunting, and touring. Motivation is involved, or else people would not do these things, but the motives are certainly not physiological.

Some years ago an experiment was done on the effects of depriving people of *sensory stimulation* (Bexton et al., 1954). College students were paid $20 a day—then a good sum—to lie on a comfortable bed for the whole 24 hours except for the time required to take care of their physiological drives. Each was in a small, lighted cubicle that was quiet except for the hum of an exhaust fan. To reduce visual stimulation to a minimum, the subjects wore translucent goggles. To reduce tactual stimulation, they wore gloves over their hands and cuffs on their forearms. All they had to do was nothing.

This might seem like an easy way to make money, but most subjects soon found it intolerable. After two or three days they wanted nothing more than to get out of the cubicle. Lying on their beds they began to have hallucinations, became disoriented in time and space, lost their ability to think clearly, and were unable to concentrate on anything for very long. In short, they were much like people suffering from certain mental disorders, and many of the symptoms lasted for some times after they left the cubicle.

Some animal studies, set up in a somewhat different way, explored a related point (Butler, 1954).

Monkeys were confined in boxes equipped with two doors. Each door was marked with a distinctive pattern, which could be changed to the other door from time to time. The door with one pattern could be opened by pushing; the other could not. Because of the way monkeys bounce around in boxes, a monkey would soon accidentally open the correct door. When he did, he could look out into the room (see Figure 3.3). After the first accidental success, he quickly learned to push whichever door had the right pattern. Yet his only reward for learning to make this discrimination was the opportunity to look out. How often he pressed the door was used

Figure 3.3 *Monkey peeping out of the apparatus used to measure curiosity motivation. If it pushed the correct door, the monkey was reinforced by being allowed to look outside for a few seconds. The reinforced response increased in frequency, while the unreinforced response declined. (H. F. Harlow, Primate Laboratory, University of Wisconsin, 1953.)*

as a measure of the strength of his motive. If there was an "interesting" scene outside—say, another monkey or a moving train—he pushed the correct door more often than if the outside room was empty.

These and other experiments make it clear that there is a motive with sensory stimulation as its goal. More than that, the motive is for *changing* sensory stimulation; we tire after a while of the same sensory situation and look for a different set of stimuli. The term we use for the motive, expressed in this way, is *curiosity.* Similarly, if something new enters our environment, we usually turn our attention to it. This is known as a *response to novelty.* Both curiosity and response to novelty are terms applying to a basic motive for sensory stimulation and for stimulus change.

Activity and Manipulation

There is a similar motive with bodily activity as its goal. Both human beings and animals spend a great deal of time moving about for no apparent reason. In fact, people provide activity wheels for their pet mice and hamsters, and the animals often run in the wheels for hundreds, even thousands, of revolutions a day.

Is such activity motivated simply by a need for activity, or does it have a physiological basis? The answer is, "Both." If we record activity at the same time that we vary physiological drives, we can see a connection. When an animal is hungry or thirsty, its activity goes up. Activity, in fact, is nature's way of ensuring that a thirsty or hungry animal will be likely to find what it needs. Similarly, when a female rat is in "heat," that is, when its sexual drive is high, activity greatly increases. Again, this is a natural reaction that increases the chances of satisfying the drive. So some activity does have a basis in physiological drive.

Not all activity arises in this way, however. Animals that are otherwise quite satisfied in physiological respects still move around a good deal. Furthermore, it can be shown that such activity is the goal of a motive. Two experiments illustrate the point. In one (Hill, 1956) an animal was confined in a small space for a period of time, then let out to run in the wheel. The longer he was cooped up, the longer he turned the wheel. This result shows a deprivation effect similar to going without food for some time. In both cases the greater the deprivation, the stronger the motivation afterward. In another experiment (Kagan and Berkun, 1954), the subjects had to push a lever to get the opportunity to run in a wheel. They learned to press the bar for this reward just about as fast as they learned to do it to obtain food. There is little doubt that activity is a goal in itself.

The motive that is involved here is not limited to gross bodily activity. It extends to the manipulation of objects, as when a kitten plays with string. More sophisticated animals, like monkeys and people, will manipulate all sorts of objects. Monkeys and chimpanzees especially like to manipulate things. And we have been able to teach them to discriminate, say, between red and green, with no other reward except the chance to unscrew a screw eye or to play with some other gadget (Harlow and McClearn, 1954).

Competence Motive

If we search for a principle in these studies of curiosity and activity, we might conclude that there is one general motive behind them—a motive for *competence*. At least one leading psychologist has reached this conclusion (White, 1961). To him organisms, whether they be people or animals, are motivated to see what they can see and do what they can do. In other words, they are motivated to use their full potentialities (Maslow, 1968), and in doing this they find satisfaction. Seeing and doing are rewards in themselves (Dember and Jenkins, 1970).

> If we watch a baby who has matured to the point of being ready to stand, we notice the enormous effort he puts into getting himself into standing position. When he does, he is likely to let out a shriek of delight, burst into laughter, and generally express joy at his accomplishment. He will do this whether or not he knows he is being watched. Obviously he has a "strong urge to stand" and gets great satisfaction out of doing it.

SOCIAL MOTIVES

Social motives are motives that involve other people in one way or another. They may or may not be learned; some are and some aren't. On the other hand, all of them are *modified* by learning, just as primary motives are. A large number of social motives have been identified by various psychologists, but systematic research has been done with only a few. It is these that will be covered here. Research on affection has been done using monkeys for reasons that will become apparent. Human subjects have been used in the other studies.

Affection and Affiliation

Affection and affiliation are two closely related, but distinguishable, social motives. The first is a desire to love others, beginning with one's mother; the second is a motive to *be with* others.

    Origin of affectional motive   Ideally, psychologists would like to study the development of a motive from its birth. If they could observe the motive from the beginning, perhaps they could tell whether it is unlearned and precisely what its goal is. The human infant is difficult to study because its motor abilities develop so slowly, but the monkey is easy because it develops early. Within 2 to 10 days after birth, a baby monkey moves around on its own and manipulates objects. Then the scientist can measure what it does and does not respond to. It can be suckled on a bottle and reared under any artificial conditions that are chosen. For that reason monkeys have been used in an interesting series of experiments on the affectional motive (Harlow, 1958).

In one experiment, monkeys were raised singly in cages that provided a comfortable environment adequate to take care of bodily needs. In each cage were two artifical mothers called "surrogate" mothers (see Figure 3.4). One was a cylindrical wire-mesh tube with a block of wood at the head. This was called the "wire" mother. The other was made from a block of wood, covered with sponge rubber, and sheathed in tan cotton terry cloth. This was called the "cloth" mother and resembled a real

Figure 3.4 *Mother surrogates made of wire and of cloth used in experiments on the affectional motive in monkeys. At left, a baby monkey huddles against a cloth surrogate mother on which it is not fed; at right, the baby monkey maintains contact with the cloth surrogate mother while feeding from the wire mother's bottle. (H. F. Harlow, Primate Laboratory, University of Wisconsin.)*

 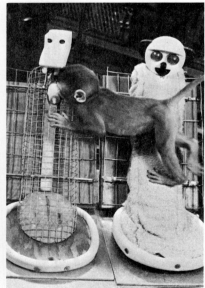

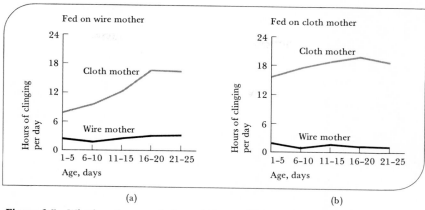

Figure 3.5 *Whether they are fed on cloth or wire mothers, infant monkeys prefer to cling to cloth mothers. (After Harlow, 1958.)*

mother much more than the "wire" mother. Behind each mother was a light bulb that provided radiant heat for the infant. Either mother could be outfitted with a nursing bottle placed in the center of its "breast."

The purpose of the experiment was to see how much time the infant spent with each mother when that mother had the bottle. This was to test the theory that love may somehow be learned through the rewarding of the hunger motive. The results are shown in Figure 3.5. The monkeys strongly preferred the cloth mother regardless of where the bottle was. They spent 15 hours or more with the cloth mother even though only an hour or so was enough for feeding.

Two conclusions can be drawn from the experiment. First, the monkey has an unlearned tendency to be near "mother." Second, this tendency is one of seeking "contact comfort" with the mother. In other words, the goal of the motive is something soft and comfortable.

Fear, curiosity, and affection Other experiments with monkeys tell us something about the relation of the affectional motive to fear and curiosity (Harlow, 1958). The monkeys were observed with and without their surrogate "cloth" mothers when strange objects were placed in the cage. Such objects tend to arouse the conflicting motives of fear and curiosity. Strangeness, as we shall see, is a natural stimulus for fear in monkeys and human infants. At the same time, strange objects are novel objects and provoke some curiosity.

The presence or absence of the "mother" made a great difference.

Without a mother, fear dominated the infant monkey's behavior; it crouched, cried, rocked, and sucked its finger. When it was with the mother, such fearful behavior was greatly reduced. In addition, the infant used the mother as a base of operations. It would cling to the mother for a while, then venture away to explore the strange objects, then return to the mother. The mother thus proved to be a haven of safety that alleviated the conflict between fear and curiosity.

The infant monkey's behavior in this situation reminds us of what we see in kittens and children. Kittens venture away from their mother to play, but they usually stay in her vicinity and return to her at regular intervals. In the same way, a small child plays securely with its mother nearby, coming to her occasionally to tug on her dress or ask for some attention. Left alone, especially in a strange situation, the infant is likely to stop playing and become afraid.

From these experiments we can draw the following conclusions: (1) The affectional motive in monkeys is unlearned; it appears in the normal course of maturation. Its object is "contact comfort." We do not know how closely the object must resemble the mother; perhaps it need only be soft and warm. (2) The affectional motive, when satisfied by a mother, allays fear in strange situations. It provides a feeling of security that can support the curiosity motive.

Affiliation   Students of human motivation consider the affiliation need, the need to be with others, as a distinct need that can vary in strength like other needs. They have a way of scoring its strength on the Thematic Apperception Test. Beyond that, however, little research has been done with it. We know that it develops early because young children, from about the time they can walk, like to be with each other. The affiliation need is probably supported in part by curiosity and manipulative motives, for the behavior of another child supplies interesting stimuli for these motives. Like the affectional motive, it is also related to fear, as the following experiment illustrates (Schachter, 1959).

Two groups of girls, none of whom knew each other, served as subjects in this experiment. When they came individually to the experimental room, they were met by a man calling himself Dr. Gregory Zilstein, who was surrounded by an impressive array of equipment. The doctor gave a brief lecture on the importance of electric shock in research. Then he gave one group of girls instructions designed to make them anxious; he said that they would receive painful, but not harmful, shocks. He told another group that they would receive mild shock. Then he explained that there would be a short delay before the experiment began. They were told that during the delay they could either wait alone or wait with some other girls in a nearby classroom. First, however, the experimenter asked them to answer a questionnaire measuring their anxiety about shock and their preferences for waiting alone or with other girls. The girls were then offered the choice of leaving or of remaining for the experiment. After each had given her decision—and before the promised delay—the experiment ended, and Dr. Zilstein explained its purpose.

These were the results: About one-third of the girls in the group that was told they would receive painful shock refused to continue with the experiment, while none of those in the other group did. This fact showed that the instructions which were intended to produce anxiety had been effective. Of the 32 girls in this group, 20 chose to wait with other girls. In contrast, only 10 of the 30 girls in the second group chose to wait with others. Thus the desire to affiliate was clearly related to anxiety or fear.

The result of this experiment fits well with common observation. People in trouble tend to seek out the company of others. Whether this is the only factor in affiliation, we do not know, but it is one factor.

Social Approval and Esteem

Social psychologists recognize another class of motives that have one thing in common: they concern a person's standing with other people. A number of terms are used to refer to this kind of motivation: social approval, self-esteem, status, prestige, and power. The concept of status is best discussed later in connection with social groups. The terms prestige and power, although useful as descriptive words, have no precise psychological meanings. The two most clearly defined motives in this class are motives for social approval and self-esteem.

Social approval   Almost any personality test, whether it is the TAT or a pencil-and-paper questionnaire, reveals a person's desire, weak or strong, to behave in socially acceptable ways. A number of scales measure the need; one that was especially constructed to study it is the Marlow-Crowne Social Desirability Scale. When ratings on this scale are correlated with other tests and with behavior in experimental situations, we obtain a fairly clear picture of the approval-dependent person (Crowne and Marlow, 1964). He favors tasks set by others rather than those chosen by himself, even when the tasks are dull. He readily conforms to social demands and is easily persuaded by others. He gives more conventional responses than the average person in tasks like word-association tests. He is also more cautious in risk-taking situations. Finally, he seeks affiliation with others more often than the average person. In summary, he depends on social approval to obtain a feeling of self-esteem. Thus the approval motive stands between an affiliation motive on the one side and a need for esteem on the other.

Self-esteem   The need for self-esteem is the need to think well of oneself. This need has a social context; it is a need to regard oneself well in relation to others, and as such is connected with the need for social approval. But it can also mean a need to respect oneself regardless of what others think of him. Hence self-esteem is a motive that can be satisfied in a variety of ways: by obtaining social approval, by finding self-respect, by attaining prestige or power, or by achieving success in some line of endeavor. This point illustrates the intertwining of social motives that makes them difficult to disentangle. The need for self-esteem can be satisfied through achievement, yet achievement may be a means of building up self-esteem.

Achievement

Although psychologists recognize self-esteem as an important motive, the motive that they have studied most thoroughly is the need for achievement (Atkinson and Feather, 1966). Those who have done the research usually call it the *achievement need.*

The strength of a person's achievement need can be measured by giving him a test like the TAT. A set of pictures is used that emphasizes achievement-related themes, and as in the regular TAT, the person is asked to tell stories about the characters and situations he sees in the pictures. His stories are then scored for the number of themes that involve achievement motivation. The resulting score can be used like an IQ, or like the score on any other test, to do research on achievement motivation.

Once strength of achievement need could be measured, several questions were asked. One was, Is achievement need related to actual achievement? Experimenters found that the answer is "Yes." People with a high achievement need do better on tasks they are given than people with a low achievement need (Lowell, 1952). The way in which the high scorers excel varies from task to task. In some cases they do better right from the start, because their high achievement need has made them more proficient in the skills required for the task. In other cases they simply learn faster. And in still others they work harder, accomplishing more in less time. But whatever form their superiority takes, they generally excel in tasks designed to discriminate between different levels of performance (Cofer and Appley, 1964).

As you might guess, achievement need correlates fairly well with intelligence: the coefficient is usually around .40. This correlation can be explained by two intertwined factors. First of all, as Chapter 9 will show, high achievement need actually increases intelligence—not a lot, but significantly. This is because high achievement need causes the person to develop some of the aptitudes that go into the measurement of intelligence. Secondly, intelligence itself affects the achievement need. The brighter a person is, the more challenged he is by difficult tasks.

Fear of failure When psychologists first began to study the achievement need, they thought they were dealing with a single motive. They began to wonder, though, when they studied the relation between the motive and actual performance. The relationship between TAT scores and actual achievement on tasks was clear enough for people who were at the extremes: the low scorers were low in achievement, the high scorers high. But people in the middle groups presented a mixed picture, sometimes performing like low scorers and sometimes like high ones. This ambiguity made research workers take another look at their scoring system.

Studying the records from the stories used for scoring, they decided that another motive, *fear of failure*, was usually mixed with the achievement need. Themes reflecting this motive had at first been scored as representing achievement need. Now the two needs were separately scored; each person received a score on achievement need and another on fear of failure. Looking at some other tests, the experimenters found that one, the Mandler-Sarason Test Anxiety Questionnaire mentioned earlier in this chapter, did a good job of assessing fear of failure. So they began to use it to obtain a score on "test anxiety."

Risk taking Many games present an opportunity to study the way in which achievement need and fear of failure are related. In one, a ringtoss game, people try to throw a ring onto a peg from some distance away (Atkinson and Litwin, 1960). Each person is allowed to pick his own distance, from 1 to 15 feet. To induce achievement motivation, the experimenter says that he wants to "See how good you are," and has the other subjects, in this case college students, standing around watching the player. The question is, What distance does a person choose?

The results of such an experiment are given in Figure 3.6. The players had been divided into four groups according to their scores on achievement need and fear of failure, which we will simply call *anxiety*. The groups represented combinations of high and low scores on the two tests: high-high, high-low, low-high, and low-low. To keep the graph uncluttered, we have shown results for only two groups—high-low and low-high. As you can see, the group that had high achievement need with low anxiety tended to choose a distance of around 10 feet, which made the task difficult but offered some chance of success. The distances chosen by the low achievement need, high anxiety group, on

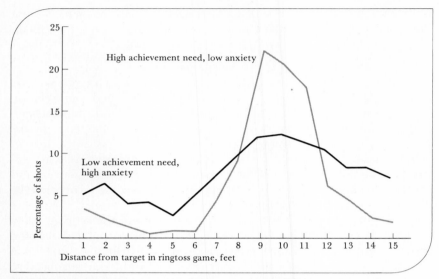

Figure 3.6 *Differences among people in achievement need and in fear of failure affect their willingness to take risks. The curves plot the percentage of shots taken by players in a ringtoss game. Players who were high in achievement need and low in test anxiety tended to shoot from intermediate distances, mostly 7 to 12 feet. Thus they balanced their chances of success with risks of failure. Players who were low in achievement need and high in test anxiety distributed their choices of shooting distances more evenly. (Modified from Atkinson and Litwin, 1960.)*

the other hand, scattered all over the place, with some players taking extremely easy shots and others very difficult ones.

A theory has been devised to account for results like these (Atkinson and Feather, 1966). It helps us understand the interplay between achievement need and fear of failure in the risks people choose to take. For a person with high achievement need, doing something easy that everyone else can do is not much of a challenge, so he shies away from easy tasks. On the other hand, if he tries tasks that are too difficult, the chances of success are slim. Not much can then be achieved with high risks. Consequently he chooses a risk that is a compromise between the very easy and the very difficult. Such a task of moderate difficulty offers the best chance of achievement.

Now let us consider the person with a great fear of failure, that is, great anxiety. The easy task is attractive because he is fairly certain to succeed. The very difficult task may also seem inviting, because no one can succeed very well on it and failure is no stigma. But he tends to avoid tasks of medium difficulty, because this is where comparisons with high achievement can be made.

Everyone has some mixture of the two motives. If fear of failure is high, it tends to cancel the risks that are chosen when achievement motivation is high. Thus risk taking has the form shown for the low-high group in Figure 3.6. On the other hand, if fear of failure is low, the effects of achievement need are more prominent, and risk taking is distributed as it is in the high-low group of Figure 3.6. To bring out the main points of this explanation, the two curves can be generalized as they are in Figure 3.7.

Origin of achievement motivation   People obviously differ quite a bit in the strength of their achievement needs—we all can observe that without using scores on a TAT. But why do they? Much effort has been given to the question without consistently clear results. Psychologists seem to find part of the answer in a person's *early* independence training. Starting with toilet training and eating habits, some parents expect a lot of their children and teach them to do things for themselves. Other parents do not. This difference in training shows some correlation with achievement need.

Aggression

Aggression is listed here among the social motives not because it is one, but because some people think it is. Since violence, war, and aggression are common in both ancient and modern societies, people often assert that aggression must be *instinctive.* Psychologists find no basis for this claim. Instead, their many studies of aggression lead to the conclusion that it is a *response* to certain kinds of situations (Berkowitz, 1968).

One of these situations involves *frustration.* If you want to see a

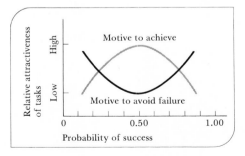

Figure 3.7 *A strong motive to achieve makes tasks with moderate probability of success more attractive than very easy tasks (no challenge) or very hard ones (too little chance for achievement). But a strong motive to avoid failure leads to avoidance of the middles range of difficulty, because this is where the person can be compared with high achievers. The motive to achieve is the dominant motive; the motive to avoid failure modifies but does not replace it. (Adapted from Atkinson and Feather, 1966.)*

display of anger, take a toy away from a child or a bone away from a dog. This and any other frustration of ongoing activity is likely to elicit some aggression. Early experiments led so clearly to this conclusion that psychologists in general, like Dollard and his associates (1939), were at first inclined to say, "Frustration always leads to aggression." But they have since found that this is not true. There are other consequences of frustration, depending on the person and the circumstances, and there are other causes of aggression.

One of these causes is aggression itself. A good way to make a dog mad is to hurt it; a good way to make a human mad is to hurt him physically or insult him verbally. Many of a person's outbursts of anger are in response to such injury, real or imagined.

Aggression is also a response that can be learned through imitation (Bandura et al., 1963). This is illustrated by an experiment in which two different films were shown to two matched groups of children. One film portrayed an adult acting aggressively, the other a nonaggressive adult. Following the movies, the children were put into a frustrating situation. The children who had seen the aggressive adult were more aggressive in their responses to frustration than the children who had seen the nonaggressive adult.

Aggression, then, is not a continuing motive. Rather, it is a response we make to frustration or to the aggressiveness of others, or an imitation of aggressive behavior seen in others.

SUMMARY

Motivation is a term covering any behavior directed toward a goal. It is usually cyclic. It begins with a need or motive, which elicits behavior that is instrumental in achieving a goal, after which the motive is satisfied.

Goals in motivation may be positive (the person approaches the goal) or negative (he avoids the goal). Goals may also be learned or unlearned. An unlearned goal, like food, is a primary goal. Something like money can become a learned positive goal when a person learns to associate it with food, the primary goal of hunger. Motives converge when one kind of activity—say, working for money—simultaneously satisfies several motives, such as hunger, affiliation, and curiosity. Motives may also conflict when the same goal is both positive and negative, or when the satisfaction of one goal frustrates the achievement of another goal.

Primary motives are unlearned motives that either are inborn or appear through maturation. Some have a physiological basis; others do not. Hunger and thirst are primary motives with a physiological basis. Sexual and maternal motives in animals are regulated by hormones, but hormones are less important in humans. Both people and animals have primary motives for sensory stimulation, for indulging in activity, and for manipulating objects. In general, organisms have a motive for competence, that is, a motive to exercise their capacities to the fullest.

Most learned motives in human beings have to do with other people; they are therefore social motives. Some social motives, however, are unlearned. One, according to experiments with baby monkeys, is an affectional motive for "contact comfort." The motives that most people develop for social approval and for self-esteem are learned. Most people also learn an achievement need for succeeding in the tasks they undertake. The achievement need is usually in conflict with some degree of fear of failure. Aggression, which is often counted among the social motives, is not really a permanent motive but a response to frustration or aggression, or an imitation of aggressive behavior that has been observed in other people.

SUGGESTIONS FOR FURTHER READING

Berkowitz, L. (Ed.) *Roots of aggression.* New York: Atherton, 1968. *A series of papers summarizing the sources of aggression.*

Berlyne, D. E. *Conflict, arousal, and curiosity.* New York: McGraw-Hill, 1960. *A systematic treatment of curiosity and exploration as motives.*

Cofer, C. N., and Appley, M. H. *Motivation: Theory and research.* New York: Wiley, 1964. *A thorough textbook on motivation.*

Fuller, J. L. *Motivation: A biological perspective.* New York: Random House, 1962. (Paperback.) *An easily read account of motivation, with special emphasis on physiological motives.*

Murray, E. J. *Motivation and emotion.* Englewood Clifs, N.J.: Prentice-Hall, 1964. (Paperback.) *An elementary textbook on motivation which covers most of the important aspects of the subject.*

4

Emotion

LEARNING OBJECTIVES

Main objective

After studying this chapter you should be able to describe the physiological changes that take place in emotion.

Other major objectives

You should also be able to

Describe the relation between physiological arousal and performance.

Outline the situations giving rise to emotions at different ages.

Show how the judgment of what emotion is being expressed depends on the kinds of information the judge has.

Minor objectives

Describe the autonomic system by naming its two subdivisions and describing the main function of each.

Describe the development of pleasure responses.

Specify the kinds of situations that give rise to humor and laughter.

Distinguish between fear and anxiety.

Trace the development of fears.

Describe the startle and orienting responses.

Emotion is a powerful force in human affairs. It is at the root of wars, murders, racial conflict, and all sorts of other conflict between people. On the other hand, emotion is the sauce of life; things would be pretty dreary without it. The fun we have at parties, our satisfaction in achieving goals, and the amusement we get out of comical situations all make life worth living.

Emotion, then, is just as important as motivation in understanding what makes people tick. But what is emotion? It is several things. For one, it is a stirred-up state of the body marked by many physiological changes. For another, it is a feeling, arising partly from the stirred-up state, that may be pleasant or unpleasant. Also, emotion is something a person expresses—with voice, face, or gesture. Finally, emotional feelings can serve as motives or goals. If they are pleasant, they are positive goals; if unpleasant, negative goals. These interrelated aspects of emotion are considered here under three main headings: (1) physiological changes, (2) emotional situations, and (3) emotional expression.

PHYSIOLOGICAL CHANGES IN EMOTION

Physiologically, what happens in any kind of emotion, whether we are happy, mad, fearful, or just excited, is that we become *aroused*. Intense emotion occurs only when we are in a highly aroused state. Conversely, when we are aroused we are more likely to react to situations with strong emotion. Even mildly emotional states involve some degree of physiological arousal. Arousal consists of increased muscular tension, and is characterized especially by changes in the autonomic nervous system.

The Autonomic Nervous System
The autonomic nervous system is composed of some centers in the brain and of nerves going out to various parts of the body (Figure 4.1). What distinguishes it from the rest of the nervous system is that it serves *glands, smooth muscles,* and the *heart muscle.* The glands served by the autonomic system are of two kinds: duct glands, like the salivary glands, and ductless (endocrine) glands, such as the adrenal gland. Smooth muscles are called smooth because they do not have the stripes found in "voluntary" muscles of the skeleton. Smooth muscles are the ones located in the stomach, the intestines, and the walls of blood vessels. The muscles of the iris of the eye that control pupil size are also smooth muscles.

The autonomic system is divided into two parts: the *sympathetic* system and the *parasympathetic* system. In most, but not all, cases, the two systems serve the same organs. A gland like the salivary gland, for example, is controlled by both systems. So is the heart. In general, the two systems have opposite effects on the organs they serve. Here are specific examples: When the sympathetic system is aroused, the pupil of the eye dilates, the salivary gland stops secreting (this is what makes your mouth dry when you are frightened), the breathing rate increases, the heartbeat speeds up, blood vessels in the stomach and

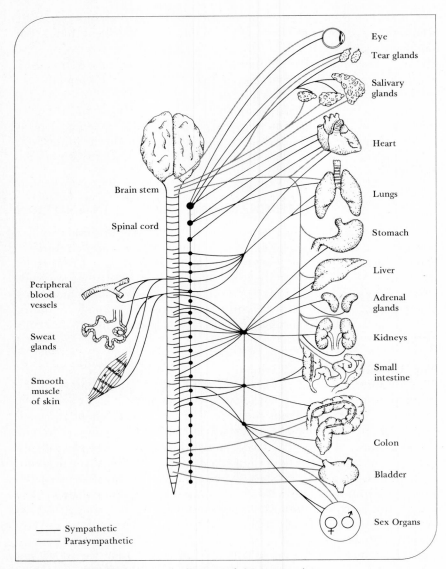

Eye

Tear glands

Salivary glands

Heart

Lungs

Stomach

Liver

Adrenal glands

Kidneys

Small intestine

Colon

Bladder

Sex Organs

Brain stem

Spinal cord

Peripheral blood vessels

Sweat glands

Smooth muscle of skin

——— Sympathetic
——— Parasympathetic

Figure 4.1 *Simplified schematic diagram of the autonomic nervous system with its nerves that link it to various parts of the body. It has two main divisions: the sympathetic system and the parasympathetic system. In general, the sympathetic system is the "emergency" system for arousal; the parasympathetic system usually acts to conserve energy.*

intestines contract, blood pressure rises, the electrical resistance of the skin falls, and the adrenal gland secretes the hormone known as adrenalin or epinephrine. On the other hand, impulses in the para-sympathetic system cause the pupil of the eye to contract, the salivary gland to secrete saliva, breathing to decrease, the heart to slow down, blood vessels in the stomach and intestine to dilate, and blood pressure to fall. (The adrenal gland is served only by the sympathetic system, so that its output hinges entirely on sympathetic activity.)

Behind these details is a general picture of how the two systems operate. The sympathetic system, acting pretty much as a whole, is the system for physiological arousal. It has sometimes been called the "emergency" system, because all the things it does prepare you for the actions required to meet emergencies. It mobilizes energy for the extreme exertion required to run away in a frightening situation or to fight off an attacker. Hence the sympathetic system is putting out when you are highly aroused with fear or anger. The parasympathetic system, on the other hand, opposes the sympathetic system and so is the system of conservation. Although there are some exceptions, its actions generally tend to conserve and build up energy stores in the body.

Measuring Autonomic Changes

Researchers in anxiety and personality frequently want to measure a person's degree of autonomic arousal. Psychologists are also asked to measure arousal for a practical reason—lie detection. In either case all they have to do is record one or more of the sympathetic responses that occur in arousal. The choice of indicators in research, however, is somewhat different from the choice in lie detection.

Measurement in research Research workers usually measure one or more of three changes: skin resistance, heart rate, or pupillary changes. Their favorite, because it is easy to measure and very sensitive to changes in arousal, is *skin resistance.* This has other names: skin conductance (the lower the resistance, the higher the electrical con-ductance) and the galvanic skin response (GSR). To measure it, they usually attach two electrodes to adjacent fingers of one hand. Any situation that causes an increase in arousal is indicated by the swing of a recording voltmeter in the direction of decreased skin resistance. *Heart rate* is measured by electrodes or amplifiers attached to recorders.

Pupillary responses, which have been used to measure autonomic changes only in recent years, must be recorded photographically or with a TV camera. Since the sympathetic system causes the pupils to dilate, the amount of their dilation is a measure of the arousal value of a stimulus. Dilation, indeed, is a sensitive measure of arousal, as the following experiment illustrates (Hess and Polt, 1960):

> Male and female subjects were shown a series of pictures, most of which were chosen to be of more interest to one sex than to the other. A few "neutral" pictures were put in as controls. The pictures included a baby, a mother and a baby, a male "pinup" figure, a female "pinup" figure, and a neutral landscape picture. While the subjects looked at the pictures, a camera snapped photographs of pupil size every 2 seconds. Control measurements of pupil size were made just before the pictures were shown.
>
> The results are charted in Figure 4.2. The pictures of the baby, mother and baby, and male "pinup" figure, which should be more interesting to females than males, did cause a much larger dilation of pupils in females than in males. Similarly, males' pupils dilated more to a female "pinup" figure. The neutral landscape caused little change in either except that it actually "turned off" the females: their pupils contracted slightly.

Results like these have been obtained in many experiments. The general rule is that any stimulus which is interesting (arousing) causes

Figure 4.2 *Pupil reactions in females and males to five pictures. Pictures most interesting to females (baby, mother and baby, and a male "pinup" figure) cause a sizable enlargement in the pupil of the eye in females, while the picture most interesting to males (a female "pinup" figure) produced a similar reaction in them. (From Hess, 1965,* Scientific American.*)*

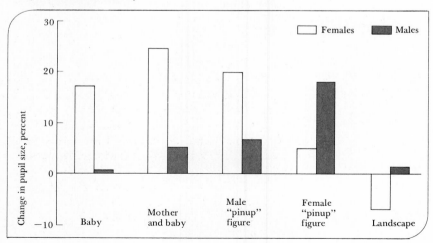

the pupils to dilate. Stimuli that are uninteresting either produce no change or cause a slight contraction of the pupil. Changes in pupil size are so sensitive and consistent that they can be used to measure the interest value of advertisements.

Lie detection   As used in lie detection, autonomic measurements frequently include breathing rate, heart rate, and the GSR. The operator presents a set of stimuli, usually words, while he watches an ink-writing device that records the autonomic responses. (Because the device is called a polygraph, the lie detector test is often called a polygraph test.) The stimuli are questions of two types: critical and neutral. *Neutral* questions are those that should have no more arousal value for a suspect than for other people. The *critical* questions are those connected with the crime of which the person is suspected. If he is guilty, these questions should make him more anxious, hence more aroused, than the neutral questions. By comparing reactions to the two kinds of stimuli, the polygraph operator tries to decide whether the person is innocent or guilty. But the test is not foolproof; some criminals feel little anxiety about their crimes and escape detection by the polygraph. Because of this fact, evidence from lie detector tests is generally not admissible for obtaining a conviction, although it may be used in preliminary hearings or as a basis for prosecution (Smith, 1967).

Psychosomatic Disorders

Sympathetic responses, we have seen, are emergency reactions. They prepare a person to exert more strength, run faster, or fight harder in emotional emergencies. But if for some reason sympathetic discharges are chronic; that is, if they continue over a long period of time, they can cause a *psychosomatic disorder.* This is a disorder of some organ of the body brought on partly by emotional tension. Constant activity in the sympathetic system results in a lot of wear and tear on the body. For example, it tends to maintain heart rate and blood pressure at high levels, and these states can injure the heart and increase the likelihood of heart ailment. High blood pressure can also cause blood vessels to burst, especially in the brain, where the bursting is called a stroke or cerebral accident. High sympathetic output to the stomach and intes-tines can lead to ulcers. In fact, we can experimentally produce ulcers in rats by keeping them in an emotional situation (Sawrey and Weiss, 1956). In human beings, however, damage to organs is seldom caused *solely* by emotional stress. Emotional tension merely aggravates a tendency toward some disorder caused by infectious or dietary condi-tions, injury, or degenerative changes accompanying aging.

Emotional Arousal and Performance

Emotional arousal also has an effect on human performance. The relationship between arousal and performance is an inverted U curve (see Figure 4.3). What this means is that up to a point arousal aids performance; beyond it arousal hinders performance.

As an example of arousal improving performance, psychologists found many years ago that achievement on such tasks as memorizing or adding columns of figures could be increased by having a subject squeeze a ball, thus raising arousal level. Common sense tells us that the more alert we are, the better we can perform. For that reason you should be reasonably aroused when you study. On the other hand, as many students know, getting too anxious can impair performance or produce "mental blocks."

As an example (adapted from Schlosberg, 1954), take the case of a sleeping man. He is near the zero level of arousal. His brain is relatively inactive, his muscles are relaxed, and the sympathetic part of his nervous system is functioning at a low level. In this state he does not respond to most stimuli. But now the alarm clock rings, waking him up and thus markedly raising his level of arousal. His muscles become active, his eyes open to visual stimuli, and his movements in bed and then puttering around the room all evoke the feedback of sensory impulses. This further increases his level of arousal.

Within an hour the man has aroused to the point of functioning efficiently. He is alert and doing well at the things he has to do. But now he looks for a book he cannot find. Frustration intensifies his arousal to the point where he is slightly irritated. He keeps on hunting for the book without finding it. As the search goes on, he becomes angrier and angrier and eventually works himself into a "blind rage." Now he is so upset that he wouldn't see the book even if he came across it.

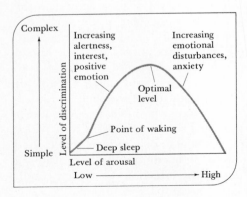

Figure 4.3 *The inverted U-shaped relationship between performance and emotional arousal. Beyond an optimal level, arousal impairs efficiency in most tasks. (Modified from Hebb, 1955.)*

EMOTIONAL SITUATIONS

So far this chapter has treated only one dimension of emotion: the dimension of arousal, which is common to all emotion. There are hundreds of shades of emotion that can be distinguished and labeled with words. Three basic kinds are fear, anger, and pleasure; and most if not all shades of emotion are some combination of these. Fear is often mixed with anger, and it can also be combined with pleasure, as when children ride a roller coaster or a mountain climber works his way up a difficult cliff. Let us consider the basic emotions in their purest forms.

Pleasure

Many different things give us pleasure, but one general principle covers them all: Pleasure is a response to the satisfaction of a motive or, in other words, to the achievement of a goal. This principle applies to both unlearned or primary motives, including curiosity and exploration, and learned or secondary motives such as social approval and status.

Development The things that give us pleasure change from birth onward, depending on the maturation of abilities and the responses we have learned. Early in life the human infant shows signs of pleasure at being physically comfortable. When he is warm, dry, and well fed, and no pins are sticking him, the baby is usually relaxed, smiling, and cooing. By the time he is two or three months old, he shows signs of pleasure when he sees a human face or hears a friendly voice. Still later he takes pleasure in exercising a new skill, as in Chapter 3's example of a child learning to stand. In general, as the baby grows into childhood, he finds pleasure in situations that are novel but not frightening, that allow for the expression of curiosity and manipulation, and that offer him some chance of success in doing what he attempts to do.

Smiling and laughing, which are the most obvious signs of pleasure, appear at the age of about 2 months. Apparently some maturation of the nervous system is necessary for this response to occur. When it does, it is first a reaction to being tickled or stroked. A little later it happens when the child hears or sees some interesting stimulus—as when a parent waves his arms, dances, stands on his head, or pulls a toy around the floor. A young child takes pleasure in physical contact with adults—clinging to them, riding piggyback, climbing all over them. When curiosity and exploratory motives are more fully matured, he takes pleasure in pulling things apart, playing with toys, and exploring. By the time adolescence arrives, the child has learned the usual social motives (such as affiliation, social approval, and achievement), and takes pleasure in satisfying these.

Humor and laughter We smile and laugh in a great variety of situations. In general these fall into two categories: One is when people express superiority, hostility, sexuality, or other usually *unacceptable* motives. Children laugh when they see a playmate in a sorry predicament or when they annoy another child by teasing him. Some adults laugh at "dirty" stories, thereby expressing sexual preoccupations that are otherwise deemed unacceptable topics for conversation. The second type of situation causing laughter is one that involves *incongruity.* A person laughs when there is some contrast or incongruity between what the situation is supposed to be and what he sees that it is.

Funny stories usually include elements of both situations. They contain expressions of superiority, hostility, or sexuality, but they rely primarily on developing incongruity. The good storyteller leads you to expect one thing, then delivers a surprise in his punch line. The stronger the expectation and the quicker the switch to a different outcome, the better the joke. To be funny, however, the switch must be reasonable; the surprise could have been the outcome of the story had we not been led to expect something different. Hence the incongruity must make sense. Something that is just different or completely implausible usually falls flat.

Fear and Anxiety

As in the case of pleasure, the situations that produce fear change with age. In infancy the main causes of fear are loss of support and something strange that occurs unexpectedly. A loud noise, for example, is not necessarily fear-producing, but it is if it comes suddenly. So are strange objects, like stuffed animals or false faces, when they appear unexpectedly.

As children grow older, Figure 4.4 shows, threats of various kinds become causes of fear. Young children may be afraid of imaginary creatures, of being left alone, or of being in the dark. Later in childhood they become fearful of social humiliation and ridicule—of social threats—and are less bothered by the strange things that scared them in infancy. As the child goes into adolescence, social threats—fears of being left out of a group, of being ridiculed, or of being disliked by the other children—become even greater sources of fear.

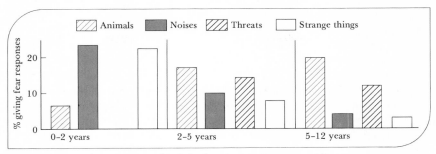

Figure 4.4 *Babies are most fearful of noises and strange things; older children, of animals and threats of harm. (After Jersild et al., 1933.)*

Factors in development of fear One of the ways a person can develop fear is through *conditioning*. As Chapter 3 said, fears are easily conditioned. For this reason each person's fears will be somewhat different from another's. If he has had a painful fall, he may go through life being afraid of high places. Or if he has been lost in a crowd as a child, he may have a conditioned fear of crowds.

Besides conditioning, fears may be acquired *symbolically* through the example of parents and the stories they tell. If a parent is afraid of something, a child observing his fright may learn to be afraid of the same thing. The child may also learn fears from stories he is told. Many children have become afraid of the dark after hearing tales about a bogeyman who might carry them off in the night.

A third factor in the emergence of fears is the child's *developing perception* of his world. The infant is not too discriminating; he does not know one face from another. But when he has learned to tell the faces of his parents from those of other people, he may be afraid of the strange faces.

Anxiety The difference between fear and anxiety will become important when we study personality and adjustment. As used by psychologists, the term *fear* applies when we can recognize what causes it; we know what we are afraid of. *Anxiety,* on the other hand, is a vague fear experienced without our knowing just what is the matter.

One cause of anxiety can be an *unconscious memory* of a fear stimulus. It is often easy to forget the particular situation in which we learned a fear. It may have happened in early childhood before our memory for events was very good. Or even if it occurred later, our memory may have rejected the fearsome experience because we do not like to think about it. We may have "repressed" it, and cannot recall it without the special probing that goes on in psychotherapy. In either case we end up with a learned fear that we have forgotten how we developed. When we encounter the situation to which fear has been conditioned, we feel an uneasy anxiety without knowing why.

Another cause of anxiety is *stimulus generalization.* As described in Chapter 3, when we learn a response to a particular situation, we have learned a response to all situations that are similar to the original one. Stimulus generalization can occur, and frequently does, without our being aware of it. A child who learns to fear his strict father may later feel uneasy or anxious in the presence of other men. He sees them as being like his father, and he has a vague fear that transfers to them through the process of stimulus generalization.

Anxiety and conflicts   A conflict arises in a person when two or more needs cannot be satisfied at the same time. It causes the frustration of a motive, and this frustration—or the fear of it—results in anxiety. The number of possible conflicts a person can experience is enormous, especially in a complex society, but they can be analyzed into three basic types.

In one kind of conflict, called *approach-approach* conflict (see Figure 4.5), a person has two needs each with a *positive* goal. He may, for example, be both sleepy and hungry at the same time. Or he may be torn between going to a basketball game or to a party. A deeper and longer-lasting case of conflict is that of a woman who wants both a family and a career. Men, too, often feel a conflict between their desires to spend time at their job and time with their family. Approach-approach conflicts are usually resolved by having "some of both." But often "some" of each is not enough to satisfy both needs.

Another kind of conflict, *avoidance-avoidance*, where a person is under the influence of two *negative* goals, is less easily resolved. A child must do his arithmetic or get a spanking. A student must spend the next two days studying or face the possibility of failure. A man must work at a job he dislikes or lose his income. These people are "caught between the devil and the deep blue sea"; they have anxiety-producing threats from two sides.

Two kinds of behavior are common in avoidance-avoidance conflicts. One is *vacillation*; the person is pushed back and forth between the two negative goals. As he shrinks from one, he comes closer to the other. In this position he is repelled again toward the first. And so on. The man thinks of quitting the job he dislikes, but then he thinks of the consequences of being without a job. This thought makes him feel that he had better hold onto his job. Another characteristic of avoidance-

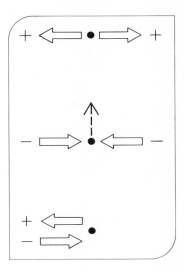

Figure 4.5 *In approach-approach conflict (top), the individual is attracted to two goals at the same time. In avoidance-avoidance conflict (center), he is caught between two threats, fears, or situations that repel him—in which case he may try to leave the situation (dashed arrow). In approach-avoidance conflict (bottom), he is attracted to a goal, but the goal also has a fear or threat associated with it.*

avoidance conflicts is an *attempt to leave the situation.* The trouble is that there are usually other negative goals that keep the person from leaving. The child who does not want to do his arithmetic or get a spanking may think of running away from home. But this is a third negative goal, inspiring enough fear to keep him where he is. Then he may try to leave the situation by indulging in fantasy or daydreams rather than doing his studying.

Although the people involved may feel that these avoidance-avoidance conflicts are the most painful, a third kind of conflict, *approach-avoidance*, is the most difficult to resolve. As Figure 4.5 shows, here the same goal is both *positive-negative*; it attracts and repels. A young woman may have acquired a dislike of bodily contact or a distaste for sex. At the same time, she wants to get married and have a family. When she comes to the point of marriage, the husband-to-be is both a positive and negative goal. Some way must be found either to reduce her fear of bodily contact or her desire for marriage and a family. Otherwise she will stay in a state of conflict, with its accompanying anxiety. Another approach-avoidance conflict that we all have to some extent was treated in Chapter 3: the conflict between achievement need and fear of failure.

Anger and Hostility

Chapter 3 summarized the causes of aggression: (1) frustration of motives, (2) injury and insults, and (3) imitation of aggression in others. The most common is frustration, or to use another term, *interference with goal-directed activity.* Frustration of any need or ongoing activity that restrains a person, or requires him to do something he does not want to do, provokes anger.

Because the things people do and do not want to do change with age, the causes of anger change too. In infants, simple restraint, which frustrates activity and exploratory motives, is a source of anger. In children, frequent provocations include being required to sit on the toilet, having things taken away, having their faces washed, being left alone, losing the attention of an adult, and failing to accomplish something they attempt. In older children and adolescents, the causes of anger broaden to include social frustrations and disappointments. Sarcasm, bossiness, social snubs, or thwarting of social ambitions become frequent occasions for anger.

Not only do the causes of anger change with age; so do the forms of expressing it. Among preschool children, anger is likely to take the forms of temper tantrums, surliness, bullying, and fighting. Among adolescents and adults, these expressions become more subtle, indirect, and verbal. They include sarcasm, swearing, gossiping, and plotting. The change in the way of expressing anger is obviously brought about by social pressures.

One important thing about anger is that we do not want to see it in *other people.* We like them to be happy and pleasant. Perhaps we can sympathize with their fears and disappointments, but we don't want them to be angry. The reason is that when another person gets mad at us, we feel threatened and angry in return. This simple fact has a couple of consequences. One is that parents try to stamp out angry behavior by punishing it, or at least by not rewarding it. Thus society attempts to teach us not to be angry. Second, we try to suppress our anger, or at least its expression, because we do not want people to be angry at us. Either way, we are under pressure to keep our temper.

But this state of affairs is frustrating. Anger functions temporarily as a motive that needs to be vented. When it is not, we suffer frustration, and frustration is the main cause of anger. Also, the punishment of angry behavior is another cause of anger. Therefore society, in its need to suppress anger, actually provokes it. The result is not so much to teach people not to be angry as to teach them not to show it. Anger smolders inside instead of coming out into the open. This smoldering anger, which can be detected in various ways, is called *hostility.*

Anger and hostility can be conditioned and generalized in the same way as fear. We get angry at whatever frustrates us, and if the same obstacle keeps blocking us, we acquire a conditioned reaction of anger or hostility toward it. To use the example of the strict father, a boy who frequently becomes angry at his father soon feels generally hostile toward him. This hostility may generalize to "father figures," that is, to all men who remind him of "father."

Interpretation of Emotions

This chapter began by saying that the physiological state of arousal is similar in all emotions. Yet we have very different feelings from time to time. In one situation we may feel cheerful, in another depressed, in another afraid, and in another angry. How can one account for these different feelings if the underlying physiological state is the same?

The answer is that we *interpret* our feelings according to the situation we are in. At least, this is psychologists' best theory—a so-called cognitive theory—of what is going on (Schachter, 1971). It is supported both by common observation and by experiment. Consider the person who has had a few alcoholic drinks. His physiological state is changed by the drug, but his feeling may be different depending on where he is. If he is at a great party, he may feel elated; if in a gloomy bar, he may be depressed. A similar effect has been noted with some of the other mood-affecting drugs. LSD, for example, produces different moods in the same individual, ranging from euphoria to fear or hostility. More precise evidence for the cognitive theory comes from controlled experiments such as this one (Schachter and Singer, 1962):

> Male college students were put in a state of physiological arousal by injecting them with epinephrine (adrenalin). Some were told what the injection was and what it would do; others were told it was a vitamin compound. The two groups were each divided into two subgroups. Subjects in one subgroup of each group were given some entertainment designed to make them happy. Subjects in the other subgroup were put into a situation intended to make them angry. Thus all the subjects had the same state of physiological arousal, but they were exposed to different circumstances. Their reactions were measured by having them fill out rating scales of their moods. The results showed that subjects who received what they thought was a vitamin compound, so that they did not know the cause of their aroused state, felt the emotion and behaved in ways appropriate to the situations they experienced. By contrast, subjects who were told about the effects of the injection interpreted their bodily state as being due to the injection; they tended not to experience emotions appropriate to the situation they were in.

EMOTIONAL EXPRESSION

When a person is very angry or very much afraid or very joyful, we can usually recognize the emotion he is feeling by the way he behaves. But which patterns of behavior distinguish one emotion from another? And how accurate are we in telling emotions apart?

Startle and Orienting Responses

The most basic emotional response is the *startle pattern.* It has been studied extensively with the aid of photography and is consistent from person to person. You can observe it yourself by tiptoeing up to a person who is deep in thought and yelling "Boo!" The reaction you get is the startle pattern. It consists first of rapid closing of the eyes with a widening of the mouth. Then the head and neck are thrust forward, often with the chin tilting up, the arms and legs are bent, and the muscles of the neck stand out. The uniformity of the response from one person to another suggests that it is an inborn response which is modified very little by learning or experience.

Another stereotyped response, more readily seen in animals than people, is the *orienting reaction.* As the term implies, this is an organism's orientation to a new stimulus or to stimulus change. It consists of a tensing of muscles and a change in the position of the head. The exact pattern of the orienting reaction depends upon the species, the animal's age, its present state of arousal, and other factors. In a cat it appears as a rapt state of attention in which the cat is ready to pounce on whatever is presenting the novel stimulus. A dog, hearing the faintest sound of another dog, perks up its ears, stands at attention, and makes ready to defend its territory. An infant turns his head and eyes toward any novel stimulus, such as a toy or strange face.

The orienting reaction is related to several concepts already discussed. First of all, it is a *reflex* response to novelty. What is novel may depend on learning or on the situation just preceding it, but the basic reaction is unlearned. Second, the orienting response is one of heightened *attention.* It readies the organism to respond to whatever follows. Third, it is linked to *curiosity* motivation. In fact, the Russians refer to it as the "What is it?" response. Finally, it is an *arousal* response that primes the organism to move speedily if the need arises.

Facial and Vocal Expression

Emotional patterns other than the startle pattern and orienting reaction differ from one person to another. Each individual has his own way of expressing himself. This fact is sometimes apparent in photos of crowds at political rallies, rock concerts, football games, and the like. The observed event is roughly the same for everyone there, but notice the great differences in facial expression. Looking at each face separately, you would not know that the people are responding to the same situation.

To see just how good we are at evaluating facial expressions, psychologists have constructed a three-dimensional system for people to judge emotion from photographs of faces (see Figure 4.6). One dimension is general level of activation or arousal, called the *sleep-tension dimension*. A second is *pleasantness-unpleasantness*. Signs of happiness are rated as pleasant, while those of sadness, fear, or anger fall into the unpleasant area shaded gray in the diagram. The third dimension is *attention-rejection*. Attention is characterized by wide-open eyes and sometimes by flared nostrils and an open mouth. In rejection the eyes, lips, and nostrils are tightly shut as if to keep out stimulation.

These three dimensions of emotional expression can be judged from photographs with reasonable reliability (Engen et al., 1958). Judgments of pleasantness-unpleasantness seem to be the easiest. In general, the mouth turns down in unpleasant emotions, up in pleasant ones. The same is true of the eyes; they slant up in mirth and drop in sadness. Leonardo da Vinci recognized this principle and made use of it in painting.

People express emotion with their voices as well as their faces, but we do not have any catalog of the vocal signs of emotion. In general, but not always, screams denote fear or surprise; groans, pain or unhappiness; sobs, sorrow; and laughter, enjoyment. A tremor or break in the voice may indicate deep sorrow; a loud, sharp, high-pitched voice usually expresses anger. Nonetheless, it is difficult to distinguish emotions just by listening to the sounds people make.

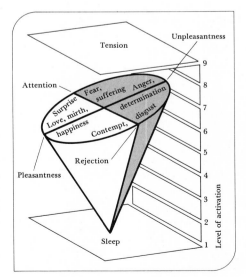

Figure 4.6 *A solid representing three dimensions of facial expression in emotion: sleep-tension, attention-rejection, and pleasantness-unpleasantness. The top surface is sloped to show that unpleasant emotions, such as anger and fear, can reach higher levels of arousal than the pleasant emotions. (After Schlosberg, 1954.)*

Posture and Gestures

Emotions are also expressed by posture and gestures. In fear, a person flees or is "rooted to the spot." In anger, he usually makes aggressive gestures and may even clench his fists and move to attack. In sorrow, a person tends to slump with face downward; in joy, he holds his head high and his chest out. Such signs of emotion are taken for granted in Western society.

But how consistently are emotions expressed in this way? Individuals actually differ widely, just as they do in facial expressions. If judges are given photographs showing only hands and forearms, they agree only for highly conventional expressions, such as worship. On the other hand, if they are permitted to see both facial expressions and gestures, their judgments agree better than for faces alone, although agreement is still far from perfect (Kline and Johannsen, 1935).

If we compare the expression of emotion in our society with that in other societies, we must conclude that gestures as signs of emotion are largely learned from the people around us. Gestures are highly conventionalized by each society; each seems to have its own "language of emotion." The Chinese, for example, frequently express surprise by sticking out their tongues, disappointment by clapping their hands, and happiness by scratching their ears and cheeks. In Western society sticking out the tongue is more likely to indicate defiance, clapping happiness, and scratching our ears worry.

Knowing the Situation

These and other studies of emotional expression indicate, first, that observing only the expression of emotion does not produce very reliable results. People simply do not react to the same situations in a consistent way. Second, the more we can observe, the better guesses we make about the emotion being expressed. If we can see both facial expression and gestures, and if we can hear the vocal expression as well, we do much better. Even so, judges often confuse emotions such as anger and fear.

In order to identify the kind of emotion another person is experiencing, we need not only to observe his expression but to know the situation giving rise to it. Then we can read his emotion pretty well because we know what we ourselves would be feeling under the circumstances.

SUMMARY

Emotion is a physiologically aroused state which involves changes in the autonomic nervous system, especially in the sympathetic system. The responses most often used as measures of emotional arousal are the galvanic skin response, heart rate, and dilation of the pupil of the eye. Prolonged emotional tension can have psychosomatic effects, aggravating such conditions as high blood pressure and ulcers. Up to a certain point, increased arousal helps performance, but when emotional tension is too high, performance deteriorates.

Situations that give rise to emotions change with a person's age; in adulthood, social situations are more important than physical conditions. Pleasure is the reaction to the satisfaction of a motive. Fears are acquired through conditioning, through watching others or hearing frightening stories, and through perceptual maturation. Anxiety is a vague fear experienced without the person's knowing exactly what causes it. One important source of anxiety is a conflict of motives. Anger is a response to the frustration of motives, to injury or insults, or to observation of other people's aggressive behavior.

Different patterns of behavior accompany different emotions. Two patterns that are inborn are the startle reaction and the orienting response. Judgments of emotion based on observing only facial and vocal expression are rather poor. They improve when we also see a person's posture and gestures, and improve still more when we know the situation to which the person is reacting.

SUGGESTIONS FOR FURTHER READING

Birdwhistell, R. L. *Kinesics and context: Essays on body motion communication.* Philadelphia: University of Pennsylvania Press. 1970. *A summary of interesting research on the communication of body movements and posture.*

Candland, D. K. (Ed.) *Emotion: Bodily change.* New York: Van Nostrand Reinhold, 1962. (Paperback.) *A set of original papers on emotion with emphasis on physiological changes.*

Darwin, C. *The expression of emotions in man and animals.* Chicago: University of Chicago Press, 1965. *A reprint of a classic and readable book.*

King, R. A. (Ed.) *Readings for an introduction to psychology.* (3d ed.) New York: McGraw-Hill, 1971. *A book of readings that supplements this book.*

Schachter, S. *Emotion, obesity, and crime.* New York: Academic, 1971. *A summary of some fascinating experiments on the cognitive theory of emotion.*

5

Principles of Learning

LEARNING OBJECTIVES

Main objective

Name and define five kinds of learning and give an example of each.

Other major objectives

After studying this chapter you should be able to explain how classical conditioning differs from operant conditioning, using an example of each.

Trace the steps involved in acquiring an avoidance response.

Define the difference between primary and secondary reinforcement.

Evaluate the relative effectiveness of reward and punishment.

Minor objectives

You should also be able to

Explain how the timing of reinforcement helps shape operant behavior.

Distinguish between the extinction and suppression of learned behavior.

Describe the different effects on behavior of the different schedules of reinforcement.

Define stimulus generalization and give two examples of it.

State how the size of reinforcement, especially punishment, affects learning.

Describe how the consistency and proximity of reinforcement strengthens responses.

Describe the relationship between punishment and the strength of the response being punished.

Indicate the value of having rewarded alternatives to the response being punished.

In man, little or no instinctive behavior is inherited. We have a few unlearned reactions (mainly the eyeblink, pupillary, salivary, and knee-jerk reflexes) that serve as signs of normality to the neurologist, but they are not important in understanding human nature. The momentous feature of the human inheritance, both for the species and for the individual, is *certain capacities for learning.* People vary greatly in these inherited capacities, but in the end it is *learning* that makes the individual as we know him.

Through learning we come to speak a particular language, acquire customs and attitudes, form certain personality traits and not others, and develop different ways of perceiving the world. Since everything we do and think comes out of learning, it is the key to understanding how most individuals behave.

This makes learning a very large subject, and indeed for many psychologists the study of learning is practically synonymous with the study of psychology. They are not far wrong; most of this book is about learning and the consequences of learning. Besides this chapter and the next, Parts II and III on personality, adjustment, and group processes all emphasize the way individuals learn to function in relation to other people. Even Chapter 9 on psychological testing concerns the measurement of things people have learned.

This chapter examines the most basic principles of nonverbal learning—principles that apply to all learning, whether by people or animals. The next chapter on human learning and memory applies these principles to human learning. It will stress verbal learning, which is uniquely human and occupies much of preschool and school education.

To begin with, what is learning? *Learning is any relatively permanent change in behavior which occurs as a result of experience or practice.* This definition has three important parts. First, learning is a change in behavior, for better or worse. If there is no change, there is no learning. But the change may not show up immediately. If you try to teach a child not to touch things that are hot, on several occasions you may say "No!" and pull his hand back from a hot object. The first few times there may seem to be no learning; the child still reaches for hot things. Something has been registering, though, for after a few trials, he obeys you and avoids the hot object when you say "No." At this point you know that learning has occurred because the child's behavior has changed.

Second, learning takes place through experience or practice. Other changes in behavior, such as those which occur through matura-tion, fatigue, or injury, do not count as learning. If a person starts to limp because he has hurt his ankle, that is not learning. If he becomes irritable because he is tired, that is not learning either.

Third, the change must be relatively permanent. If it is not, it is probably due to a transitory change in motivation, to fatigue, or to adaptation. A person entering a dark movie house on a bright afternoon stumbles around because his eyes have been light-adapted. He needs to dark-adapt in order to find a seat; when he does, it is not learning but simply a temporary change in behavior due to adaptation.

BASIC KINDS OF LEARNING

In the final analysis all learning is of two basic kinds: *classical conditioning* and *operant conditioning.* In both, a specific response to a stimulus or stimulus situation is acquired. Classical and operant conditioning differ in three ways: (1) the nature of the stimulus, (2) the kind of response learned, and (3) the relation of the response to reinforcement.

1 *Stimulus.* In classical conditioning the stimulus is a specific event, such as the flash of a light or the sound of a tone, which is briefly presented. But in operant conditioning the stimulus is not a specific event; it is a longer-lasting situation which has several features, only one or a few of which prove relevant to learning.

2 *Response.* In classical conditioning the response, like the stimulus, is a specific one. Moreover, it is usually a reflex or an innate reaction to a situation. But in operant conditioning the responses are at first varied, random movements in the stimulus situation.

3 *Response and reinforcement.* The most important difference is the relation of reinforcement to the response made. The concept of reinforcement, introduced in Chapter 3, refers to the satisfaction of a goal. Food is a positive goal of the hunger motive; escape or avoidance is a negative goal of a fear- or pain-producing situation. In classical conditioning the reinforcement is always presented following the conditioning situation, regardless of what the person or animal does. It does *not* depend upon the response made. But in operant conditioning reinforcement *does* depend on the response. If the subject does the "right" thing, he is reinforced; otherwise he is not.

Classical Conditioning
Classical conditioning gets its name because it was the first kind of conditioning to be studied experimentally. It was made "classical" by the pioneer studies of the Russian psychologist Ivan P. Pavlov. In 1904 Pavlov received the Nobel prize for his work in the physiology of digestion, and it was this work that led him into experiments on conditioning.

Salivary conditioning   In studying the role of saliva in the digestion of food, Pavlov found, as scientists often do, that something was getting in his way. Salivation was occurring *before* food was placed in the mouth of the dogs that he was using as experimental animals. The normal, reflex response is salivation after food is put in the mouth. Just bringing a dog repeatedly into a standard experimental situation, he noticed, was causing it to salivate. Realizing that some kind of learning was going on, he decided to make a systematic study of it (Pavlov, 1927, 1960).

Pavlov devised an operation and an apparatus for measuring the flow of saliva in a dog's mouth (Figure 5.1). The operation consisted of diverting the flow of saliva to the outside of the mouth. Here drops of saliva were picked up in a cup. Then they ran down a tube, displacing air in the tube, which in turn displaced a colored fluid in an instrument that looked something like a thermometer. This gave Pavlov a precise way of measuring the salivary response whenever it occurred.

For the conditioning part of the experiment, he placed the dog in a soundproof room with a one-way screen, so that he could see the dog but the dog would not be distracted by watching him. He also hooked up a pan that could be swung into and out of the dog's reach. As an alternative arrangement, powdered food was puffed into the dog's mouth. The apparatus was also constructed so that Pavlov could present several kinds of stimuli to the dog, including the sounds of a buzzer, bell, or metronome.

Figure 5.1   *Pavlov's apparatus for studying the conditioned salivary response. The dog is in a soundproof room with a one-way vision screen between it and the experimenter. The experimenter can sound the bell (CS) and present food (US) by remote control. (After Pavlov, 1928.)*

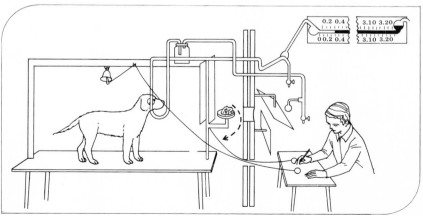

The experiment consisted of pairing one of these stimuli with food, allowing a brief time interval in between. Pavlov would, for example, sound the bell and then, after a few seconds, present the food. He continued pairing the bell and food while measuring the amount of saliva the dog secreted in response to the bell.

In this way Pavlov could chart the course of conditioning as it is shown in Figure 5.2. A key diagram for classical conditioning, the graph makes many points that you will be referring to later in the chapter. For now, concentrate on the first panel with the conditioning curve. Note that the ordinate (vertical axis) of the graph is labeled *strength of conditioned response*. This is a general term psychologists have adopted to indicate how fully something has been learned. In Pavlov's study, the amount of saliva secreted on a trial measures strength of response. In other experiments, strength of response might be indicated by how accurate a person is on a test of some sort, or how often he makes a response to some stimulus.

Here are some other important terms. Any reflex response, before it is conditioned, is called an *unconditioned response* (UR). In Pavlov's experiment, food placed in the dog's mouth before conditioning caused the response (UR) of salivation. The stimulus which causes the response, in this case food, is called the *unconditioned stimulus* (UC). Finally, the stimulus used to condition the response, in this case a bell, is called the *conditioning stimulus* while the experiment is going on, and

Figure 5.2 *Schematic diagram of the course of conditioning, extinction, reconditioning, and reextinction. Spontaneous recovery after a rest period is shown by the vertical arrow. (After McGeoch and Irion, 1952; adapted from Gregory A. Kimble and Norman Garmezy,* Principles of General Psychology, *3d ed. Copyright © 1968, The Ronald Press Company, New York.)*

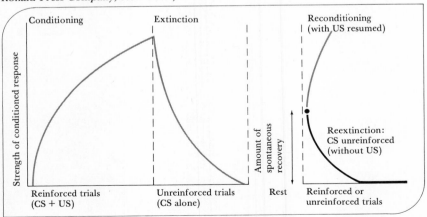

later after conditioning has made some progress, the *conditioned stimulus.* In both instances it is given the shorthand label CS.

Salivary conditioning has been described not because it is so important in everyday life, but because it illustrates the way in which important conditioning can take place. All the same, most of us really have acquired conditioned salivary reactions. Dinner bells do not ring the way they used to down on the farm (producing salivary responses and a stampede to the table), but in modern life the smell of food, talk about food, or the thought of food can still make our mouths water.

Fear conditioning Another kind of conditioning—*fear conditioning*—plays a bigger part in everyday life. Most of us have had a good many fear-conditioning experiences, and these fears become part of our adjustments—and sometimes our maladjustments—to the world. As an example of fear conditioning in man, the case of Albert, an 11-month-old boy, is famous in psychology (Watson and Rayner, 1920).

> At the beginning of the experiment, Albert had no fear of animals. When shown a white rabbit, he acted delighted and made no effort to get away (Figure 5.3). Later, however, he was shown a white rat and at the same time heard a loud noise. As Chapter 4 said, loud noises are usually fear stimuli (USs) for young children, if not for all of us. The loud noise made Albert shrink back. The procedure of presenting the white rat (CS) and sounding the noise (US) was repeated on several occasions. Next, the white rabbit, which formerly caused no fear, was presented to Albert again. This time he was frightened by the sight of the rabbit alone, and he fought to get away. He had developed a conditioned fear to a white animal. His fear even extended to other white furry objects, including a white beard on a man. (The switch from the rabbit to the rat to white furry things demonstrates stimulus generalization, discussed in Chapters 3 and 4. This chapter too will have more to say about it.)

All that is required, then, to condition fear is to pair some neutral stimulus (CS) with some natural or unconditioned stimulus (US) for fear. An important feature of fear conditioning is that it happens *fast.* Salivary conditioning takes many trials, but fear conditioning takes very few. Rats can regularly be conditioned in five trials; under some circumstances, one will do.

In people, too, fear conditioning may require only one trial. It often happens that a person who once nearly drowned has a desperate fear of water. In a case written up in the book *The Locomotive God* (Leonard, 1927), a child wandered a few blocks from home to some railroad tracks. A passing train scalded him with steam. Years later, as

Figure 5.3   *Conditioning and generalization of fear in a baby. Upper left, before conditioning, Albert approaches a white rabbit without fear. Upper right, a loud noise, which startles and scares him, is paired with the presentation of a white rat. Lower left, after conditioning, Albert appears to be afraid of the rabbit. Lower right, he is afraid of other white furry objects. (After Watson and Rayner, 1920.)*

an educated man (a professor and a poet), he had an intense fear of leaving home and its immediate neighborhood.

Operant Conditioning

As explained earlier, operant conditioning differs from classical conditioning in (1) the stimulus situation involved, (2) the response made, and (3) the relation of reinforcement to response. These differences can now be made a little clearer.

In operant conditioning the stimulus is a box, a room, or a situation, rather than a brief stimulus such as a bell or a light. The organism in operant conditioning *emits* responses—it wanders around, sniffs, looks at things, pushes them; it does not give a specific elicited response as in classical conditioning. Finally, some one of the responses it emits obtains a reward or avoids punishment. To put all this together, we can say that operant conditioning consists of learning to perform some act that leads to reward or avoids punishment. Operant conditioning can be illustrated by seeing what takes place in a box which used to be called a Skinner box but which nowadays, in deference to Professor Skinner, is called an operant chamber.

This is a chamber (Figure 5.4) that can be outfitted in many ways—with two or more levers, two or more lights, a feeding place into which pellets can be dropped, a drinking place for water, and a metal-grid floor for applying electric shock. The operant chamber permits us to study all sorts of learning. Reduced to the bare essentials, however, it consists merely of a box with a lever protruding from one wall and a food cup below it for rewarding the animal with food.

Attached to the lever through an electrical circuit is a device that makes a recording on paper each time the rat pushes the lever (Figure 5.5). It is called a *cumulative recorder*, because one response moves the pen one unit, another response another unit, a third response a third unit, etc., and the responses are cumulative—they add up. Since the paper moves at a constant speed, a steep line on the record means that the rat is making responses in quick succession. A relatively flat line means that it is making very few responses.

Suppose now that a hungry rat is placed in an operant chamber hooked up to a cumulative recorder. Since the box is unfamiliar to the rat, and unfamiliar things tend to evoke fear in animals, the rat at first shows signs of fear. But these signs soon fade as the box becomes more familiar, and

Figure 5.4 *A rat in an operant chamber pushes the bar that delivers a pellet from the feeder. The pellet constitutes the reinforcement. (Courtesy of Pfizer, Inc.)*

Figure 5.5 *A cumulative recorder, through which the learner "draws" a record of his responses. Each response causes the pen to move a very small distance to the left as we view the recorder in the photograph. The paper moves at a constant rate under the pen. The rate of response is shown by the slope of the lines on the paper. Here, the short tick marks indicate when reinforcement was given. After the pen reaches the right edge of the paper, it is reset to the left, and the record continues. The record is thus a continuous one; it is broken up simply to keep it on the paper. (Ralph Gerbrands Co.)*

the rat starts to explore. It does many things—sniff at walls and crevices, paw at the floor and the walls, stand on its hind legs, and run along the floor. Eventually it depresses the lever, perhaps by leaning on it, or by bumping it with its head, or by grasping it with its paws. When the lever is depressed a pellet of food is released and falls into the food cup. There is a click of the feeding mechanism and a sound of the falling pellet.

This is the rat's first correct response and first reward in the chamber. In the case shown in Figure 5.6, the period between the time the rat was placed in the box and the time it made the first rewarded response was 15 minutes (Skinner, 1938). And there was another minute or so before the rat noticed the food and ate it. The rat didn't learn much from this first experience. But the food pellet, which the rat ate because it was hungry, aroused it and caused it to explore with greater vigor. As luck would have it, the rat did not strike the lever again for 20 minutes —altogether, 35 minutes after the experiment began. At 47 minutes, it made a third response; at 71, a fourth. At this point the rat began to "get the idea." Speaking more strictly, *it had become conditioned.* Responses started coming rapidly. From then on, it alternately pushed the lever and ate the pellet about as fast as a rat can.

This experiment illustrates the conditioning of an operant response. The rat's operant behavior—its repertoire of responses—at the beginning of the session had many components: sniffing, pawing, running, standing, and incidentally pressing the bar. But only one of the responses, pressing, was rewarded. This response was the one it learned after a few trials of pairing the response with the reward. Note carefully that the rat *was required to emit the response himself;* it was not a reflexlike response that was elicited, as it is in classical conditioning.

OTHER FORMS OF LEARNING

Every kind of learning known to us can be analyzed satisfactorily into some combination of classical and operant conditioning. But except for fear conditioning, we seldom see pure classical conditioning outside the laboratory. The learning most common in everyday life is some form of operant conditioning, often combined with classical conditioning. Here are some examples (Deese and Hulse, 1967).

Discrimination Learning

When we learn to make one response to one stimulus and another response to another stimulus, it is called discrimination learning. This kind of learning may be either classical or operant. Pavlov could teach

Figure 5.6 A record of responses from a rat in an operant chamber. After about 80 minutes, the rat got the point that it could press the bar for food. Its rate of response then was high and fairly steady; it had become conditioned. Note that low rates of response produce shallow slopes; high rates produce steep slopes.

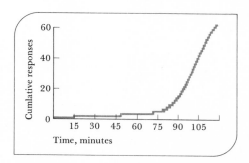

his dogs to discriminate between a bell and a buzzer simply by reinforcing one with food, and not reinforcing the other. The usual procedure is to train the dog to give a conditioned response to a bell; then the experimenter intermittently sounds the buzzer, without following it with food. At first when the buzzer is sounded, the dog responds with salivation—an example of stimulus generalization, because the sounds of the bell and the buzzer are similar. But as trials with the buzzer go unrewarded, the dog salivates to it less and less, while continuing to salivate to the sound of the bell. Eventually the dog never salivates to the buzzer, but always does to the bell. It has learned a conditioned discrimination.

Operant situations can also be arranged to teach discrimination learning. The experimenter may wire an operant chamber so that pressing the bar produces food only when the chamber is lighted. After a while the rat learns to discriminate between light and darkness, and pushes the bar only when the light is on. Or two alleys, leading from a starting place, may be arranged so that the dark one leads to food while the lighted one does not. After enough trials, a hungry rat learns to discriminate the light from the dark alley.

Everyday life abounds with learned discriminations. The child learns to discriminate a cup of milk from a piece of bread, a dog from a bunny rabbit, mommy from daddy. Older children learn to discriminate red traffic lights from green, apples from oranges, bears from lions, and on and on. It is hard, in fact, to think of anything we do that does not involve some kind of learned discrimination. The greater part of education consists of learning discriminations between words and concepts. But what we do in all discrimination learning is simply to attach different responses to different stimuli.

Motor Learning

Simple operant learning requires knowing *what* to do to achieve a goal. Motor learning, sometimes called psychomotor learning or skill learning, is learning *how* to do something well. Everyday life is also full of activity that demands motor learning: eating with fork and spoon, talking, handwriting, typewriting, driving a car, driving a golf ball, playing a musical instrument. In all these skills practice is required for the individual to make his responses with speed and accuracy.

In motor learning, stimuli are as important as they are in discrimination learning, but in a somewhat different way. A good golfer needs a certain stimulus situation—a feeling in his wrists and legs, eyes over the ball, feedback stimuli from shoulders and arms as he raises his club—in order to swing well. Pianists and typists must get into certain positions where "things feel right" in order to perform. In other words, motor skills require *coordination* between environmental and internal bodily stimuli and the act to be performed. The emphasis in motor learning, however, is on the particular way the response is executed.

Motor learning is usually measured by the speed and the accuracy with which a response is produced. In typing tests, for example, typing speed is scored against the number of errors made. And when the daily test scores of a person who is learning to type are plotted on a graph, they form a learning curve that looks very much like a typical conditioning curve (for example, the first curve shown in Figure 5.2). That is, the curve is usually steep at first when rapid progress is being made, then becomes flatter as mastery is approached. As learning progresses, more and more practice is required to inch one's way toward perfection.

Avoidance Conditioning

Learning to avoid some person, object, or situation is a combination of classical and operant learning linked in a special way. Before avoidance conditioning can occur, fear and escape conditioning must have taken place.

Fear conditioning, we have seen, is classical conditioning in which some neutral stimulus (CS) is paired with a stimulus that naturally causes a fear response (US). The pairing, in good Pavlovian fashion, soon produces a conditioned fear. Fear conditioning of a child to a white, furry object was shown in Figure 5.3. Once fear has been conditioned to a situation, however, an organism's natural (inborn) reaction to a fear-producing situation is to escape from it. This is true whether the fear is produced by an unconditioned stimulus or a conditioned stimulus. How to escape, however, is not always so obvious to a naïve organism; it frequently must be learned. Escape conditioning is a special form of operant learning, as illustrated by this experiment with dogs (Solomon and Wynne, 1953).

> A dog was placed in a compartment with two halves divided by a fence he could easily jump over. The floor had a grill through which the experimenter could administer an electric shock. The experimenter began a training procedure designed to teach *avoidance conditioning* (not specifically escape conditioning, as will become clear below). He turned on a buzzer and then, 10 seconds later, he sent an electric current into the floor on the side of the box where the dog was. The experimenter wanted the dog to learn to jump over the fence during the 10-second interval, or "warning period." If the dog did, the buzzer was turned off, and no shock was given. If the dog did not, both the buzzer and the shock continued until the animal jumped the fence.
>
> As the record shows (Figure 5.7), from the beginning the dog always

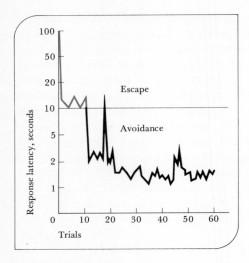

Figure 5.7 A dog acquires an avoidance response to a buzzer. The fairly sudden transition from escape to avoidance is typical. It shows that learning to avoid punishment takes place rather abruptly after a period of fear conditioning and escape conditioning. (Modified from Solomon and Wynne, 1953.)

managed to escape, but not to avoid, the shock. A shock evokes a variety of reactions—sometimes merely sitting and yelping, other times moving around the compartment. Sooner or later, the movement gets the dog over the fence and away from the shock. Hence it learns very quickly to escape shock—about as quickly as fear conditioning is learned. This rapid learning characterizes both fear and escape conditioning.

But the experimenter's main purpose was to teach the dog to *avoid* the shock by responding promptly to the buzzer. How does this happen? The record shows that avoidance conditioning took a few more trials, but when it happened it too did so rather abruptly.

The learning curve in Figure 5.7 does not look like the rather smooth curve seen in other learning experiments that do not involve emotional responses. Why? Analysis of the situation reveals an interesting linkage. During the early trials, two kinds of conditioning are going on: emotional (fear) conditioning and escape conditioning. While the dog is learning to escape, it is also being fear-conditioned to the buzzer. The two types of conditioning gradually become linked: the feeling of fear becomes conditioned to the escape behavior. As this connection becomes stronger, it reaches a point where the fear produced by the buzzer now becomes a kind of stimulus that evokes the escape responses. When these occur before the shock arrives, the animal *avoids* the shock—he does not just escape it after he feels it. Thus avoidance conditioning is a two-step process in which fear conditioning to the buzzer and escape responses to the shock are learned, and then the two together produce avoidance. This effect has been studied in great detail, and psychologists are quite sure that the two-step mechanism is the explanation (Solomon, 1964).

The same analysis applies to human avoidance. A child usually needs to touch hot things a few times, each time reflexly withdrawing his hand (escaping) before he learns to avoid hot objects. In the meantime he is acquiring a conditioned fear of stoves, cigarettes, or flames (whatever the hot objects are), and this causes the avoidance. Adults too avoid situations in which they have been afraid, because they have been conditioned to avoidance through fear and escape conditioning.

Conditioning of Attitudes

Many attitudes, though not all, are formed through simple conditioning. If we are in an unpleasant situation, the negative feelings it arouses become conditioned responses to the stimuli connected with the situation. A person who has been painfully poor has negative feelings about signs of poverty and is likely to react by avoiding them. Conditioning can also produce favorable attitudes. If we have had a good time—felt pleasure—in the presence of another person, he tends to make us feel good and we have a favorable attitude toward him. If a child has had pleasant meals while using his mother's pink dinnerware, a pleasant feeling will be conditioned to pink (another example of stimulus generalization). Chapter 12 will explore attitudes in much more detail.

CONDITIONS OF LEARNING AND RETENTION

So far, this discussion of the kinds of learning that can take place in animals and people has outlined what happens when the simple conditions for learning exist. The conditions themselves, however, can be altered in many ways that make a difference in how effective the learning is and how well it is retained. By studying these conditions psychologists can see what is necessary for learning to take place and what can speed it up or slow it down.

Arousal and Motivation

One of the important conditions for learning is arousal: the organism must be aroused but, as Chapter 4 explained, not too aroused. If a subject is in a very low state of arousal—if he is asleep, for example—he does not learn. (Although it has been claimed that some learning can take place in sleep, the amount is so small as to be debatable.) Certainly for learning to proceed very efficiently, the subject must be wide awake and alert to his environment.

Up to a certain point, the higher the arousal level, the better the learning. Beyond that point, when the organism is in a highly excited state, most forms of learning are retarded. The general relation between arousal and learning, then, is an inverted U curve—the same curve as the one back in Figure 4.3 showing the relation between arousal and performance. Learning becomes increasingly better as arousal rises to a fairly high level, but beyond that it becomes increasingly worse. When the high arousal is one of great anxiety or emotional excitement, learning is seriously hampered.

For example, if an experimenter is conditioning a rat, dog, or other animal for avoidance, he must be careful not to make the electric shock too strong. Weak shocks that "keep the animal on its toes," just sufficient to motivate it to escape and avoid the shock, are best. A very strong shock makes an animal so emotional that it bounces around the cage without paying attention to the warning stimulus. This slows learning so much so that in many cases the animal never does learn. Students getting ready for examinations may find themselves in the same boat. If they put off studying for too long, they may find themselves in a panic, unable to concentrate and learn what they could learn in a moderate state of arousal. The block that some students get in the examination itself is a similar phenomenon, even though the problem here is one of retrieving what they have learned rather than of original learning. The effect of too high a state of arousal, as we shall see (page 136), is to lower overall academic performance.

In most learning situations the subject must be not only aroused but *motivated*. The relationship between arousal and motivation is circular. An aroused subject is easily motivated by external stimuli—lights, sounds, odors, and novel objects in the environment. They evoke his curiosity and exploratory responses. On the other hand, a subject with internal motivation, such as hunger or thirst, is aroused by that motivation to be active and to explore his environment.

Motivation is important because it gets the organism to make responses, either specific or general, that can be rewarded. An animal must be hungry, for example, if it is to make the specific response of searching for food (in the natural condition) or salivating to food (in the Pavlovian laboratory situation). Otherwise the response is not present to be rewarded by food. Or in operant learning, motivation brings out a whole series of initially undirected or "random" responses in the operant box, one of which, the pressing of a bar, can be rewarded with food.

Suppose a mother wants to teach her child, who is a little thirsty, to say "milk" when a glass of milk is shown to him. One way of doing this, when he is ready to learn, is to show him the glass while she says "milk." If the child repeats the word after her, he is given a sip of milk as a reward. If he is motivated, he tries many things. He may grab for the glass, he may cry, he may shake his head, he may stick his tongue out at his mother, or he may imitate the word "milk"—the correct response. If he is not motivated, these responses are less likely to occur, so that he may never emit the correct one and never have a chance to learn it.

Motivation, then, is a critically important condition for learning because it both arouses the subject and makes him responsive to his environment. In those circumstances when an appropriate response does occur, it can be rewarded.

Primary and Secondary Reinforcement

Up to this point we have talked about "reward" and "punishment." The modern psychologist, however, does not often use these words. He uses a more general term to cover both cases: *reinforcement.* To him, *a reinforcement is anything that strengthens a response*—anything that promotes learning. A reward is a positive reinforcement; a punishment is a negative reinforcement. In either case, *reinforcement is the key to learning.* If it is not present and *if* it is not applied in the right way at the right time, there is no observable learning. Discrimination learning may sometimes take place without observable reinforcement, however, as we shall see later (see Modeling, p. 249).

Reinforcement means somewhat different things in classical and operant conditioning. In classical conditioning, reinforcement is the presentation of the unconditioned stimulus (US), which *elicits* a specific unconditioned response (UR). When the US is paired with a neutral, conditioning stimulus (CS), reinforcement causes the CS to become attached to the UR. Hence the UR becomes a conditioned response (CR).

But in operant conditioning, there is no specific UR to be reinforced by a US. Rather, the reinforcement is anything that strengthens some one of the responses emitted in a situation. To strengthen a response, a positive reinforcement must be relevant to the motive; if the animal is hungry, then food is the relevant reinforcement. A negative reinforcement is a punishment that is *both* motivating (it makes the animal try to escape or avoid it) and a reinforcement. The reinforcement, as analyzed in the experiment where the dog learned to avoid electric shock, really consists of reducing the fear of punishment.

The concept of reinforcement can be broken down into primary and secondary reinforcement. A *primary* reinforcement is an *unlearned* reinforcement. Shock or any unpleasant stimulus is a natural, unlearned primary (negative) reinforcer. Food is an unlearned primary (positive) reinforcer for a hungry animal.

A *secondary* reinforcement, on the other hand, is a *learned* reinforcement. And the rule for learning a secondary reinforcement is that some stimulus must be paired with a primary reinforcement. This is the same rule as for classical conditioning. Thus through classical conditioning, the conditioning stimulus comes to be a secondary reinforcement (or reinforcer) because it is paired with the primary reinforcement.

> Suppose that a rat is placed in an operant chamber, but in this case the experimenter does not try at the beginning to teach it to press a bar. Instead, the rat is simply put through a series of trials in which first a buzzer sounds and then a pellet of food is released into the food tray. The first time this happens, the rat does not perceive the connection between buzzer and food. But in wandering around the box it discovers food in the tray, and it quickly learns to stay nearby to wait for the delivery of pellets. While doing this, the rat begins to associate the buzzer with the delivery of food. The sounding of the buzzer comes to mean, "Food is on the way." The rat thus learns to wait for the buzzer signal. In between trials it wanders around the box paying little attention to the food tray, but when the buzzer sounds it runs to the tray to get food. The buzzer has been learned as a secondary reinforcement for food.
>
> The full meaning of secondary reinforcement can be illustrated by taking the experiment into a second phase. Here the secondary reinforcer (the buzzer) can, by itself, serve as a reward for pressing the bar.
>
> In phase 2 the food tray is disconnected, and the buzzer is wired up so that it sounds when the bar is pressed. The experimenter proceeds as he did in the original experiment of teaching the rat to press the bar, except that now the rat's reward is nothing but the sound of a buzzer. The significant thing is that this sound alone is enough to get the animal to learn. It will learn to press the bar just to hear the sound of the buzzer. The buzzer has become a learned secondary reinforcement with sufficient reinforcing power to promote learning. It is not as powerful as the primary reinforcement, food, and the rat will not keep doing this forever, but it does serve as a reinforcement.

In summary, a secondary reinforcement is a stimulus that has been associated with a primary reinforcement. When the association has become strong, the previously neutral stimulus can be administered as a reward that will serve to strengthen a response. The best example of a secondary reinforcer in modern society is money. Because it can be used to buy things (primary reinforcements) that satisfy primary motives, it acquires secondary reinforcing power. Then it in turn serves as a reward for work (operant behavior).

Timing and Shaping
In the learning situations described in this chapter the term *pairing* has been used repeatedly, because pairing the reinforcement with the

response to be learned is the most essential requirement of conditioning, both classical and operant. Many studies have indicated that the
best interval for such pairing is about $1/2$ second. Longer delays
between the response to be learned and the reinforcement greatly
retard learning.

In classical conditioning it is easy to use the optimum interval, for
the US promptly elicits the desired response and the experimenter
knows just how much before the US he needs to provide the CS. In
operant conditioning, however, there may be a considerable interval
between the time when an animal first presses a bar and the time that
he finds food. The problem, then, is how to get the correct response
and the reinforcement closely paired.

A solution to this problem combines *secondary reinforcement* and
shaping. Shaping is somewhat like the parlor game in which a person is
trying to find a hidden object, and the spectators, who know where it is,
say "warmer," when he gets closer to it and "colder," when he moves
away from it. In such a case the spectators are *immediately* reinforcing
any response that is in the "right direction," thus strengthening that
response. Hence shaping keeps the subject moving closer to his goal
rather than wandering around until he accidentally finds it.

Shaping, initiated by secondary reinforcement, promotes very
rapid learning. To use secondary reinforcement, a rat is first "magazine trained." The experimenter gives it a few free pellets in its food
tray to strengthen the response of staying near the tray. As each pellet
is dropped, the magazine clicks, thereby pairing the sound of the click
with *immediate* reinforcement. Thus the click becomes a secondary
reinforcer. As soon as the rat hears a click, it promptly goes to the food
tray. At this point the shaping begins. First the animal is given a pellet
for going to the general vicinity of the bar. After a few reinforcements
strengthening this response, the rat is rewarded only when it approaches the bar. Again after a few trials, it is reinforced only for bar
pressing. Handled in this way, a rat can be shaped to press a bar in a
few minutes rather than in the hour or more required when it is
reinforced from the beginning only for pressing the bar.

The technique of shaping is very effective in teaching things to
pets or children. To teach a dog to "stand," the trainer can begin by
rewarding the animal for simply approaching him, then for sitting still,
then for reaching upward for the food, then for standing briefly, and
finally for holding a standing position for several seconds. Or to return
to the example of teaching a child to say "milk" when his readiness for
learning to speak has matured, the mother can first reward him for
making almost any sort of vocal sound, then for something remotely
resembling "milk," and finally for something that is pretty close to

"milk." Animal trainers have long used this method to teach stunts and tricks much more quickly than they could by other techniques that fail to keep correct responses and reinforcements closely paired (see Figure 5.8).

Extinction and Suppression

Studies of learning deal not only with the training or *acquisition* of responses but with the *weakening* of responses that have previously been learned. This is an important matter, because responses that have been learned in everyday life often do weaken over time. Then, too, many habits that people acquire are not desirable, and they wish to weaken or get rid of them altogether. How can a learned response be weakened?

Forgetting   One way is simply to permit the subject to forget. If we test him some days or months after he has learned something, the chances are that he will not know it as well as he did immediately after the learning trials. This loss of something learned is called *forgetting* or *lack of retention.* Psychologists now know a good deal about forgetting—when to expect a lot of it or just a little of it. Forgetting is most conspicuous in verbal learning, so the next chapter will devote a major section to it. It is much weaker in nonverbal habits. The strength of a nonverbal habit weakens somewhat after a long period of disuse, but a few reinforced trials normally restore it to full strength.

Extinction   A second way to weaken a response is to extinguish it. *Extinction,* the key term here, is both a procedure and the result of that procedure. The critical feature is that we stop reinforcing the behavior we want to extinguish. All the rest of the extinction procedure remains

Figure 5.8 *Shaping animal behavior for a circus act. The trainer (off camera at right), using a pole, teaches the tiger to ride the horse. (Krone Circus.)*

the same. In Pavlovian or classical conditioning, the experimenter keeps ringing the bell for the conditioned animals, but he no longer accompanies it with food. In operant conditioning, he lets the animal push the bar but does not reward its efforts with food. The procedure is the same whether the learning which is to be extinguished is avoidance learning, motor learning, or discrimination learning. To extinguish it, you discontinue the reinforcement, whatever it was.

Extinction causes a learned response to become weaker. In Pavlovian salivary conditioning, the number of drops salivated to the bell becomes smaller. In bar pressing, the presses become less and less frequent. In maze running, the speed of running slows down and just about stops. If the results are plotted on the same kind of graph that is used to chart learning, an extinction curve looks like a learning curve in reverse (you can see this in Figure 5.2). The extinction curve starts out steeply, because responding is very rapid at first, as it was at first after learning. But the responses drop fairly rapidly, and after a time slow down almost to zero.

These statements about extinction need some qualification. They are true of learning with positive reinforcement, but not so true where the reinforcement is *negative*, that is, where punishment has been used. Fear conditioning, although it is rapid in the first place, does not extinguish easily. Indeed, all emotional responses are difficult to extinguish, and this fact is important in psychotherapy with people who have excessive fears and anxiety. But in classical conditioning, fear conditioning does extinguish—slowly—the experimenter simply does not pair the punishment (US) with the conditioned stimulus (CS).

Avoidance conditioning is an extreme case; it is very resistant to extinction. In some animals and situations, it may not be extinguished after thousands of trials. This was true in some prolonged experiments with dogs that were required to jump over a fence when a buzzer sounded. Two factors make avoidance conditioning unique. First, it is linked to fear conditioning, and that kind of conditioning extinguishes slowly. Second and even more important, in avoidance the subject that is responding well does not know when reinforcement is absent. It has learned to give an avoidance response whenever it hears (or sees) a warning signal. Taking away the punishment means nothing until the subject accidentally fails to avoid and on that occasion receives no shock. Even such occasional experiences tend to have little effect. Eventually some extinction takes place, but usually it is far from complete.

Suppression A third way to weaken a response is through *suppression*: a punishment is used as a negative reinforcement whenever the previously learned response is made. Suppression is really passive avoidance learning that weakens a previously conditioned response. A rat, for example, may have been conditioned to bar-press for food in an operant chamber. To weaken this response, the animal can be both extinguished by omitting the food reinforcement *and* punished by shock each time he pushes the bar. Usually the punishment will temporarily suppress the learned response, but it may not do so permanently. It turns out that the rules for suppressing behavior with punishment are rather complicated. The section on reward and punishment will explain why.

Spontaneous recovery   Another factor complicating the extinction and suppression of responses is the tendency of responses to recover spontaneously. Pavlov noticed that a day or so after he gave his dogs a series of extinction trials, salivary responses bounced back; they were stronger than they had been at the end of extinction (see the right-hand curve in Figure 5.2). He named this comeback *spontaneous recovery*. It is a kind of forgetting in reverse—a tendency to forget the extinction that has occurred. Spontaneous recovery, together with the slowness of forgetting and extinction and the relative ineffectiveness of punishment, makes it difficult to eliminate responses that have been learned.

Partial Reinforcement

Another factor retarding the elimination of responses is the effect of *partial reinforcement.* In all the experiments described up to now, the use of reinforcement was consistent. In the conditioning and learning experiments, it was administered on every trial. In the extinction experiments, it was omitted on every trial. In experimental situations psychologists can be as consistent or inconsistent as they choose.

In everyday life, however, things are seldom consistent. A child playing with fire does not always get close enough to be burned. Parents, because they vary in their moods or in the amount of attention they can pay to the child, are seldom consistent in providing rewards and punishments. Consequently the child is sometimes rewarded or punished for a particular act, but not every single time. Partial reinforcement is the reinforcing of responses only some of the times they are made. When they are reinforced every time, it is called continuous reinforcement. What does it matter whether reinforcement is partial or continuous?

There are several answers to this question, depending on how the partial reinforcement is arranged (Ferster and Skinner, 1957). Any particular arrangement is called a *schedule of reinforcement*—a term which, in practice, is almost synonymous with partial reinforcement. One schedule can be tied to time in such a way that a reinforcement is given at intervals of, say, 10 minutes. This is done no matter how many responses the subject makes, so long as he makes at least one response before the appointed time of reinforcement. This general type of plan is called an *interval schedule*. Another kind of plan, a *ratio schedule*, calls for giving a reward after so many responses are made—say, after every tenth response.

When a schedule of reinforcement is arranged so that the time interval between reinforcements is always the same (an interval schedule) or the number of responses between reinforcements is the same (a ratio schedule), the schedule is a fixed one. Then psychologists speak of a *fixed-interval schedule* or a *fixed-ratio schedule* (see Figure 5.9). It is also possible to have *variable-interval* and *variable-ratio* schedules, in which the interval or the ratio varies from one reinforcement to the next.

One of the things that happens with schedules of reinforcement is that they get more responses out of a subject once he has learned the required response than continuous reinforcement does. When intervals or ratios are reasonably large, he emits many more responses than he would with continuous reinforcement. Responses per hour on

Figure 5.9 *Payday: A fixed-interval reinforcement schedule. (Omikron.)*

these schedules may number in the thousands when under continuous reinforcement they might amount to a hundred or so. This increase in the number of responses emitted is especially prominent in extinction following a schedule of reinforcement. During extinction there is no reward, and therefore no time at all is spent in eating or drinking. And extinction is slower after learning with partial reinforcement than after learning with 100 percent reinforcement.

Another result of schedules of reinforcement is that the pattern of responding changes depending on the particular schedule. A subject on an interval schedule slows down immediately after a reinforcement. Then as the time draws near for another reinforcement, he speeds up, so that he is responding at a high level just before the next reinforcement. But a subject on a fixed-ratio schedule gives a fairly high and steady rate of response throughout. Since this subject must make a certain number of responses for one reward, each response is as important as any other, and he works just about as rapidly as he can in order to keep reinforcements coming rapidly.

There are parallels between these facts and everyday life. Ratio schedules are like paying an employee for piecework; he is paid for so many units of work. Such a schedule tends to maintain high and steady levels of output. Interval schedules are like paying a salary at fixed intervals. Because close supervision tends to mitigate the natural effect of a salary schedule, a person on salary usually works at a steadier pace than he would in an operant chamber. But this schedule tends to make people more interested in their work near payday than earlier in the pay period. Perhaps the most important parallel comes from the effect of partial reinforcement on extinction (called a PRE). Habits learned by partial reinforcement—by the inconsistent application of reinforcement—are much harder to weaken through extinction than habits acquired with continuous reinforcement. This is why some nasty habits in children are often so difficult to break—a subject considered in more detail below.

Stimulus Generalization
As mentioned earlier, Pavlov discovered that if he conditioned an animal to salivate at the sound of a bell, it would also salivate, though a little less, at the sound of a buzzer or the beat of a metronome. The conditioned response was *generalized* from the original CS to other stimuli that were similar. Likewise, the baby reacted fearfully to all white, furry objects when he had been conditioned to one particular object (Figure 5.3). Stimulus generalization also occurs in operant conditioning, and its importance in all learning is hard to over-emphasize.

Except in rigidly controlled laboratory experiments, two situations are almost never exactly alike. Yet we are forever generalizing from one to another. If it were not for such stimulus generalization, learning would be pretty useless. What we learned could not be applied except in a case identical to the learning situation, so that we would have to learn things over and over again. Fortunately, generalization makes a learned response useful in many different situations.

Animals in laboratories are pretty much limited to the learning experiences we plan for them. Otherwise they live drab, though usually comfortable, lives in pens where they are supplied with food, water, and occasionally something interesting to play with. Not so with most people. From childhood on, a human being has many opportunities to learn. He is being taught something, by nature and by other people, many hours of each day. This means that he is taught not just one or two habits, as animals are, but hundreds, even thousands, of them. Some of his learning situations are similar to others he has experienced, and in these cases what he learns in one situation *transfers* over to the others.

Learning Sets

Stimulus generalization is one important case of transfer; another is called a *learning set.* It can be studied in the laboratory by attempting to give animals something comparable to the varied learning experiences of a child. The experimenter presents the animal with a whole series of learning problems to see how one bit of learning transfers from one problem to another. In a program of this sort carried out with monkeys, the animals were provided with a sequence of discriminations to learn on as few as a half-dozen trials for each problem. The series ran as high as 344 problems given to a single monkey. Many of the problems were just different kinds of discriminations. When the monkeys were rewarded for choosing, say, a tobacco can instead of a doll, or a toy car instead of a toy automobile, they learned to make many discriminations.

The result of such a program is that the subjects actually speed up their learning. On the early problems they make very little progress; later they "catch on" quickly. They *learn to learn,* or form *learning sets.* Their progress in learning to learn can be charted by simply scoring them on the *second trial* of each problem, as Figure 5.10 does. (The first trial is like an instruction trial; it reveals which stimulus is correct and which is incorrect. If the discrimination can be learned in one trial, the learning will show up in the second trial.) As the graph demonstrates, learning to learn gradually improves among monkeys from hardly more than chance (50 percent) in the early problems to nearly 100

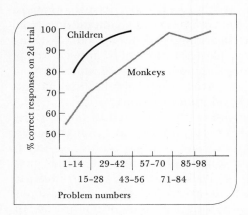

Figure 5.10 We "learn to learn" by transferring previous problem-solving experience to problems that are new but of the same general kind. The curves show learning-to-learn by children and monkeys. In this graph the percentage correct on the second trial of a problem was plotted against the number of problems. (Modified from Harlow, 1949.)

percent in the later ones. Children who are given the same series of problems start at a higher level of performance, but their curve too shows rapid improvement as they learn to learn.

What the children and monkeys learned here is a way of playing the game. On the first trial, the subject finds out what is correct or incorrect. On this or on subsequent trials, he learns a rule: If he is correct, stick with the same response; if incorrect, switch to the other response.

Knowing the rules of the learning game is what enables educated subjects to learn more rapidly and effectively than naïve subjects. Not only do educated learners generalize from previous stimuli, but they transfer a way of going about a learning problem. As a result, they often learn so quickly that they appear to have immediate "insight" into a problem (see page 179). These experiments suggest what their insight, or very rapid learning, really is. It is a transfer of previous experience with solving problems to a new situation—a transfer that enables the subject to grasp the problem quickly and solve it with ease.

USES OF REWARD AND PUNISHMENT

Almost all, if not all, learning involves reinforcement. Sometimes the reinforcement is subtle—a teacher's "Good," or our own feeling of a job well done. Often we are unaware of the reinforcements, either positive (rewards) or negative (punishments), affecting our behavior; but they are there all the same.

Society in general and parents in particular use both rewards and punishments, with varying degrees of success, to teach the habits they consider desirable. Starting with feeding schedules and moving on to toilet training, eating behavior, and "manners," parents combine the two forms of reinforcement according to their best judgment to shape the behavior they consider to be "good" behavior. Sometimes they succeed; sometimes they fail. Why? How are reward and punishment best used to produce learning responses?

Reward versus Punishment

Both parents and psychologists have held varying opinions about the relative effectiveness of reward and punishment. Some have argued that reward alone is sufficient and punishment should be avoided. They feel this way partly because punishment can be damaging both physically and psychologically, and partly because reward, properly applied, often seems to do the job. They subscribe to a theory that undesired responses will drop out through extinction if they are not rewarded, whereas desired responses can be strengthened through simple positive reinforcement.

The problem, now that it has been extensively studied (Solomon, 1964; Glaser, 1971), turns out to be more complicated. There are cases where responses linger on despite efforts at extinction. A child may continue to cry or throw temper tantrums even though the mother tries to ignore, and thus to extinguish, such behavior. It is also true that punishment is often ineffective; a child may continue to put his fingers in an ash tray even though his hand has been slapped repeatedly for doing it. Certainly using punishment successfully can be tricky. However, psychologists have learned some of the rules for using both reward and punishment in the right way at the right time. The following sections summarize them.

Size of Reinforcement

Animals and people learn more quickly, and work harder, for large rewards than for small ones. So if you wish to teach a particular habit, give a significantly large reward—significant to the subject, that is. If praise is used with children, as it often can be, it should be used in ample quantities to reinforce the behavior that the parents want to encourage.

The general rule behind this is that a response is strengthened in proportion to the size or intensity of reinforcement. It applies equally to punishment. If punishment is strong enough, it will completely —and usually permanently—suppress the behavior being punished. A child who burned his finger in a fire will probably never stick them in the fire again. And if all unwanted behavior could be as strongly punished, parents could easily stamp it out.

The trouble is that we tend to scale down the intensity of punishment because we don't like to hurt anyone, particularly children and pets. Then we are in for trouble, because mild punishments tend to be ineffective. They may suppress undesired behavior briefly but not for long (as in the case of punishing a rat's bar-pressing, the behavior tends to stop for a while and then reappear). And light punishment which is also *inconsistent,* as discussed below, is worth almost nothing.

Consistency and Contiguity

Since continuous reinforcement promotes better learning than partial reinforcement does, *consistency* is necessary for reward and punishment to be most effective. Even mild punishment, though ineffective if given only a few times, will do the job when it is regularly administered. This is one of the places where parents go wrong. In many cases they cannot be present each time the child behaves a certain way; in others their will to provide regular reward and punishment simply weakens.

Closely related to consistency is the *contiguity* of reward and punishment to the response being reinforced. Experiments discussed earlier have demonstrated that very close pairing of the reinforcement and the response is required for the most rapid learning. Ideally, the reinforcement should follow within 1 second after the response. The farther removed the reinforcement is from the behavior one wants to alter, the less likely it is to do any good. A delay of as much as 10 seconds can make a reinforcement totally ineffective. Well-intentioned parents who do not wish to punish a child when they are angry or embarrassed often violate this principle by delaying punishment.

Strength of Response

Also important in changing behavior by using reinforcement is the *strength of response*—the strength of the tendency to do something. If a person wants some goal very badly—that is, if he is highly motivated (see Chapter 3)—then rewarding him for behavior directed at this goal will make a powerful impression. He will usually learn quickly what he is supposed to do. On the other hand, if the behavior to be changed is a strongly ingrained habit—ingrained because it has been well rewarded—the habit will be difficult to eliminate with punishment.

Consider the behavior of a professional robber. On the one hand, robbery is highly rewarding. By the simple act of taking money from someone else, a robber obtains more reward more quickly than a man does who makes an "honest" living. Such a large reward so easily acquired greatly strengthens the behavior called "stealing." Unless the robber can be quickly caught (contiguity) and surely punished (consistency), his fear of the punishment he may eventually receive simply is not strong enough to suppress the strong response of robbing. If he succeeds in robbery a good many times without being caught and punished, the habit becomes very strong. The fact that he is later punished, even with long imprisonment, will not break it. This is one reason why the recidivist—the "repeater," or habitual criminal—is so hard to reform.

Adaptation

Small rewards, regularly administered, come to be taken for granted. Also, they do not seem as attractive as they did when they were first given. This is the phenomenon of adaptation to reinforcement. Similarly, people tend to adapt to pain and punishment, especially if these are mild. Punishment that at first suppresses a response may after a while have little or no effect. Children have been known to persist in punished behavior, even though punishment has been consistent, simply because they come to regard the punishment as "not so bad." They suffer it because it is more than offset by the reward they get from the forbidden behavior.

Out of the research on reward and punishment comes some useful advice. Parents do not need to go to extremes in training children, but they should couple punishment of unwanted behavior with reward for approved behavior. In punishing a child, parents should not stop with the punishment and leave him on his own. Rather, they should try to immediately provide him with an opportunity to do something for which he can be rewarded.

Punishment of Consummatory Responses

So far, all the examples in this section have dealt with responses that are *learned* by reward or punishment. The effect of punishment on unlearned consummatory responses is a special case. By a *consummatory response* a psychologist means a response that satisfies a need for food, water, or sexual activity. The response itself is thus the reward, and the question is, How does punishment affect this kind of response? You might think offhand that a consummatory response, being innate, would be hard to change, that it would withstand punishment better than a learned habit. But this is not true. A rat receiving shock at its food tray quickly learns to avoid the tray, no matter how hungry it is. It may even starve itself to death without venturing back to see if the shock is still there. The reason, psychologists believe, lies in the principle of *contiguity.* Shocking an animal as soon as it makes a consummatory response gets a conditioning stimulus and a response about as close together in time as they can be. Hence learning is very fast.

Even more dramatic results are seen when punishment of one consummatory response is combined with the rewarding of another

(Solomon, 1964). If puppies, for example, are given a healthy swat when they start to eat horsemeat, but are allowed to eat pellets without punishment, they quickly learn to eat only pellets and to shun the horsemeat. The learned aversion is so strong that they starve to death if presented only with horsemeat.

Reward and Punishment as Cues

In human societies not many rewards or punishments take the form of physical acts. We do not reward people with food as we do dogs, and except in extreme cases we do not apply physical punishment to adults. Instead, most reinforcements are symbolic—words of praise or reproof; increases in salary; fines for speeding; grades and diplomas (see Figure 5.11). None of these are primary reinforcements: they do not reward or punish physiological motives. They have, however, been conditioned to physiological motives; they are signs of potential primary reinforcement. What they are, in fact, is *secondary reinforcements.*

We have seen that secondary reinforcements strengthen and weaken responses. But they do more than that; they serve as *cues* for desired behavior. By an early age a human being has acquired a large stock of responses; he knows all sorts of things to do in various situations. What he needs to learn is which ones are "right" and which are "wrong." By providing signs of reward like the words and symbols

Figure 5.11 *Olympic swimming champion Mark Spitz with five golden examples of secondary reinforcement. (Den Hanna.)*

"right," "good," "excellent," and "A+," or signs of punishment such as "incorrect," "bad," "naughty," "F," we give cues to the behavior which is wanted and to that which is not. Most of the time such cues do the job; they strengthen and weaken appropriate responses, and they do it without making it necessary to use physical reward and punishment.

SUMMARY

All learning is of two basic kinds: classical conditioning and operant conditioning. In both, reward and punishment (called reinforcements) must be paired with the occurrence of a response. In classical conditioning, the reinforcement is always given along with a conditioning stimulus. But in operant conditioning, there is no specific conditioning stimulus, and reinforcement is given only when the desired response is made.

Other common forms of learning are discrimination learning, motor learning, and avoidance conditioning. In discrimination learning, one response is made to one stimulus, and another response (or no response at all) is made to a different stimulus. In motor learning, the subject learns to make a response more rapidly and more accurately. In avoidance conditioning, there are two stages: first, the organism learns to escape from punishment; secondly, it learns to avoid punishment by responding to the signal that comes before the punishment.

Some conditions are better than others in promoting learning. To learn well, an organism must be aroused and motivated to learn. Too much arousal, however, can impair learning. Initially, learning depends on primary reinforcement, that is, on something which satisfies a primary unlearned motive. A secondary reinforcement, which is a stimulus regularly associated with a primary reinforcement, can also serve as a reinforcement for learning responses. If reinforcement is discontinued—a procedure called extinction—a response gradually weakens through a process also called extinction. Responses can also be suppressed, usually temporarily, by punishing them. After both extinction and suppression, the response is likely to reappear; that is, it tends to recover spontaneously.

In partial reinforcement, a response is reinforced only part of the time it occurs. A response well learned and given only partial reinforcement is made more often than with continuous reinforcement. It also extinguishes more slowly. All conditioned responses show stimulus generalization, in which a response conditioned to one stimulus is made in other similar stimulus situations.

Reward is usually better than punishment in conditioning responses. Punishment can, however, be effective if used correctly: It should be strong enough to suppress the undesired behavior, and it should be given consistently at the time the response occurs. But if the tendency to make a response is very strong, even strong punishment consistently applied may not be effective. People tend to adapt to punishment, especially if it is weak, so that it gradually becomes less effective. Punishment is most effective when a reward is also given for an alternative desired response. Punishment is extremely effective with consummatory responses. Reward and punishment, finally, may serve as cues for correct and incorrect responses, and in this way aid learning.

SUGGESTIONS FOR FURTHER READING

Birney, R. G., and Teevan, R. C. (Eds.) *Reinforcement.* New York: Van Nostrand, 1961. (Paperback.) *A book of readings giving different points of view on the way reinforcement works.*

Deese, J., and Hulse, S. H. *The psychology of learning.* (3d ed.) New York: McGraw-Hill, 1967. *An introductory textbook on animal and human learning.*

Hill, W. F. *Learning: A survey of psychological interpretations.* San Francisco: Chandler, 1963. (Paperback.) *Some of the major psychological theories of learning are discussed.*

King, R. A. (Ed.) *Readings for an introduction to psychology.* (3d ed.) New York: McGraw-Hill, 1971. (Paperback.) *A book of readings that supplements this textbook.*

Pavlov, I. P. *Conditioned reflexes.* New York: Dover, 1960. A reprint of *Conditioned reflexes.* (Trans. by G. V. Anrep) London: Oxford, 1927. *A description of Pavlov's classical experiments on conditioning. Not difficult to read after the fundamentals in this chapter have been mastered.*

Human Learning and Memory

6

LEARNING OBJECTIVES

Main objective

After studying this chapter you should be able to describe the major conditions that affect human verbal learning.

Other major objectives

You should be able to

Distinguish four different kinds of verbal learning.

Give four rules governing transfer from previous learning.

Outline five general methods used in a good strategy of study.

Describe five major features of learning material that affect ease of learning.

Outline the three principal factors that determine how much we retain.

Minor objectives

Describe the role of imitation and operant learning in word learning.

Compare associative learning methods with those used in organized learning.

Explain how learning should be distributed to be most efficient.

Describe the four major features of a programmed learning system.

Compare conceptual and associative similarities, and conceptual and associative hierarchies, in learning material.

Describe four differences between short-term and long-term memory.

Explain how interference affects retention.

Account for the phenomenon of forgetting.

Except for the rare experiment in which a chimpanzee has been taught a few words (page 39), animals do not learn words in any form. But humans, although they acquire many nonverbal skills, spend most of their time in verbal learning. Verbal learning is any learning that makes use of words as either stimuli or responses. Even nonverbal human skills, such as learning how to fix an engine, swing a golf club, or make an end run in football, depend heavily on verbal instructions.

The result of verbal learning is the acquisition of language. Language is a set of symbols used according to certain rules for communication and thinking. The symbols are usually words, and verbal language is the richest of languages (compared, say, with mathematics) because the possibilities of constructing different words and sentences are endless. Chapter 5 concentrated on nonverbal learning in both animals and people; this chapter applies the principles of learning laid down in Chapter 5 to the characteristically human activity of verbal learning. Chapter 7 on thinking will treat the conceptual aspects of language, since these are vital to the thinking process.

KINDS OF VERBAL LEARNING

Verbal learning involves several steps. The first is simply learning to say a word. The next is using the word as a name for a particular object. After that, other words can be learned for the common properties of objects: concepts such as "red," for instance. Finally, words are put together in grammatical sequences to make sentences. The first step of learning to speak words must, of course, come first. But the other steps can overlap, so that a child begins to string certain words into sentences while he is still acquiring other words and learning to use some of them as names for concepts.

Word Learning

When normal children's progress in learning words is charted, it shows an orderly sequence (McCarthy, 1946), just as children's learning of other skills does. (Look again, for example, at Figure 2.2.) At birth the child has no vocabulary, only an assortment of cries, grunts, and breathing sounds. Within a month or so, these sounds begin to have some meaning; they become somewhat different for pleasure, discomfort, hunger, and pain—different enough for the mother to tell pretty well what they represent. By 2 months some vowel sounds start to appear—sounds like *ah, uh, ay.* Two or three months after that, the baby goes into the stage of babbling and cooing, in which he makes many sounds. By the age of 4 to 6 months he is talking to himself, with sounds like *ma, mu, do, na.* Gradually these merge into repeated sounds, like *mamama-mama, booboo, dadada.* By 9 or 10 months he can use them to imitate similar sounds made by adults. At about 1 year of age, give or take a couple of months, the child says his "first word": usually "mama."

These are the stages in a child's learning to say "one word"—that is, to make a verbal response. At the same time, he is learning some verbal discriminations. Preceding the first verbal response, usually by a month or two, he learns to understand simple commands like "Hold the spoon," or "Look at the doll." And he can understand and use simple gestures like that for "bye-bye." So an auditory discrimination is being learned along with, and to some extent preceding, the word response.

What is going on here? What are the mechanics of this early verbal learning? As well as psychologists can analyze it, the learning occurs through a combination of imitation and operant conditioning.

Imitation   A baby obviously has a genetic predisposition to make sounds, for he makes them spontaneously before he knows how to use them as words. It is only necessary that maturation (discussed in Chapter 2) proceed in a normal way. When it does, the sounds come tumbling out. During the babbling stage, in fact, babies make all the sounds known to any language, including some they will later have no use for (because few languages contain all sounds). This is a species-specific behavior that occurs only in human infants. Without it there could be no further verbal learning.

But how does the baby, spontaneously babbling sounds, come to make the correct sounds for a particular object—to use words meaningfully? The explanation lies pretty much in the establishment of a conditioning circle that sets up imitation. The circle consists of the infant's hearing his own sound whenever he makes one. This is a classical conditioning situation in which a stimulus (CS) is closely associated with a response (CR). Through such conditioning, the hearing of a sound comes to elicit the sound. This accounts for the repetitive sounds heard late in the babbling stage, like *mamamamama-mama.*

The next step is imitation. The mother or someone else makes the same sounds (or says the same words) the baby has been saying. And the baby responds to the other voice as he does to his own. So when his mother says "mama," the baby imitates with "mama." By eliciting such imitation, the mother can start to control the sounds made by the baby to make them appropriate to the situation. She can say "doll" when she holds up a doll, and the child will imitate "doll." This, of course, sets up a new conditioning situation in which the baby says "doll" when he sees a doll, and comes eventually to use the word "doll" as a name for the object.

Operant learning The classical conditioning of imitation, however, is not the whole story. Learning to talk also involves operant learning based on various sorts of reinforcements. If the baby says "cup" when he is thirsty and if mother then gives him a cup of milk, this reinforcement helps shape his response of "cup"; that is, helps elicit the response of "cup" by him. A parent who is interested in getting his infant to talk can offer all sorts of subtle reinforcements, from rewarding his bodily needs to giving him attention and praise for saying the "correct" words. Thus the baby's learning to say words is not just classical conditioning, especially as the learning becomes more sophisticated. He is also being rewarded for the verbal responses he emits.

Concept Learning

Words are learned, then, through a combination of classical conditioning, which elicits imitation, and operant learning. In the process, the infant learns to use a certain word as a name for an object and comes to know that the word "means" that object. But if this were all he learned, vocabularies would be limited, and our ability to communicate would be even more so. What is necessary next in verbal learning is to learn *concepts.* A concept is some property that several objects, otherwise not necessarily alike, have in common. Examples are "red," "cold," "girl," and "tree." Most of the words in any language are names for concepts rather than specific objects.

A concept is learned by a form of discrimination learning (see page 107) in which the name of the concept is used for any and all objects having the correct property. "Red" is applied by the mother to "red doll," "red house," "red wagon," and so on. At first this is confusing to the child, for red when used alone with doll could just as well be the name of that object. But when he hears it enough times for enough different objects, the child eventually learns to associate "red" only with the property of red and to ignore other features of the object.

Associative Learning

After learning to use words as names for objects and concepts, a child goes on to learn sentences. Certain words become strongly associated with one another simply because they describe common events—"Dada go bye-bye," "Mama go store." Many words also become associated because they refer to the poles of concepts. Examples are "black-white," "good-bad," "rich-poor," "strong-weak." Other associations are learned because they consist of concepts commonly related to each other: "green-grass," "bright-sun," "dark-night." And there are still other kinds of associations, so that the child learns many different ways of linking words.

Such associations have both advantages and disadvantages for psychological research. On the one hand, because people in a given culture build up very similar associations, the scientist can use their associations as a test of the normality of thinking. Several such tests have been constructed. In one (Kent-Rosanoff), a hundred fairly common words are given to a subject one at a time. He is asked to respond quickly with the first word that comes to mind. If he usually gives the words that most people do, he is normal. But if most of his associations are bizarre, as they are in schizophrenics, for example, then something has gone wrong with his learning and thinking.

The disadvantage of built-in associations is that they get in the way when the psychologist wants to study the process of association itself. If his subjects already have strong associations, say, with the word "black," how does the experimenter chart the formation of a new association with "black"? The old associations get in the way, and he cannot see the associative process "in the raw." To get around this, experimenters long ago devised the *nonsense syllable,* and along with it, certain standard ways of studying association. Many kinds of nonsense syllables can be constructed. The most common is the CVC syllable—C for consonant and V for vowel, so that the sequence is consonant, vowel, consonant. Some examples are given in Figure 6.1. Nonsense syllables are used to provide stimuli which have a minimum of prior association in the

Stimulus (S)	Response (R)
QEW	
QEW	– ZAJ
KEZ	
KEZ	– FUH
QOS	
QOS	– MIF
XAJ	
XAJ	– NUX
GUX	
GUX	– PIW
WUJ	
WUJ	– BOF
DAQ	
DAQ	– ZUY
CEJ	
CEJ	– KOJ

Figure 6.1 *Nonsense syllables arranged for paired-associate learning. The stimulus member of each pair is presented first, and the task is to learn the response which goes with each stimulus. Thus when QEW appears, the correct response is ZAJ.*

subject's learning history. With them the psychologist can study the formation of associations in the abstract.

The method of studying the learning of associations illustrated in Figure 6.1 is known as paired associates. Pairs of nonsense syllables are shown to the subject, and he must learn to associate the first member of a pair, the stimulus (S), with the second or response (R) member. In other words, he must learn a series of S-R associations in a manner similar to classical conditioning. This kind of learning is rather like learning a foreign-language vocabulary list, in which the stimuli are the words of one language and the responses are words of another language. In the case of nonsense syllables, however, both "words" are "foreign."

Organized Learning
In recent years, psychologists have tended to dispense with nonsense syllables and devise studies based on more meaningful materials. Instead of trying to get around the meanings that words have acquired in everyday learning, they have decided to attack these meanings head on and see how they are organized.

To do so, they frequently use the *free recall* method. For experimental control, the material to be learned is often restricted to a list of words selected so that it has certain properties. It may include, say, four color names, four occupational names, and so on. It may also be arranged in various ways to provide more or less "organization." The subject is then allowed to read over the entire list for a period of time and use whatever devices he chooses in order to learn it. Afterwards he is asked to recall the words in any sequence that comes to mind. The disadvantage of free recall is that it does not let the experimenter identify the internal stimuli the subject is using in recall. On the other hand, it does permit him to see how the subject organizes his responses. Later this chapter will describe some of the things that have been learned by the free-recall method of studying verbal learning.

ABILITY TO LEARN

Psychologists have examined human verbal learning with a fine-toothed comb, ferreting out just about every conceivable factor that could be involved in it. Out of their assiduous effort have come tens of thousands of experiments—more than a thousand now appear each year—and countless facts. Some of the work is "pure," being concerned with basic principles; much of it is applied, being designed to find ways of improving the learning of students at all educational levels. This and the following sections distill the existing knowledge, giving both the basic principles and some pointers on effective study.

The factors known to aid or to hinder learning can be classified into three main groups. First is the learner himself—the factors that endow him with greater or lesser ability to learn. Included in these personal factors are the amount and kind of his previous learning. Second is his methods of learning—how he goes about it. And third is the kind of material he has to learn.

As for the learner himself, individuals naturally vary in all sorts of ways, psychological and otherwise. Some of their psychological characteristics have little to do with their ability to learn; others are very important. Four big factors can be distinguished: (1) intelligence, (2) age, (3) arousal and anxiety, and (4) transfer from previous learning.

Intelligence
A person's level of intelligence, as measured by an intelligence test, makes a great difference in how readily he can learn. Intelligence, in fact, is defined by some psychologists as a measure of the ability to learn.

Chapter 2 (page 40) described the way in which children's progress in learning to read was correlated with their intelligence—that is, with their mental age. And Figure 2.3 showed that at a mental age (not an actual age) of 6 to 6½, children make good progress in reading, while below that level they make hardly any at all. The formula for the intelligence quotient (IQ) is mental age/chronological age. When a child's mental age is much higher than his chronological age, he is very bright; when it is much less, he is retarded. All children within the normal range of intelligence reach a mental age of 6, so they will all eventually be able to read. But the same intelligence factor is at work in all verbal learning, and only the rather bright person will be able to master some of the more difficult verbal skills (such as acquiring a large vocabulary).

Age
Some years ago a student activist asserted that people over 30 have deteriorated greatly in intelligence. What this student thinks now that he is over 30 has not been reported. In any case, he was incorrect. Verbal learning ability is, of course, zero at birth, but it grows steadily up to 17 to 20 years of age. Thereafter it remains constant until about age 50, when it begins to drop, at least as far as the learning of new material is concerned.

On the other hand, tests of intelligence that give more weight to the ability to *use* what has been learned show very little drop in a person's later years. Therefore, effective intelligence remains practically constant throughout life after it has reached its maximum in the early twenties. (There are some important differences between people under and people over 30, but these are in the domain of attitudes and attitude change that will be described in Chapter 12.) The time when age is important in IQ is in the growing years, since verbal learning ability is increasing then. If intelligence is high, this ability reaches a high maximum; if intelligence is low, verbal learning levels out on a low plane.

Arousal and Anxiety

People can be aroused without being anxious, but anxiety is always accompanied by arousal. Both states are related to the ability to learn.

To learn anything, an individual must be well aroused. Verbal learning in particular requires arousal because it involves the most intricate operations of the brain. In college study you cannot expect to learn very much unless you are fully awake, with your full energies focused on the task. Any tendency to relax, say, by studying in bed, is for most people a hindrance to learning, because it lowers their general level of arousal. On the other hand, too much arousal also impedes learning. As shown in Figure 4.3, no one can perform well when he is emotionally upset.

Anxiety, like arousal, is important in learning, but the relationship between the two is not simple. It depends on academic aptitude, as can be seen in one large-scale study of how students with varying anxiety levels did in their college work (Spielberger, 1962). The results of the study are summarized in Figure 6.2. Note that the two graph lines meet at the far left and far right of the scholastic aptitude scale. This means that anxiety makes very little difference for students of either very low or very high aptitude. In one case, low aptitude is the main thing hindering them. In the other, they find learning so easy that anxiety does not affect it. But in between, for students of moderate aptitude,

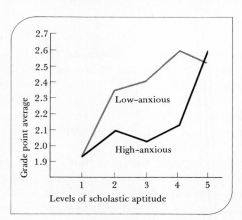

Figure 6.2 Grade point averages for college students of different aptitudes scoring high or low on a test of anxiety. For students with very poor or very good scholastic aptitude, anxiety made no difference. But for average students, high anxiety was a hindrance to learning. (Spielberger, 1962.)

anxiety level makes a great difference. Those with high anxiety do much worse than those with low anxiety.

The reasons for this relationship are complex. The high-anxiety student may be so anxious about nonacademic matters that he does not do enough studying. Or he may become so anxious in a test situation that he "blocks." But a crucial factor in the relationship is attention. High anxiety tends to prevent a student from keeping his mind on his work. Specifically, it blinds him to exactly what he should be learning.

To summarize: In order to learn best, a person should be wide awake and well aroused so that he puts all his energy into learning. He should not be too anxious, however, for anxiety disrupts effective learning.

Transfer of Previous Learning

Another important characteristic of the learner is the previous learning that he brings to a particular task. The fully grown learner never learns anything from scratch. He has had years of learning both in and out of school, and any new learning always builds on the old. This effect, which has been called *transfer of training*, can be either a help or a hindrance. If the transfer is helpful, it is called positive transfer; if it is a hindrance, negative transfer.

The rules that control positive and negative transfer have been carefully worked out. They depend on the *similarity* between the *stimuli* and the *responses* present in previous learning and those involved in the current learning situation. A classical experiment has outlined the rules governing positive and negative transfer (Bruce, 1933):

> The subjects learned two sets of paired-associate tasks. The first task was considered "old" learning because it was learned before the second task; the second task was "new" learning. The question was how the old learning affected the new. Several different lists of stimulus-response nonsense syllables were formed for each of the two tasks. As shown in Table 6.1, there were four experimental conditions. In condition 1 the stimuli in the two tasks were different, but the responses to be learned were identical. In condition 2 the stimuli were identical, but the responses to be learned were different. In condition 3 the stimuli were *similar* (but not identical) while the responses were identical; condition 4 had identical stimuli and similar responses. The results are shown in the last column of Table 6.1.

Out of this experiment and many like it (see Deese and Hulse, 1967), come some rules for predicting how much transfer there will be between old and new learning, and whether the transfer will be positive or negative. These are the rules:

TABLE 6.1
Sample stimulus-response items from an experiment on trans-
fer. The psychologists' understanding of transfer of knowl-
edge—including the ability to predict *how much there will be*
and what direction it will take—is based on experiments like
this one.

Experimental condition	Relation of S-R items in the two tasks	Task 1 Stimulus	Response	Task 2 Stimulus	Response	Direction of transfer
1	Stimuli dissimilar— responses identical	LAN	QIP	FIS	QIP	Slightly positive
2	Stimuli identical— responses dissimilar	REQ	KIV	REQ	ZAM	Negative
3	Stimuli similar— responses identical	BES	YOR	BEF	YOR	Very strongly positive
4	Stimuli identical— responses similar	TEC	ZOX	TEC	ZOP	Slightly positive

Source: Modified from Bruce, 1933.

1 Positive transfer occurs when a person learns to make the same responses to different stimuli. In Table 6.1 this result appears in condition 1 (where QIP was the response to the stimulus LAN in task 1 and also to FIS in task 2) and in condition 3 (where YOR was the response to BES in task 1 and to BEF in task 2).

2 Negative transfer occurs when the subject must learn to make dissimilar, opposite, or antagonistic responses to similar stimuli in the two tasks. In condition 2, for example, learning the response ZAM to REQ in task 2 was hindered by having learned the response KIV to REQ in task 1.

3 Stimulus similarity in the two tasks determines the *amount* of transfer, either positive or negative, between the two. The greater the similarity of stimuli in the tasks, the greater the transfer. Positive transfer, for example, was greater in condition 3 when the same response, YOR, was given to BES in task 1 and BEF in task 2.

4 Response similarity largely determines the *direction* of transfer: whether it is positive or negative. The more similar the responses, the more positive the transfer; the more dissimilar the responses, the more negative the transfer. In condition 2, for example, where dissimilar responses of KIV and ZAM in the two tasks were learned to the same stimulus, REQ, the transfer was negative. But in condition 4, when the similar responses ZOX and ZOP were associated with the same stimulus, TEC, the transfer was slightly positive.

Similarity of stimuli   Positive transfer between old and new tasks is favored by similarity of stimuli. In other words, similarity of stimuli makes the learning of a new task easier. This is another instance of stimulus generalization (page 120). In Pavlov's classical conditioning experiment described in Chapter 5, a dog that was conditioned to salivate to a bell also salivated to a buzzer and a metronome, because these were stimuli similar to the bell.

The same principle applies to all learning. Here are two practical examples, one from nonverbal learning, the other from verbal learning: After a person has learned to drive one make and model of car, he usually has little trouble transferring what he has learned to another car. Instruments on the dashboard of the second car may be arranged somewhat differently, the windshield may be a little higher or wider, and at first the car may seem a little strange to handle. In general, however, the stimulus situations presented by the two cars are similar; hence positive transfer takes place. In the same way, positive transfer occurs in learning a foreign language that is similar to a language previously learned. It is easier to learn French if you know Greek or Latin, since many of the roots are similar in the three languages. Latin also helps in learning Italian or Spanish, because these Romance languages have Latin as a common parentage.

Similarity of responses   Positive transfer is also favored by similarity of responses in two tasks. The best examples of this principle come from nonverbal learning. In switching from one automobile to another, transfer is usually easy not only because the stimuli are similar but because the responses are too. In both situations, for example, the driver uses his right foot to brake and to accelerate. A person who has learned to play tennis learns quickly to play ping-pong or badminton, because similar responses and skills are involved in all three games.

But when opposite responses are required in somewhat similar situations, negative transfer occurs. The previous learning retards new learning so much that it would have been better if the learner had never had any experience before. If a person has steered a snow sled, he may have trouble learning to pilot a plane, because extending the right foot makes a sled go left but a plane go right. Many people find it difficult to steer a boat with a tiller because pushing the tiller to the left makes the boat go right, and that seems unnatural at first (see Figure 6.3). In the early days of airplanes, pilots often made mistakes—sometimes fatal ones—when a new airplane's controls were located in different positions from the old model. Designers have become aware of this important human factor and now standardize the location of controls in cockpits.

Transfer of training in education   Educators have always put great trust in transfer; otherwise they would have little faith in education. The whole idea of education is that learning at one level will prepare the person to learn at a higher level. This is why some college courses are prerequisites for others. Another basic assumption in education is that what is learned in school will transfer to tasks outside school and in the working world. That is what education is all about.

Educators' ideas of transfer, however, have changed with their

Figure 6.3   *Top, an example of positive transfer. The motions involved in playing tennis are very similar to those used in playing badminton. Bottom, an example of negative transfer. If you want to go to the right on a bicycle, you turn the handlebars in that direction. But if you want to go right (to starboard) in a boat, turning the tiller to the right causes you to go wrong.*

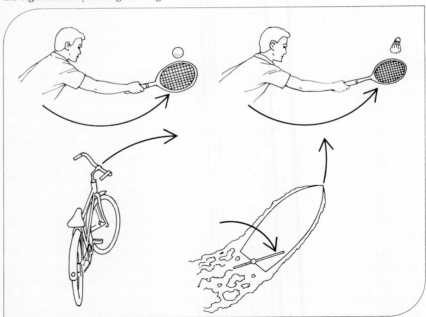

right or wrong. The problems are presented in a prearranged order that has been worked out to make an efficient sequence for learning. Transfer is maximized by building one response on another: that is, the response required for one question makes use of the answer that has just been learned.

By forcing the learner to respond, not just to read passively, learning programs require *active recitation.* Active responding in itself provides motivation for learning, since people are almost always more involved in a situation when they are participating than when they are passive. If a student has to answer questions or solve problems, he is more interested than when he merely sits, reads, and listens. Unfortunately, not all programmed texts and machines are interesting and motivating—they sometimes bore students, especially bright ones. Good learning programs, however, are certainly more motivating than dull lectures and textbooks.

Another feature of programmed learning is that it permits students to *proceed at their own pace.* In contrast, lectures demand the same amount of time from everybody; they are too slow for the fast learner and too fast for the slow one. This is also true of class recitation techniques. But learning programs are given to students individually, and each one can work away at the program as rapidly or as slowly as his abilities and work habits permit.

In addition, learning programs provide *small steps* in learning; the material is broken up into units so small that almost anyone can learn them. This may be a little boring for the student who can grasp a lot quickly, but it helps the student who cannot. It ensures that whatever a person learns, he has learned well so that he is ready to go on to the next step. Small steps also reduce the number of wrong responses a person makes—responses that may impede the shaping of the final product. Lectures and textbooks, on the other hand, frequently go in steps that are too large for the slower and less well-prepared student.

A final important feature of learning programs, as mentioned in the section on feedback, is their emphasis on *knowledge of results.* Because they require responses that can be compared immediately with the correct answers, the student knows as he goes along whether he has been right or wrong. Neither lectures nor textbooks do this nearly so well. A student can study lecture material by checking himself against his lecture notes, but they may be wrong or inadequate. He can study a textbook by checking himself against the book, but even when he has the discipline to do it, he cannot be sure exactly what he is supposed to be learning. The learning program shows him what is to be learned and how well he has learned it.

THE LEARNING MATERIAL

Besides the characteristics of the learner and the strategy used in learning, the third main factor in verbal learning is the material to be learned. Some material is easy, some hard. The learner cannot do too much about the material itself, though he can analyze what makes it easy or hard and can sometimes revise his learning strategy to match. Where such revisions are possible this section will point them out, but the emphasis will be on what factors make material more or less learnable.

A number of characteristics affect the rate at which verbal material can be learned. One minor feature is pronounceability; it is easier to learn words that are easy to pronounce. It follows that a student should pronounce the words which he finds relatively strange; this way he will be more likely to remember them, how they are spelled, and what they mean. Besides pronounceability, five major features affect the learnability of verbal material: (1) perceptual distinctiveness, (2) associative meaning, (3) categories of concepts, (4) conceptual hierarchies, and (5) associative hierarchies.

Perceptual Distinctiveness

Something that stands out from the material which surrounds it is easily learned. Suppose, for example, that you are presented with the following items: *gub, kev, 406, dac, rul, hot.* One item, *406,* stands out because it is different; it is said to be perceptually distinctive. For that reason you can learn to remember it more easily than the rest. In addition, one item, *hot,* is a real word, while the rest are nonsense syllables. Noticing that makes it easier to remember. The important factor here is attention; distinctiveness catches attention, and the more attention you give something, the more readily you learn it.

If you think about the experiences in your life that you remember best, you will find that many of them were so different from your daily routine that they stood out as perceptually distinctive. Distinctiveness does not account for all indelible memories—other factors such as the intensity of an experience or the emotion connected with it are also important—but it is significant.

Usually a student must learn what he is assigned; he has no control over the features of the material. You can, however, learn better if you keep distinctiveness in mind and look for it along the way. Then you will note distinctions that might slip by, and you will learn the distinctive material better than you otherwise would. But be careful: Not everything that is distinctive is worth learning; it might be irrelevant or unimportant. So don't just learn everything that is distinctive, but use distinctiveness, where it occurs, as an aid to learning.

Associative Meaning
Psychologists long ago formulated a general rule about learning verbal material: The more meaningful it is, the easier it is to learn. The fact that nonsense syllables are harder to learn than English words is an example of this rule. Having established the rule, researchers have gone on to see just what "meaningfulness" means: What makes material meaningful? They have found that there are three basic kinds of meaning: *associative, conceptual,* and *hierarchical.* These are not mutually exclusive but may be combined to give material more or less meaning.

Associative meaning refers to whatever you are reminded of when you study verbal material. If you have many associations with the material, it is highly meaningful. Your ability to learn is influenced by the amount of such associative meaning in the material, as the following experiment shows (Noble, 1952a).

> A long list of two-syllable words, some of them ordinary English words, others nonsense words, was presented to a large number of subjects. They were instructed to give all the associations to a word that occurred to them in a 60-second period. The number of their associations was averaged for each word to provide an index of its meaningfulness. For example, one nonsense word, *gojey,* got an average of 0.99 associations, showing that it was not very meaningful. But the word *kitchen* was quite meaningful, drawing an average of 9.61 associations. Several hundred words and nonsense syllables were given indexes in this way.
>
> A second experiment was devised to see how these indexes of associative meaning affect ease of learning (Noble, 1952b). Three different lists were constructed, one with an average index of 1.28, another with 4.42, and a third with 7.85. The lists were presented to a group of subjects by the method of serial anticipation. The list with the low index of meaning took almost three times as many trials to learn as the list with the high index. The list with the intermediate index was between the extremes. Conclusion: The more associative meaning a word has, the easier it is to learn—in this case, to associate with another word high in meaning.

There is every reason to believe that the principle illustrated by this experiment holds true for everyday verbal learning. The more experience you have had with the words in a sentence, the easier the sentence is to understand and remember. This is a kind of transfer of your previous learning to new learning. Meaningfulness, in fact, is really positive transfer. Certain words and phrases are more meaningful than others because you have already learned things about them. You can get some practical use out of this point in studying if you put things into your own words. By writing lecture notes or making outlines of textbook material in your words rather than the author's, you capitalize on the associations you have with these words and make learning easier.

Conceptual Similarities
What we have been talking about so far is associations from *outside* the material to be learned—associations that come from the past experience of the learner. But most verbal learning involves *internal* associations: associations between the items being learned. These items have different degrees of association with each other, and the meaningfulness generated by their relations is called *organization* (Mandler, 1967). Organization contributes much to each verbal learning task.

There are two kinds of organization—conceptual and hierarchical—and they can operate separately or in combination. To understand conceptual organization, first note that a *conceptual category* is a class which includes a number of members (see page 169). Names of men, names of animals, names of occupations, and names of dances are all conceptual categories, for they contain many individual members. These particular categories have been used in an experiment on conceptual organization (Underwood, 1964).

> Four lists of 16 words each were read to subjects at the rate of one word every 5 seconds. During this period the experimenter spoke each word twice. Two of the lists had low conceptual similarity because the words in them were drawn from many conceptual categories. Two had high conceptual similarity because the words were members of only four conceptual categories. An example of each list is given in Table 6.3. On the left is the "low" list; on the right the "high" list, where every fourth word is related. The subjects were told nothing about these differences between the lists. After each was read, they were simply asked to reproduce as many words as they could in any order.
>
> Two related facts came out of the experiment. First, the high list was much easier to learn than the low list. Many subjects recalled the high list on just one run-through, perfectly while hardly any got a perfect score on the low list. Second, in recalling words from the high list, people wrote them category by category. They would first write, say, the names of men (Bob, Bill, Joe, and John), then the names of animals (cow, horse, dog, cat). Thus they *clustered* words to be learned according to their conceptual similarity. This clustering undoubtedly accounted for the ease with which they learned the items in the high list.

TABLE 6.3
*Word lists used in an experiment on learning items low and
high in conceptual similarity. List 2, where every fourth word
belongs to the same conceptual category, was much easier to
learn than list 1.*

List 1 (low)	List 2 (high)
apple	Bob
football	rabbi
emerald	cow
trout	rumba
copper	Bill
theft	priest
hat	horse
table	foxtrot
cruiser	Joe
trumpet	bishop
doctor	dog
head	tango
wide	John
blue	minister
gasoline	cat
cotton	waltz

Source: Modified from Underwood, 1964.

The subjects described here were not told to cluster; they did it on their
own. Noticing the similarity of certain items, they could remember
them better by pigeonholing them according to the concepts they
represented. Other groups of subjects who were told in advance to look
for certain conceptual similarities learned the "high" lists more easily
still.

Conceptual Hierarchies

Organizing items into similar conceptual categories is one step in
tapping the meaningfulness of material you must learn. Another step is
to organize the items into *hierarchies* wherever this is possible. Concepts
can be large or small, and one large concept may include a number of
smaller ones. These in turn can encompass even smaller ones. The net
result is a hierarchy, or "tree," of relationships with two, three, or more
branchings. The value of conceptual hierarchies for learning is illustrated by another experiment (Bower et al., 1969).

Subjects were given a total of 112 words to look at for a total of about 4
minutes. The words were arranged in four trees, of approximately 28

words each, on four separate cards. Looking at the four cards for the 4 minutes constituted one trial, and four trials were run. Between each trial the subjects were asked to report orally all the words they could remember.

The subjects, however, were divided into two groups. For one group, the words on the tree were arranged in a conceptual hierarchy as you see it illustrated at the top of Figure 6.5. For the other subjects, a "random" group, the same words were arranged randomly on the tree, thus obscuring their conceptual relationships.

The results were striking. The group that had the words arranged in a conceptual category learned with lightning speed. They recalled an average of 72 words after the first trial and 106 after the second, and they had perfect scores of 112 by the third. The "random" group that had words arranged randomly on the trees learned at a snail's pace. At the end of the first trial, they had only 21 correct responses. On each subsequent trial they got more, but even after the fourth they averaged only about two-thirds correct (70).

This experiment illustrates the powerful effect of conceptual organization on learning. Although the material to be learned was exactly the same for the two groups, its arrangement in a hierarchy helped one group learn it about three times faster. The lesson should not be lost. Teachers and textbook writers should try to exploit their material by

Figure 6.5 *Examples of word "trees" arranged in hierarchies. Top, a conceptual hierarchy for "minerals." Words arranged in conceptual hierarchies are the easiest of all to learn. Bottom, an associative hierarchy for "cheese." This arrangement is less easy to learn than a conceptual hierarchy, but easier than random words. (Modified from Bower et al., 1969.)*

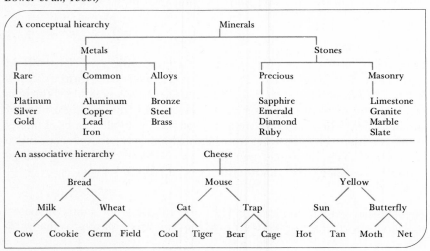

carefully arranging the concepts they teach into hierarchies. (The headings and subheadings of this book, for example, form a hierarchy of concepts.) Those who ramble with their associations make learning much more difficult. The student, for his part, should attempt to perceive the hierarchies being taught and to learn the material by hierarchy rather than by random sequences. He can add strength to his learning by carefully outlining what he hears and reads so that it makes an accurate "tree" of the concepts being presented.

Associative Hierarchies
The bottom of Figure 6.5 illustrates an intermediate form of organization called an associative hierarchy. In it the tree consists of items that are associated, but not necessarily in a conceptual hierarchy. Fortunately, nobody tries to teach much by offering this kind of hierarchy, so it is not a practical problem for the learner. It is another possible arrangement of material, however, and it has been studied experimentally.

The experiments on associative hierarchies are much like those on conceptual hierarchies (Bower et al., 1969). One group is shown items arranged in a hierarchy; another "random" group has the same items randomly arranged in the tree. Then the learning rate of the two groups is compared, and as you might guess, the group that is shown the hierarchical arrangement learns faster than the "random" group. Hence some kind of hierarchy is better than no hierarchy at all. But the group with the associative hierarchies does not do nearly so well as a similar group with conceptual hierarchies. The conceptual hierarchy is therefore the more "organized" and meaningful of all possible arrangements. It is definitely the easiest arrangement to learn.

REMEMBERING AND FORGETTING

How wonderful it would be if we could remember everything we learned! We would all be gigantic storehouses of information, yet we would spend much less time in learning because we would not have to relearn what we had forgotten. But the fact is that we forget most of what we learn, and forget it rather rapidly. This section takes a close look at the problem of forgetting. First it deals with the amount that is remembered (or forgotten), then with the changes that take place in remembering and forgetting, and finally with the causes of our forgetting.

Measures of Retention
First, some remarks about terminology. Assume that you have learned something perfectly. At that point in time, we might say that you have

100 percent retention and 0 percent forgetting. Some hours or days later, you take a test of retention and find that you have forgotten, say, 75 percent of what you originally learned. We might express that fact in another way by saying that you now have 25 percent retention. *Retention* (or the amount remembered) is thus the difference between 100 percent learning and the amount forgotten. One hundred percent minus one figure equals the other. So, although this section will be using several different terms—memory, remembering, retention, and forgetting—it is always looking at the decline from the 100 percent mastery you had at the point of complete learning to some lower amount of retention. This *curve of forgetting*, as it is named, can be measured in one of three ways: recall, recognition, or savings.

Recall   To measure retention and forgetting by the method of recall, just ask the person to reproduce what he previously learned either by writing it down or by saying it aloud. This is the method psychologists most frequently select for their experiments. It was used, for example, in the experiments on serial anticipation, paired associates, and free recall that were considered earlier in the chapter. It is also the method used in the essay or completion types of examinations.

The method of recall gives lower retention scores than the method of recognition, because it is harder to recall something than to recognize it. Since the recall method gives relatively low scores, it is also very sensitive in measuring *forgetting*; it will reveal forgetting when the other measurements may not. For this reason it would be the preferred method in examinations—if it were not so difficult to use. It is more time-consuming than the recognition method, and it is usually less reliable, because a grader must examine the results and decide (often subjectively) whether they are correct. The recognition method, which is traditionally cast in multiple-choice or true-false form for easy scoring, is more widely used.

Recognition   In the method of recognition, the subject is merely required to decide whether a response presented to him is correct or not. In the true-false version he indicates whether a response is or is not true. In the multiple-choice form he picks out one response from an array of several alternatives.

The great advantage of this method of measuring retention is that it is inexpensive to score. Even by hand, a grader checking responses against a key can whip through hundreds of responses in a matter of minutes. The method also lends itself to machine scoring, which further reduces the time and effort required. There are two arguments against the recognition method: First, it is considerably easier to do well on a recognition test than on one measuring recall. A person can often recognize a correct answer when he would not be able to recall it. Second, the results are inflated by chance; a person who knows nothing can achieve a chance score based on the number of alternatives presented to him. This method therefore is considerably less sensitive than the method of recall.

Savings   The important feature of a third method, the method of savings, is the *relearning* of material previously learned. What psychologists measure is the number of trials (or errors) taken to relearn, in comparison with the number originally required. The two numbers are put into an equation like this:

$$\frac{\text{Number of trials (or time) to learn originally}}{\text{minus number of trials (or time) to relearn}} \times 100 = \text{savings score}$$

From this equation you can see that if the number of trials (or amount of time) required to *relearn* is small, then the numerator is large, and the savings will approach 100 percent. On the other hand, if the number of relearning trials is large, then the numerator becomes smaller and approaches zero. Suppose, for example, that it took 20 repetitions to learn to repeat a certain poem without making any errors, and that after a period of a month, it took only 10 repetitions to relearn the poem. The equation would look like this:

$$\frac{20 - 10}{20} \times 100 = 50$$

Thus the savings would be 50 percent.

The main advantage of the method of savings is that it is extremely sensitive in measuring what has been *remembered*. It may show some retention when other methods do not. On a test of recall, for example, a person may score practically zero—indicating that he remembers nothing. Yet when he is required to relearn, he may take considerably fewer trials that he did originally and thus show some savings.

This saving of what has been learned is one of the main benefits of formal education. It is a dismal disappointment to test by the method of recall, or even recognition, what a student has learned in a course a few months—or even days—after the course has ended. Most of what we learn in courses fades mighty fast, for reasons given below. This is especially true when the measure is of recall. On the other hand, the student can still recognize later some things he cannot recall. Even more important, he can relearn what he has forgotten at a much faster clip than was required the first time. What this means in practical terms is that we can relearn quickly, if we need to, what we once have learned even though we may not recall much of it. It is these savings that, for the most part, make the years of education worthwhile.

Short-Term and Long-Term Memory

The retention that has been discussed so far (and will be considered again in the last sections of this chapter) is long-term memory—memory that lasts hours, days, or even years. For the most part, this long-term memory is what psychologists are interested in studying, and what teachers are interested in promoting in the classroom. But there is another kind of retention called short-term memory that tells us something about memory processes.

Consider the example of a telephone number that you look up in the directory. Having found it, you perceive it and perhaps think you know it. But when you close the book, you may start to dial and realize that you haven't remembered it. The number has been lost from your short-term memory. If you are to remember it for even a little while, you must make more effort—do a little memorizing. Then you can dial the number and complete your call. At this point it may go out of your mind; you had put the number into short-term memory long enough to use it, but did not get it into long-term memory. Such a loss is very likely to occur with nonsense items like telephone numbers. To remember them permanently after only one exposure, you usually need to rehearse (recite) them a few times and make a definite effort to memorize. More meaningful items, like a sentence describing a person's appearance, may not be lost so easily. Nevertheless, there is a difference between short-term and long-term memory.

Short-term memory, for one thing, has a limited capacity, while long-term memory is very, very large. This fact can be demonstrated by a test of memory span, traditionally a part of intelligence tests. One gives a person a series of digits and sees how long a string he can repeat back. The average person can handle only 6 or 7 items, the bright one up to 10. Either quantity is small compared with the amount of information we store in long-term memory.

There is a way of enlarging short-term capacity, and that is by "chunking." In chunking, a person groups the numbers, say, into threes, and remembers not one set of nine numbers, but three sets of three each. Chunking is a good device for extending your memory span—try it with a telephone number—but it requires you to adopt a *strategy* in memorizing.

Another interesting characteristic of short-term memory is that it is extremely susceptible to disruption. Most of us have had the experience of being interrupted while we are dialing a telephone number, only to wind up with the wrong number. Long-term memory, by contrast, is much more resistant to distractions.

Another difference between short-term and long-term memory is in *retrieval*. If you lose something from short-term memory, it is really lost. There is no point is searching for it; the only thing to do is to refresh your memory by referring again to the material to be remembered. But in long-term memory, there is a difference between remembering something and retrieving it. You may know a person's name very well, but when you try to say it, you are unable to recall it—to retrieve it. It is in your memory, but you cannot pull it out. In that case, the effort to remember may produce results. You search your memory, making repeated attempts to retrieve the name, often coming up with a name that is similar but not quite right. Then at some point, the name bursts forth—you have retrieved it from your memory. Hence having something in long-term memory and retrieving it can be quite distinct.

Amount Retained

The rest of this chapter is about long-term retention—specifically, about the *amount* retained after material has been learned. The amount of retention depends upon a number of things, but three are most important: *meaningfulness* of the material, *how well* the material was learned in the first place, and *interference* from other learning.

Meaningfulness of material   The material that is learned, especially in psychological experiments, can vary widely in meaningfulness all the way from nonsense syllables of low association value to material organized into conceptual hierarchies. If the psychologist measures retention for material varying in meaningfulness, he typically obtains negatively accelerated curves. The curve for highly meaningful material, however, does not fall as fast or as far as it does for nonsense material.

Earlier, we saw that it is much easier to learn sense than nonsense. Now we see that it is much easier to remember sense than nonsense. Actually, one is the consequence of the other. The reason we do not remember nonsense or difficult material is that it was hard to learn in the first place (Underwood, 1964).

Degree of learning   In most experiments on learning and retention, the psychologist takes subjects to the 100 percent point of learning. He runs learning trails until one trial is completely correct. But if he is interested in the best possible retention, he goes further, because people will retain more by *overlearning* the material. Figure 6.6

gives the results of an experiment in which subjects in different groups learned a list of two-syllable nouns to three different degrees: 100 percent, 150 percent, and 200 percent (Postman, 1962). In the 150 percent group, for example, subjects continued on after 100 percent learning to rehearse the lists for 50 percent more trials. The groups were then retested at various intervals after the original learning. The overlearning of the material greatly aided retention. The superior performance of the overlearning groups was considerable after one day and remained that way after several days. The difference narrowed, however, as time went on.

Research of this kind demonstrates, first, that overlearning is a good thing. The student who is preparing for an examination should plan to overlearn his material. To know it well is not enough; he should go over it enough times to know it "cold." A few hours or days later, he will retain much more for use in the examination. Second, there is a law of diminishing returns from overlearning. Something around 200 percent is probably the limit beyond which more overlearning profits little. The value of overlearning varies, moreover, with the kind of material learned. Overlearning aids retention more for nonsense or difficult material than it does for easy, highly organized material.

Interference We have seen that short-term memory is easily disrupted by interfering activity. The same is true of long-term memory though not to the same degree. Nevertheless, interference is probably the most important single factor in forgetting. Here interference means the same thing that was earlier called *negative transfer*, but here we are talking about retention rather than learning. In negative transfer, learning one set of stimulus-response relationships interferes with learning another set. In interference, learning which occurs either *before* or *after* other learning adversely affects the retention of that learning. If the interference comes from something learned afterward,

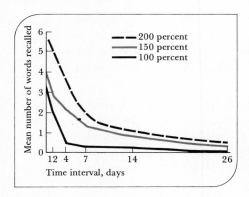

Figure 6.6 *Retention curves after different amounts of practice show that overlearning aids memory. The 100 percent curve means that learning proceeded to a criterion of one perfect repetition; 150 percent means that half again as many trials were given as were needed to reach criterion; 200 percent means that twice as many trials were given as were needed to reach criterion. (Data from Krueger, 1929; figure from Hovland, 1951.)*

it is *retroactive* interference; if from something learned before, it is *proactive* interference.

Suppose you go to a large party where you are introduced to many new people. By the time the evening is over, you will probably have forgotten, or at least mixed up, the names of many people you met. Your ability to remember the names you heard earlier in the evening is interfered with by the names you heard later. This is retroactive interference. On the other hand, you had difficulty remembering the names of the people you met later because you had heard so many names earlier. This is proactive interference.

Interference can be studied in the laboratory by using one experimental design for proactive interference and a slightly different one for retroactive interference (McGeoch and Irion, 1952). In each case there is a control group to provide a basis for comparing the retention that occurs without interference, and an experimental group that undergoes interfering activity. The proactive design is as follows:

Control group   Rest   Learn 2   Measure of retention 2
Experimental group   Learn 1   Learn 2   Measure of retention 2

The numbers 1 and 2 in this design refer to different learning tasks. If the retention of task 2 is poorer for the experimental group, because it had previously learned task 1, than for the control group, the reason is proactive interference.

The retroactive design is as follows:

Control group   Learn 1   Rest   Measure retention of 1
Experimental group   Learn 1   Learn 2   Measure retention of 1

If the experimental group does not retain task 1 as well as the control group does, it is because of the retroactive effect of learning task 2 on the retention of task 1.

Designs like these frequently reveal interference effects. Whether the effects appear or not depends on the similarity of the two tasks. In many, many experiments using such designs with different kinds of tasks, psychologists have learned the rules for predicting fairly well when interference will occur.

    1   If the interpolated material—that is, the extra task learned by the experimental group—is very similar to the other material, interference will be very small. Indeed, there can be positive transfer. This is because the learning of the extra task is very much like having some trials on the other task.

2   If the two tasks are very dissimilar, the interference will be small, but greater than when the tasks are very similar. This is because very little transfer, either positive or negative, occurs between dissimilar tasks.

3   If the two tasks are somewhat similar, but not very much so, interference will be greatest. In this case the subject has a tendency to confuse what is learned in the interpolated material with what is learned on the other task.

In college you can use these rules in scheduling the sequence of study in various subjects. Rule 1 can be largely ignored, because college students seldom have subjects so similar that the learning of one is like the learning of the other. But rules 2 and 3 can be used to minimize interference between the subjects studied. Try to schedule subjects close together that are very dissimilar, like German and physics, and avoid back-to-back study of such similar fields as psychology and sociology.

Why We Forget

Psychologists have been most interested in the rules governing interference, not for their limited practical value, but for their bearing on the nature of forgetting. The rules explain in part why we forget, because they tell us that much forgetting is due to the interference of things we learn with other things we want to remember. But just how much forgetting do they account for?

Theoretically there can be two causes of forgetting: interference is one; the other is simple decay of the memory. Both theories have been proposed formally, the second one sometimes being called the "leaky-bucket hypothesis" (Miller, 1956). Offhand, this one seems the most attractive—at least, most people would say we just "naturally" forget. Still, experiments have demonstrated that the effect of interference is powerful in forgetting, so that all forgetting cannot be simply a decay of the memory trace (Underwood, 1957). How much can we ascribe to each factor?

There is no way of constructing a crucial test of these theories, because there is no way of arranging life so that it is free of interference, even in the laboratory. Other activities, some of them similar to the task given a subject to learn, have occurred in his past (proactive interference) and occur between the learning task and the test of retention (retroactive interference). All that the psychologist can do is to keep interference to a minimum or try to assess its influence when it occurs.

One way of cutting down on retroactive interference is to have a person sleep between the time he learns something and the time his retention of it is tested. An early experiment along these lines is now a classic in psychology (Jenkins and Dallenbach, 1924).

> Subjects learned lists of 10 nonsense syllables just before going to bed in the laboratory. At various times after going to sleep (1, 2, 4, and 8 hours), they were awakened and their retention was tested by the method of recall. The same subjects at other times learned comparable lists and were tested in the same way after 1, 2, 4, and 8 hours of normal daily waking activity. Retention was considerably better after sleep. In both cases, it fell rather sharply in the first couple of hours. It continued to fall to nearly zero when the subjects were going about their daily affairs, but it leveled off at about 50 percent when they slept.

This kind of experiment has always been used as a strong argument against decay theory and in favor of an interference explanation of forgetting. But the experiment dealt only with retroactive interference, not with proactive effects.

A different type of experiment is needed to study proactive interference. Suppose that a subject learns a single list of nonsense syllables and is tested for recall 24 hours later. Typically, he has forgotten 65 percent of the list by then. This is a great deal of forgetting to be explained by the retroactive effects of what he has been doing in the meantime. Indeed, his activity outside the laboratory is so dissimilar (rule 1 above) that little interference should be expected. But how about his previous verbal learning? He had had a lot of that over the years, and this could cause proactive interference.

Psychologists cannot get at this possibility directly, because they cannot measure precisely the relevant prior learning that might interfere. They can, however, run experiments in which they have subjects learn two or more lists (Underwood, 1957). Then they can see how the retention of one list is affected by the number of lists learned before it. This kind of analysis, illustrated in Figure 6.7, shows a powerful effect of prior learning. The more lists learned previously, the poorer the retention of the list tested. Retention, therefore, depends very much on the existence of prior learning that interferes proactively with new material learned. Extrapolating this result to learning outside the laboratory, we can conclude that prior learning, and particularly strongly ingrained habits, are sources of interference in the retention of verbal material. Whether this accounts for 100 percent of forgetting, we do not know and may never be able to find out. An informed guess is that people forget mainly because they have learned so much in the past, but also partly because they learn other things afterward.

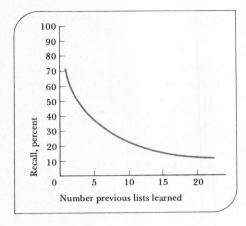

Figure 6.7 *Recall depends upon the number of lists learned prior to the list which is being tested. This curve is a summary of the results obtained by many experimenters over many years. (Modified from Underwood, 1957.)*

SUMMARY

The same principles apply to both animal and human learning, but human learning is largely verbal, using words as both stimuli and responses.

A baby learns words through a combination of imitation, classical conditioning, and operant conditioning, in which reinforcement shapes the word responses learned. Later, through discriminative learning, he learns words as labels for concepts. He forms words into sentences by serial associations referring to common events and also by the relations of concepts that the words represent.

A person's ability to learn depends on his intelligence, age, and state of arousal. The higher his intelligence, the more rapidly he learns. Ability to learn increases with age up to early adulthood, levels off, and declines slightly in middle and old age. In general, a high state of arousal is necessary for the best learning. But too much arousal, especially if it is accompanied by anxiety, is detrimental to learning. A person's ability to learn also depends on his previous learning. Previous learning can be helpful or detrimental, according to the similarity between old learning and new learning of the stimuli and responses to be learned.

Certain strategies for learning are better than others. In general, spaced practice is better than massed practice. Also, immediate knowledge of results helps learning. In studying material in school, a substantial amount of time should be spent in active recitation rather than in simply reading. Sometimes it is better to approach a learning task as a whole; at other times studying it in parts is the best strategy. Learning programs are designed to make use of the best strategies in learning.

The nature of the material learned affects ease of learning. Things that are perceptually distinctive from other things are readily learned. Material that has the most associations for the learner is also easily learned. Best of all is material that can be organized into conceptual hierarchies.

Three principal measures of forgetting are recall, recognition, and savings. Of these, recall yields the least material remembered, and savings the most. Short-term memory stores less and is more easily disrupted than long-term memory. Items in long-term memory may sometimes be difficult to retrieve. The amount we remember depends on the meaningfulness of the material, the degree to which it was learned in the first place, and interference from things learned later. It is such interference that accounts for most forgetting.

SUGGESTIONS FOR FURTHER READING

Adams, J. A. *Human memory.* New York: McGraw-Hill, 1967. *A summary of the facts and theories about human memory.*

Deese, J., and Hulse, S. H. *The psychology of learning.* (3d ed.) New York: McGraw-Hill, 1967. *A short textbook on learning.*

King, R. A. (Ed.) *Readings for an introduction to psychology.* (3d ed.) New York: McGraw-Hill, 1971. *A book of readings that supplements this text.*

Melton, A. W. (Ed.) *Categories of human learning.* New York: Academic Press, 1964. *A symposium on different types of human learning.*

Morgan, C. T., and Deese, J. *How to study.* (2d ed.) New York: McGraw-Hill, 1969. *An application of learning principles to techniques of study.*

7

Thinking and Problem Solving

LEARNING OBJECTIVES

Main objective
After studying this chapter you should be able to explain the nature of thinking and describe the kinds of thinking that take place.

Other major objectives
You should be able to
Describe the roles of the following in thinking: images, muscle movements, concepts, and language.
Outline the ways in which concepts are learned, how they are best learned, and ways of testing their meaning.
List four steps in creative thinking.

Minor objectives
Define simple concept, conjunctive concept, disjunctive concept, and relational concept.
Explain why most thinking is verbal.
Outline the factors that make problem solving easier.
Explain the difference between logical and illogical thinking.
Explain why so much of our thinking is illogical.

The term *thinking* refers to a wide range of activity. In its simplest form, it means very little more than remembering some fact or event. Suppose that you see a road sign saying, "Think—speed kills." All this asks you to do is to remember that fatal acidents may be caused by fast driving. At the other extreme, thinking can be the kind of highly complex activity involved, say, in engineering or science, where a person spends hours or days in juggling mathematical formulas, drawing diagrams, or merely imagining various ways in which a problem might be solved. This chapter will consider the various forms of thinking, from simple to complex.

THE THINKING PROCESS

Although scientists cannot inspect the actual processes that go on, they are quite sure of what thinking is, at least in general. Thinking is the use of *symbolic processes.* A symbolic process is something taking place within the person that *represents* his previous learning and experience. Another term that is frequently applied to this activity is *mediating process*, which means something that forms an intervening link, beyond simple learned responses, between the situation a person is in and what we see him do. Whatever term we use, we are talking about events within the person that symbolize or represent his past experience, immediate or remote.

Just what is a symbolic process? This is a hard question to answer for any given period of thinking in a particular individual. But we do know that thinking involves images, implicit movements, conceptual thinking, and verbal thinking.

Images

Early in the history of experimental psychology, when structuralists believed that their business was to study conscious experience, they assumed that thinking consists of *images.* They conceived of images as we do now, regarding them as processes in the brain that represent past experience. And they set out to trace the sequence of images occurring in any particular bit of thinking.

The structuralists carried out some rather simple experiments: for instance, they would, ask a person what he had had for breakfast. After he had told them, they would ask him to report the images he had experienced in arriving at the answer. They were disappointed by what they found; for although some people did report vivid images of what they saw as they remembered their breakfast table, other people reported no images at all. They simply recalled from memory what they ate without using images to do it. This was so disturbing to the psychologists that it caused a great controversy. Eventually, however, all psychologists came to accept the idea that images are sometimes involved in some people's thinking, but that a great deal of thinking is accomplished without them. This conclusion led to other ideas that will be described later. For the moment, let us see what images are like and how they are used when they exist.

Short-term traces   The simplest kind of symbolic mediating process, it now appears, is a memory trace that lasts a brief time after a stimulus is experienced. If a problem is presented to a person to solve after he has seen the stimulus, he can use the trace as a cue. The action of memory traces was explored in the following experiment (Sperling, 1960).

A device called a tachistoscope was used to present visual stimuli for a very brief moment—50 thousandths of a second. The stimuli were groups of letters arranged in a 3 × 3 block like that at the left in Figure 7.1. Subjects were instructed to recall as many as possible when they were given a signal at a brief interval following the flash. Under these circumstances, subjects could recall only about one-third of the letters. Then the experiment was changed to give a signal for recalling the letters in a particular row. A high tone was the signal for the top row, a middle tone for the middle row, and a low tone for the bottom row. The signal was given at various points in time, from just before the flash up to a second or so after the flash. This greatly improved performance, as can be seen in the right-hand part of Figure 7.1.

What was going on here? The flash was too short to do any reading or rehearsing during its presentation. To recall any of the letters, the

Figure 7.1 *Left, a 3 × 3 block of letters used in the experiment. Right, the results of the experiment. First, the 3 × 3 letter block was flashed for 50 milliseconds (at the point where the dashed line intersects the time scale). Subjects could recall very few of the letters about a second after the flash (degree of recall is indicated by height of black bar at right). Next, various tone signals, each indicating that a particular row of letters in the 3 × 3 block would be the "recall target," were given at various time intervals before and after the letter block was flashed. Recall of the letters was markedly greater with the tone signals than without them, as the graph curve shows. (After Sperling, 1960.)*

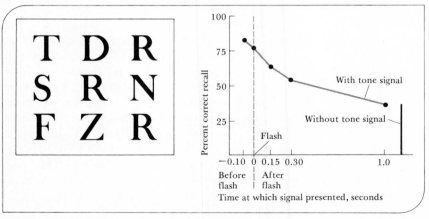

Figure 7.2 *A picture for a test of eidetic imagery. (G. W. Allport.)*

subjects must have had an "image" in their brain that could be scanned after the flash. Subjects did report having such fleeting images, which decayed quickly during the first second after the flash. The value of the signal was that it directed the subjects to scan a portion of the decaying image.

Long-term traces   Also involved in thinking are images of events occurring in the more distant past—or at least more than a second ago. An extreme case of such imagery, found in a few people, is an ability called *eidetic* (or sometimes *photographic*) imagery. Some people, most often young children, have a photographic memory for things they have seen. They have, for example, almost perfect imagery for visual material (Haber, 1969). To test yourself, look at the picture in Figure 7.2. Do not read further until you have inspected the picture for 35 seconds.

Now, without looking at the picture, can you spell the German word in it? In one experiment 3 out of 30 English children, unfamiliar with German, could spell the word forward and backward; 7 spelled it with only two mistakes. They and other "eidetikers" often hesitate a moment before recalling their answers. During this time they seem to "project" their image on a "mental screen," inspect it, and then read it as if it were actually there. Some people can recall a page of print so accurately that they can repeat any word or line on demand, shifting to different parts of the page as requested.

Most of us do not have eidetic imagery. Either we never had it, or we had it in childhood but lost it as adults. Instead, we have selective or partial imagery. We can imagine only certain features of past experiences, and we forget most of the details.

Imagery in thought Many experiments over the years have studied imagery in thinking. They show that imagery exists—more in some people than in others—but that it is not the whole of thinking. Take, for example, an experiment in which a person is blindfolded and asked to learn a maze by repeatedly tracing his way through it until he can do it without an error (Davis, 1932). Afterwards he is asked how he learned the maze. Many people in such an experiment report truly functional imagery; they solve the maze by constructing a "mental map" of it as they go along. They can quickly draw a map of it, showing not only the correct path but blind alleys as well. Other persons solve the maze by purely verbal methods. They count or name correct turns by learning a sequence like RRLRLLRL, but they do not "see" the maze as a whole in their mind's eye. So there are marked individual differences among people in the way they use imagery or verbal symbols to solve a problem.

Implicit Movements

When it became clear that images are far from the full explanation of thinking, psychologists considered other alternatives. John B. Watson, who believed that all behavior could be explained in terms of conditioned reflexes, offered a behavioral explanation of thinking: Thinking, he reasoned, is the outcome of conditioned responses. These responses, practiced over and over again, become smaller and smaller. Eventually they become very small movements in the muscles that represent larger movements learned earlier.

Watson's hypothesis was put to experimental tests about as early as recording instruments were available to do it. In one (Jacobsen, 1932), subjects were told to imagine hitting a nail with a hammer either one or two times. Electrical recordings were made from muscles in their arms, and sure enough, a burst of electrical activity indicating hidden muscle movements showed up on the record—one burst for each blow. In a parallel experiment (Max, 1937), deaf-mute subjects were studied because they use their hands and fingers for "talking." When told to do multiplication problems mentally, nearly all of them made small, recordable movements with their hands.

There is evidence, then, that very small movements, called *implicit movements*, often accompany thinking or imagining. Are they absolutely necessary? Probably not, for other experiments tell us what happens when movements are impossible. In one heroic experiment (Smith, 1947), a subject was completely paralyzed with the drug curare. He literally could not move a muscle, and his breathing was done for him in an "iron lung." He was given certain problems to solve, and he solved them correctly, reporting the answers after the drug wore off.

He could also clearly remember everything that took place while he was under the drug.

Psychologists have concluded, therefore, that implicit movements are not necessary for thinking, although they often accompany it. Possibly they are an aid in some kinds of situations. Try, for example, to answer the question of which way you turn the key to unlock the door of your room or apartment. Observe yourself, or have someone else observe you, while you do it. The chances are that you do not remember this verbally. What you probably do is make small movements, as you would in really opening the door, and then you give the answer, "To the right," or "To the left." In this case you have a motor habit, and by checking that habit, you obtain a cue for answering the question.

There seem to be other situations in which neither imagery nor implicit movements are involved in thinking. The process is something implicit, that is, not seen—an unconscious process in the brain. Have you ever struggled to recall a name, given up, and found later that the name suddenly popped into your mind, even when you were not thinking about the problem? This happens frequently to some people. Their attempt to recall the name apparently leaves them with a "set" to produce the name. Then some sort of unconscious process goes to work and eventually turns up the result. This sort of process, as we shall see later, is frequently reported by creative thinkers trying to solve a problem.

So far three kinds of processes that are involved in thinking have been described: images, implicit muscle movements, and unconscious (also implicit) processes. Now consider another activity going on in thinking—the use of concepts.

Conceptual Thinking

Some of the things a person thinks about are specific. He might think about the house he lived in as a boy, or the football game on homecoming day. Much of the thinking people do in everyday life is in this category. On the other hand, much of their thinking, and especially the thinking involved in college work, is about abstractions: politics, economics, learning, motivation, and the like. These general or abstract "things" are called *concepts.* The thinking people do in which concepts are the symbolic processes is called *conceptual thinking.*

What is a concept? A concept is the mental process people have that corresponds to some common property or properties of objects. "Common property" means some feature that is the same in several otherwise different situations. Examples of concepts are man, red, triangle, meticulousness, atom, anger, learning. In fact, most of the nouns in our vocabulary are names for concepts. The only exception is proper nouns, that is, names for specific things or persons.

The ability of human beings to form concepts enables them to divide things into classes. With a concept of red, they can sort objects into "red" and "not red." With a concept of fruit, they can classify things into "fruit" and "not fruit." The common property forms the concept, and this is the basis for making classifications. Since the number of common properties we find in the world around us is practically unlimited, there is almost no end to the number of classes or concepts that can be formed.

The examples given so far are simple concepts. Each refers to a single common property of objects. Other more complex concepts may be formed, although not so easily. There are three kinds of more complex concepts recognized by psychologists.

Conjunctive concepts   This kind of concept is defined by the joint presence of *two or more* common properties among objects. Consider the patterns shown in Figure 7.3. They are drawings of some cards used in an experiment on concepts. All the cards with three gray squares, for example, make up a conjunctive concept. In this case the concept is defined as the joint presence of three of something, grayness, and squareness. A football team is another example of such a concept. It consists of eleven men wearing certain clothes who kick or pass a ball of a certain shape according to certain rules. Such concepts are fairly easy to learn.

Disjunctive concepts   A disjunctive concept is defined by specifying two or more properties, *any one* of which is in the class of the

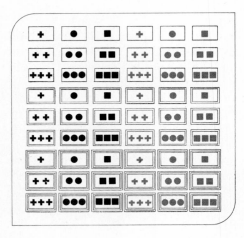

Figure 7.3 *Cards used in a story of concept formation. Note that they differ in three ways: in the number of figures, in the shape of the figures, and in the number of borders. (After Bruner et al., 1956.)*

concept. Suppose that in Figure 7.3 a class includes three of anything *or* anything gray *or* anything square. This would be a disjunctive concept, even though it does not make much sense. A more familiar example is the concept of a strike in baseball (Bruner et al., 1956). A strike is a swing of a bat that misses the ball, *or* a pitch that is not swung at but comes over the plate between the batter's shoulders and knees, *or* a foul ball if there are less than two strikes on the batter, *or* a foul bunt if the batter already has two strikes. Disjunctive concepts, as you might guess, are rather difficult for people to learn.

Relational concepts   The last kind of concept is a fairly simple one. It is *any* relationship between the elements in a situation. In Figure 7.3, it could be all cards with more borders than figures. In everyday use it includes such concepts as "more than," "heavier than," "taller than," "higher than," and so on.

Verbal Thinking

In principle, it is not necessary to have words connected to concepts. Rats and monkeys have been taught such concepts as triangularity. All that is needed is some discriminative response on the part of the animal to tell us whether or not the animal has the concept. The discriminative response can be pushing a lever or any other act that can be scored in terms of the concept tested. Psychologists test the concept by presenting different instances of it. If the animal responds to a common property such as triangularity, they can say that it has formed a concept.

Humans, however, have come to use words as labels for concepts. Although the child may learn some concepts before he has words for them, in a few years he has words for all the concepts he has learned. When he thinks of a triangle, he also thinks of the name for it. When he visualizes red, he also thinks the word "red." In fact, most formal education is concerned with the dual process of learning concepts and at the same time learning the words that label the concepts. The result of this schooling is *thinking*, which links together each concept and its word label. Hence most conceptual thinking also becomes verbal thinking. People who do a lot of thinking with imagery may omit some of the verbal counterparts. Even so, when they go to record the result of their thinking, they do it in words.

Thinking, then, for most people most of the time is a verbal affair. The symbolic processes involved in thinking represent words as well as the concepts for which the words stand. Moreover, the sequence followed in thinking is controlled by rules that people have learned to use with words. These rules are called *grammar.* In learning grammar, humans come to use nouns, verbs, adjectives, and so on, in certain relationships to each other. These relationships become ingrained habits. When people think, they think verbally, and pretty much according to the rules of grammar they have learned.

CONCEPT LEARNING

Since concepts with their verbal labels form much of the stuff of thinking, the way people learn concepts is a subject of major study for psychologists. In most college courses, especially in the sciences, what teachers and textbooks are trying to teach is concepts. The thinking you do as you listen or read is directed at learning concepts. Specifically, how do you learn them?

Methods of Learning Concepts

Three different methods of learning concepts can be distinguished: discrimination, context, and definition. All these are used by all of us at some time in our lives.

Discrimination learning   To teach a rat or a monkey a concept, psychologists must use the method of discriminative learning. They present pairs of objects, one of which has the common property they are interested in—say, triangle—while the other does not. They reward the animal only for choosing the "correct" stimulus containing the common property. When the animal performs more or less perfectly, they say that it has learned the concept.

A similar process goes on in children's learning, except that the child is also taught word labels for the common property. Suppose that whenever an apple is offered to little Charlie, whoever is teaching him says "apple." The teacher says nothing at all, or says something else, whenever he offers Charlie a ball, a cup, or a triangular block. This gives Charlie a chance to associate "apple" with the fruit. In addition, the teacher may reward him for saying "apple" by giving him an apple. The apples Charlie associates with "apple" in this way will vary somewhat in size and shape. But they all will be more or less round, they will be edible, and they will have stems.

Having learned this, Charlie has the conjunctive concept of apple. His concept, however, may not be the same as our concept of apple. If "apple" is the first concept of fruit he learns, and he is presented with a pear, he may very well confuse "apple" and "pear." He may mix up the two because he *generalizes* the concept of apple to other similar fruits. To straighten him out, more discrimination training is required. In due course he will learn the difference by associating the word "pear" with a pear, the word "orange" with an orange, and so on.

This example illustrates the way in which our early concrete concepts are formed. It also illustrates the fact that concepts can be learned imperfectly. Most people get the names for common fruits straight, but something like "gravity" may be more difficult. They may learn that gravity makes apples fall to the ground, but further learning is required to understand that gravity also holds the moon in the sky and the earth in its orbit around the sun. Even then they may fail to grasp other instances of gravity—that it holds air to the earth, for example. A person's concept of fruit may also be an imperfect one—he may generalize it, for example, to tomato—until he takes a course in botany and learns a much more conjunctive concept of fruit.

Context   Early in school, in kindergarten and in the first grade, the teacher explains concepts by showing children pictures of things and giving their names. This is essentially discrimination learning. As time goes on, however, children pick up many concepts by hearing new words and inferring what they mean from the *context* in which they are used. As an example, see if you can form the conjunctive concept of "corplum" (Werner and Kaplan, 1950).

> A corplum may be used for support.
> Corplums may be used to close off an open space.
> A corplum may be long or short, thick or thin, strong or weak.
> A wet corplum does not burn.
> You can make a corplum smooth with sandpaper.
> The painter uses a corplum to mix his paints.

In an experiment with these sentences, the psychologist read them one at a time and after each sentence asked the subjects what they thought a corplum was. Very few got it in the first couple of sentences. More got it by the fourth, and all had it by the last sentence. In this case, of course, the concept of corplum is the same as the concept given another word in our language. But if you were not familiar with the properties of the material, you would learn the concept of corplum through context.

Definition   As a child's education progresses, he acquires more and more concepts by the method of *definition.* That is, he uses already learned concepts to build a new concept. This is exactly what a dictionary does. It.is also what a teacher does in much of his classroom instruction. A six-year-old, for instance, many never have seen a zebra, but he has seen horses or pictures of horses, he has seen things that are striped, and he has an idea of what is meant by "wild." Possessing these concepts, he needs only to be told that a zebra is an animal that has stripes, looks like and runs like a horse, and is usually found in the wild. Thus he gets a pretty accurate concept of zebra by using other concepts to define the animal conjunctively.

This illustrates one of the powerful advantages of language. Once a certain limited number of concepts are learned by discrimination learning and context, they can be used in different combinations to teach an almost unlimited number of other concepts. The trick, however, is in learning *correctly* the combinations that specify a conjunctive concept. If a student learns, say, three of the defining properties of a conjunctive concept but forgets the fourth, he has learned it imperfectly. This is exactly what has happened much of the time when students miss questions on examinations. They failed to master *all* the qualifications that define a concept.

Aids to Concept Learning
A number of factors can help or hinder us in learning concepts. Two of the most important are distinctiveness and transfer.

Distinctiveness   When a concept is acquired through discrimination learning, the *distinctiveness* of the property to be learned is important. If the cue is embedded in a lot of other material, it is difficult for a person to discover what the common property is.

In a classical experiment (Hull, 1920), Chinese characters similar to those in Figure 7.4 were used. Some characters, like those in the first row, had a common part, or "radical." Each time the experimenter presented such a character, he gave it a nonsense name like *oo*. Other sets, like those in the second row, also had a particular part in common. The experimenter presented these with another nonsense name, say, *yer*. The cards, however, were in mixed order, and the subjects did not know which cards contained the common property. Their only cue was the name given. Concept learning under these circumstances was extremely difficult. You might judge that by trying to figure out the common part among the

Figure 7.4 Characters used in a study of concept formation by discriminative learning. (After Hull, 1920.)

characters in each row of Figure 7.4. Yet you have the clue that there is something in common in each particular row, whereas the subjects did not.

In this experiment concept learning was slow because the common parts were not very distinctive; they were embedded in other lines and dots. If they had been more distinctive, the concepts would have been learned more rapidly. In summary, the more distinctive a common feature is, the more easily the concept can be formed.

Transfer   Chapters 5 and 6 on motor and verbal learning showed that positive transfer speeds up learning and negative transfer slows it down. The same is true, but even more so, in concept learning. When students see the similarities between new concepts and the concepts they have previously learned, concept learning is easy. But this method of learning concepts has its dangers. If the student grasps only the similarities between concepts, he will confuse the old and the new and so learn the new concept imperfectly. To offset this, the teacher must point out clearly both the similarities and differences between new and old concepts. In teaching the concept of zebra, for example, the teacher is using transfer when he says that a zebra looks like a horse, has stripes, and is found in the wild. From this description, however, the learner might conclude that a zebra is a wild, striped horse unless the teacher points out that a zebra looks like a horse but is not a horse.

Other factors   Although distinctiveness and transfer are probably the most important aids to concept learning, two others should be mentioned. One is *manipulation of the material.* If a person is permitted to rearrange, redraw, or reorganize the materials containing the common properties, he is more likely to grasp the correct concept of them. A child, for instance, will learn the concept of ball more quickly if he can play with a ball than if he is merely shown a picture of one or given a verbal definition. Another aid is *instruction* or *purpose.* If a person is instructed to learn a concept and told to search for the common property in various situations, he will discover the concept more rapidly than he would if he were not given a general purpose.

Meaning of concepts

In the natural sciences, concepts have very precise meanings. "Mass," "force," and "acceleration" are examples. In the social sciences and humanities, meanings become less precise. "Status" is a key term in sociology, but different sociologists define it differently. And the meanings of concepts acquired by people in everyday life are even less precise. What, for example, is the meaning of "liberal," "honesty," or "politician"? People have very different concepts of these terms—that is, the terms mean different things to different people.

Where concepts have precise meanings, teachers can be interested in how *correct or incorrect* a student's particular concept may be. In the fuzzy areas, where even experts cannot agree on what a concept means, social scientists may want to find out what it means *to a particular person.* For whichever purpose, methods are needed for measuring the meaning of concepts. There are four such methods.

Free response The most straightforward way to find out what a concept means to a person is to ask him what he thinks it means. This is the free-response method. The quality of the results depends on the instructions given and the particular concepts tested.

A child's concept of dog can be tested by asking him to describe a dog. His description can be scored as "accurate," "too general," "abstract," "concrete," "irrelevant," and so forth, with a fair degree of agreement among scorers. In fact, items like this are used on intelligence tests with good reliability. When a description avoids irrelevancies and includes only the generally accepted meaning, we call the response a *definition.* The definition, however, need not be verbal. A child may be asked to draw a picture of a dog, or a student may be asked to make a diagram of a vector. In many cases this kind of free response may provide a more accurate measure of a person's concept than a verbal response.

Discrimination The free-response method, being subjective, often does not produce scorable results. Moreover, it may not tell whether a person knows what a concept *is not.* A child may describe a dog as a furry animal that barks and sometimes bites. From this, or from a picture he might draw, you could not be sure that he knew the difference between a dog and a wolf.

One practical test is to require a set of discriminations. A person is shown a variety of objects, some of which are examples of the concept and some of which are not. He is then asked to identify which ones are which. Alternatively, he may be shown the objects with the instruction to classify them according to such and such concepts.

The methods of free response and discrimination do not always give the same results. A person may give a good verbal definition of a concept and make mistakes in choosing instances of it, and vice versa. The explanation is that if he has learned concepts by context or definition, he is likely to do well with the free-response method. But if he has learned his concepts in a practical setting, he will do best with the discrimination method. This is one of the reasons why strictly formal education, limited to books and the classroom, can turn out students who do not understand "practical" concepts. And it is one of the reasons why schools try to supplement classroom instruction with laboratories and other more lifelike methods of teaching concepts.

Word association   Another method for finding out the meaning of a person's concepts is to ask him for his association(s) with a particular concept word. This approach is best suited to studying the normality or idiosyncracy of a person's concepts. Most people, when asked what they associate with "black," will say "white." To "table" they will say "leg" or "chair." These answers are not getting at the precise meaning of the word "black" or "table," but they are indicating what concept class a person puts the word in. On the other hand, if a person gives the word "funeral" to "black," or "poison" to "table," he is putting the words into different concept classes from the classes most people use. Many responses of this kind suggest that something is wrong with a person's mental processes. Thus word-association tests are frequently used in the diagnosis of disturbances in thinking.

Semantic differential   The fourth method of obtaining the meaning of a concept is called a semantic differential (Osgood et al., 1957). Its great advantage is that it provides a *profile of the meaning* of many concepts on a few (usually three) common dimensions. The three dimensions most often used are called evaluation, potency, and activity. (They were chosen after statistical studies showed that most people can, and do, classify concepts on these dimensions.) *Evaluation* refers to a good-bad continuum; *potency* to a weak-strong one; and *activity* to an active-passive one.

To obtain a semantic differential, people are given the three scales and a series of concepts. They are asked to rank each concept by indicating a number from 1 to 7 on each scale. The concepts can then be arranged in a three-dimensional space.

Figure 7.5 gives the average position of an assortment of concepts on two dimensions, since the page of a book has only two. To suggest the third dimension of good-bad, the words falling on the bad side are printed in heavy black, and those on the good side in lighter type.

PROBLEM SOLVING

Much of the thinking we do is directed at the solution of problems. A problem is basically a conflict situation in which a person experiences frustration in achieving a goal (see Chapter 4). The frustration may be a barrier to a goal, and the problem is to find the best way around the barrier. Or the frustration may be a conflict of goals, as in approach-

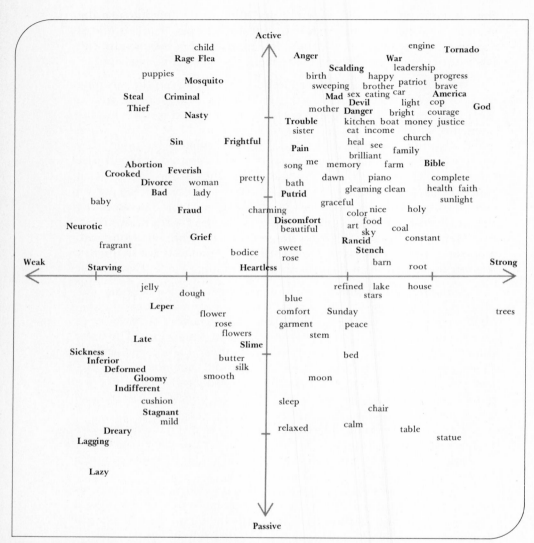

Figure 7.5   *Concepts may be located in "meaning space." Here each term (which is also a concept) is placed with respect to three factors derived from the semantic differential. The three factors are activity (active-passive), potency (weak-strong), and evaluation (good-bad). The position of the concept with respect to the axes locates it on the activity and potency dimensions. The evaluative factor is represented by the way the words are printed: "Good" concepts are in light type; "bad" concepts in dark type. For instance,* **Anger** *is rated as strongly active, slightly strong, and "bad." (From Carroll, 1964. Based on data from Jenkins et al., 1958.)*

avoidance conflict (page 90). In trying to make up his mind about how to vote in an election, a person may experience both positive and negative feelings about each candidate. The problem is to resolve the conflict.

A problem is not a problem just because someone says it is. To produce thinking, it must be regarded as a problem by the person himself. He must have a goal he wishes to attain, one that he will try to think his way toward. Then the processes he uses to attain his goal can be analyzed. This field of study includes the major steps in problem solving, the individual factors affecting solutions, and finally the processes of reasoning and logical thinking.

Stages in Problem Solving

One way of studying what goes on in problem solving is to examine the ways in which outstanding thinkers solve problems. This has been done in a number of cases using such sources of information as diaries, interviews, and questionnaires. Although each person has his own way of thinking, and although the methods that he follows depend on the kinds of problems to be solved, great thinkers seem to have a recurring pattern of approach to problem solving (Wallas, 1926). They tend to proceed in four stages: (1) preparation, (2) incubation, (3) insight or illumination, (4) evaluation and revision.

In stage 1 the thinker works out what his problem really is, and collects the facts and materials that he decides are relevant to it. This is the step of *preparation.* He tries to solve the problem but may find he cannot, even after hours or days of working on it. He may then give it up for a time, hoping that he will have more success later. This puts him in stage 2, *incubation.* Now some of the ideas that were getting in the way of a solution fade away. At the same time, he is doing and learning other things, some of which may provide a solution to the problem. Unconscious processes are also at work. In stage 3, *illumination,* the thinker often has an insight—a sudden and completely new idea for a solution. "Aha! I have it," is his reaction. At this point he has produced a novel solution—novel to him, at least—through thinking. Most of us have had this experience at one time or another. Next in stage 4, *evaluation,* he tests his idea to see if it really works. Sometimes it does not, and he is back where he started. In other cases he has the right idea, but it needs some revision or requires the solution of other minor problems.

Individual Factors

The success a person has in solving problems depends on a number of personal factors—factors within the individual rather than in the problem itself. One is *intelligence.* The brighter he is, the better he is at solving problems. In fact, ability to solve problems is one of the ingredients of intelligence, and intelligence tests contain many standardized problems to be solved. Problem-solving ability also depends on motivation, set, and functional fixedness.

Motivation A person must be motivated to solve a problem, or else his thinking will be aimless and he will probably not arrive at the solution. Motivation gives *directness* to his thought, so that he entertains only those thoughts that seem relevant to the goal of the problem.

Motivation is most important in the early and late stages of problem solving. A person must be motivated in stage 1, preparation, in order to formulate the problem and assemble information for solving it. But in stage 2, strong motivation may be a hindrance; it may keep him working fruitlessly at "wrong" solutions instead of laying the problem aside and allowing incubation to do its work. However, once he has gotten through the period of incubation (stage 2) and has arrived at insight (stage 3), motivation is again necessary for the work of evaluation and revision (stage 4).

Motivation thus helps the thinker get started and helps him tidy up the solution to the problem. One form of motivation may arise from the problem itself—its inherent interest as a puzzle. As Chapter 3 said, human beings possess curiosity motives and related motives to explore and manipulate. Once a person gets into a problem, he often becomes interested in solving it. And when people gain satisfaction from their solutions of problems, they may develop a general motivation for problem solving. This is the case with great thinkers such as scientists, artists, writers, and inventors. They develop a lifelong interest in solving problems just for the sake of solving them.

Set Early research on thinking revealed the importance of habit and *set* in problem solving. The way people are used to doing things (habit) produces a readiness (set) to go about a new problem in a particular way. Sets are the basis of many trick jokes and puzzles. In one trick, for example, you spell words and ask a person to pronounce them. You use names beginning with Mac, like MacDonald and MacTavish; then you slip in "machinery" and see if he pronounces it "MacHinery." With a set for names, he may fall into your trap.

Set can be produced in a variety of ways: by the immediately preceding experience, as in the spelling problem above; by the instructions a person is given for solving a problem; or by established habits. Set biases the thinker at the start of his problem by directing his thinking in one direction rather than in another. It may help him—that is, provide positive transfer—if the problem requires responses along the lines of his bias. But it may hinder him—produce negative transfer—if the problem requires different responses from those he is set to give. An illustration of the role of set in problem solving is provided by a famous experiment (Luchins, 1946).

It is sometimes called the water-jar experiment, because it requires a subject to use water jars of different sizes to measure a given amount of water. First he is given the practice problems stated in Table 7.1. In problems 1 through 5, you can see, the correct answer is obtained by filling the B jar, then filling the A jar once, and then filling the C jar twice. In the sixth problem, the test problem, the subject is asked to say how he would measure 20 quarts of water when he has only three jars holding 23, 49, and 3 quarts. With the set he has acquired in the practice problems, he is very likely to use the same method as before. But this will be the "long way round," for the problem can be solved simply by filling A and then C. In the original experiment, 74 percent of the college-student subjects took the long way after working on the practice problems.

Functional fixedness   Related to set is a tendency to think of objects in the way they usually function. When we are given a problem in which they must function in a different way, we have trouble seeing it. For example, we normally use knives to cut things with; that knowledge may keep us from using one as a screwdriver. The following experiment shows how *functional fixedness* impedes the solution of problems (Adamson, 1952).

Subjects were asked to find a way of mounting three candles on a vertical screen. They were provided with the candles, three small pasteboard

TABLE 7.1
Practice and test problems demonstrating negative transfer caused by set. The five practice problems require a roundabout method of solution; the test problem can be solved easily. But most subjects who acquired a set by solving the practice problems used the long method of solving the test problem; they were blind to the easy method.

Problem number	Given the following empty jars as measures			Obtain this amount of water
	A	B	C	
1. Practice	21	127	3	100
2. Practice	14	163	25	99
3. Practice	18	43	10	5
4. Practice	9	42	6	21
5. Practice	20	59	4	31
6. Test	23	49	3	20

Source: Luchins, 1946.

boxes, five thumbtacks, and five matches. One group of subjects was given these materials with the candles, thumbtacks, and matches *lying in the boxes*. For another group of subjects, all the objects were *laid out separately on a table*. The solution to the problem is rather simple; it consists of sticking the candles on the boxes with melted wax, then tacking the boxes to the wall with the thumbtacks. The first group had much more difficulty reaching the solution than the second. With the candles in the boxes, they thought of the boxes as containers, which boxes usually are. With this function of boxes in their minds, they could not think of them as platforms.

Reasoning

The four stages of problem solving that are typical of great thinkers include insight, or illumination. Yet many, if not most, everyday problems do not get solved by insight but by two other general methods: mechanical means or reasoning. Mechanical solutions may be either trial and error or rote. In trial and error, people try one solution, then another, without much reason, until they hit on the arrangement that works. In a rote solution they simply apply the methods they have used successfully in the past. If the new problem is similar to the ones they have previously solved, then they can solve it with very little thinking.

The kind of problem solving that requires the most thinking is the one based on *reasoning* methods. Perhaps you tend to use the words *"reasoning"* and *"thinking"* as though they mean the same thing; people frequently do in everyday talk. However, there are many instances of thinking that do not involve reasoning. At the extreme are dreams, which are a type of thought but do not follow logical rules. Strictly speaking, only when the rules are followed can thinking be called reasoning.

Logical thinking Most human reasoning makes use of verbal symbols; we use words to reason with. Yet word meanings are often vague or ambiguous, and we can be led astray by them. Also, when we reach a conclusion through words we often cannot tell whether we are right or not, because we do not have a chance to check our conclusion with reality. To help us reason correctly, rigid standards have been developed over the centuries by philosophers and mathematicians. These are the *rules of logic*. They limit what a particular statement can imply, and what conclusions can be drawn from a series of statements. Let us see how they relate to human reasoning.

Suppose a psychologist, in conducting a test of reasoning in children, asks a child the question: "If all 6-year-olds are in school, and if Johnny is 6, then where is Johnny?" The psychologist should not be surprised if the answer is "I hate school" or "He's home sick with a cold." To the logician, these are "unreasonable statements," because they are not logical. To the psychologist, however, the statements are logical, because they are simple associations with a stimulus. This is what people learn long before they learn to reason, much less to reason by the formal rules of logic.

Children gradually learn to be more logical: they keep their associations within certain bounds. I may, for instance, instruct a high school student to respond with a word, whenever I say a word, that is a class name for objects of the same kind. If I give him the word "table," he will give me "furniture" or some comparable word. He will not say "chair," because that violates the rule I gave him of responding with class names. He has learned to follow a rule.

Now for a more complex case. In school the student may learn syllogisms, one form of which is

1   All A is B. (All men are mortal.)
2   All C is A. (All farmers are men.)
3   Therefore, all C is B. (All farmers are mortal.)

This syllogism (see Figure 7.6) follows one of the rules of logic, and the student can learn it, perhaps by memorizing it. But he will immediately have trouble when he tries to apply it to daily situations. In these,

Figure 7.6 *Simple diagrams sometimes aid logical thinking. These circles—sometimes called Euler's circles or Venn diagrams—are used to represent simple logical problems.*

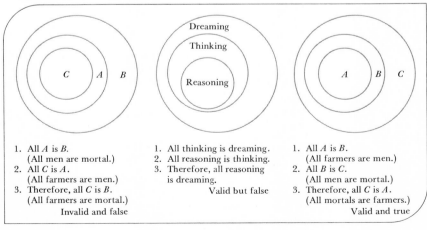

1. All *A* is *B*.
   (All men are mortal.)
2. All *C* is *A*.
   (All farmers are men.)
3. Therefore, all *C* is *B*.
   (All farmers are mortal.)
   Invalid and false

1. All thinking is dreaming.
2. All reasoning is thinking.
3. Therefore, all reasoning is dreaming.
   Valid but false

1. All *A* is *B*.
   (All farmers are men.)
2. All *B* is *C*.
   (All men are mortal.)
3. Therefore, all *C* is *A*.
   (All mortals are farmers.)
   Valid and true

emotional factors cloud our thinking, and often we cannot tell whether our premises are true or false. Even the simplest syllogism seems complex. For instance, the form of the syllogism above *looks* suspiciously like the following:

1 All A is B. (All farmers are men.)
2 All B is C. (All men are mortal.)
3 Therefore, all C is A. (All mortals are farmers.)

The conclusion is unsound because it does not follow from 1 and 2. The verbal discriminations involved are difficult, even when put in symbol form. They are even harder in the form of words. For this reason many of the statements made in politics, business, and everyday life seem to be valid syllogisms when they are really fallacious. A political candidate, for example, may say:

> We have high taxes.
> High taxes lead to tax scandals.
> So let's cut taxes.

And people may respond with, "I want lower taxes. Say, he makes good sense!"

Illogical thinking As illustrated in the example above, one reason why it is hard to think logically is that it is hard to tell when verbal reasoning is logical and when it is not. Another reason is that ordinary conversation is not made from a logical mold—and how dull it would be if it were!—but from the interplay of personal and motivational factors. People learn to use language for purposes that are not necessarily logical: to sell a magazine subscription, to persuade a reluctant parent, or to stimulate a mood. Seldom do they use words to "think straight."

In the instances where we are illogical, our trouble is the same as that of the 6-year-old who replied with "I hate school." We respond to "logic" stimuli with free associations—and often do so when we are trying our level best to be logical. Free associations distort our reasoning, leading to illogical rather than logical thinking. Three factors in a situation are especially important in distorting thinking: the complexity of the situation, an atmosphere effect, and an opinion effect.

The simpler a situation, the more likely people are to be logical. The more *complex* it is, the more likely they are to be illogical or to accept illogical conclusions. In experiments on this point, psychologists find that if a logical fallacy is presented to people in a complex way, or if it is presented along with many facts and statements, they are less likely to detect it.

An *atmosphere effect* can also make people accept false conclusions (Sells, 1936). This is the effect of the language in which a set of statements is expressed. Quite apart from its logical implications, its language may predispose a person to answer one way or another. If, for example, the premises of the syllogism are presented in the affirmative—"All *p*'s are *q*'s, and all *q*'s are *t*'s"—people tend to reject any negative conclusions containing "no" or "are not." But if the premises are split so that one is stated negatively and the other affirmatively, people are more likely to accept a negative conclusion. Atmosphere effects are very common, even in college students.

The so-called *opinion effect* can distort logical thinking when the statements presented to a person call forth strong prejudices, beliefs, or opinions. Then he may not be able to make the discriminations necessary for logical thinking. In other words, emotionally loaded words in the premises can prevent the correct use of logical rules in reasoning.

In conclusion, while the rules of logic help us solve problems, they do not guarantee correct solutions. Our learned associations and emotional reactions often override logic. The causes are psychological; they lie in the learning history of the individual. Thus humans are usually more psychological than logical, even when they reason.

SUMMARY

The thinking process consists of symbolic activities within the person that represent his previous learning and experience. Images may be a part of thinking, but not all thinking consists of images. Implicit muscle movements and unconscious processes in the brain are also involved. Much of people's thinking is done with concepts. A concept is a mental process that represents some common property of objects. Because human beings use words as labels for concepts, much of their conceptual thinking is verbal thinking.

Concepts are learned through *discrimination learning*, with many different objects representing the concepts; through the *context* in which words are used; and by verbal *definition*. We learn concepts more rapidly if (1) the common property is distinctive, (2) positive transfer from previously learned concepts takes place, (3) we can manipulate the objects involved, and (4) we are instructed in what to look for. The meaning of concepts can be tested by the methods of free response, discrimination, word associations, and semantic differential.

Creative thinking is characterized by four stages: (1) preparation, (2) incubation, (3) illumination or insight, and (4) evaluation and revision. Success in problem solving hinges on several factors. The most important are motivation, set or expectancy, and functional fixedness. Reasoning is thinking according to certain rules. Logical thinking follows the rules of logic, but it is very easy for people to slip into illogical thinking both because they tend to respond to stimuli with free associations and because many situations are too complex for them to know what is "logical."

SUGGESTIONS FOR FURTHER READING

Carroll, J. B. *Language and thought.* Englewood Cliffs, N.J.: Prentice-Hall, 1964. (Paperback.) *An introduction to thinking which stresses language as the symbolic system most important in thought.*

Duncan, C. P. (Ed.) *Thinking: Current experimental studies.* Philadelphia: Lippincott, 1967. (Paperback.) *A representative set of current studies in problem solving, set, originality of thinking, and concept learning.*

Ghiselin, B. (Ed.) *The creative process: A symposium.* New York: Mentor, 1955. (Paperback.) *Selections from creative artists and scientists who talk about their own creative processes.*

Ray, W. S. *The experimental psychology of original thinking.* New York: Macmillan, 1967. (Paperback.) *A text and a set of readings on problem solving.*

Thomas, R. *The psychology of thinking.* Baltimore: Penguin, 1969. (Paperback.) *An elementary textbook.*

Wertheimer, M. *Productive thinking.* (rev. ed.) New York: Harper, 1959. *A classic analysis of thinking with many ideas about ways of solving problems.*

8

Perception

LEARNING OBJECTIVES

Main objective
After studying this chapter you should be able to explain the stability of our perceptual world in terms of the perceptual constancies.

Other major objectives
You should also be able to
Outline the major factors influencing perception.
Describe the innate organizing tendencies in perception.

Minor objectives
Describe the principal cues in depth perception.
Define different kinds of visual movement.

How does the sensory information that we use to learn and think with get from the outside world into our heads? We process this information at two levels: the levels of sensation and perception. A *sensation* is an elementary experience such as the brightness of a light, the pitch of a tone, the warmth of coffee, or the pain of a pinprick. Sensations are the raw stuff of which experience is made; yet experience is much more than a series of sensations. In daily life we are forever *interpreting* the sensory information we receive. We interpret a sequence of tones as a melody, a large red cubical object as a red house, a cold and wet sensation as rain. This process of interpreting sensations—making them meaningful—is called *perception*.

Since the study of sensation is connected with the physiology of human sense organs and the human nervous system, sensation is treated in a separate place (Chapter 14) just preceding the chapter on the nervous system and behavior. But perception is concerned with the *meaning* of experience and is best considered here along with the chapters on learning and thinking.

More is known about perception than any other area of psychology, so the material in this chapter represents only the highlights of a very rich field of scientific knowledge. Because human beings perceive the world through all their senses, they have perceptions corresponding to each sense—visual perception, auditory perception, and so on. Normally they rely heavily on visual perception, which has been the most extensively studied of all kinds of perception and which will be emphasized here.

OBJECT PERCEPTION

A striking fact about all perception is that it is always converting sensory information into *objects*. A large red image is seen as a barn. A series of pressure sensations on the arm is perceived as a crawling bug. A wailing sound in the distance is heard as an approaching ambulance. Thus people are always perceiving objects, not just sensations or collections of stimuli.

The perception of objects is partly learned. Certainly a person's ability to name them and give their function is learned. But besides learning, a basic tendency to organize stimuli into objects is an innate property of a human being's sense organs and nervous system. The factors involved in this natural ability to perceive objects have been called *organizing tendencies*.

Figure-Ground Perception
The main organizing tendency in people's perception of objects is the separation of *figure* and *ground*. This tendency causes everyone to see objects as standing out from the background. Pictures hang *on* a wall, words are *on* a page. In these instances the pictures and words are seen as *figures*, the wall and the page as *grounds*. In looking at the left-hand drawing of Figure 8.1, you automatically see the dark area as an object, although it may not look like any particular object you ever saw. Or looking at the drawing on the right, you see either two faces close together or a vase. This is an example of a reversible figure—it can be perceived as either one of two objects. But the point is that you cannot help seeing an object—a figure or a ground.

This perception of figure-ground relationships also characterizes senses other than vision. When people listen to a symphony, they perceive the melody or theme as a figure while the chords form the

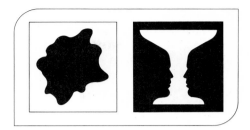

Figure 8.1 *Left, the dark area is automatically perceived as a figure on a ground. Right, sometimes a figure becomes a ground, and vice versa.*

ground. In rock music, the guitarist uses repetitive chords as ground against which he sings a more or less varied song, or figure. A tickling sensation that a person feels in the skin of his arm is perceived as a bug crawling *on* the arm. The tendency to perceive the figure-ground relation thus pervades all perception.

Grouping

Another organizing tendency in the perception of objects is a tendency to group stimuli into some pattern. Grouping may make use of various cues in the situation. In Figure 8.2*a*, for example, you see three pairs of lines. Here the cue is the *nearness* of one line to another. In part *b* of the figure, you will probably see one triangle superimposed on the other. Here you group the items together that are *similar* to each other. Otherwise you would see a six-pointed star, as in part *c*. Grouping according to similarity also occurs in part *d*, where most people perceive the Xs as being close together and the circles close together, with extra space separating the circles from the Xs.

Grouping by similarity, however, does not always happen. Part *e* of Figure 8.2 is more easily seen as a six-pointed star than as one figure composed of dots and another of circles. Here similarity is competing against another strong grouping tendency, *symmetry*, which is a habit of forming a balanced or symmetrical figure. Grouping, finally, may occur by *continuation*, as illustrated in part *f*. This tendency makes you see a curved line as continuing in a curved path, and a straight line as continuing in a straight path. Thus in part *f* you will tend to see three figures: a straight line, a semicircle, and a jagged line. Only with effort can you see a straight line suddenly becoming curved at one of the junction points.

Closure

Psychologists have discovered several other organizing processes in object perception, one of which is the tendency toward *closure*. This tendency makes people organize the visual world by filling in gaps in stimulation so that they perceive a whole object, not disjointed parts. Such a tendency is involved in the perception of parts *b*, *c*, and *e* of Figure 8.2. It is also illustrated in Figure 8.3, where the left and middle figures are perceived as a circle and a square. We also see the right-hand as an object rather than as disconnected lines (most people see a man on horseback).

PERCEPTUAL CONSTANCIES

Besides the strong tendency to perceive objects, human perception also has remarkable *stability*. The size of a man does not appear to change as he walks toward you, even though his image on the retina of your eye grows larger. The dinner plate does not look like a circle when viewed from one angle and an ellipse from another, even though these are the shapes of the retinal image. When you stand in front of a window its image on the retina is a rectangle; when you move to the side the image becomes a trapezoid, yet you continue to see it as a rectangle. In all these instances you recognize the object for what you have learned that it is—its appearance remains constant in perception despite differences in physical stimulation. This kind of stability is known as *perceptual constancy*.

Shape Constancy
Two of the examples given above—the dinner plate and the window—illustrate the principle of *shape constancy*. If we know what an object is, its shape remains constant no matter how we view it. Put another way, the shapes of *familiar* objects are perceived as constant

Figure 8.2 *Examples of perceptual grouping in vision.*

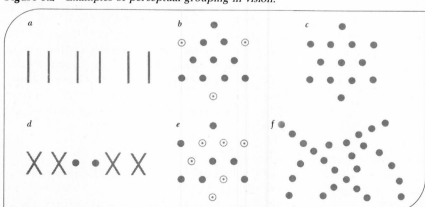

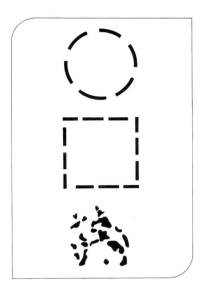

Figure 8.3 *Perceptual closure fills in the gaps: We tend to perceive a complete object even though it may not be all there.*

under various viewing conditions. It is the familiarity—our knowledge of what the object should look like—that is important. If for some reason we cannot identify an object, we lose shape constancy.

Size Constancy

The size of the retinal image of an object grows smaller as the object moves farther away. Yet people normally perceive the object as remaining the same size. This is the phenomenon of *size constancy*. Here two factors are at work. One, as in shape constancy, is the familiarity of the object, that is, a person's previous learning of what an object is. A man perceived as a man will also be perceived as constant in size no matter how far away he is. Another factor is *distance*. If an object is unfamiliar or if it could be any size—for example, a sheet of paper or a rock—you can preserve size constancy only by knowing how far away it is. Distance cues thus become important. If a depth cue is artificially reversed, as in Figure 8.4, you lose size constancy. There the large envelope looks farther away, and for this reason seems "larger," when in fact it is closer than the "small" envelope. The figure legend explains how the trick was worked.

Brightness Constancy

Perceptual constancy is also found in the perception of brightness: objects appear constant in their degree of whiteness, grayness, or blackness. Brightness constancy is independent of the amount of light

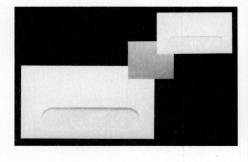

Figure 8.4 Size constancy is destroyed by reversal of the depth cue. These envelopes are the same size. The "large" envelope is actually much closer than the "small" one, yet you see it as farther away because it seems to be behind the gray card, which is in turn behind the "small" envelope. But in fact the gray card is not interposed between the two envelopes; it is behind both of them. It seems to be in front of the "large" envelope because the corner of the envelope has been cut out. (Fundamental Photographs.)

falling on the object. People see coal, for instance, as black both in moonlight and in bright sunlight; they see snow as white under the same conditions. The main reason is that perceived brightness depends on the *ratio* of brightness between the object and its background (Wallach, 1963). Normally the ratio remains the same regardless of the illumination. Increasing or decreasing the amount of light merely makes both the object and its background brighter or dimmer, and so people perceive the object's brightness as a constant.

DEPTH PERCEPTION

Human beings can judge the relative distances of objects, and more than that, can see objects in three-dimensional space. Yet the retina on which objects are imaged is a two-dimensional surface. The question that used to puzzle scientists was, How is two-dimensional information converted into three dimensions to give people a perception of depth?

Today they know the answer, but it is not a simple one. The fact is that people utilize a large number of *cues*, or features of the environment, which are related to depth. Many of these cues require only one eye and are called monocular cues. Other cues are supplied by the use of two eyes; these are the binocular cues to depth.

Monocular Cues
If you look at any picture, it may not seem to have as much depth as the scene it depicts, but it usually gives the impression of three dimensions. You can tell which parts of the picture are far and which are near because you have learned to use certain cues that signal depth.

Linear perspective   Objects of known size appear closer together when they are far away than when they are near. Imagine that you are standing between some railroad tracks and looking down them as they recede in the distance. The ties seem to become gradually smaller, and the tracks to run closer together, until they appear to meet at the horizon. This is an example of linear perspective. Part of the depth effect in Figure 8.5 is due to this factor.

Clearness Clearness of the air varies with distance, and this serves as a cue. When there is some haze in the air, you see far objects as blurred but can make out the fine details of near ones. If you have spent time in a mountainous region where you have a pretty good idea of the distance of a peak or range, on a brilliantly clear day you have probably noticed how close it looks. On most days, however, it is much dimmer than the hills closer by. Some of your perception of depth in Figure 8.5 comes from the cue of clearness.

Interposition The monocular cue of interposition occurs when one thing obstructs your view of another thing. As you can see in Figure 8.5, if one object is partly covered by another, the first object is perceived as being the nearer.

Shadows Because people are accustomed to seeing things lighted from above, shadows are often very strong cues to depth. The sun is the overhead light out of doors, and artificial lighting is usually arranged in the same way. People come to expect, then, that shadows fall below and behind things, and this expectation becomes so ingrained that they immediately perceive depth from shadows without even realizing why.

Figure 8.5 *Three monocular factors in depth perception. The buildings and the street appear to move closer together in the distance (linear perspective); more distant heights show less detail than the closer areas (clearness); and some parts of buildings are behind others (interposition). (Fundamental Photographs.)*

Texture Imagine that you are standing on a rocky desert looking 100 yards or so away. Because of size constancy you will perceive the rocks of similar size as indeed being much the same in size, whether they are near or far away. The rocks farther away form smaller images on the retina, but the "grain" or texture of the visual image becomes finer with increasing distance. This change in texture, which is related to linear perspective, is another cue to depth.

Movement Whenever you move your head, you can observe that the objects in your visual field move relative to you and to one another. And if you watch closely, you will find that the objects nearest to you appear to move in the opposite direction, whereas distant objects appear to move in the same direction as your head. This effect, called *motion parallax*, is an obvious cue to the relative distance of objects. Furthermore, with all movement, whether it is real or caused by the motion of your head, the relative *amount* of movement appears less for far objects than for near ones.

Binocular Cues

Because our eyes are separated by a few inches, they view objects from slightly different angles. This difference in angle causes a slight difference—called *retinal disparity*—in the retinal images. Although small, it is a powerful cue for depth.

The value of this cue is easily demonstrated with a stereoscope—a device, very popular before the days of radio and television and still available in many stores, for viewing two slightly different pictures, one with one eye and the other with the other eye. When the eyes focus on the two pictures, the scene appears as one picture with as much depth as a scene viewed in real life.

Conflicting Cues

In general, monocular and binocular cues are mutually supporting; they help rather than hinder one another. But there are cases where they conflict, and when they do, we lose some of the depth that might otherwise be perceived. A painting of a pastoral scene hanging on a wall or reproduced in a book, for example, has most of the monocular cues for depth. Yet we do not perceive all the depth of the real scene because the binocular cues tell us that the picture is flat. Thus our perception is a compromise.

In the case of conflicting cues, we can increase depth by eliminating the one that is hindering perception. For example, you can see much more depth in the picture in Figure 8.5 by eliminating binocular cues. Take a piece of paper, roll it into a tube, and look at the photograph through the tube, using only one eye and closing the other. This increases your perception of depth by blocking out the frame (the edges of the picture), which is a conflicting cue. You will see even more depth if someone else holds the tube for you, because that eliminates conflicting cues from your arms and body.

MOTION PERCEPTION

When an object moves across your visual field, you see it as moving. Nothing is strange about that; everyone would expect an image moving on the retina to be perceived as moving. But there are several instances in which movement is seen when there is no real movement of the retinal image. These cases of apparent movement reveal interesting facts about the way people perceive movement.

Stroboscopic Movement

This is the kind of apparent movement you see at the movies. Film consists of a number of separate pictures, or frames, that are shown in quick succession, each picture forming a slightly different image on the retina. This effect is even more dramatic in time-lapse photography: A slow event, such as the growth of a plant, can be made to seem like a continuous movement by taking separate pictures at different stages in the growth cycle, then putting them together and showing them in a movie projector. The apparent movement seen in this case is impressive—sometimes grotesque.

Induced Movement

People may perceive a stationary spot as moving when its background or frame of reference moves. For example, the moon is often seen as racing through the sky when it is observed through a thin layer of moving clouds. The movement of the framework of clouds "induces" movement in the relatively stationary moon.

Real Movement

Perceptual constancy applies to movement as well as to object, size, and shape perceptions. For example, if two objects move at exactly the same speed but one is some distance behind the other, a person will perceive the velocity of the two as being the same. This happens despite the fact that the speed of the images moving over the retina is very different.

However, the background of the field in which an object moves affects its perceived speed. Movement through a complex, structured field seems faster than movement through a homogeneous field. Also, if the object is relatively small in comparison with stationary objects in the field, it will seem to move more quickly than if it is large. This relationship is sometimes known as the "scurrying mouse effect" (Teuber, 1960).

INFLUENCES ON PERCEPTION

As we have seen, the brain has a strong tendency to organize various stimuli into objects which are seen as figures on grounds. Stability in our world is provided by our various perceptual constancies. We perceive depth because we make use of several monocular and binocular cues. And we perceive motion when slightly different images fall on the retina in quick succession. These general principles help us to understand how perception works.

In addition, there are several other influences that determine what is perceived. These include attention, preparatory learning set, motivation, and the organism's stage of development.

Attention

One of the most obvious characteristics of perception is its selective nature. At any given moment, a person's sense organs are bombarded by an indescribable number of stimuli. Yet at one time he perceives only a few of these clearly. He perceives a few others on the margin of his attention, and the rest form a hazy background of which he is only partially aware or else not aware of at all. In other words, among the various things going on at any moment, people *attend* to only a few. Hence attention is a major factor in what they perceive.

Focus and margin Attention divides your field of perception into a focus and a margin. The things you perceive clearly are in the *focus*; the things you are vaguely aware of are in the *margin* of your experience. Shading off from the margin are events you do not perceive at all, at least for the moment.

Imagine that you are at a football game on a cold fall afternoon. As the teams scrimmage, you focus your attention on the ball carrier and follow his movements intently. In the margin of your perception is the tangle of players at the scrimmage line. While you are watching, you are bombarded with many other stimuli. Maybe your feet are cold, unpleasant sensations are coming from your stomach as a result of the last hot dog you ate, and the man next to you is puffing on a strong cigar. While the play is going on you are not aware of these things, but when time out is called, you realize that your feet are numb, the hot dog was a mistake, and the smell of cigar smoke is so strong you can taste it.

This narrowing of attention that occurs in the natural course of things is intensified in the special case of hypnosis. The hypnotist gets the subject to concentrate on (attend to) a visual stimulus such as a light or pendulum and to listen to (attend to) his instructions. If he successfully induces a "trance," he gets the subject's attention focused entirely on what he instructs the subject to do. The narrowing of attention is a central feature of the hypnotic state.

Shifting of attention As the example of the football game illustrates, attention is constantly shifting. Even in a concentrated activity like studying or playing a musical instrument, your attention shifts from one part of the activity to another, and every once in a while you become aware of other things around you. Nothing dominates attention for very long, and consequently our perceptions are constantly changing.

These changes are not random or chaotic; as any good advertising man can tell you, certain rules determine the direction of attention. Some of the principles of attention getting depend on factors in the external situation and are listed below. Others depend on factors that are inside the person—his set or expectancy, and his motivation—and are discussed in the following sections.

1 *Intensity and size.* The brighter a light or the louder a sound, the more likely it is to capture your attention. Similarly, a full-page advertisement is more likely to get attention than a smaller one. The factors of *intensity* and *size* influence perception most strongly when you encounter something new or unfamiliar. In general, if two stimuli are competing for your attention, you will notice the one that is biggest, brightest, or loudest first.

2 *Contrast.* Things that are different—things that *contrast* with the rest of the environment—tend to get attention. When you come into a room, you may notice the ticking of a clock, but you soon habituate to it (tune it out). Then if the clock suddenly stops ticking, you notice that. If you are studying in a quiet room and someone turns on the radio next door, you notice it. In time, though, you get used to it, and it drops out of awareness. The general principle is that any marked change in your present environment directs ATTENTION to it. The word just printed in capital letters is another example of the contrast effect. You probably noticed it several sentences back because it contrasts with the lowercase letters that are normally used.

3 *Repetition.* You are more likely to perceive a stimulus if it is repeated. A person calling a meeting to order pounds the gavel several times, a mother calling her child to dinner calls his name more than once, and an advertisement that appears twice in a magazine has a better chance of getting attention than an ad that appears once. The advantage of repetition is twofold: First, a stimulus that is repeated has a better chance of catching you during one of the moments when your attention is not on something else. Secondly, the first stimulus gets into the margin of your awareness and makes you more sensitive or alert to later repetitions.

4 *Movement.* Human beings, like most animals, are extremely sensitive to movement. You have an inborn orienting reaction to anything that moves, especially if nothing else is moving at the time. Your eyes are involuntarily attracted to movement in much the same way that a moth is attracted to a flame. Advertisers know this and often use movement in signs to attract attention.

Preparatory Set

Besides the external factors in the environment that attract attention, there are factors within the individual that make him attend to one thing instead of another. One is his *preparatory set*—his readiness to respond to one kind of stimuli and not to other kinds. If a geologist and a bird fancier go on a field expedition, they are set to look for different things and so will notice different things. A doctor may hear the phone ring in the night but may not hear the baby crying. His wife is more likely to hear the baby than the phone.

Another example of the influence of set is given in Figure 8.6. If a person has been counting numbers before he looks at the drawing, he will probably see it as 13. If he has been reciting the alphabet, he will probably see it as a B. (Try it out on some people who have not read this chapter.) The different responses to the drawing are examples of short-term set induced by the activity just preceding the perception. On the other hand, the difference between the geologist and the bird fancier illustrates long-term set built up through previous learning.

Figure 8.6 What a person sees is influenced by what he is set to see. The drawing can be perceived as either a B or a 13, depending on what you expect.

Closely related to preparatory set is the *meaningfulness* of information in the stimulus. On a Saturday afternoon in the fall, an avid football fan is likely to hear (notice) the words "football scores" spoken by a radio announcer when he is paying little attention to the rest of the news. Someone who is reading while half listening to a news program will immediately take notice of an announcement that an important person or a person whom he knows has died. The reporting of routine traffic deaths, in contrast, may go unnoticed. In other words, people are more likely to pay attention to things that interest them—things that are meaningful to them—than things that are not.

Learning

Just about everything we learn is partly a learning of new perceptions. And our previous learning affects our present perceptions, especially when the learning has been emotional or unusually meaningful. A gun may be perceived quite differently by a woman whose husband has been killed in a hunting accident and by a child who is fascinated with cowboys. To the child the gun is a toy associated with pleasurable excitement, with fantasies of range wars and of galloping horses. To the bereaved wife the gun is a deadly weapon associated with sadness and fear.

The influence of prior learning is not limited to emotional experiences; it is also evident in our perception of space. How, for instance, do we see the world as right side up? The images on the retina are actually inverted—they are upside down and reversed from left to right. Yet we interpret them so that we perceive the world as right side up and "correctly" positioned with regard to left and right. How does that come about?

To study the question, psychologists as early as 1897 (Stratton) began conducting experiments in which they reversed a person's visual world by giving him goggles with lenses that interchange up and down and right and left. When the subject first puts the goggles on, the effect is bewildering. He is severely disoriented, and his eye-body coordination is badly disrupted. Every time he moves his head the whole world appears to swim. When he attempts to avoid walking into a chair that appears to be on the left, he steps to the right and bumps into it. To pick up an object appearing on the left, he must learn to reach to his right.

But subjects learn to adjust to all this. As they continue to wear the glasses, walking about and locating objects in the topsy-turvy world become easier and more automatic. They can turn their heads without the world appearing to move. Sounds begin to seem as if they come from the place where the object actually is. On psychomotor tests such a subject does almost as well as normal subjects. One subject, an

Austrian professor, rode his bicycle to and from classes as usual and carried on his ordinary routine (Kohler, 1964).

A great deal of learning clearly takes place in these experiments, but there is a question about just what kind of learning it is. Two kinds are possible: One is learning *motor* adjustments to the reversed world—simply learning to make movements that are the opposite of normal ones. The other is learning a new *perception* of the world—the subject learns to see the world as he did not before. Motor learning certainly occurs, as proved by the nearly normal skill of the subjects who have adjusted. Perceptual learning occurs to some extent, but not completely. Subjects get so they are often unaware of the reversed world, but when they are asked, they recall how it looked before; and they still perceive it as being upside down.

Sensory Deprivation

Changes in perception can also be induced by depriving people of normal sensory experience. Chapter 3 on motivation described an experiment in which subjects were isolated from as much sensory input as possible. Each lay in a partially soundproof cubicle and wore translucent goggles, gloves, and cardboard cuffs which covered the lower arm and hand. This experiment has been repeated by several investigators. After several days of isolation, the subjects always experience dramatic effects on perception organization. As illustrated in the following report, apparent movement is one:

> The whole room is undulating, swirling. . . . You were going all over the fool place at first. The floor is still doing it. The wall is waving all over the place—a horrifying sight. The center of the curtain over there—it just swirls downward, undulates, and waves inside. I find it difficult to keep my eyes open for any length of time, the visual field is in such a state of chaos. (Heron et al., 1956, p. 15)

In addition, there were distortions in shape and color. Vertical and horizontal edges often were seen as curved; colors appeared to glow; they were bright and saturated. Some subjects reported hallucinations, but this has not always been confirmed (Zubek, 1969). The main point demonstrated by the experiment is that sensory deprivation can seriously distort perception.

Motivation

There is an old saying, "People see what they want to see." It implies that our perceptions are strongly influenced by our motives, and there are plenty of everyday examples to support it. A girl in love with a homely boy is likely to think him handsome. And if we want to believe in a person, we emphasize his good points and overlook his faults. Thus if we are strongly in favor of a political candidate, the things he says are all good, while we might disregard or pooh-pooh the same things said by an opponent. If we think highly of an artist, a painting of his may seem to us very good even if we would consider the same painting by an unknown to be poor. All these examples, you will recognize, are instances of prejudice. Indeed, selectively perceiving what we want to see is an important means of maintaining prejudice as Chapter 12 will show. To put it another way, prejudice is motivated and so makes a person want to see things that reinforce his prejudice.

The basic idea that people perceive what fits their motivation can be demonstrated experimentally (Lambert et al., 1949):

> Nursery school children aged 3 to 5 were used as subjects, one at a time. A machine with a crank on it was set up in front of them. For each 18 turns of the crank a subject received a poker chip. By putting the chip into a slot, he obtained a piece of candy. Thus the poker chip came to be perceived as something of value, that is, something the children were motivated to obtain.
>
> Before the experiment, the subjects estimated the size of the poker chip by telling the experimenter when a spot of light of variable size matched the chip. After the children had been rewarded with candy for cranking out poker chips, the same comparison was made. The poker chip now seemed significantly *larger* to the children. Following that, the children's response was extinguished by giving them no more chips, no matter how much they cranked. Now in their estimates, the chip shrank back to its former size. The chip's desirability had thus influenced its perceived size.

The effects of motivation on perception in this experiment and others like it are small, even though they are statistically significant. Objects like poker chips are *unambiguous,* and therefore perceptions of them are hard to influence. In our social and interpersonal relationships, however, we come across many *ambiguous* situations. It is in these that motivation most affects perception. How many times, for example, have you pondered what a friend meant by a remark? The meaning of some remarks is not clear, nor are the meanings of some of the things people do. Then our perception of the situation will be strongly influenced by whether we like the person, whether we feel insecure in the situation, and in general how we are motivated. Everyone remembers times when a comment was perceived as a slight by one person and a compliment by another.

Perceptual Development

Now look at the problem of nature versus nurture in perception. Earlier when this chapter spoke of man's "organizing tendencies," it said that they were inborn features of the brain. But later in the discussion of learning, it concluded that perception can be changed through learning. To what extent are perceptual abilities inborn, to what extent learned? Psychologists cannot give a precise answer except to say that there is some nature and some nurture in perception.

Maturation   To study the development of a perceptual ability, the scientist must have some way of measuring it early in life. A device called the *visual cliff* does this for depth perception. The visual cliff is a drop-off from a platform to the floor. The entire surface is covered with a checkerboard pattern which enhances depth perception, as shown in Figure 8.7. Stretching over the shelf and out over the floor at the same level is a heavy piece of glass that can support the weight of the subject being tested. The experimenters merely place him on the shelf or "shallow" side and see whether he will venture out over the deep side. All that is necessary for this test is that the subject be old enough to walk or crawl around.

The test has been used with human infants, kittens, monkeys, rats,

Figure 8.7   *The visual cliff, a test of depth perception that can be used with almost any organism, human or animal, as soon as it can crawl or walk. At this stage, most organisms tested have good visual depth perception: they avoid the "deep side" even though they can tell by touch that the glass would support them. (From Gibson and Walk, 1960; William Vandivert,* Scientific American.*)*

lambs, goats, and many other animals. It gives consistent results in all species: All animals or infants that are mature enough to test are able to perceive depth, for they are unwilling to cross the glass when the well below it is deep. They refuse to cross even though they can touch the glass and tell that it can support them. (We know that they can tell because they are willing to crawl around on the glass over the "shallow" side.) Apparently they trust their eyes rather than their sense of touch.

From such experiments psychologists conclude that depth perception matures in time to be useful to an organism when it can move about. In the case of a lamb this is mighty fast, for it can walk within a day of birth and at that time shows depth perception on the visual cliff.

Sensory experience   We might conclude from the visual cliff evidence that depth perception is inborn or matures with little or no learning involved. But there is another way to get at the problem: The experimenter can control the visual experience of an animal from the day of birth until it takes the test.

Many experiments have been done with animals reared in the dark. From the first, a special problem was encountered. Certain cells in the retina need normal stimulation in order to stay normal; otherwise they degenerate and impair the animal's ability to see anything. To get around this problem, animals are given some light each day, but given it in unpatterned form. If they wear translucent goggles, for example, they will have experience with light, but they will not see objects. Tests after animals have been reared in this way reveal marked differences among species. Rats show depth perception as soon as the goggles are removed. Cats and chimpanzees, on the other hand, require several days of experience with objects or with "patterned" light before they pass the tests.

Scientists cannot, of course, rear babies in the dark or even make them wear translucent goggles. The only way to study this problem in humans is to find people who are born with cataracts, which are very much like translucent goggles. Fortunately cataracts can be removed surgically, and people can be tested after the operation to find out what their innate perceptual abilities are. The tests show that these people are at first overwhelmed by the flood of visual imput. They are able to perceive vague figures against a ground, and they see that "something is out there." Their object vision, however, is practically nonexistent. They slowly learn to distinguish a circle from a triangle by scanning it with their eyes. After weeks or months of such laborious scanning, they come to distinguish the shapes that a normal person can. Thus their vision becomes normal only very slowly.

Experiments like these have led psychologists to conclude that in man and the higher animals, visual experience is necessary for normal object and depth perception. Exactly what kind of visual experience, and how much, science does not yet know.

Extrasensory Perception

Is there any way of perceiving (knowing) events when the information has not come in through our senses? Some people have long believed that there is, and many dramatic stories have been recorded in support of their belief (Murphy, 1969). In the 1930s, J. B. Rhine at Duke University started reporting scientific experiments in which he found evidence for "extrasensory perception." His experiments and others like them have continued to this day and, on the surface, appear to support his belief (McConnell, 1969).

Very few psychologists put faith in the evidence, however. Most of them point to problems with the experimental and statistical methods used. The early experiments of Rhine were quickly shown to have experimental faults (Kennedy, 1939). In one case, subjects could get cues from the backs of the cards they were guessing. In another, the experimenter was unconsciously giving whispered cues to the subject as he concentrated on "sending the message." And in another, errors of recording accounted for the results. These particular faults were controlled in most later experiments, but the later ones in turn have been criticized on statistical grounds. The criticisms are complex, but they boil down mainly to complaints that the investigators selected data which agree with their premise while ignoring data which do not. For this reason, only a small minority "who want to believe" see the evidence as supporting the belief.

SUMMARY

Perception consists of the interpretation of sensory information. People perceive objects, not just collections of stimuli, and object perception is determined in part by innate organizing tendencies. These include the tendency to perceive a figure on a ground, the tendency to group objects together, and the tendency to create closure—to fill in missing elements. Stability in our perceptual world is maintained largely through perceptual constancies in shape, size, and brightness. Depth perception relies on both monocular and binocular cues. The principal monocular cues are linear perspective, clearness, interposition, shadows, texture, and movement. The main binocular cue is retinal disparity of the images seen by the two eyes. Motion perception can consist of either real or apparent motion. Stroboscopic apparent movement, like that seen in motion pictures, is perceived when successive images fall on different places on the retina.

Several factors influence perception: Attention divides our field of peception into a focus and a margin. Preparatory set gives us a readiness to respond to one kind of stimuli and not to other kinds. Motivation gives us a tendency to see what we want to see. Previous learning strongly affects perception, especially the recognition of objects. Perceptual development depends in part on maturation and in part on previous sensory experience.

SUGGESTIONS FOR FURTHER READING

Dember, W. N. *The psychology of perception.* New York: Holt, 1960. *A textbook on perception.*

Gregory, R. L. *Eye and brain.* New York: McGraw-Hill, 1966. (Paperback.) *A colorful and intriguing book written in popular style.*

Hochberg, J. E. *Perception.* Englewood Cliffs, N.J.: Prentice-Hall, 1964. (Paperback.) *An interesting and well-written introduction to perception.*

Von Fieandt, Kai. *The world of perception.* Homewood, Ill.: Dorsey, 1966. *Includes some unusual examples of the perception of pictorial art and perception of the self.*

Zubek, J. P. *Sensory deprivation: Fifteen years of research.* New York: Appleton Century Crofts, 1969. *An account of the major experiments on sensory deprivation.*

PART II

Individual Differences

The chapters in Part I describe the way organisms (animals and people) are motivated, how they learn new ways of behaving in various situations, and how they come to perceive and think about their world. But people do differ in their genetic endowments, and they differ in their learning experiences. As a consequence, they differ in their learned motivations, in what and how much they learn, and in their ways of interpreting their experiences. Such individual differences are described in this part of the book.

Individual differences are studied in two basic ways. One way is with psychological tests, and Chapter 9 is devoted to this topic. Next, in Chapter 10, the use of psychological tests in the study of personality is considered.

A second way of studying individual differences is through clinical observation. This is the method most relied upon in studying the behavior disorders—the topic of Chapter 11, which concludes this part of the book. Chapter 11 also discusses various therapies for treating the behavior disorders.

9

Psychological Testing

Psychology's first, and perhaps greatest, contribution to human affairs came in the form of psychological tests. Some tests were devised in the late 1800s, and public interest in testing began to flourish early in this century. By 1916 the first fully standardized test of intelligence appeared (Stanford-Binet), making it possible for the first time to predict with some assurance how children would fare in school. Almost instantly came the large-scale use of intelligence tests in World War I. These enabled the U.S. Army to screen out individuals who were mentally unfit for service. Since then thousands of tests of many kinds have been used for all sorts of purposes with literally millions of people.

Although psychologists have been proud of their contributions through testing, tests have met increasing criticism in recent years. Many people, some of them quite enlightened, feel that society has come to rely so much on tests in daily affairs that it has been treating the "victims" of tests unfairly. To be sure, the use of tests has sometimes been abused. Any tool can be. The criticism, however, stems from a misunderstanding of how tests should be, and ordinarily are, used. This chapter examines the proper use of tests and surveys some of the major tests in common use.

USES OF TESTS

Why have psychologists gone to the trouble of developing tests, and why do people use them so much? As Chapter 1 said, the alternative to a test is *natural observation* of a person. This, although sometimes useful, is both time-consuming and imprecise. It can provide mountains of data, after hours and hours of work, without telling what is important or trivial. As a matter of economy, people usually want to know quickly the things that are important about an individual. They need a crisp description, not a book. And for precision, they would like to have the description in the form of a number or numbers.

But a numerical description of a person's important characteristics is in itself little more than an interesting fact. If the description is any good—if it is meaningful—it can be used to make *predictions* about people. If, for example, we know that one person is bright and another is dull, we can predict something about their abilities to succeed in school, in a job, or in adjustment to life. Feeling that we can make such a prediction, we go ahead and make some *decisions* about the people being tested. We advise them to do such and such, or we even decide to admit one person to school and to keep another person out. This decision making is the real purpose of psychological testing. And this is what the critics of testing say tests should not be used for.

Decision making on the basis of test results, the psychologist argues, is both a necessary and a good thing to do if certain conditions are met: (1) the right kind of test is used to make the decision, (2) the test is a "good" test, and (3) the right kind of decision is made on the basis of all available evidence, not just the test alone.

Kinds of Tests

What sorts of human characteristics do psychological tests measure? The answer shows what kinds of tests have been developed. First, tests measure what a person has learned to do—the skills, such as reading and arithmetic, he has acquired and the information he has learned. These are called *achievement* tests. Standardized achievement tests have been developed for various educational levels from first grade to college. Since they are mostly of interest to the student of education rather than the psychologist, they will not be treated here. Two other kinds of tests are more in the domain of the psychologist: tests of ability and tests of personality.

Ability tests   Often we need to measure what a person is *able* to do at his very best, not necessarily what he has done. An ability test is a test of potential rather than of achievement, of what the individual can learn, not what he has learned. There is one qualification, however: a test measures what a person can do on the test, so that in a sense any test is an achievement test. And a test of ability presumes that a person has had adequate opportunity to learn certain things required to take the test—the language, for example. But ability tests are constructed to *minimize* differences in achievement among the test takers and *maximize* differences in the potential for achievement.

Few tests of ability are actually called that. They are usually labeled as tests of intelligence or of aptitude, two terms that need to be distinguished. *Intelligence* is the more general term; it refers to overall capacity for learning and problem solving. In actual fact, as we shall see, intelligence is a mixture of abilities. But a good intelligence test does a good job of measuring the potential of a child for school learning or the ability of an adult to cope successfully with general intellectual problems encountered in the world. *Aptitude,* on the other hand, refers to ability to do the required work in some specified school or vocation. Aptitude tests are divided into two classes: scholastic aptitude tests and vocational aptitude tests. Scholastic aptitude is a person's predicted ability to do the required work in some specified school—a college of arts and sciences, engineering school, graduate school, medical school, or law school. Vocational aptitude is ability to learn the skills of a particular vocation.

Personality tests   With this second general kind of test psychologists attempt to measure *personality characteristics.* As Chapter 10 will explain, a personality characteristic is some way in which a person normally or usually behaves. The personality test does not attempt to explore what he can do, or what he does only occasionally. It aims to find out what he typically does. The questions on personality tests are framed accordingly: "Do you generally prefer to be alone or with people?" "Do you prefer reading a book or the conversation of friends?" Such questions get at characteristic differences among people.

To summarize, ability tests and personality tests are the two general varieties of psychological tests used to make decisions about people. To utilize tests wisely, we must know what it is we are trying to measure and choose the right test for the purpose.

Characteristics of a Good Test

To make good decisions with tests, we need to use not only the right test but a "good" one. Tests vary considerably in "goodness"; some are virtually worthless, especially when made or given by amateurs. Even the best tests that psychologists have constructed are not uniformly good. We need to know just how well they do their job when we try to interpret their results. What makes a good test? The following four characteristics are required.

Reliability   A good test should be highly reliable: this means that different forms of the same test, or repeated measurements with the same form, should give the same result. Reliability can be measured by a correlational method (page 29) in which repeated results are compared. Psychological tests are never perfectly reliable, but the good ones—such as a good intelligence test—give correlation coefficients in the neighborhood of .90. Not all tests, especially personality tests, achieve this high reliability. When they do not, we must be aware that predictions, and hence decisions, made from them have considerable error.

Validity   A good test must be valid (page 29): this means that it should measure what it is supposed to measure. An intelligence test, for example, is not a good test for measuring college potential, although it has some value in this respect. A better test is one which has been both designed for the purpose and validated: the well-known Scholastic Aptitude Test (SAT).

Validation, like determining reliability, is done by using a correlational technique. To measure validity, test results are correlated against the criterion—in the case of the SAT, success in college. Validity correlations are never as high as those for reliability; a validity of .50 or .60 for a single test is quite good. (Testers can frequently achieve higher validities by using several tests.) This, however, is fairly good validity, and is good enough to *help* in making proper decisions about admitting students to college.

Standard administration   Even when a test meets the first two requirements of reliability and validity, it may not do its job well unless it is administered by a standard procedure. This is especially important for tests (such as the Stanford-Binet) that are given by an individual tester to testees one at a time. Individual tests require highly trained persons to administer them in a uniform way under varying circum-

Group Tests of Intelligence

In hospitals or in counseling situations where individual problems are being analyzed, expert testers are usually available and an individual test of intelligence is convenient to use. In many other situations, however, it is necessary to administer tests in large groups.

The best known of the group tests is the Army General Classification Test. Standardized in World War II, it was the offspring of the intelligence test that the Army devised in World War I and has since been restandardized as the Armed Forces Qualification Test. It is a paper-and-pencil test that can be given to any number of people assembled in a room, as a regular college examination might be.

The AGCT and its successor, the AFQT, are standardized to yield an average score of 100, just as individual tests of intelligence do. Their other scores, however, have been assigned somewhat differently from IQ tests. An AFQT score of 120, as shown in Figure 9.1, is the equivalent of an IQ of 115; hence the AFQT score and an IQ score are not quite the same. Nevertheless, it is a test of general intelligence.

The test has been used by the Armed Forces for two general purposes: the screening of inductees and the selection of officer candidates. To screen inductees a low cutoff score is used; individuals who score less than this are considered, on the basis of past experience, to be too low in intelligence to make normal progress in military training. To select officers a higher cutoff score is set. Individuals who make scores near the cutoff point are eligible for officer's training if they seem to show capacity for leadership.

Besides the Armed Forces test, several other major group tests have been developed, principally for use in selecting employees in industry. One of the best known is the Otis Self-Administering Test of Mental Ability (Otis SA). This is a short four-page pencil-and-paper

TABLE 9.2

Distribution of intelligence quotients on the Wechsler Adult Intelligence Scale.

IQ	Verbal description	% of adults
Above 130	Very superior	2.2
120–129	Superior	6.7
110–119	Bright normal	16.1
90–109	Average	50.0
80–89	Dull normal	16.1
70–79	Borderline	6.7
Below 70	Mentally retarded	2.2

Source: Modified from Wechsler, 1958.

test that can be given simply with a stopwatch under testing conditions that are relatively easy to keep standard. It can be taken and scored with either a 20-minute or a 30-minute time limit. Its results correlate fairly well with IQs determined on the Wechsler scale, the WAIS.

Scholastic Aptitude Tests

All tests that are used to help predict success in some particular school are called scholastic aptitude tests. Two that are widely given to students headed for liberal arts college are the American College Test (ACT) and the Scholastic Aptitude Test (SAT). It is very likely that any student reading this book has already taken one or the other of these. As already pointed out, schools normally do not rely entirely on the test results to make decisions about admissions. They require a *combination* of a certain standing in a student's high school class and a minimum score on the aptitude test, because analysis regularly shows that this combination predicts college success better than either criterion taken separately.

Tests similar in purpose to the ACT and SAT have been developed for all major schools of higher education: engineering, medicine, dentistry, nursing, and law. Several tests have been devised for students planning to do graduate work for the master's or doctor's degree in such specialties as psychology, economics, and physics. The one most frequently used for this purpose is the Graduate Record Examination (GRE). Primarily an aptitude test, it also includes achievement tests for each of the fields of specialization.

A common feature of most scholastic aptitude tests is a provision for two kinds of scores, one for *quantitative* aptitudes involving arithmetic and numbers, and the other for *verbal* aptitudes. This two-score system is used because (1) verbal and quantitative aptitudes do not correlate very highly—a person may be high on one and low on the other, (2) different courses of study tap these aptitudes in different degrees—for example, quantitative aptitude is more relevant for studying mathematics and the physical sciences, but verbal aptitude is more relevant for studying social science and literature.

Vocational Aptitude Tests

Scholastic aptitude tests measure a person's aptitude for success in relatively prolonged training such as college. The great majority of jobs in business and industry, however, do not require or make good use of such training. Success in these jobs can be forecast best from a knowledge of specific vocational aptitudes without much regard for intelligence or scholastic aptitude.

Hundreds of vocational aptitude tests are available today. Not all of them are good tests in the sense that they have been validated (proved to be good predictors of success in a particular vocation). Many are slight variations of another test, designed to serve some special purpose. In fact, because such tests are commonly very specific, it is a good idea to develop a new form of a test for each intended use. To do this the test constructor devises a test that meets the four requirements of a good test that were outlined above—reliability, validity, standard administration, and norms. His final product should be one that predicts success or failure well in the particular jobs for which applicants are to be selected.

The many vocational aptitude tests that exist can be divided roughly into three general types: mechanical ability tests, psychomotor tests, and tests of logical thinking.

Mechanical ability tests Many tests that are intended for mechanics, machine operators, assembly-line workers, repairmen, and similar workers involve mechanical knowledge or ability to manipulate objects. A relatively unique factor is common to these tests—the factor of mechanical ability—because people who score high on one test tend to score high on other tests. On the other hand, different jobs require different combinations of mechanical ability, so several different tests are in use.

Psychomotor tests Unlike mechanical ability, there seems to be no unique or common psychomotor ability: a person who has good manual dexterity is not necessarily good at the kind of coordination involved in running a tractor or flying an airplane. So psychomotor tests have had to be developed and proved for many individual jobs and occupations. These tests involve such psychomotor tasks as manual dexterity, steadiness, muscular strength, speed of response to a signal, and the coordination of many movements into a unified whole.

Tests of logical thinking The aptitude tests just mentioned are designed for conventional jobs found in offices and manufacturing plants. However, modern technology is creating many jobs that require logical thinking and complex problem solving. Such abilities are involved, for example, in computer programming and in diagnosing malfunctions on complex systems. Hence aptitude tests have been developed in recent years to measure the ability to think logically. One such test is the LAD (Logical Analysis Device), which consists of an operator's display unit plus a central logic unit, problem plugboards, and control and recording units. An examiner can present standardized problems of varying complexity for an operator to solve. This kind of test has proved to have fairly high validity for choosing individuals for computer programming jobs.

Test Batteries

To select people for a particular job, employers normally use one good test designed for that purpose. But in counseling people the psychologist does not have a specific job in mind; he is trying to discover what general line of work and what kind of education they are best suited for. Generally he finds it desirable to use not just one test but a battery of them. The battery is put together to provide information about both scholastic and vocational aptitudes.

One widely accepted battery is the Differential Aptitude Tests (DAT), which contains tests of verbal reasoning, numerical ability, abstract reasoning, space relations, mechanical ability, clerical speed and accuracy, spelling, and the use of language in sentences. The person who takes such a battery does not come out with just one score but a *profile* of scores showing how he compares with other people on each of the abilities test. The profile for a high school girl given in Figure 9.2 shows that she is extremely good in spelling and rather good in most other abilities, but mediocre in verbal reasoning and poor on clerical tasks. On the basis of these results, the counselor would advise her to prepare for occupations involving abilities in which she is high, and to steer away from those requiring verbal reasoning and clerical skills.

DIFFERENCES IN INTELLIGENCE

The fact that individuals differ greatly in the abilities they possess raises a number of questions. How do different abilities correlate with one another? What is the effect on a person's functioning in life to have high or low abilities? How are such differences related to age, home environment, and cultural environment? The answers that psychologists have been able to discover are given in this section.

Relationship among Abilities

Is a person who is high on one ability also high on another? Or are the various abilities completely independent of one another? The question is complex. To arrive at a general answer, psychologists have had to consider the nature of intelligence as well as the possible relationship between intelligence and creativity.

Kinds of intelligence The intelligence of various individuals clearly varies in *kind* as well as in amount. This fact is recognized in the

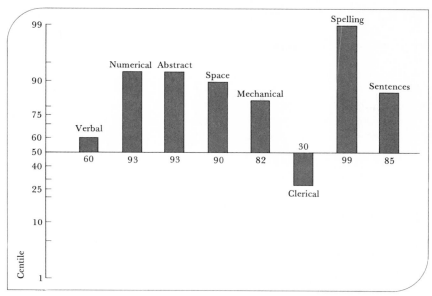

Figure 9.2 *A Differential Aptitude Tests (DAT) profile put together from a high school girl's scores on the battery of tests. The centile scale is bunched in the middle and stretched out on the ends because many more cases fall in the middle of a normal distribution than at its ends. This profile was obtained from a girl interested in majoring in science in college. If you were a counselor, would you advise her to go ahead? (Modified from Bennett et al., 1951.)*

division of the Wechsler scale, the WAIS, into verbal and performance tests. It is also indicated by the separation of verbal (V) and quantitative (Q) scores on such scholastic aptitude tests as the SAT and GRE. The distinction between vocational and scholastic aptitude tests is another illustration of differences in the kind of intelligence that different people have.

We can see such differences in children in school and in the people we know. Susie is good in music but not mechanical things. Joe is good at mathematics but not at English. Ruth excels in English and history but has a hard time with physics. And so on. These differences seen in individuals can, of course, be influenced by training and parental pressures, but they do exist, and they represent different patterns of abilities.

Psychologists long ago asked, "Just how many kinds of intelligence are there?" The answer, they learned, depends on how they sample people's abilities. Even tests that are limited to verbal abilities can be analyzed to show different factors (kinds) of intelligence (Thurstone and Thurstone, 1941). When psychologists sample a very wide range of abilities and look for the most significant differences in intelligence, they find two major kinds: concrete and abstract—sometimes called level 1 and level 2 (Jensen, 1969). Standardized tests of intelligence and of scholastic aptitude stress abstract intelligence—the ability to manipulate words and concepts. In contrast, tests of vocational aptitude, performance tests on the WAIS, and other tests designed for the purpose emphasize concrete intelligence—the ability to manipulate and solve problems with real objects in everyday situations.

Intelligence and creativity Is intelligence the same thing as creativity? It would seem that they are related, because intelligence tests require a certain degree of creativity. But are they identical?

To get at this question, tests have been specifically designed to measure creativity. Examples are association tests, in which a subject gives as many definitions as possible for fairly common words, and tests of the "uses of things," in which the subject thinks of as many possible uses as he can for a common object such as a brick. How do these tests of creativity correlate with the results of intelligence tests?

In one experiment 500 public school students in grades 6 to 12 were given both kinds of tests (Getzel and Jackson, 1962). Then the experimenters selected a group of students who were in the upper 20 percent on creativity but not in the upper 20 percent on intelligence. They compared this group with another group consisting of students in the top 20 percent on intelligence but not on creativity. Despite a difference of 23 points in IQ, the two groups performed about equally well in school. But the students who were high in intelligence were considered more "achievement-oriented" by their teachers, while those high in creativity were regarded as more original and more playful.

Studies like this tell us that creativity and intelligence are not highly correlated—at least not in people who are above the average level of intelligence. Thus creativity and intelligence as measured by psychologists are not the same thing. People who are not highly intelligent may be creative and through their creativity may contribute new things to society.

Individual Differences in Intelligence

A distribution of intelligence scores or IQs can be divided in many possible ways. One fine-grained method is to group scores in seven categories, as was done with the Wechsler scores back in Table 9.2. Then, as in the Wechsler table, each of these categories can be given a descriptive name like "very superior," "superior," and so on. A simpler way is to divide the scores into three groups: very low, very high, and in between. What can be expected of people in these three general groups? How do their differences in intelligence affect their educational and occupational achievement?

Mental retardation Individuals with low IQs are said to be mentally retarded. The cutoff for this category of people is set rather arbitrarily at 70. Those just below 70 are called "mildly retarded," those between 36 and 52 "moderately retarded," those between 20 and 35 "severely retarded," and those below 20 "profoundly retarded." Altogether, 2 to 3 percent of the population falls into the general category of mental retardation. Fortunately, the majority are in the "mildly retarded" group; only a small number are "profoundly retarded."

A description of the *intellectual* level of the retarded, however, does not give a fair account of their abilities. IQ tests tend to weight verbal factors; they do not evaluate the social skills that are important in adjusting to life. Hence in general, IQs tend to underestimate what a person will be able to do. Many people of subnormal intelligence function quite adequately in day-to-day living.

Mental retardation has two general causes: one is a matter of inheritance, the other injury or disease. In the first case, the individual is sound physically; he has simply inherited a set of genes endowing him with low intelligence. Since other members of his family are frequently low in intelligence too, this kind of retardation is called *familial.*

Mental retardation stemming from injury or disease may have many causes: injury to the brain at birth, diseases of the mother during pregnancy (such as German measles, toxemia, or syphilis), or inborn errors of metabolism or of glandular function. Retardation caused by injury or disease is frequently called *mental deficiency.*

Some instances of mental retardation with a medical basis can be prevented or sometimes cured if caught early enough in life, but these are relatively rare. For most retardates there is no treatment or education that will change their IQs significantly. All that can be done is to make the most of their limited capacities. Fortunately, since the majority of retardates are only mildly retarded, there is some hope for most of them. When they are patiently taught elementary social and occupational skills, they can eventually take care of themselves fairly well and do useful tasks that keep them from being a great burden on their families and society.

The mentally gifted At the other end of the spectrum of intelligence, at a cutoff point usually set at 140, is approximately 1 percent of the population with very high IQs. The mentally gifted have been studied in two ways: One is by analyzing the biographies of well-known people, determining at what age they were able to do the things called for on an IQ test, and estimating their IQs. The results of such a study are given in Table 9.3. Reading down this list you can see that many of the most famous names in history were among the mentally gifted.

A second way of studying the mentally gifted is to take children who score about 140 on intelligence tests and follow them through life. One such experiment was carried on for over 35 years (Terman and Oden, 1959), with interesting results. A breakdown of the kind of homes they came from showed that a third were children of professional people and half were children of business-class parents; less than a tenth came from the working classes. This agrees with other studies that have found a positive correlation between intelligence and socio-economic class.

A second major finding of the experiment was that the gifted children became outstandingly successful adults. Of those who could be contacted 25 years later, about 20 percent were prominent people as judged by such things as listing in *Who's Who*, the positions they held, and the awards they had received. Most of the others, though less eminent, were far more successful than people of average intelligence. A small percentage were unsuccessful—vocational misfits or even

TABLE 9.3
The IQs of some eminent men, estimated from biographical data.

Francis Galton	200
John Stuart Mill	190
Johann Wolfgang von Goethe	185
Gottfried Wilhelm von Leibniz	185
Samuel Taylor Coleridge	175
John Quincy Adams	165
David Hume	155
Alfred Tennyson	155
René Descartes	150
Wolfgang Amadeus Mozart	150
William Wordsworth	150
Francis Bacon	145
Charles Dickens	145
Benjamin Franklin	145
George Frederick Handel	145
Thomas Jefferson	145
John Milton	145
Daniel Webster	145

Source: Cox, 1926.

criminals. A comparison of the unsuccessful group with the other subjects revealed that personality factors were responsible for the differences. The least successful were more poorly adjusted emotionally and less motivated to succeed. Despite these exceptions, the fact was that the gifted children had an outstanding record of social and intellectual achievement.

The middle groups   The huge majority of us—about 95 percent fall in the middle groups of intelligence, those between the retarded and the gifted. Within this middle range, what difference do differences in our IQs make? The many statistics available on the IQs of people in various vocations can be summarized in two ways: by comparing averaged IQs or by comparing ranges of IQs.

If you look only at averages, you will be impressed with the importance of IQ in occupational success. The professional classes average about 120; farmhands average about 90; other occupations fall in between. Not only that, but these differences are nearly as great in the *children* of people in different occupations. Children of professional people average about 115, while those of day laborers are in the middle to upper 90s. Such differences are the result of a combination of hereditary and environmental influences (see Chapter 2).

If you now turn to the *range* of IQs in various occupations, you will immediately become less impressed with the importance of IQ. (Range in this case includes the middle 80 percent of each group.) Accountants, for example, average 120 but range from 110 to 140. Farm workers range from less than 70 to more than 115. Similarly broad ranges are found for intervening occupational groups such as salesmen, machinists, and day laborers; in all cases the overlap is great. This means that some minimum IQ is necessary to work in a given occupation, but the minimum is not high compared with the average. Put another way, a person with a given IQ, even if it is not very high, has a wide range of occupations to choose from.

Group Differences in Intelligence

Besides the variation in average IQ with occupation, there are many other group differences in intelligence. The principal ones are age, home environment, and cultural environment.

Age   The IQ was devised to be a stable measure of intelligence. As it was originally conceived by the pioneering developers of intelligence testing, a person's IQ was supposed to remain the same throughout life—at least, within the error of measuring it. In general, the intelligence quotient comes close to this ideal, but there are in fact measurable changes in it throughout life.

In the first place, the IQ can be fairly erratic in the first years of life. From the time it can first be measured at about two years of age, it can shift around quite a bit for the next few years. It tends to settle down at 7 to 8 years of age when a child has acquired his basic language skills. But beyond this point, shifting may still take place as the child grows up. And in about half the cases the shift is as much as 10 to 15 points.

In general, the IQs of boys tend to rise during the period between early school age and adolescence, and those of girls tend to fall. This gives a hint, which experiments confirm, about what causes the shifting: a shift in achievement motivation. If motivation is high, the IQ tends to rise; if low, to fall; and with increasing age, achievement motivation usually rises higher in boys than in girls.

Intelligence scores rather than IQ scores are, of course, increasing as the child grows up. This increase slows and comes to a stop in adulthood. Just where it stops depends on what test the person takes. If it is the highly verbal Stanford-Binet, the peak is hit at age 16, but if the Wechsler (WAIS) is the measure, the peak appears later. On the performance tests of the Wechsler, it comes in the late twenties; on the verbal part, in the early thirties.

Thus as Chapter 6 explained, young people who think intelligence declines rapidly after 30 are wrong; it is just topping out then. After the early thirties there is indeed some decline, but it is not great and it is selective. In tests of vocabulary and general information, there is no decline at all unless aging brings on some brain damage. On the other hand, in tests that require people to work rapidly or to adapt to novel situations, there is a measurable decline in intelligence from about 30 on.

Two points about these differences should be kept in mind. First, the *average* change is not great; it moves a person's percentile position in the population by just a few points. Secondly, there is a great deal of variability and overlap. Bright old people are still brighter than average young people. The effects of age, therefore, by no means erase the spread of intelligence in the general population.

Home environment   Both this chapter and Chapter 2 have noted the high correlation between a child's intelligence and that of his parents. This fact could be explained by either inheritance or the home environment, or both. Through techniques described in Chapter 2 (and summarized back in Table 2.2), psychologists have learned that an important component in the correlation is genetic.

On the other hand, intellectual influences in the home also make a difference, as shown by studies of children who were placed in superior foster homes. In one of the more dramatic research reports, children whose true mothers had an average IQ of 91 scored an average of more than 109 when measured at an average age of 13. This was usually 10 or more years after they had been placed in the superior homes (Skodak and Skeels, 1949). Without knowing what their IQs would have been if they had been reared by their true mothers, it is impossible to say how much of the difference was caused by rearing in the superior homes. It is probably fair to estimate, however, that children may gain as much as 10 to 15 IQ points when they are brought up in superior homes.

Cultural environment If the home environment can make a substantial difference in a child's IQ, what about the other features of his environment? Do superior schools, bright playmates, and other kinds of stimulation make a difference in IQ? Conversely, does an impoverished cultural environment hold down IQ?

Many studies are relevant to these questions, but none gives a conclusive result. One thing is clear: IQ does correlate positively with the richness of cultural environment. Of course, it is known too that genetic differences create some differences in the environment: brighter parents, having higher socioeconomic status, are able to provide better environments. So we are left with a chicken-and-egg problem. But since we know that heredity and environment interact in determining IQ, we can assume that the cultural environment does make a difference. Social justice, of course, requires us to do all we can to erase cultural disadvantages. To the extent that we succeed, we can expect some favorable effects on IQ.

PERSONALITY TESTS

Ability tests are tests of maximum performance—in the sense that they measure performance—because people try to do their best on them. Personality tests, on the other hand, are intended to measure *typical* performance (Cronbach, 1970). There are no right or wrong answers on personality tests; people are asked what they usually do, or what is typical of them.

There are many personality tests that take many forms, but in general they fall into four categories: (1) interviews and rating scales, (2) interest tests, (3) questionnaires, and (4) projective tests.

Interviews and Rating Scales

The interview is one of the oldest methods for attempting to evaluate personality. It is regularly used in two different settings: the employment interview in which the interviewer attempts to determine the suitability of a person for employment, and the counseling interview where the purpose is to assess personality as a preparation for counseling or psychotherapy. We will consider only the second.

In a counseling interview a clinician tries to sample as wide a range as possible of the person's feelings and attitudes by getting him to talk about his personal experiences. The interviewer notes not only what things the person talks about, but the way he talks about them. He observes whether some topics appear to make the person uncomfortable, and whether he avoids some subjects altogether. From observations in the interview and from other facts of the case, the clinician attempts to construct a picture of the person's major motives, his sources of conflict, and the areas of poor adjustment. Sometimes he goes a step further and uses a set of rating scales to put his conclusions into a more quantitative form.

Rating scales come in several forms. One of the simplest is a 7-point scale that rates the person on such characteristics as honesty, reliability, sociability, and emotionality. Another scale provides the rater with a number of alternative descriptions so that he can check the alternative that seems most appropriate.

Interviews and rating scales are so simple that anyone can use them to record his impressions of almost any aspect of personality. Their simplicity, however, should not fool us. They supply only crude measurements that can be unreliable and invalid. Rating scale techniques need to be subjected to the same rigorous analysis that—reliability, validity, standard administration, and norms—used with more objective tests.

Interest Tests

A somewhat more objective way of assessing personality is to find out with a standardized test what a person likes or dislikes—what he prefers or avoids. This is an interest test, commonly presented as a pencil-and-paper quiz. Interest tests that are used in vocational counseling to determine what kinds of work a person might like or dislike are called vocational interest tests. Other tests are designed to give a more general picture of interests.

Vocational interest tests   Two tests of interests that were standardized many years ago, with later revisions, are in common use: the Strong Vocational Interest Blank and the Kuder Preference Record.

Strong developed his Interest Blank by contrasting a sample of people in general with groups of successful people in many different occupations. He tried out several hundred items that might conceivably distinguish the interests of those in the special occupations from those of people in general. The items were set up so that a person could mark whether he liked (L), disliked (D), or was indifferent to the item (I).

After these intitial trials, Strong retained the items that distinguished between people in general and one or more of the successful occupational groups. Then he constructed different scoring keys for each occupation in order to give different weights to items, depending on their ability to discriminate between an occupational group and people in general. A person who takes the test can select certain occupations in which he is interested and have his test scored for them. The answers come out in the form of an A-B-C rating for each occupation.

Kuder has two tests: the Kuder Preference Record: Vocational, and the Kuder Preference Record: Personal. The Kuder tests differ from the Strong in that the Kuder measures a limited number of interests. From these Kuder obtains a profile of a person's pattern of interests, which can then be matched with the profiles that characterize different occupations. It is a procedure that gives somewhat more generalized guidance than the Strong. For this reason it is often used in high school counseling, where only general guidance is needed. The Strong test, on the other hand, is more often used when a person wishes to choose between specific occupations.

Allport-Vernon-Lindzey scale   Another test of interests first constructed by Allport and Vernon, then revised by Lindzey, is known as a "Study of Values." It measures and then charts a profile of a person's major values and interests: theoretical, economic, esthetic, social, political, and religious (see Figure 9.3). In one part of the test, the person marks whether or not he agrees with certain statements; for example, "The objects of scientific research should be applications." In another part, he must rank four alternatives in the order of his agreement with them. He would, for example, express his agreement with these statements by indicating a rank order:

Do you think that a good government should aim chiefly at

(a) More aid for the poor, sick, and old?
(b) The development of manufacturing and trade?
(c) Introducing more ethical principles into its policies and diplomacy?
(d) Establishing a position of prestige and respect among nations?

Personality Questionnaires

In a third kind of personality test frequently called a questionnaire or inventory, a person is asked to indicate with "yes" or "no" whether a particular statement applies to him. For example:

I generally prefer to attend movies alone.
I occasionally cross the street to avoid meeting someone I know.
I seldom or never go out on double dates.

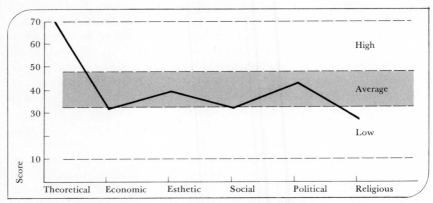

Figure 9.3 *A profile of scores from the Allport-Vernon-Lind-zey Study of Values test. Note the highest and lowest scores. What do you suppose some of the other characteristics of this person might be?*

Two widely used personality tests of this type are the Minnesota Multiphasic Personality Inventory and the Edwards Personal Preference Record.

Minnesota Multiphasic Personality Inventory This test, abbreviated MMPI, was constructed by comparing the responses of normal subjects with those of abnormal individuals classified into several diagnostic categories. Items were given different weights depending on how well they distinguished normal subjects from individuals in a category. In this way 8 different scales were built. In addition, a scale for masculinity-femininity was constructed by scoring items that differentiate men from women. Finally, a tenth scale was derived by using items that distinguish socially introverted from socially extraverted people. The names of the 10 scales and what they measure are as follows:

1 *Hypochondriasis (Hs)* Exaggerated anxiety about one's health, and pessimistic interpretations and exaggerations of minor symtoms

2 *Depression (D)* Feeling of pessimism, worthlessness, hopelessness

3 *Hysteria (Hy)* Various ailments such as headaches and paralyses which have no physical basis

4 *Psychopathic deviation (Pd)* Antisocial and amoral conduct

5 *Masculinity-femininity (Mf)* Measure of masculine and feminine interests; especially a measure of feminine values and emotional expression in men

6 *Paranoia (Pa)* Extreme suspiciousness of other people's motives,

frequently resulting in elaborate beliefs that certain people are plotting against one

7 *Psychasthenia (Pt)* Irrational thoughts that recur and/or strong compulsions to repeat seemingly meaningless acts

8 *Schizophrenia (Sc)* Withdrawal into a private world of one's own, often accompanied by hallucinations and bizarre behavior

9 *Hypomania (Ma)* Mild elation and excitement without any clear reason

10 *Social introversion (Si)* Avoidance of other people and removal of oneself from social contacts

Since it was standardized on hospital patients, the MMPI is widely used in the diagnosis of psychiatric patients. It measures tendencies toward abnormal or disturbed behavior fairly well. Consequently it is also helpful in counseling and in the selection of subjects for experiments who are high or low on certain personality traits.

Edwards Personal Preference Schedule The EPPS does not measure abnormal traits, as does the MMPI. Rather, it is designed to characterize the dominant needs or motives of a person as given by Murray's list of needs (see page 242). In constructing his inventory, Edwards wanted to avoid a bias found in many personality inventories: the tendency for a subject to make what he considers to be socially desirable responses, whether they are true or not. Edwards presents items in pairs, both equally desirable, that require the person to choose between them. The resulting test has proved a useful one for personality counseling. As might be expected, however, the MMPI is a better hospital instrument when a clinician is attempting to diagnose a patient's illness.

Projective Tests

By presenting the subject with an ambiguous stimulus and asking him to interpret it, the projective test induces him to project his own feelings and needs into his responses. The most widely used projective tests are the Thematic Apperception Test (TAT) and the Rorschach Test.

Thematic Apperception Test The TAT consists of a series of twenty pictures. An example (but not one used in the actual test) is shown in Figure 9.4. When each picture is presented, the subject is asked to make up a story about what is happening in the picture. In doing so, he usually identifies with one of the characters in the picture, and his story becomes a thinly disguised autobiographical sketch or a scene from his own life. In this way he reveals feelings and desires that he would hesitate to discuss openly or would be unwilling to admit to himself.

The TAT has no standardized scoring. The tester simply notes recurring themes in the stories and from these decides on what is being revealed. The emphasis in the interpretation is on the dominant needs of the person.

Rorschach Test The Rorschach is somewhat more objective than the TAT. At the same time, it is more ambiguous. It consists of a series of 10 inkblots similar to the example (not used on the test) in Figure 9.5. As each inkblot is presented, the subject is asked to say what he sees in it. After going through the 10 blots once, he is asked to go through them again and point out what part of each blot suggested his responses to it.

Some of the scoring is objective. For example, the number of responses made to a *part* of a blot are tallied and compared with the number of responses made to the *whole* blot. Counts are also made of things like responses to color or responses that refer to movement. On the other hand, the clinician interprets not only the scores for different kinds of responses, but also the pattern of responses. This is more subjective.

Clinicians use projective tests as one way of discovering what may be bothering a person. Their judgments from such tests are put together with other data from interviews and objective tests to form a picture of the personality.

SUMMARY

When a good test of the right kind is chosen, testing is useful in decision making. There are two general kinds of tests: ability tests and personality tests.

Figure 9.4 *A picture similar to those used on the Thematic Apperception Test (TAT). The subject is asked to tell a story about it—to explain the situation it shows, discuss events that led up to the situation, indicate the feelings and thoughts of the characters in the picture, and describe the outcome of the story. (After Murray, 1943.)*

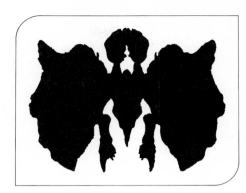

Figure 9.5 On the Rorschach Test a person is shown 10 inkblots similar to this one and asked to describe what he sees in them.

A good test should be (1) reliable, (2) valid, (3) administered by a standardized procedure, and (4) provided with group norms for populations like the one it is to be used with. Test results aid in decisions made in selection of personnel, counseling and psychotherapy, and commitments and judicial proceedings.

Intelligence tests measure general ability to function in school and adult life; aptitude tests measure ability to succeed in a particular kind of training. Intelligence tests have been developed for individual testing and for group testing. Scholastic aptitude tests measure ability to succeed in college or professional school; vocational aptitude tests measure the likelihood of success in vocational training or in an occupation.

There are many different kinds of intelligence; two general categories are abstract and concrete intelligence. Among people of above-average IQ, abstract intelligence and creativity are poorly correlated. Individual differences in intelligence can be classified into three general groups: the mentally retarded, the mentally gifted, and the middle groups. When group differences in intelligence are compared, the differences are found to correlate with age, home environment, and cultural environment.

Personality tests fall into four main classes: (1) interviews and rating scales, (2) interest tests, (3) personality questionnaires, and (4) projective tests.

SUGGESTIONS FOR FURTHER READING

Anastasi, A. *Psychological testing.* (3d ed.) New York: Macmillan, 1968. *A review of the principles and types of psychological tests.*

Cronbach, L. J. *Essentials of psychological testing.* (3d ed.) New York: Harper & Row, 1970. *A comprehensive introduction to the field of psychological testing.*

Lyman, H. B. *Test scores and what they mean.* Englewood Cliffs, N.J.: Prentice-Hall, 1963. (Paperback.) *A very readable account of the use and interpretation of psychological tests.*

Mischel, W. *Personality and assessment.* New York: Wiley, 1968. *A textbook on personality and its measurement.*

Telford, C. W., and Sawrey, J. M. *The exceptional individual: Psychological and educational aspects.* Englewood Cliffs, N.J.: Prentice-Hall, 1967. *An analysis for the nonspecialist of the problems of very superior and retarded children.*

10

Personality

LEARNING OBJECTIVES

Main objective
> *After studying this chapter you should be able to* describe personality as a system of behavior for satisfying motives and adjusting to conflicts between motives.

Other major objectives
> *You should also be able to*
> Compare three general approaches to a theory of personality.
> Describe the ways in which personality as a set of habits is learned.
> Outline several different kinds of coping behavior.

Minor objectives
> Explain how traits are defined and measured.
> Describe the role of the family and social influences in personality formation.

People talk a lot about personality, but most are hard put to define it. They are apt to say that it is something a person "has," and to describe the personalities of particular people in words like "friendly," "nice," "forceful," or "aggressive." So what they must mean by personality is some way that a person usually behaves with other people.

This is not far from a scientific definition: psychologists would say that personality consists of an individual's *characteristic* and *distinctive* ways of behaving. Characteristic, because they represent his usual or typical behavior. Distinctive, because they differentiate him from other people. There are many ways in which people in a society are much the same: in ours, most children of school age go to school regularly, and most people eat three meals a day. But in the study of personality, only the ways in which one person differs from another are important. If a schoolchild plays hooky a lot, or if a person eats far too much or too little, these are distinctive personality characteristics.

THEORIES OF PERSONALITY

Most psychologists would accept the definition of personality given above, although some would phrase it somewhat differently. What they have strongly differed and still differ on is how to *discover* and *label* characteristic and distinctive ways of behaving. The problem has proved to be very difficult; many approaches have been taken to it, and they have resulted in a number of different theories of personality. At the present time, however, psychologists seem to be reaching a solution which more and more of them agree on—and this chapter presents that solution. Since there are still differences of opinion, in fairness these will be sketched in terms of the categories they generally fall into: trait theories, state theories, and finally, the current solution that seems to be most satisfactory, social behavior theory.

Trait Theories

The oldest psychological approach to the problem of identifying characteristic and distinctive ways of behavior is to establish a limited number of *traits* that can be measured by personality tests or rating scales. In fact, characteristic and distinctive ways of behaving have been defined as traits. The assumption of trait theories is that traits can be measured by giving people personality tests or by having judges who know a person rate him on a number of traits. What needs to be done is to select the "correct" traits for the purpose.

Webster's unabridged dictionary contains approximately 18,000 adjectives that describe how people act, think, perceive, feel, and behave (Allport and Odbert, 1936). It also contains about 4,000 nouns that might be accepted as trait names—for example, "humility," "sociability," "honesty," and "forthrightness." With such an enormous number of trait names available, how does the psychologist pick out a limited number of the "right" ones?

Factor analysis   A scientific way of selecting and measuring a limited number of traits is called *factor analysis.* A mathematical procedure that is essentially a correlational technique (see page 27), it shows how the items on a personality test correlate with each other. Suppose the experimenter starts with several hundred questions designed to describe a person. In each question is a key adjective or phrase that means a trait. Take the following examples: Is the person *friendly*? Does he *like people*? Does he prefer to work *alone* or with *others*? Does he *belong* to many organizations? Now the psychologist rates a large number of people on the traits and analyzes the results. Suppose he finds that when the answer to one of the questions above is yes, the answer to the others is usually yes, and when one is no the others are too. This result is known as a correlation among items. When he finds such a correlation, he has identified a common factor or trait measured by the various items.

A typical factor analysis of items on personality tests or rating scales produces a number of factors—often as many as 12. But usually several of the factors are not very significant; they refer to correlations among a small number of items. Much of the time, about 5 factors will account for virtually all the correlations among items. Such a case is illustrated in Table 10.1. This example is based on 20 trait-rating scales which factor analysis reduced to the 5 factors listed. The names of the factors given in the first column did not come from the factor analysis; they were devised by the psychologist doing the study (Norman, 1963). After he identified a factor, he looked at the trait-rating scales that measured it and decided from the nature of the items what the factor should be called: "extraversion," "agreeableness," and so on.

Primary traits? When a psychologist has performed a factor analysis and identified, say, five factors, he is tempted to think he has isolated "the" traits that can be used to measure characteristic and distinctive ways of behaving. As it turns out, the five factors listed in Table 10.1, or very similar ones, are found in many different studies, so long as the items on the scales are very similar. This fact increases the experimenter's temptation to think that primary traits have been discovered. But are primary traits really discovered by such a method? There are problems, it seems, with this way of constructing traits (Mischel, 1968).

One problem which psychologists have long been aware of is that the factors identified depend on the items in the test. Factor analysis only gives out what has been put into it. If the experimenter changes the kinds of items, or the number of items of a particular kind, he obtains a different set of factors. This dependency of traits on the items used to measure them leads to the suspicion that the traits are in the heads of the test makers rather than in the personalities of the groups being tested.

And the suspicion is confirmed by research. In one study, judges rated fellow college students who were complete strangers (Passini & Norman, 1966). The judges were in the same room with the persons

TABLE 10.1
Factor names and descriptions based on twenty trait-rating scales.

Factor names	Scale dimensions
1 Extraversion	Talkative/Silent Frank, open/Secretive Adventurous/Cautious Sociable/Reclusive
2 Agreeableness	Good-natured/Irritable Not jealous/Jealous Mild, gentle/Headstrong Cooperative/Negativistic
3 Conscientiousness	Fussy, tidy/Careless Responsible/Undependable Scrupulous/Unscrupulous Persevering/Quitting, fickle
4 Emotional stability	Poised/Nervous, tense Calm/Anxious Composed/Excitable Not hypochondriacal/Hypochondriacal
5 Culture	Artistically sensitive/Artistically insensitive Intellectual/Unreflective, narrow Polished, refined/Crude, boorish Imaginative/Simple, direct

Adapted from Norman, 1963.

being judged for only fifteen minutes, and no verbal communication was permitted. The five main factors that emerged from their ratings were very similar to the list given in Table 10.1, which was obtained on subjects well known to the judges. This is strong evidence that the traits represent established ways of thinking about personality characteristics—factors that judges use whether they know the individuals or not. Put another way, such results suggest that "personality factors" are concepts which most of us share about the way to judge people rather than characteristics of people's *behavior*.

There are other weaknesses of personality tests as ways of measuring traits (Mischel, 1968). One, already mentioned in Chapter 9, is a tendency of the person taking the test to respond with socially desirable choices—he gives the answer he thinks he should, rather than describing how he actually behaves. As Chapter 9 said, the Edwards Personal Preference Inventory attempts to overcome this weakness by pairing items in such a way that the alternatives are equally desirable. Thus the person is forced to choose between alternatives on some other basis—on his actual way of behaving, the testers hope. But most personality tests do not compensate for the bias of social desirability.

Personality tests are also vulnerable to people's tendency to agree with statements—sometimes called the tendency toward acquiescence. People who are inclined to go along with whatever statements are on the test help produce not their own personality traits, but traits that were imagined by the test maker.

Probably the greatest weakness of the trait approach, as measured by personality tests or rating scales, is that the traits measured do not correlate well, if at all, with actual behavior. Experiments that objectively measure some bit of behavior—say, a sample of honesty—show that this behavior does not have much to do with the trait of "honesty" as measured on a personality test. The reason, psychologists now know, is that the *behavior* of people is not very consistent even if their responses on paper-and-pencil tests of personality are. The significance of one classical study of honesty has become clear only in recent years (Hartshorne and May, 1928):

> Thousands of children were placed in different kinds of situations—at home, at parties, in games, and in athletic contests—where they could lie, cheat, or steal. Unknown to the children, the investigators had ways in every case of detecting the cheating.
>
> Moral conduct, it turned out, was very inconsistent. A child would be honest in one situation but cheat in another, and different children were dishonest in different ways. On the other hand, given pencil-and-paper tests to find out their opinions about cheating, the children were fairly consistent. In other words, what they say they did and what they actually did were two different things.

These criticisms of personality measures are not meant to damn them. Personality tests do have predictive value in some situations, as was emphasized in Chapter 9. The point here is that they are not good ways to get at *primary* traits, partly because of biases in the making and taking of tests, and partly because primary traits of actual behavior are not measured well by such tests. You will see the implications of this conclusion in this and the next section.

State Theories
Historically, state theories have their origin in the Freudian conception of personality. Freud thought that people have underlying needs, urges, or "instincts" of which they are largely unaware. He also emphasized anxiety as a basic "trait" giving rise to different behaviors that attempt to allay it. Thus he believed that different ways of

behaving in different situations are really consistent when the underlying needs or anxieties are known. The problem, according to Freudian theory, is to discover these needs—usually frustrated needs—and through them to trace the consistency in behavior that otherwise appears to be illogical.

Psychoanalysis, according to Freud, is the method through which the underlying states or needs can be discovered. In this kind of psychotherapy, which will be described in the next chapter, the therapist uses free association and dream analysis to delve into a person's past and uncover unsatisfied, repressed need states that account for his present problem.

But from the personality psychologist's point of view, even if psychoanalysis can discover a person's underlying need states, it is a long process and obviously cannot be used to study needs in large groups of people. To do this, investigators who accept the Freudian approach have constructed projective tests (page 233). These are based on the assumption that underlying need states can be identified by giving people ambiguous tasks—the sort that require responses which are not part of an individual's habitual reactions to clear-cut situations. The theory is that he will then *project* his underlying state into the ambiguous situation. This is the theory behind such projective tests as the TAT and the Rorschach test.

Classification of needs Of the two tests, the TAT is the one specifically designed to uncover need states. An exploratory study developed a list of needs, many of which are described in Table 10.2. Then the stories told by people in response to the pictures of the TAT were analyzed to give scores for the strengths of various needs. A total of 28 needs were used for this purpose, but the table omits some because they are difficult to understand and not very important. The list was not chosen by factor analysis or by any sophisticated techniques. It simply represents the best judgment of a team of investigators, headed by Murray (1938), analyzing material from the TAT given to a large group of Harvard students.

Is Murray's list of 28 needs the "right" list? No one knows. In view of the fact that needs may converge in the same behavior, there probably is no "right" list. Indeed, other investigators have devised other lists of primary needs. Murray's list has proved useful, however, in a great deal of personality research, especially on need achievement (page 74).

Anxiety According to Freud, anxiety is a consequence of the frustration of needs, particularly the frustration that occurs in conflict situations (page 90). Freudian theory also says that a person is largely

TABLE 10.2
*A classification of major personal motives, based on extensive
tests and interviews of a large number of young men.*

Motive	Goal and effects
Abasement	To submit passively to others. To seek and accept injury, blame, and criticism.
Achievement	To accomplish difficult tasks. To rival and surpass others.
Affiliation	To seek and enjoy cooperation with others. To make friends.
Aggression	To overcome opposition forcefully. To fight and revenge injury. To belittle, curse, or ridicule others.
Autonomy	To be free of restraints and obligations. To be independent and free to act according to impulse.
Counteraction	To master or make up for failure by renewed efforts. To overcome weakness and maintain pride and self-respect on a high level.
Deference	To admire and support a superior person. To yield eagerly to other people.
Defendence	To defend oneself against attack, criticism, or blame. To justify and vindicate oneself.
Dominance	To control and influence the behavior of others. To be a leader.
Exhibition	To make an impression. To be seen and heard by others. To show off.
Harmavoidance	To avoid pain, physical injury, illness, and death.
Infavoidance	To avoid humiliation. To refrain from action because of fear of failure.
Nurturance	To help and take care of sick or defenseless people. To assist others who are in trouble.
Order	To put things in order. To achieve cleanliness, arrangement, and organization.
Play	To devote one's free time to sports, games, and parties. To laugh and make a joke of everything. To be light-hearted and gay.
Rejection	To remain aloof and indifferent to an inferior person. To jilt or snub others.
Sentience	To seek and enjoy sensuous impressions and sensations. To enjoy the arts genuinely.

Source: After Murray, 1938.

unaware of the sources or causes of his anxiety, but that psychoanalysis
helps the patient uncover the sources of conflict in his previous history.

Since psychoanalysis is prohibitively expensive as a means for
"measuring" anything in large numbers of people, tests of anxiety have
been developed. One is the Mandler-Sarason Test Anxiety Question-

naire; another is Taylor's Manifest Anxiety Scale, which puts into test form a number of items from the MMPI that are related to anxiety. But these do not really measure a general state of anxiety, for they do not correlate well with general behavior other than test responses. On the other hand, they do sometimes correlate with specific responses in specific situations. For example, the Manifest Anxiety Scale correlates with the rate of eyelid conditioning—light being the CS and a puff of air to the cornea being the US (Spence and Spence, 1964). And the Mandler-Sarason test does seem to measure fear of failure in achievement situations (page 75). Most of the time, however, anxiety turns out to be a response to specific stimulus situations, not a general characteristic measurable with tests (Mischel, 1968).

Weakness of state theory Thus state theory, like trait theory, has its weaknesses. In psychoanalysis we never know whether the interpretations made by the therapist are correct. He may decide that certain needs have been frustrated and that the patient's anxiety arises because of certain early experiences, but there is no way of checking on his interpretations. The notion that a person's anxieties often stem from learning experiences is not wrong. It is only that there is no way of knowing whether the therapist has uncovered these experiences with the techniques used. Similarly, there is no way of knowing whether the states or needs he thinks a person has are what the person actually has.

Social Behavior Theory

Trait theory and state theory have failed to predict actual behavior. And because it is actual behavior—characteristic and distinctive ways of behaving—that constitutes personality, psychologists are gradually discarding these theories (Mischel, 1968). In their place social behavior theory is becoming the prevailing way of looking at personality.

The tenets of social behavior theory are as follows: People learn social behavior in the same way and according to the same principles as any other kind of behavior. Furthermore, they learn to make different responses to different situations. Through their learning experiences, anxiety may be aroused by one situation and not by another. Or they learn to be honest in one situation and not in another. The only way, then, to discover characteristic and distinctive ways of behaving is to find out what a person does in specific situations.

Social behavior theory further assumes that the way to find out what a person does is either to watch him or to ask him. Watching behavior in everyday situations, of course, takes a lot of time and may be as expensive as psychoanalysis. But there are other ways of finding out what actual behavior is. One is to present pictures of situations and to measure autonomic changes in the person's response to them. Another is to have people play certain roles—be actors—in certain situations and note what seems to cause them trouble. Another is by self-report—to ask the person what he does in different situations, either in interviews or on paper-and-pencil questionnaires. If it is done by questionnaire, the items must refer to responses in specific situations, not to general traits or ways of reacting. The use of interview techniques will be described when Chapter 11 considers personality diagnosis for the purpose of conducting psychotherapy.

THE SHAPING OF PERSONALITY

Social behavior theory does not attempt, as psychoanalysis does, to reconstruct critical experiences in a person's life. Instead it concentrates on the here and now, that is, on the way a person behaves in specific situations. It recognizes, however, that he is a product of hereditary influences and of his learning experiences. It assumes that there are different kinds of social learning, and that these correspond to the basic kinds of learning described in Chapter 5. Knowing these differences, the therapist can use them to teach a patient to drop out previously learned responses and to learn new responses in specific situations. This section outlines the ways in which people learn social behavior. But first a word about the role of inheritance and of abilities in the formation of personality.

Inherited Predispositions
Scientists have not yet worked out all the ways in which inheritance influences personality, but they are sure that it does. Chapter 2 showed that a person's genetic endowment strongly affects a number of his characteristics—intelligence and emotionality, for example. Further evidence can be found both in "commonsense" observation and in systematic research on schizophrenia, one of the psychoses.

Everyone has noticed that striking differences exist among infants in the early days of life before they have had much opportunity to learn anything. One baby comes into the world extremely active, another sluggish. One cries and fusses most of the time; another is so placid that its mother calls the pediatrician to see if anything is wrong. Sometimes these differences in the "personality" of infants have to do with diet or temporary physical conditions, but sometimes they do not—they seem to indicate strong genetic influences.

Systematic research on the inheritance of personality characteristics is sparse—so sparse, in fact, that it yields few sound conclusions. But the role of inheritance shows up strongly in the incidence of certain behavior disorders such as *schizophrenia* (Chapter 11), a personality disorder for which people are frequently hospitalized. Contrary to popular belief, often fostered by the movies, schizophrenia is not a "split personality" in the Dr. Jekyll–Mr. Hyde sense. Rather, it is marked by some combination of confused, bizarre, and rigid patterns of thought, inappropriate emotional responses, a deficiency in feeling pleasure or displeasure, and sometimes suspiciousness of people. Schizophrenic patients sometimes, but not always, have hallucinations (that is, they see or hear things which are not there) and delusions (they develop bizarre ideas of grandeur or persecution).

To determine whether a disposition to schizophrenia is heritable, many investigators have compared pairs of identical (Mz, or monozygotic) twins. Their studies are summarized in Table 10.3, where you can see that if one identical twin is schizophrenic, the chances are about 46 percent that the other will be too. A second important finding is that if the other twin is not schizophrenic, he is very likely to have some other serious behavior disorder. Only about 12 percent of the identical twins of schizophrenics are normal. Compare these figures with an incidence of about 1 percent in the general population. Furthermore, among schizophrenic patients' brothers and sisters, who have a somewhat similar heredity and environment, the incidence of schizophrenia is about 12 percent.

These figures by themselves would not prove anything, since the higher incidence of schizophrenia in twins or siblings of schizophrenics might be because they shared similar environments. But other studies have been made of identical twins and of siblings reared apart

TABLE 10.3
The incidence of schizophrenia and related disorders in pairs of identical (MZ) twins. The findings summarized here provided strong evidence that schizophrenia itself and related behavioral problems are inherited.

Investigator	MZ twin pairs	Schizo-phrenia	Other significant abnormality	Normal, or mild, abnormality
Essen-Möller	9	0	8	1
Slater	37	18	11	8
Tienari	16	1	12	3
Kringlen	45	14	17	14
Inouye	53	20	29	4
Gottesman and Shields	24	10	8	6
Kallmann	174	103	62	9
Totals	358	166 (46.4%)	147 (41.1%)	45 (12.6%)

Source: Based on Heston, 1970.

(Rosenthal and Kety, 1968). And though the incidence of schizo-phrenia is somewhat lower in these situations, it still remains high, even when siblings have had otherwise good environments. So the argument for a large factor of inheritance in schizophrenia is a strong one.

Caution: Note that the personality disorder of schizophrenia is not directly inherited. All adults of whatever personality are the outcomes of years of learning. No one would argue that schizophrenia, or any aspect of behavior, is solely the product of inheritance. Instead, what is inherited is a predisposition—a tendency—to develop a certain kind of personality. Whether any one person does develop in that way depends both on his predisposition and on his learning history. On the basis of the research with schizophrenia, and some other personality disorders as well, psychologists believe that personality is always influenced by inherited predispositions. But in most cases they do not know how great the influence is.

Abilities

Although we sometimes don't think of it because they are separately measured, a person's abilities are really part of his personality. Being "bright," for example, is a personality characteristic; in fact, intel-ligence is a trait that can be measured when other traits are in doubt.

Abilities are not only parts of personality, but an important influence in the shaping of personality. Superior intelligence, for instance, helps a person make better adjustments in handling conflicts (Terman and Oden, 1959). The brighter a child is, the sooner he can learn to understand that his mother may be cross and grouchy because she has a headache rather than because he is a naughty, unlovable boy. And he can learn sooner to see into the future—to forgo a satisfaction now for a greater one later.

A person's abilities also influence his personality by providing him with a means of gaining recognition. The bright child is rewarded by his parents and teachers for his accomplishments. The child with mechanical ability wins recognition for building a ham radio set. Intelligence and special abilities permit children and adults as well to develop areas of competence from which they acquire confidence and self-esteem.

Moreover, abilities provide motivation, since a person with a special talent usually has strong motivation to exercise it—he has a kind of competence need. The father of the great composer Handel strongly opposed his son's interest in music, but even when faced with threats of punishment, the child would sneak to the garret at night to practice the harpsichord. According to *Life* magazine (1971), many of today's superstars of rock music had similar experiences. As a consequence of such strong drives to exercise their talents, children with outstanding abilities usually show them at an early age.

Social Learning

Social behavior theory simply applies the principles of learning that were described in Chapter 5 to the learning of habits that make up personality. The theory recognizes classical conditioning and operant conditioning as the two basic kinds of learning. In addition, it stresses a special kind of discrimination learning called *observational learning* or *modeling*, in which a person acquires a response to a situation simply by observing others making the response. Let us see how the principles of learning apply to the shaping of personality.

Classical conditioning Classical conditioning, you will remember (page 100), takes place when a neutral stimulus (CS) is paired with an unconditioned stimulus (US). By following this simple procedure in the laboratory, psychologists condition all sorts of responses—salivation, eyeblinks, knee jerks. Although such responses are sometimes conditioned in the course of human development, the responses

Figure 10.1 *The famed violinist Yehudi Menuhin, like many others with a great ability, demonstrated his talent early. Here he is shown at age 10 in Paris, where he "held the audience spellbound at the Concerts Lamoureux. . . . In spite of his prodigious musical ability, young Menuhin is like other boys and plays with all the fervour of youth when not practising." (Acme.)*

Figure 10.2 *Modeling in the family. The boy is learning to act like his father, who was a college and professional football player. Perhaps more important, he is learning to value many of the same things. (Courtesy of Henry Ford.)*

most often conditioned and those that are important in the study of personality, are emotional responses, both pleasant and unpleasant. As pointed out earlier, a person is very likely to have experiences in which some neutral stimulus, say, water, becomes conditioned to a fear, say, of drowning. Hence conditioned fears are often "characteristic" ways of behaving in certain situations.

A human being, unlike an animal, can also acquire "conditioned" reactions indirectly; he does not need to have a conditioning experience. One indirect way of acquiring them is through language. Many words carry negative, unpleasant meanings: for example, "dirty," "nasty," "bitter," "painful," "terrible," "loathsome," "disgusting." When such words are paired with certain events, the emotional attitudes connected with the words become attached to the events. This is one way that prejudice is taught: the mother says to her child, "Negroes are dirty," which, repeated a few times, conditions the child to have an aversive response to blacks. Thus a person can learn conditioned responses, usually negative ones, to many objects and situations.

Another indirect way of acquiring "conditioned" responses is through observational learning. A person sees someone else reacting emotionally to a situation and learns to react the same way. A girl who sees her mother being inhibited with her father can adopt an inhibited attitude toward men without herself having an unpleasant conditioning experience with a man. Fear of snakes, which is very common, is more often acquired in this way than by direct experience. A child sees a snake and at the same time sees an older person shrink back in horror. One or more such experiences are enough to "condition" a fear in the child.

Operant conditioning   As explained in Chapter 5, the reinforcement in classical conditioning is simply the US paired with the CS. But in operant conditioning, the reinforcement is food, shock, or anything which increases the likelihood that a response will be made (page 104). Many personality characteristics are acquired through operant conditioning. A familiar case is the child who throws temper tantrums. If the mother rewards the tantrums with attention or with a lollypop, the behavior tends to be learned, and later in life the child is likely to show signs of temper whenever he wants something he does not have. If, on the other hand, he receives no reward for his temper tantrums—if he is given extinction training—he will abandon this kind of operant response. The general rule is that certain responses to situations may or may not become characteristic ways of behaving depending on whether or not they are reinforced.

Operant responses, like classically conditioned ones, can be acquired indirectly through observational learning or modeling. When we see someone else do something and see him praised (reinforced) for it, we quickly acquire similar responses. Experiments have demonstrated that an observer who sees another person praised for his aggressive behavior increases his tendency to be aggressive, whereas he becomes less aggressive when he sees someone else punished for aggressiveness (Bandura et al., 1963).

Modeling   Thus human beings learn their characteristic ways of behaving not only through classical and operant conditioning, but also through the essentially human means of modeling or observational learning. Some animals can learn some responses through modeling too, but humans acquire a great many of their characteristics in this way. Some social behavior theorists feel that learning by modeling is the major channel through which personality characteristics are developed.

Family Influences

The family is the most important of all environmental influences in the shaping of personality. The family administers the rewards and punishments through which characteristic responses are acquired. It also, especially in the early years, provides models for observational training.

Learning in the family   Normally, a child's parents are the first teachers he has. They reinforce some kinds of behavior and discourage others, thus helping to determine his habits, goals, and values. One child may discover that his mother will let him have his own way if he screams and turns purple. Another child in another family may find that screaming does not work but that playing sick does. The techniques a child learns in dealing with his parents carry over into his contacts with other people. The grown man who sulks because he is angry with his wife probably learned this response in dealing with his mother.

Children also learn something more general in most families: *sex typing,* or the development of responses and interests appropriate to one's sex. Boys are rewarded by their parents for rough and aggressive play, for showing emotional restraint, and for an interest in mechanical things. Girls are usually rewarded for being more submissive, "sweet," and emotionally expressive, and they are usually discouraged from acquiring interests in mechanical things. Parents may or may not administer this training consciously. Nevertheless, the pressure is there, and it produces some of the personality differences we see between boys and girls.

Parental attitudes and the self-concept   Parents who are themselves well adjusted, and who love and respect their child, give him a feeling of self-worth and self-confidence. With their praise and love they help him come to regard himself as a desirable person.

Unfortunately, many parents reject their child, enmesh him in the cross fire of their own emotional problems, or take out on him the ill-treatment they experienced in their own childhood. In fact, as studies show, many mothers and fathers unconsciously relive their own childhood problems through their children. For example, a mother may react to her son with the same resentful feelings she herself felt as a child toward her older brother. Instead of giving him encouragement, love, and praise, she rejects and criticizes him, and the child comes to have a poor regard for himself—sometimes so poor that he develops severe inferiority feelings.

Modeling in the family   A child's parents are his first models as well as his first teachers. Children learn both general attitudes and specific responses by using their parents as models. Watching his father, a son learns how to act like a man; watching her mother, a daughter how to act like a woman. In the process of modeling, children copy many of the personality characteristics of their parents and take over their moral and cultural standards as well.

Social Influences

Your culture and subculture vary according to whether you live in the United States or the jungles of New Guinea, in a city or on the farm, in an upper or a lower socioeconomic class. Wherever it is, each culture has its distinctive values, morals, and ways of behaving. It lays down the rules for child training and the relationships within the family. Thus culture influences personality because through a process called *socialization,* it dictates many of the characteristics a person will acquire. The parents are the first agents of socialization. Later in childhood, other agents take part in the socializing process—playmates, teachers in school, television. In adolescence, peer groups—that is, companions of the same age and status—become an important force in personality development. (Their role in attitude formation is discussed in Chapter 12.)

Continuity of Personality

Although culture is a pervasive influence in shaping personality, do not forget that each personality is *unique.* Every person's characteristic ways of behaving are different from every other person's, because he has a unique biological endowment and a unique set of learning experiences.

Moreover, personality has continuity: habits and motives that are learned over a number of years are not easily forgotten or supplanted by new ones. Thousands and thousands of learning trials make up the history of any particular individual. Continuity is also provided by biological factors, to the extent that they determine personality. And continuity is further enforced by the roles a person is called upon to play. His family, friends, social class, and economic circumstances are all relatively constant. These make continual demands on him for certain ways of behaving, called roles, which will be discussed in Chapter 13.

Over a period of time, however, personality usually does change to a certain extent—some people's more than others'. An individual may discover new ways of adjusting to a situation, or he may alter his way of life and find satisfactions that he had not known before. Sometimes, too, relatively sudden personality changes occur as a result of religious experience, moving away from home, changing jobs, or achieving success in a new line of work. In some instances a deliberate attempt is made to change personality as in psychotherapy for a person who is so incapable of making social adjustments that a change is urgently needed. When successful, psychotherapy enables him to discard old habits and learn new ones that reduce motivational conflict and provide satisfactions for his needs (more on this in Chapter 11).

COPING BEHAVIOR

You have now seen that personality characteristics are largely learned, since it is through learning that the individual acquires many habitual ways of reacting to situations. On the other hand, new situations continually arise, and they cannot always be successfully handled by using established habits. The person must solve problems as they come along, and in the process he is likely to experience frustration and anxiety. By definition a problem is frustrating, because it presents some barrier to attaining a goal. And as explained earlier, frustration causes anxiety because it threatens us with the possibility of not reaching the goal. So frustration and anxiety go together. At the same time, anxiety is unpleasant; we do not like it, and getting rid of it is in itself a problem to be coped with.

To a Freudian, coping with anxiety is the central theme of existence. A person acquires many conflicts (page 90), which produce frustration and the consequent anxiety. Freud described a number of ways in which people typically behave to avoid or lessen anxiety. These he called *defense mechanisms*—devices to defend the person against anxiety. Other theorists have placed less emphasis on anxiety; to them a person simply learns characteristic methods, like those described below, for attempting to cope with his problems.

Forgetting (Repression)

To Freud, *repression* was the fundamental technique that people employ to allay anxiety caused by conflicts. Repression in his theory is an active mental process in which a person "pushes" down into his subconscious any thoughts that arouse anxiety. As psychologists think of it today, repression is simply a refusal to think about something because we find the thought unpleasant. If we don't think about it, we don't *rehearse* it—which is what we need to do to preserve something in long-term memory (page 156)—and so we forget it.

Forgetting, then, is a kind of coping behavior used to take our minds off unpleasant memories or thoughts. A person can forget to pay a bill if paying it would make his bank balance uncomfortably low. Or he can forget an appointment with the dentist because he is afraid of the drill. In these instances he represses the memories of things he should do; in other cases he might forget someone's name because he dislikes him or has had an unpleasant experience with him. In still other instances, repression distorts a person's perception of situations or his interpretation of his own and others' behavior.

Reversing Motives (Reaction Formation)

Another method by which a person attempts to cope with conflicts is to perceive one of his motives as the *opposite* of what it really is. The true

trait-rating scales and personality questionnaires. Trait theories of personality concentrate on doing this. State theories, in contrast, emphasize underlying needs in the person. The trouble with both kinds of theory is that people behave in characteristically different ways in different situations. Social behavior theory recognizes this fact and attempts to describe personality in terms of learned responses to situations.

Personality depends in part on inherited predispositions and abilities. It is shaped through classical conditioning, operant conditioning, and modeling through observational learning. Early in life the family is the most important influence in teaching responses; later other social influences become more important.

A person is continually experiencing anxiety and frustration because of a conflict of motives. Several patterns of behavior are typical of attempts to cope with these conflicts and to reduce anxiety: forgetting, reversing motives, blaming others, making excuses, "kicking the dog," fantasy, identification, acting childish, and sublimation and compensation.

SUGGESTIONS FOR FURTHER READING

Allport, G. W. *Pattern and growth in personality.* New York: Holt, 1961. *A revision, easily read, of one of the classic texts on personality.*

Bandura, A., and Walters, R. *Social learning and personality development.* New York: Holt, 1963. *A text that applies social behavior theory to personality development.*

Hall, C. S. *A primer of Freudian psychology.* Cleveland: World, 1954. (Paperback.) *A clearly written systematic description of Freudian theory.*

Hall, C. S., and Lindzey, G. *Theories of personality.* (2d ed.) New York: Wiley, 1970. *A comprehensive treatment of major personality theories.*

Lundin, R. W. *Personality: A behavioral analysis.* New York: Macmillan, 1969. *Behavior theory applied to personality.*

Mischel, R. *Personality and assessment.* New York: Wiley, 1968. *An analysis of trait and state theories and the use of social behavior theory in diagnosis and psychotherapy.*

Sarason, I. G. *Personality: An objective approach.* New York: Wiley, 1966. *A general book on personality from an empirical point of view.*

11

Behavior Disorders and Therapy

LEARNING OBJECTIVES

Main objective

After studying this chapter you should be able to distinguish among psychoneurotic reactions, psychotic reactions, and personality disorders by stating the major characteristics of each.

Other major objectives

You should also be able to

Define five major psychoneurotic reactions.

Describe five principal types of psychotic reactions.

Name and describe four kinds of personality disorders.

Outline five major types of psychotherapy.

Minor objectives

Explain how repression is involved in conversion reactions and dissociative disorders.

Define four kinds of schizophrenia.

Describe two major kinds of medical therapy.

Describe how psychoanalysis attempts to treat a patient with motivational conflicts.

Name and describe three varieties of behavior-modification therapy.

Just what is abnormal behavior? In most cases, no sharp line divides it from normal behavior. The difference is a matter of degree and circumstances. Most of us have some of the symptoms of abnormal behavior, but they are not serious enough to require hospitalization or treatment. Even when the symptoms are serious, a person's particular circumstances are important. If he is surrounded by a loving and tolerant family, he may function fairly well. If the family is less loving and less tolerant, they may pack him off to the hospital. Similarly, certain kinds of abnormal behavior can be tolerated in some jobs and not in others.

Even when a person's behavior is clearly abnormal to every bystander, the behavior is difficult to classify (diagnose) with any precision. Many studies show that when the same patient is diagnosed by two or more psychiatrists, the agreement between them is poor (see Mischel, 1968). They agree readily only on very general categories, such as classifying the patient's symptoms as a psychotic reaction, an organic disorder, or a personality disorder. Attempts to classify behavior disorders are largely abstractions; the diagnostic categories represent "ideal" or "pure" cases that almost never exist in real patients. Most people showing abnormal behavior display a mixture of symptoms, and people in different diagnostic categories often behave in the same way.

But attempts to classify the behavior disorders continue. Every patient admitted to a mental hospital gets some kind of label attached to him. Indeed, state law often requires it. The label, though it might be different if assigned by another psychiatrist, is usually based on an "official" classification published by the American Psychiatric Association: *The Diagnostic and Statistical Manual of Mental Disorders* (rev. ed., 1968). That classification will be used in this chapter, but keep in mind the relatively low reliability of classifying behavior disorders.

Several terms are used in talking about abnormal behavior: behavior disorders, behavior disturbances, mental disorder, mental illness, and mental disease. All can be found in the psychological and psychiatric literature. "Behavior disorders" is the most general and is preferred by many psychologists. "Mental disorder" implies something more serious than a mild behavior disorder, and tends to be used more by psychiatrists.

Descriptions of behavior disorders can cover a large territory, but this chapter will not attempt to present them all. Most of them can be classified under three general headings: psychoneurotic reactions, psychotic reactions, and personality disorders.

PSYCHONEUROTIC REACTIONS

Psychoneurotic reactions, sometimes simply called neurotic reactions, are patterns of behavior in which *anxiety* is prominent. In some cases anxiety is so strong that anyone can see what the trouble is. In others anxiety may not be so obvious, but the person feels it and his attempts to cope with it are expressed in his neurotic behavior.

The last chapter described defense mechanisms that people use in attempting to cope with anxiety. Psychoneurosis can be regarded as a failure of the defense mechanisms. They may fail by simply not keeping anxiety down, or by being so exaggerated that they themselves produce abnormal behavior. Examples of both types of failure are given here.

Anxiety Reactions

Of the psychoneurotic reactions, anxiety is most prominent in the disorders labeled *anxiety reactions* (see Figure 11.1). The anxiety may be persistent and uncomfortably high, or it may come in sudden attacks that last for a few hours or a few days. The precise reason for the anxiety is not clear either to the victim or to his family and friends; the cause must be ferreted out by an expert, as in the following case (Coleman, 1964):

> A successful business executive began having acute anxiety attacks every two or three months. When he saw a therapist, these facts came out. His family was poor, and he had been insecure as a child. Later he had married a rich woman eight years older than he. Her wealth and connections had much to do with his business success. But she had become physically unattractive to him, and he began casting eyes at younger women. In time he met a girl with whom he felt he was in love. The relationship grew to the point where he considered a divorce. It was then that the anxiety attacks started. Piecing these facts together, the therapist

Figure 11.1 *The intense suffering of the anxiety neurotic. (Meade Johnson Laboratories.)*

could see that the attacks were related to his conflict about his wife. The threat of losing his present security and style of life, if he divorced her, caused the attacks.

Anxiety reactions can take other forms. In one, the person becomes *hypochondriacal*: he develops physical complaints that are groundless or grossly exaggerated. In this way he takes his mind off feelings of inadequacy that would otherwise cause unbearable anxiety. Another anxiety reaction is *neurasthenia:* literally, "nervous weakness." The person is chronically unable to do anything because he feels "too tired." Actually he is worn out by anxiety, but his symptoms relieve his anxiety somewhat by giving him an excuse for not doing things that cause him anxiety.

Phobic Reactions
As most people know, a *phobia* is an intense, irrational fear of something. Actually, the fear is rational in the sense that it has arisen in the person's learning history. He has repressed the circumstances of the learning, and the existing fear makes no sense, so the fear has become irrational.

There are many kinds of phobias: fear of small enclosed places, of high places, of the dark, and of certain animals, among others. Phobic fears of one or more objects are fairly common, but when they are mild or when they don't interfere with normal living, they do no harm. The author, for example, has an intense fear of high places, but since he has no need to be in them, he gets along all right. If a person has a phobia about things he cannot avoid, his misery can be intense. His phobia may disrupt his life, as in the famous case of the poet and professor at the University of Wisconsin, William Ellery Leonard (1927).

> Leonard had a phobia of going more than a few blocks away from his home and the university. For years his phobia kept him a virtual prisoner in this small geographic area, although he did not know why he was afraid. Then during the course of psychoanalysis he was able to remember a frightening incident in his childhood. He had wandered away from his home and had gone to the railroad tracks, where a passing train had scalded him with steam. His fear, it turned out, originated in this incident, and it proved to be the real motive for his staying near home. The phobia was so powerful that it dominated his whole life. It was never completely eradicated, even though he recognized its source and could be objective enough to write a book about it— *The Locomotive God.*

The history of people with phobias, when it is revealed, usually provides instances of frightening, or "traumatic," events. As in

Leonard's case there may be a single episode, but often a phobia arises from frightening situations in a person's early life that are repeated many times. In either case, the phobia is rooted in a fear that has been classically conditioned (page 100) and has generalized to situations or objects like the original one. In other instances, the fear may have been acquired vicariously—through modeling—from other people (Bandura, 1963).

Obsessive-Compulsive Reactions

Another psychoneurotic disorder is the *obsessive-compulsive reaction*, which may include obsessions, or compulsions, or both. An obsession is an *idea* that constantly intrudes into a person's thoughts. An obsessive mother may think constantly that something has happened, or will happen, to her children. A person may be obsessed with the idea that he will kill himself, or someone else, in an auto accident. A compulsion, on the other hand, is an *act* that intrudes into a person's behavior. One compulsive person may wash his hands every few minutes; another must count all the steps he climbs; another cannot sleep at night until he has neatly stacked the day's change on the bureau—quarters on the bottom, then nickels, then pennies, and dimes on top. But some people are compulsive in a more general way; they cannot tolerate disorder or uncertainty, and they strive for orderliness of thought, in dress, and at work. Indeed, any undue emphasis on "doing things the right way" is in some degree compulsive. The following case illustrates a typical compulsion (Masserman, 1961):

> A twice-married business executive had two children of his former wife enrolled in a private day school. He should have known that they were about as safe as children can be, yet he felt impelled to interrupt his work and call the school two or three times a day to ask if they were all right. Naturally this behavior got on the nerves of the principal and caused a flare-up between them. The man also felt compelled to take home some present each night to his second wife and children—usually something they did not want. Therapy revealed that the cause of his compulsive behavior was a conflict between his feeling of responsibility as a husband and father and his intense dislike of these duties. To reduce the anxiety generated by the conflict, he showed excessive concern about the children's safety and overdid the present-giving.

In this instance the cause of the compulsive behavior lay in a *present* conflict; in others a person may feel guilty about something he did in the *past*. The guilt lingers on, causing anxiety. In either case, the compulsive behavior takes on features of reaction formation (page 252): the person reduces his anxiety by acting as though his motive is the opposite of an unacceptable motive. (The business executive became oversolicitous when what he really wanted was to forget about his family.) Obsessive-compulsive behavior may also be riddled with *rationalizations.* A person with a hand-washing compulsion, for example, may try to rationalize his unreasonable behavior by giving silly reasons for his hands being dirty.

Conversion Reactions
If a conflict is unusually severe, and if its nature is largely repressed, a person may develop symptoms of some physical illness. He has no real illness—a doctor can find nothing organically wrong—but he thinks he does, and he feels and acts sick. Such a reaction to conflict is called a *conversion reaction*, because it converts a psychological state into physical symptoms. It is also sometimes called a hysterical reaction, but the meaning of hysteria in this instance is different from the common meaning of hysteria (an outbreak of uncontrolled emotional behavior). Here is a case of hysterical or conversion reaction:

> A woman was admitted to a hospital with a paralysis of the legs: they were extended rigidly and close together, like two stiff pillars. Neurological examination indicated no physical disorder, so physicans looked into other aspects of her problem. They discovered that she was the mother of several children, that her doctor had warned her not to have any more, that her husband desired frequent sexual intercourse, and that she had strong prohibitions against both practicing birth control and denying her husband's sexual demands. Here were all the elements of a complex conflict situation. The conversion reaction was a response that reduced the anxiety associated with the conflict.

Like other neurotic behavior a conversion reaction is learned. It is adopted because it is reinforced by the reduction of anxiety. The learning does not have to be conscious; indeed, usually it is not, because awareness of the "lie" would itself cause anxiety. Thus the person learns a reinforced response while conveniently repressing his or her awareness of the reasons for the learning.

Dissociative Reactions
A great deal of repression is also involved in dissociative reactions, but the repressed material is *memories* that evoke painful anxiety. In mild form, a dissociative reaction is no more than dividing one's thinking into compartments. A businessman who is a vigorous competitor and not too scrupulous about it may be a good family man, a fervent churchgoer, and a pillar of the community chest. He simply compartmentalizes his business thinking so that it does not get in the way of his

other roles. In more extreme form, however, dissociative reactions are bizarre and incapacitating. They furnish the most dramatic instances of neurotic behavior.

   Amnesia One well-publicized type of extreme dissociative reaction is amnesia, the subject of many movies, books, and news stories. A person suffering from amnesia usually forgets what his name is, where he lives, who his relatives are, and what he has been doing for some weeks, months, or years. Amnesia can be caused by a blow on the head or an injury to the brain. As a neurotic disorder, however, amnesia represents extreme repression. To cope with painful conflict, the person unconsciously represses the memory of his own identity and things closely connected with it.

   Multiple personality Occasionally repression works in such a way as to dissociate two or more relatively complete personalities. A fictional case is the story of Dr. Jekyll and Mr. Hyde, where one personality is evil, the other good. In the story the transformation from Jekyll to Hyde is made by drinking a potion. But in real cases of multiple personality the change is tripped off by stress or emotional trauma, and it stems from a deep-seated conflict of motives. Though often dramatized and talked about, split or multiple personality is relatively rare. Only a few cases have been found and studied by competent clinicians. One famous case is reported in the book, *The Three Faces of Eve* (Thigpen and Cleckley, 1957), later made into a movie. (Subsequently, it appeared that this case might not be genuine.)

Depressive Reactions
Neurotic depression (so called to differentiate it from psychotic depression) is like this:

> The neurotically depressed individual gives the outward general appearance of being dejected, discouraged, and sad. He many have an extremely sorrowful expression on his face or a dull, masklike one. He seems to see only the dark side of everything, seems uninterested in any pleasurable activities, may stay by himself, may just sit and stare. Although his thinking is not slowed up, he may complain of difficulties in concentrating. He may have trouble sleeping, feelings of restlessness, irritability, and inward tension. (Kutash, 1965, page 967.)

Neurotic depression is usually brought on by some unusual event—the death of a loved one, breakup of a marriage, loss of a job, or entrapment in some impossible situation. The depression may simply represent an overreaction to the situation. On the other hand, the person may also have feelings of guilt connected with his own actions. But as time passes and the situation recedes in his memory, he tends to "snap out of it," for neurotic depression usually does not last long. While the person is in the depths of depression he is miserable, and suicide is a danger, but spontaneous recovery is the rule rather than the exception in this type of neurotic disorder.

PSYCHOTIC REACTIONS

Psychotic reactions are different from neurotic ones in a couple of ways: (1) The neurotic *overreacts* to the world of reality; he is too sensitive to it. This is because the world arouses anxieties in him that he attempts to cope with. A psychotic person, in contrast, *underreacts* to reality. Anxiety may play some part in his disorder, but his response to it is to withdraw into his own world. (2) The *thinking* of a neurotic is reasonably normal, distorted only by the defense mechanisms he uses to reduce anxiety in particular situations. In the psychotic, on the other hand, thinking is distorted and confused, often having very little to do with reality. The psychotic constructs a world of his own to live in—he is *autistic*—rather than live in the real world. In addition, psychotics may have, but do not always have, delusions and/or hallucinations. A *hallucination* is an experience for which there is no sensory basis. A *delusion* is an idea that has no basis in fact.

The psychotic reactions can be described under five main headings: affective reactions, paranoid reactions, schizophrenic reactions, involutional reactions, and chronic brain syndromes.

Affective Reactions

The major characteristic of one variety of psychosis is *extremes of mood.* Hence it is called affective psychosis—one in which marked disturbances of mood or emotion take place—or sometimes, *manic-depressive psychosis.* Affective reactions often appear as relatively short psychotic episodes in the otherwise normal behavior of a person. These episodes, which may be either manic or depressed, tend to last about 6 months. On the average the depressed episodes are more prolonged than the manic ones. Most people who suffer from this disorder experience several such psychotic episodes in their lives.

As the term manic-depressive implies, the psychosis is sometimes cyclical: the patient is manic for a period and then swings into a depression. The cycle may be repeated rapidly, or a period of months may intervene. It may be repeated more than once. On the other hand, manic states may never swing over into depressive ones, and vice versa. There are many patterns of affective disturbance: cycles of mania followed by depression, mania with no depression, or depression alone.

The manic individual is wildly elated and active. He may sing, dance, run, talk a lot, and generally expend more energy than seems humanly possible. He may also exhibit obsessions and delusions. Frequently he is aggressive and hard to handle: he may break chairs, attack people, use vile language, and generally put life and property in jeopardy. Or occasionally he may try so hard to be helpful that he becomes extremely troublesome.

The depressed individual feels melancholic, worthless, guilty, and hopeless. Some depressed patients cry a good deal of the time, some keep talking about terrible sins they imagine that they have committed, some are so depressed that they take no food or water and must be forcibly fed through a tube. Patients in this state usually also refuse to dress or take care of their toilet needs. The extremely depressed patient is often on the verge of suicide and must be watched closely to see that he does not harm himself.

Note that this description differs in several respects from the one of the neurotically depressed person. In the first place, a psychotic depression is not linked to any observable cause; it is simply an expression of the patient's physical state. Secondly, psychotic depression can be much more severe. Suicide is a danger in both neurotic and psychotic depression, but neurotically depressed people usually do not have to be dressed, fed, and cleaned up after by others. Thirdly, the psychotic has distortions of thinking; he may imagine, for example, that he has committed serious sins. Usually the neurotic merely feels unreasonable guilt about something that did in fact happen.

What causes an affective psychosis? For one thing, it has a strong genetic basis—just about as strong as schizophrenia (Kallmann, 1951). It runs in families. The fact that it occurs in episodes which are not closely related to casual events also indicates that it has a physiological basis. One theory has it that the basic disorder in the psychosis is depression, and that mania is a flight into activity to ward off depression. Whether this is correct, nobody knows. Psychologists have yet to disentangle the biological and psychological factors in affective psychosis.

Without special treatment, about 70 percent of manic-depressive patients recover enough within one year to be released from the hospital (White, 1964). And with modern treatment, nearly 100 percent can be released within the first year. The treatment in this instance is almost always medical. Electroshock (regulated jolts of electrical current passed through the brain) is used with considerable success in the affective psychoses; it seems to shorten the period of depression. Besides electroshock (discussed in more detail later), antidepressant drugs have been developed for the depressive patient, and calming drugs for the manic.

Paranoid Reactions

Paranoid reactions are marked by *delusions,* usually some combination of imagined *grandeur* and/or imagined *persecution.* A paranoid patient may tell you he is George Washington or Napoleon and spin quite a tale to prove it. He may also have the delusion that someone is persecuting him. For example, a paranoid may be convinced that someone has invented a machine which is slowly destroying him by some sort of wave, or that someone has organized a plot to deprive him of his rights as President of the United States.

Except for his delusion, the paranoid psychotic usually shows almost no disorder in thinking. (This is unlike paranoid schizophrenia, discussed below.) He appears normal until something happens to trigger the delusional thinking. In general, his delusional system is well worked out and often plausible. Given some of the false premises in his thinking, it might even be true.

Schizophrenic Reactions

The word "schizophrenia" is constantly being misused to describe people who behave in inconsistent, but by no means psychotic, ways. For example, newspapers will label the inconsistent behavior of politicians as schizophrenic. The term is also incorrect when it is used to mean "split" or multiple personality. As explained earlier, the multiple personality is a relatively rare neurotic disorder characterized by repression and dissociation.

Then what does schizophrenia mean? The medical language of the American Psychiatric Association gives the symptoms of the various disorders which are lumped together under the term schizophrenia.

> This large category includes a group of disorders manifested by characteristic disturbances of thinking, mood, and behavior. Disturbances in thinking are marked by alterations of concept formation which may lead to misinterpretation of reality and sometimes to delusions and hallucinations, which frequently appear psychologically self-protective. Corollary mood changes include ambivalent, constricted, and inappropriate emotional responsiveness and loss of empathy with others. Behavior may be withdrawn, regressive, and bizarre. The schizophrenias, in which the mental status is attributable primarily to a *thought* disorder, are to be

distinguished from the *major affective illnesses* which are dominated by a *mood* disorder. The *paranoid* states are distinguished from schizophrenia by the narrowness of their distortions of reality and by the absence of other psychotic symptoms. (American Psychiatric Association, 1968, page 33.)

Although schizophrenia may occur at any age, it tends to develop early in life. The highest rate of admission to mental hospitals for schizophrenia is among people in their late teens and early twenties. Moreover, this disorder is no rarity; it is the most common of all psychotic reactions, affecting about 1 percent of the population.

Schizophrenia is also the most crippling of the psychoses. Although modern therapeutic techniques have helped some patients, a substantial number of schizophrenics steadily "deteriorate" and need to be taken care of for years. About 15 to 20 percent of people admitted to mental hospitals for the first time are diagnosed as schizophrenics. Their average stay in the hospital is *13 years* (Wolman, 1965). Because they stay so long, while other psychotic patients are released much sooner, half or more of the patients in most mental hospitals at any one time are schizophrenics.

Types of schizophrenia   Traditionally, psychiatrists have identified four types of schizophrenia. *Simple schizophrenia* consists mainly of withdrawal from contact with the world. The patient is apathetic and indifferent, talks very little with others, pays little attention to anything going on—generally does nothing. In *hebephrenic schizophrenia* the patient regresses to childish levels of behavior. Like a little child he often giggles or cries for no apparent reason, and he has the eating and toilet habits of a child. *Catatonic schizophrenia,* perhaps the most dramatic of the four, is characterized by muscular rigidity. For many minutes or even hours, the patient stays fixed in some strange position, say, in a crouch, or with arms outstretched. *Paranoid schizophrenia* has some features of the paranoid psychosis; the patient may have delusions of grandeur or persecution. It differs from paranoid psychosis in that the delusions are confused and *unsystematized:* the patient does not defend them with elaborate rationalizations.

Causes and treatment of schizophrenia   Schizophrenia seems to be caused by a combination of genetic and environmental factors. The evidence for a genetic factor has already been presented (page 244). But inheritance cannot be the entire cause of the disorder; it can only endow a person with a *predisposition* to develop schizophrenia. What precipitates it in people with a predisposition for it is not clear. Theories abound, but about all we really feel sure of is that stress in early family relationships is important. Dissension between parents and conflicting demands on the child cause some children to withdraw into their own worlds. This withdrawal may not be severe enough to cause hospitalization until the person encounters some stressful situation in adult life.

As said earlier, schizophrenics tend to stay in the hospital a long time. How long depends on the patient's previous history as well as on the treatment. If the schizophrenic symptoms have been coming on for some time, the outlook is not very good. A patient with this history is said to be in *process schizophrenia.* In contrast, if the patient seems to have been pretty normal most of his life and the schizophrenia has appeared suddenly in response to a stressful situation, the chances are good. A disorder with this history is called *reactive schizophrenia.*

Treatment in the hospital nowadays can take any or all of three forms. One is *drug therapy.* In some cases, particularly when the patient is somewhat agitated, the appropriate drugs can cause full or partial remission. (In partial remission, the patient is at home some of the time and in the hospital some of the time.) A second approach is to provide a more normal *social environment* in the hospital—helping patients form friendships, having them participate in sports and dances, and permitting them to spend time at home with their families and friends. A third approach is to *motivate* the patient to do things for which he is rewarded. One form of this treatment is the "token economy," which will be described later.

Involutional Reactions
Whereas schizophrenia is a psychosis that develops mainly in young people, involutional psychosis begins later in life. It may occur in women during menopause—known as the involutional period, and hence the name—at 45 to 55 years of age. In men, the onset is more often at 55 to 65.

The behavioral symptoms that occur in involutional reactions are of two main types: paranoia and agitated depression. In the paranoid type, the symptoms are similar to the paranoid reactions described earlier. Agitated depression is characterized by crying, moaning, wailing, restless pacing, wringing of the hands, and attacks on one's own body—hair pulling, for example.

Despite the fact that involutional reactions tend to appear at a time when physiological changes are going on in the body, their causes seem to be mainly psychological. The period of life involved is a time of crisis for both men and women. For some women, menopause is a sign that life is coming to an end and that their sexual attractiveness is fading. By the time of menopause, many of the adjustments a woman has made previously are no longer appropriate. For instance, after years of having children at home, suddenly, it seems, they are grown, and the mother may feel lonely and left out. Men too may fear that the approach of old age means the end of sexual attractiveness and the end of the job which has given them purpose and identity. For both men and women, worries about financial security in old age, regrets over opportunities lost, and so on, may become intense.

The depressed patient tends to blame himself for the predicament he is in, whereas the paranoid patient blames others. The outlook for a cure is fairly good for the depressed reaction, although some degree of depression may last for years. Various drugs, as well as electroshock therapy, frequently help. Hope for paranoid patients is not so good; they frequently deteriorate as they grow older.

Chronic Brain Syndromes

The psychoses described so far have sometimes been called *functional* psychoses, meaning that nothing is physically wrong with the patient, that his disorder is a matter of psychological function. In contrast, the *organic* psychoses are caused by an organic disorder. Since in the end the brain is the organ that is always affected, these psychoses are also called chronic brain syndromes.

They can result from all sorts of brain damage: physical blows to the head, disturbances of the blood supply to the brain, brain tumors, disorders of metabolism, physical changes in the brain with old age, and chemical agents such as poison, drugs, or alcohol. Two types of damage are by far the most common. One is *senile psychosis* caused by physical changes in the brain with old age; the other is *intoxication psychosis* caused by the overuse of alcohol.

Senile psychosis Old people may develop psychotic behavior that is characterized by delusions, defects of memory, and general disorientation. For example, a person may think that he has been talking to someone who really was not there. Or he may imagine that people are boring holes in his head. As his memory grows worse, he may forget what he has just said, and at the same time remember things which never happened. Frequently in senile psychosis the person hardly knows where he is, where he has been, or what is going on; he is generally disoriented.

Senile psychosis is due to brain damage, which may be caused by general deterioration of the brain. Apparently as we grow older we are constantly losing nerve cells that are not replaced—a process which speeds up in old age, in some people more than others. The damage may also be due to impaired circulation of blood to the brain. In so-called "hardening of the arteries," fatty deposits gradually stop up blood vessels. Nerve cells, being starved for oxygen and nutrition, then die.

Intoxication psychosis (alcohol)   The long-term effects of heavy drinking—a pint to a fifth a day for 10 to 30 years—can bring on this psychosis. (It is not the same as *delerium tremens,* which occurs in the wake of acute alcoholic intoxication.) The symptoms include disorientation, confusion, memory disorders, and impulsiveness. Similar symptoms can arise whenever there is any widespread damage to the cerebral cortex. A severe concussion, for example, may produce essentially the same behavior.

Hospital Admissions

What kinds of patients are committed to mental hospitals? Figure 11.2 gives statistics based on more than 175,000 persons admitted to state and county mental hospitals in the year 1968 (National Institute of Mental Health). There you can see that the psychotic reactions, including chronic brain syndromes, account for about half of all patients entering the hospital for the first time. Personality disorders (discussed in the next section) make up about 25 percent of admissions. Actually, the great bulk of personality disorders are not severe enough to require hospitalization. Nor do most psychoneurotic patients end up in mental hospitals. Still, there are enough acute neuroses to account for about 10 percent of first admissions.

Note that the statistics in Figure 11.2 are for first *admissions;* they do not show what hospital *populations* are like. In these populations the schizophrenic disorders, which account for the major share of the psychotic reactions, are usually the largest single category. That is because schizophrenia tends to develop early in life, and therapies so far are relatively unsuccessful, although the prospects seem to be improving. As mentioned earlier, schizophrenics tend to live in hospitals for many years of their lives. The next largest group in mental hospitals are patients with chronic brain syndromes, most of them senile cases who are old when they enter and live on in the hospital for a few years. Psychoneurotics and people with personality disorders are a minority in hospital populations, because many of these improve fairly rapidly and can be discharged.

PERSONALITY DISORDERS

Some of the symptoms of a personality disorder resemble those of psychosis, but the person maintains contact with reality—he does not,

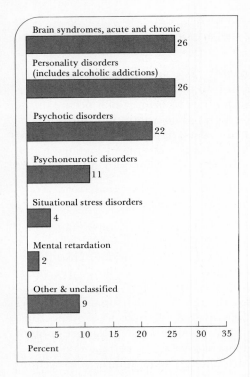

Figure 11.2 Most patients who are admitted for the first time to mental hospitals have brain syndromes, personality disorders, or psychotic disorders. (Biometry Branch, National Institute of Mental Health.)

for example, have delusions or hallucinations. Such a person would usually be termed "odd" by the layman. His main problem is that he had developed deviant lifelong personality traits. A few of them are described in this section.

Schizoid Personality

In some respects a person with a schizoid personality is like a schizophrenic, but he has not developed delusions. Some psychologists would say that he is a person with the genetic predisposition for schizophrenia who has not suffered the stresses which precipitate the full-fledged disorder. However that may be, the schizoid is characterized by withdrawal from other people, eccentric thinking, and a lack of normal aggressiveness in his relations with others. The general picture is that of the eccentric fellow who lives in a back room down the block and is rarely seen in the neighborhood, preferring to come and go when people are not about. Descriptions of skyjackers and political assassins usually fit the picture of schizoid personalities. A formal description of schizoid patients in *The Diagnostic and Statistical Manual* speaks of their

. . . coldness, aloofness, emotional detachment, fearfulness, avoidance of competition, and day dreams revolving around the need for omnipotence. As children, they were usually quiet, shy, obedient, sensitive, and retiring. At puberty, they frequently become more withdrawn, then manifesting the aggregate of personality traits known as introversion, namely, quietness, seclusiveness, "shut-inness," and unsociability, often with eccentricity. (American Psychiatric Association, 1952, page 35.)

Passive and Aggressive Personalities

Three varieties of passive and aggressive personalities are commonly described: passive-dependent, passive-aggressive, and aggressive. The *passive-dependent* person clings to others in the same way that a dependent child clings to adults. He is helpless, and he expects and wants other people to dominate him.

The *passive-aggressive* person expresses his feelings of rebellion and resentment by passive means such as "pouting, stubbornness, procrastination, inefficiency, and passive obstruction" (American Psychiatric Association, 1952). This description fits some members of certain protest movements witnessed in recent years, although they are probably more conscious of their obstructive tactics than the typical passive-aggressive person.

The *aggressive* person burns with resentment and irritability. He is prone to temper tantrums and violent attacks as he acts out his hostility by striking at the world. He can be extremely dangerous, especially if his attacks often come without any visible provocation.

Antisocial Reaction

People in this category have little feeling for others or for the rights of others. They display no sense of responsibility, loyalty, or conscience. Older terms for the antisocial personality are the "morally insane" and the "psychopathic deviate." The antisocial person, although adept at rationalizing his immoral behavior, lacks any responsibility for living "by the rules" of society and frequently winds up in jail.

One variation of this disorder is the suave "con man," superficially convincing, glib, even charming, but not at all constrained by conscience. Another antisocial pattern is the person who acts impulsively without regard for his obligations to others. One day a New York bus driver, bored with his route, drove across the George Washington Bridge and continued down the East Coast to Florida. When picked up by the police, he explained his 1,500-mile trip by saying, "I just wanted to get away from New York" (Kisker, 1964, page 231). Then there is the case of the gas station owner who, after his Coke machine took his money without delivering a Coke, shot the machine with his gun.

What causes such behavior? No one really knows. Certainly the learning experiences of the antisocial person have not given him a sense of responsibility, a sense of self, a conscience, or a tolerance of anxiety—the things healthy people have learned.

Drug Dependency

Excessive dependence on drugs, an important category of the behavior disorders, takes two forms: *addiction* and *habituation.* The major differences between the two are shown in Table 11.1. In both cases the person has a need for the drug. But in addiction, a physical need develops; the physiology of the body is so changed that *withdrawal symptoms* occur when use of the drug is stopped. An addicted person deprived of his drug can become so agitated, depressed, or otherwise miserable that he can think of nothing but getting another dose. The need for the drug has become a powerful physiological drive.

Some drugs, such as heroin, are strongly addictive—after a few doses or a period of days on these drugs, the person is "hooked." Other drugs, such as marijuana, do not seem to be addictive; their intermittent use produces habituation but not addiction. However, almost any

TABLE 11.1
Drug addiction versus drug habituation.

Drug addiction	Drug habituation
Drug addiction is a state of periodic or chronic intoxication produced by the repeated consumption of a drug (natural or synthetic). Its characteristics are:	Drug habituation is a condition resulting from the repeated consumption of a drug. Its characteristics are:
1 An overpowering desire or need (compulsion) to continue taking the drug and to obtain it by any means	1 A desire (but not a compulsion) to continue taking the drug for the sense of improved well-being or effect it produces
2 A tendency to increase the dose	2 Little or no tendency to increase the dose
3 A psychic (psychological) and generally a physical dependence on the effects of the drug	3 Some psychic dependence on the effect of the drug, but no physical dependence and hence no abstinence syndrome
4 A detrimental effect on the individual and on society	4 Detrimental effects, if any, primarily on the individual

Source: After Jones, Shainberg, and Byer, Drugs and Alcohol *(Harper & Row, 1969). (Modified from Seevers, 1962.)*

drug taken in quantity over a long period changes the physiology of the body so that the need for it becomes an addiction. Even the caffeine in coffee, Coke, and Dr. Pepper can become addictive.

The most common drug dependency in the United States today is, of course, dependence on alcohol. Whether a person's dependency is considered habituation or addiction depends on how much he drinks. The line between the "heavy drinker" and alcoholism, however, is not easy to draw. If a person depends on alcohol to "solve" basic problems of adjustment but is not regularly drunk, he has a habituated dependency on it. If he is constantly or regularly drunk and craves liquor when he is briefly without it, he is an alcoholic addict. Why people become alcohol-dependent has not yet been determined. The problem is the subject of increasing research, but it will probably be some years before science has a clear answer.

For most people, the occasional use of nonaddictive drugs does not create dependency. For others, drugs like alcohol become crutches for calming anxieties and releasing strong needs. There is not yet enough data concerning dependency on nonlegal drugs such as LSD and marijuana to say how many people are becoming dependent on them or how the dependency starts.

PSYCHOTHERAPY

Therapy is the name used for any attempt to treat a disease or disorder. Most therapy for behavior disorders employs psychological techniques and is therefore called *psychotherapy*. In certain behavior disorders, however, medical treatment has also proved effective and so will be described in this section.

The Problem of Validity
It is an axiom of medical practice that half to two-thirds of patients with physical illnesses recover at about the same rate whether they see a doctor or not. This fact makes it difficult to assess the effectiveness of medical treatment.

A similar problem arises in assessing therapies for the behavior disorders. People with psychological problems often get over them in the course of time, so how do we know whether any particular form of therapy is working? This question poses the problem of validity, which is similar in principle to the validity problem encountered in constructing and evaluating tests (page 212).

To answer the question, some sort of *control* data are needed. One kind of control is a *base rate* consisting of the number of patients who get well or improve without any treatment at all. This number can then be compared with the number of patients who get well when given treatment. In the case of medical therapies conducted in hospitals, the base rate can be the rate of patient remissions (discharges) without treatment. The history of the particular patients being treated is also important. If a patient has been in a hospital for many years without improvement, and if a new treatment helps him enough to permit his discharge, and if the same improvement occurs in many patients, then we can feel sure that the new treatment has some validity: it substantially increases the number of improved patients.

To study the validity of therapy for patients treated outside the hospital, we need to get ratings of their improvement as well as ratings of improvement in a control group who have the same problems but are not receiving treatment. Unfortunately, most psychotherapists *must* believe in their therapeutic attempts; otherwise they would quit. Believing their techniques to be effective, they do not bring themselves to test for validity. But several validity studies have been made, and unfortunately, the results are not encouraging for the traditional forms of interview therapy such as psychoanalysis (see Mischel, 1968). In general, these studies show that some patients in psychotherapy get better, some get worse, and some change very little, so that the average outcome is no better than the outcomes of untreated groups.

In recent years all sorts of new therapeutic methods have sprung up—primal therapy, psychosynthesis, psychocybernetics, and encounter groups, to name a few. Since the validity of these methods is at present unknown, they will not be covered here. This section will treat certain medical therapies, psychoanalysis, client-centered therapy, behavior modification, and various group therapies.

Medical Therapy

Drugs, surgery, or other physical means are used to treat the patient in medical therapy, which is practiced only by psychiatrists who hold the M.D. degree and who are trained in these techniques. The two forms of medical treatment most widely employed in behavior disorders today are electroshock therapy and drug therapy.

Electroshock   In electroshock therapy a patient is put through a series of convulsions, typically three or four times a week up to a total of 20 treatments. Each treatment consists of a brief, carefully regulated jolt of electrical current passed through the brain. It causes a convulsion followed by a period of unconsciousness, but except for slight feelings of apprehension before the shock, a patient has no unpleasant memory connected with it. Indeed, he has little memory of the events immediately preceding the shock session.

Electroshock therapy seems to be most effective with individuals suffering from depression; often it alleviates their guilt feelings, suicidal tendencies, and feelings of worthlessness. Sometimes the patients seem entirely normal after a series of electroshock treatments and can be discharged without further therapy. Shock treatment is frequently combined with psychotherapy, since in many cases the electroshock leaves the patient lucid enough to make progress through psychological treatment. Even if a depressed patient would snap out of his depression in time, electroshock often hastens his recovery.

Drugs Psychiatrists have long employed drugs as aids to psychotherapy, often with questionable results. But today drugs such as the tranquilizers, antidepressants, and others discovered recently have been so effective in severe disorders that they constitute a major therapeutic breakthrough. The tranquilizers quiet a person's anxieties and keep him from feeling so miserable. They do not, of course, get at the cause of his anxiety, but they can keep under control the agitated behavior that brought him to the hospital and so can make it possible to release him. They also frequently enable him to undergo psychotherapy. It does sometimes happen that these drugs are "overused," because they are convenient and require so little staff to administer.

Thus medical therapy and psychotherapy can be combined in the treatment of some disorders. In other cases the two forms of therapy are used separately because they are effective with different kinds of patients. Psychotherapy is practiced primarily with the less severe disorders—the psychoneuroses. Medical therapy, on the other hand, is used more widely with severely disturbed psychotic patients who have been admitted to mental hospitals. The rest of this section will discuss psychotherapy.

Psychoanalysis

Psychiatrists practiced psychotherapy for years before the advent of Freud. The typical non-Freudian psychiatrist dispensed, and still dispenses, what has been called *directive* therapy. He talks with the patient about his problems and gives advice on the best ways of handling them, often issuing fairly direct instructions to do certain things in certain situations. Much of the counseling now performed by psychologists is also directive.

Freud produced a major revolution in psychiatry with his concept of repression and his techniques for dealing with it. His basic assumption was that a patient, usually a neurotic patient, is beset with unconscious conflicts. The patient does not understand the conflicts, which stem from early experiences, because he has repressed the memories connected with them. The aim of psychoanalysis is to help him acquire insight into his emotional conflicts, thereby gaining relief from anxiety and/or finding healthier ways to react in conflict-related situations. In other words, the attempt is to take someone who, because of repression, is stupid about the sources of his anxiety and to "wise him up" (Dollard and Miller, 1950). As the previous section explained, the validity of psychoanalysis has not been proved. Also, most psycho-analytic therapy requires four or five hours a week for many months or even years. Therefore only people with the money and the time for long treatment can afford it.

Free association   Psychoanalysis begins with the therapist's ex-planation of its general procedure and aims. The patient is told that he should not expect recovery in a specific period of time, that his attitude may depend on emotional factors of which he is unaware, and that these must be traced back to their unconscious motivations. The method of doing this will be *free association*, in which the patient must say whatever he thinks, regardless of how irrelevant or objectionable it may be. A patient often takes some time to "learn" to associate freely. To make it easier for him, he frequently lies on a couch facing away from the analyst so that he will be relaxed and undistracted by the therapist's presence.

Resistance   During free association the patient often shows signs of *resistance*, which is an inability to remember important events in his past or to talk about certain anxiety-charged subjects. These signs of resistance are grist for the analysis. From them the therapist gets clues about the patient's motivational conflict. He then makes a tentative interpretation of them to help the patient continue his free association. Eventually the patient overcomes his resistances and talks freely about the subjects they involve.

Dreams   The patient is asked to report his dreams at any time in the analysis, since dreams are supposed to be shortcuts to the uncon-scious. They are interpreted as *disguised fulfillment of wishes* and therefore cannot be taken at face value. Rather, the analyst interprets them according to principles developed in psychoanalysis.

Transference   During the course of psychoanalysis, the patient generalizes to the therapist the attitudes he acquired toward other people in childhood. This *transference* appears at a time when the therapist and the patient have established good rapport. The therapist may become a *father figure* and be regarded by the patient with the same emotions as those he felt toward his father. These emotional attitudes may be either positive or negative.

To the analyst, transference is significant in two ways. First, if it is positive, it gives the patient a feeling that he is protected and so makes it easier for him to overcome his resistances. Secondly, it helps the analyst understand the patient's problem. The transference substitutes a conflict between the patient and the therapist for a conflict that has gone on within the patient and thus brings the problem out where the therapist can look at it.

The last stages of analysis are reached when the patient appears to have insight into the sources of his anxieties. But psychoanalysis cannot be ended until the transference situation has been broken up and a normal doctor-patient relationship is restored. This is sometimes a very difficult achievement.

Client-Centered Therapy

Like psychoanalysis, client-centered therapy takes place in an interview; it is a "talking" therapy rather than a behavior therapy like those that will be described in the next section. But it has different and simpler assumptions than psychoanalysis (Rogers, 1951); in fact, it is not based on any personality theory at all. The therapist simply attempts to get the person to talk about his problems, with the idea that the talking, aided by warmth and friendliness, will help him work them out. This kind of therapy seems to have some validity; at least, many patients show improvement in the way they regard themselves (Truax and Carkhuff, 1965).

Client-centered therapy begins with the counselor's explanation of the roles he and the client will play in order to work out the patient's difficulties together. The therapist takes pains to establish a relationship that is warm and permissive. He puts no pressure on the patient to follow any prescribed course, does not criticize or judge what the patient says, and aims mainly to help the patient express his feelings freely. In the process, the client gains the ability to accept his feelings without fear and gradually finds it possible to express feelings that were formerly repressed. He begins to see new relationships among his emotional attitudes. He also comes to react positively to situations in which he used to respond negatively.

Behavior Modification

Therapies based on social behavior theory, which was explained in Chapter 10, are called *behavior modification* therapy (Bandura, 1969). The emphasis is not on gaining insight, as it is in psychoanalysis, or on feelings, as it is in client-centered therapy. Rather, behavior modification therapy focuses on responses in specific situations. In essence, it attempts to use carefully controlled reinforcement (or extinction) to reduce a person's symptoms and teach him more normal ways of behaving. The three kinds of learning (classical conditioning, operant conditioning, and modeling), through which the patient has learned his abnormal behavior, are employed to correct that behavior. The techniques of behavior modification are essentially self-validating, because they focus on behavior change: if the change occurs, the technique has worked.

Counterconditioning   Techniques that use reinforcement as it is used in classical conditioning are called *counterconditioning*. This approach is chosen when the behavior disorder consists of an abnormal response to a stimulus that must have arisen in the patient's learning history. Counterconditioning consists of conditioning a response to stimuli that are *incompatible* with the undesirable response. Here is a case (Raymond, 1956):

> The patient had a strong fetish—he was sexually excited by the sight of baby carriages and women's handbags. He could have satisfactory sexual intercourse with his wife only when imagining handbags. His fetish was a problem, because he often attacked baby carriages. Since other methods of therapy are not generally successful with this type of disorder, counterconditioning was tried. Handbags, baby carriages, and a movie of baby carriages being pushed were used as the conditioned stimuli. At the same time that the patient was shown these stimuli, he was made nauseous by the injection of a drug; the aim was to condition the sight of the sexually exciting objects to nausea. The treatment was successful in removing the fetish. After some days, the patient, referring to the handbags and baby carriages, said over and over, "Take them away." A follow-up 19 months later showed that he had continued to be free of the fetish.

This type of counterconditioning is sometimes called *aversion therapy*. It is often used as the first step in treating alcohol addiction.

Other counterconditioning techniques aim at *desensitization*, which makes the person feel comfortable in situations where he has previously been anxious or fearful. Under special "safe" conditions he is led to face the anxiety- or fear-arousing stimuli so that other responses can be conditioned to them. In a variation of this method, called *reciprocal inhibition*, a mildly fear-producing stimulus is presented to a patient when he is relaxed (Wolpe and Lazarus, 1966). Since relaxation is incompatible with fear, the mild fear can extinguish. When that has happened, progressively stronger fear-producing stimuli can be used, until all fear is gone.

Operant conditioning   In operant conditioning, reinforcement, either positive or negative, is contingent upon what a subject does

Figure 11.3 *An example of the counterconditioning technique called desensitization. The people lying on the mats are looking at color-slide projections designed to help them overcome their fear of dogs. In the early sessions of this experimental study, they viewed slides of small, friendly looking dogs. In later sessions they looked at slides of bigger and bigger dogs. Finally they were exposed to slides showing large, lunging dogs. In this way they learned how to relax in the face of a stimulus that had previously made them afraid. After gaining confidence from looking at the slides, some volunteers could walk up to a leashed dog and pet it. The study was conducted by Judith Sills, a Ph.D. candidate in psychology at The New School. (The New York Times.)*

(page 100). By choosing the appropriate reinforcements and supplying them when a desired response is emitted, an experimenter can shape behavior to produce a large number of the responses. This principle is being used today to eliminate annoying and disruptive responses in cases of psychosis. The case of a schizophrenic woman who had been in the hospital for 9 years makes an interesting example (Ayllon, 1963).

The woman had a number of deviant behaviors: overeating and stealing food, hoarding towels, and wearing up to 25 pounds of clothing in the form of extra layers of garments and a peculiar headdress. All these were eventually eliminated by operant conditioning. Here is how the technique was applied to wearing extra clothing:
The therapist made eating contingent upon the amount of clothing

she wore. She was weighed in before each meal with all her clothes on, and her actual body weight was subtracted from her clothed weight. At first, the level was set at 23 pounds or less of clothing—a reduction of 2 pounds from her usual clothing weight. If she had more than this on, she did not eat. She went hungry for a few meals, but she eventually met the standard. Then the limit was set lower and lower, until after several weeks the clothing weight was stabilized at 3 pounds. Besides taking off her excess clothing, the patient now removed her headdress and began to arrange her clothes more normally.

Modeling   The two actual cases of behavior modification just described adapted basic learning methods to the aims of psychotherapy. One used classical conditioning, the other operant conditioning. A third technique, *modeling* (described in Chapter 10), combines *perceptual learning* with *extinction*. It is especially effective against phobias and abnormal fears. The general idea is that the therapist or model shows the patient by his own behavior that there is nothing to fear. In this way he gradually gets the patient to approach and handle the feared object. The method is illustrated by an experiment with small children (Bandura et al., 1967).

> Preschool children who were intensely afraid of dogs were the subjects. Another child who was not afraid of dogs served as a model. In the course of eight brief sessions, the children watched while the model gradually increased contact with a dog. The model began by petting the dog while it was in its pen, then gradually handled the dog more and more until, in the final session, the model got into the pen with the animal, hugging and feeding it. After the last session, the children were tested for their fear by observing how they behaved toward the dog. Most of them increased their approaches to the animal.

Group Therapies

The therapies described so far are individual therapies: one therapist works with a single patient at a time. This one-to-one relationship is expensive. Besides, individual therapy occurs outside the social situation in which a patient's problems arise. For these two reasons various kinds of group therapy have been devised.

The traditional form of group therapy is to assemble a group of people with problems and have them talk with each other under the guidance of a therapist. The therapist tries to keep the discussion focused on certain topics without himself dominating the conversation. Mostly he wants to get group members to talk about their own problems and then have other members comment, so that each member gradually contributes some of his own experiences, attitudes, and feelings. The aim is to help the members look at interpersonal situations from different points of view. In this way a person may get rid of feelings of isolation or rejection, overcome self-consciousness, relax too strict a conscience, give vent to aggression, or in general learn more satisfactory ways of behaving in social situations.

In recent years other forms of group therapy have been tried. The *T(training)-group method*, like traditional group therapy, employs conversation among group members, but it is more highly structured than the traditional form. Another method, the *encounter group*, involves physical contact among members as well as talk. The aim of these methods is to get people to drop the "facades" they frequently hide behind. In the early sessions of such groups, negative attitudes, aggressive behavior, and confrontations between people are common. The idea is to work through these negative feelings by seeing how each person appears to other people. As people come to know each other better, their negative feelings give way to positive ones. Then people who felt lonely may begin to be accepted warmly by others. That, at least, is one of the major goals of the group encounter.

We do not know how well any of the group therapies actually work. We only know that many people who go through them feel helped by them. But so do people who go to doctors and get placebos ("sugar pills"). It remains to be seen whether group therapies have any scientific validity.

Token Economies

Another kind of group therapy, the *token economy*, does have some validity, for it can produce remarkable changes in behavior. Like behavior modification, the token economy is based on learning principles. In the hospital ward, tokens are used for money to purchase

Figure 11.4 *Emotions often run high in encounter-group sessions. (Hella Hammid.)*

things the patients want: more privacy, leave from the hospital, or little luxuries. Obtaining tokens is made contingent on the patient's doing certain things, including work. Thus the basic principle of operant conditioning, *contingent reinforcement*, is used in the management and treatment of patients, and the hospital becomes much more like the outside world. One study of the token economy was done with 44 schizophrenics (Ayllon and Azrin, 1968).

The patients were paid in tokens for serving in such jobs as waitress, janitor, recreational assistant, secretarial assistant, and so on. As they got used to the new system, their work output gradually increased to a satisfactory level (see Figure 11.5).

Then, as a test of the value of contingent reinforcement, the same number of tokens they had been earning was given to them regardless of how much they worked. In other words, tokens were made *noncontingent* on performance. As the graph shows, their work dropped drastically to almost nothing. After this test the tokens were again made contingent on their output, and the amount of work the patients did jumped back to its previous level.

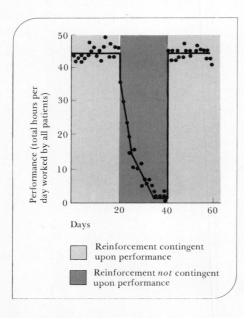

Figure 11.5   *The token economy is a successful form of therapy, as shown by this experiment with a group of 44 schizophrenics. For 20 days they were "paid" in tokens for doing certain jobs in the hospital ward. With the tokens they could buy privileges and small luxuries. Then the system was changed: they were just given the tokens, whether they worked or not. Work fell off to almost nothing. But when they were required to work for tokens again, their output improved to the old level. In a token economy patients do not simply sit and deteriorate, but relearn behavior that will fit them for life outside the hospital. (Modified from Ayllon, T., and Azrin, N. H. The measurement and reinforcement of behavior of psychotics. Journal of the Experimental Analysis of Behavior, 1965, 8, 357–383. Copyright © 1965 by the Society for the Experimental Analysis of Behavior, Inc. Additional information and related experiments can be found in The Token Economy: A Motivational System for Therapy and Rehabilitation, by T. Ayllon and N. H. Azrin, published by Appleton-Century-Crofts, 1968.)*

Because they work so well, token economies are being introduced in more and more mental hospitals. Instead of just sitting and deteriorating, as they often did in the past, patients in a token economy relearn behaviors that will fit them for life outside the hospital. This technique, combined with other therapies, is helping to reduce the number of people staying in mental hospitals.

SUMMARY

Abnormal behavior can be divided into three main categories: psychoneurotic reactions, psychotic reactions, and personality disorders.

Psychoneurotic reactions are mild disorders not usually requiring hospitalization. They consist of anxiety reactions, in which anxiety is prominent; phobic reactions, which are irrational fear responses; obsessive-compulsive reactions, in which some idea or act constantly intrudes; conversion reactions, which convert a conflict into a physical, but not real, disorder; dissociative reactions, marked by amnesia for certain events; and depressive reactions.

Psychotic reactions are severe disorders often requiring hospitalization. Among the psychoses the affective reactions are disorders of mood expressed as extreme mania, depression, or both at different times. In paranoid reactions, a person is suspicious of other people and suffers from delusions of persecution or grandeur. Schizophrenic reactions, the most prevalent of the psychotic reactions, consist of disorders of thought and feeling accompanied by withdrawal from reality. Involutional reactions sometimes occur with "change of life" and may take the form of depression or paranoia. The principal chronic brain syndromes are senile psychosis and intoxication psychosis (the result of prolonged alcoholism).

Personality disorders fall into four principal groups: the schizoid personality, marked by "loner" tendencies and peculiar behavior; passive and aggressive personalities; antisocial reactions, in which a person acts irresponsibly and without conscience; and drug dependencies.

Many forms of therapy have been devised for behavior disorders. Most of them lack established validity. Medical therapies that sometimes prove effective for certain cases include electroshock and drug therapies. Psychoanalysis utilizes free association and dream analysis in an attempt to produce insight into unconscious conflicts. In client-centered therapy, a patient tries to work out his problems by freely expressing his feelings to the therapist. Behavior modification applies the principles of learning to the task of changing behaviors that occur in specific situations. It uses the three main techniques of counterconditioning, operant conditioning, and modeling. In group therapies, the aim is to improve a person's social behavior by having him talk about his problems with other people who also have problems. Token economies are arrangements in hospital wards that "pay" a person with tokens for doing work and behaving in more normal ways. The tokens can then be exchanged for things or privileges the patient wants.

SUGGESTIONS FOR FURTHER READING

Buss, A. H. *Psychopathology.* New York: Wiley, 1966. *A text emphasizing theories of behavior disorder.*

Coleman, J. C. *Abnormal psychology and modern life.* (3d ed.) Chicago: Scott, Foresman, 1964. *A popular textbook on abnormal psychology.*

Harper, R. A. *Psychoanalysis and psychotherapy.* Englewood Cliffs, N.J.: Prentice-Hall, 1959. (Paperback.) *A succinct summary of several systems of psychotherapy.*

Mischel, W. *Personality and assessment.* New York: Wiley, 1968. *An appraisal of personality assessment and psychotherapy, with descriptions of social behavior theory applied in psychotherapy.*

Rabkin, L. Y., and Carr, J. E. (Eds.) *Sourcebook in abnormal psychology.* Boston: Houghton Mifflin, 1967. *A selection of stimulating articles on the behavior disorders and psychotherapy.*

Rogers, C. R. *On becoming a person: A therapist's view of psychotherapy.* Boston: Houghton Mifflin, 1961. *A personal account, by the founder of the method, of the processes involved in client-centered therapy.*

Wiener, D. N. *A practical guide to psychotherapy.* New York: Harper & Row, 1968. *A helpful book describing systems of psychotherapy and ways of finding a psychotherapist if you need one.*

PART III

Group Processes

The chapters up to this point have stressed the behavior of individuals in particular situations. Some of these situations involved other people and thus concerned social behavior. In this part, however, the emphasis will be on social behavior itself—on the reactions of people to other people. The material is divided into two chapters. Chapter 12 discusses attitudes, and Chapter 13 looks at behavior in groups.

An attitude, like a thought, is not itself behavior. Rather it is a potential for behavior. It is a readiness to react in a certain way. If we know what that readiness is, we have a pretty good idea of what the behavior will be. Thus it is important to understand the nature of attitudes, how they develop in early childhood through young adulthood, and how they change or resist change when persuaders attempt to change them. Chapter 12 describes how prejudices are acquired and the social harm they cause.

Chapter 13, on social groups, shows how groups form social structures in which people are expected to play particular roles. How and why people learn conforming behavior is then discussed. This chapter concludes with an analysis of the factors involved in our liking and disliking other people.

12

Attitudes and Social Conflict

LEARNING OBJECTIVES

Main objective

After studying this chapter you should be able to describe the nature of an attitude and the general way in which attitudes develop.

Other major objectives

You should also be able to

Describe the ways in which attitudes can be measured.

Trace the influences operating at different ages on the development of attitudes.

Outline the factors that affect attitude changes on specific issues.

Explain how prejudices are acquired and maintained.

Minor objectives

Give three characteristics of an attitude source that affect the changing of an attitude.

List four characteristics of a message that determine its effectiveness.

Describe three characteristics of a person that affect how much his attitude may be changed by a message.

We cannot see attitudes directly; we infer them from the things people do. Invisible though they are, attitudes have a powerful influence on people's likes and dislikes. A businessman needs favorable attitudes to keep his company going. A politician needs favorable attitudes to get elected. And all of us try much of the time to creat favorable attitudes in the people we meet.

NATURE OF ATTITUDES

This first section of the chapter will define a few terms, describe a modern theory of attitudes, and explain how attitudes are measured.

Definitions

An attitude is a tendency *to respond to some person, object, or situation in a positive or negative way.* To simplify the discussion, the word *object* will stand for whatever an attitude is directed toward. Think of this object as a learned goal—positive or negative—because attitudes are learned just as other behavior is learned. Like other personality characteristics, they may be learned through classical or operant conditioning, or through observational learning and modeling (page 249). Attitudes are, in fact, part of an individual's personality characteristics.

An attitude has both an emotional and an intellectual component (Fishbein and Ajzen, 1972). The emotional component is a feeling of being for or against, liking or disliking, or approaching or avoiding the object of the attitude. The intellectual component of the attitude is a *belief* about the object. A belief is the *acceptance of a statement.* If you have an unfavorable attitude toward something, you will also have a belief or beliefs about it. The belief may be a vague statement, such as "*A* is bad," or it may be more specific, such as "Inflation leads to high taxes."

The belief aspect of an attitude affects its emotional component, and vice versa. If a person comes to believe that the Establishment works in the interest of large corporations and against the rights of minorities, he acquires a negative emotional reaction to the Establishment. Or if he starts out with negative feelings about the Establishment, he is more likely to accept statements—adopt beliefs—about it that are unfavorable. So although there is a difference between attitudes and beliefs, they go hand in hand. Beliefs are the verbalized statements that accompany the emotional aspects of attitudes. This does not apply to all beliefs, of course. Some are not connected with attitudes; for example, "The world is round." To separate the two kinds of beliefs, the word *opinion* is used to indicate a belief associated with an attitude.

The term *prejudice* refers to an attitude that is unjustified—"prejudice" comes from "pre-judgment." To some extent all attitudes are prejudices, because we seldom have enough firsthand information to fully justify our attitudes. But when attitudes are fairly strong, usually in the unfavorable direction, and are clearly not in line with the facts, they are called prejudices.

Attitude Theory

A great deal is known about the specific factors that cause attitudes to be formed and to change. Much of this chapter is about such changes. Psychologists naturally have tried to devise theories to account for the many known facts. So far, no single explanation fits all the facts (Feshbein and Ajzen, 1972), but one general theory, known as *consistency theory*, is gaining wide acceptance. The basic idea of the theory is that an attitude provides some consistency for response tendencies that otherwise would be incongruous or inconsistent. Take an example:

> Suppose Mr. Smith has a new neighbor, Mr. Jones. Soon after their first meeting, Smith hears Jones say some kind words about the last President Johnson. Knowing only this, Smith classifies Jones as a Democrat. Smith has previously formed beliefs about Democrats: He thinks they favor high taxes and socialism, goals toward which he has unfavorable attitudes. Out of this "generalization" Smith forms a mild dislike for Jones. Later on, however, Smith learns that Jones is a good father, a helpful neighbor, and a regular churchgoer—all of which Smith regards favorably. What is Smith's attitude toward Jones now?

Attitude averaging A model that fits this example and many other data has been called the *attitude averaging model* (Anderson, 1968). Smith's unfavorable attitude toward Jones as a Democrat is averaged out with his favorable attitudes toward Jones as a father, neighbor, and churchgoer. Some people can verbalize two attitudes simultaneously toward the same object—regard Jones favorably in one respect and unfavorably in another—but mostly they don't. Instead, their attitude toward an object has one dimension. On this dimension the different components of the attitude add and subtract from each other to produce an attitude with a certain degree of favorableness or unfavorableness. In the end, Smith feels mildly favorable toward Jones for his "good traits," but not quite so favorable as he would if he did not regard Jones as a Democrat.

Cognitive dissonance The averaging model is supported by considerable research (Anderson, 1970). There are two kinds of situations, however, in which something more than simple averaging is involved. In one, a large discrepancy exists between the favorable and unfavorable components of an attitude. In the other, a person is forced to make a choice between two objects about which he has mixed feelings. In both situations *cognitive dissonance* is aroused (Festinger, 1957). The person recognizes a discrepancy between two or more things that he knows about an object. Such a discrepancy, or dissonance, as it is called, is not tolerated; he feels impelled to reduce the dissonance by "making things fit." To return to Smith and Jones:

> Suppose that Smith, as he comes to know more about Jones, hears that Jones is a crooked businessman—something about which Smith has a very unfavorable attitude. How can this fact (belief) be made to fit with the favorable categories of good neighbor and churchgoer? It is hard to resolve the discrepancy by saying, "He's crooked, but otherwise a fine person." Smith is more likely to think, "Jones goes to church to make people think he's not crooked," and "He's nice to me as a neighbor in order to get my business." In this way Smith revises his beliefs—his interpretation of the facts—to make them fit with his highly unfavorable attitude toward Jones as a crooked businessman.

In the second kind of situation in which attitudes are revised rather than averaged, a person must commit himself to one of two objects toward which he has mixed attitudes (Brehm and Cohen, 1962).

> Suppose a man is thinking of buying either a sedan or a station wagon. He carefully considers the merits of each and finds certain features of both attractive. Then he settles on a station wagon. But having made the choice, he is bothered by perceptions of dissonance between the good features of the rejected sedan and those of the wagon. To reduce this dissonance he alters his attitudes so that he emphasizes the "bad" features of the sedan and the "good" features of the wagon. He may also begin to pay closer attention to advertisements of station wagons, especially his own brand, to convince himself that he has made the correct choice. Thus he modifies his attitudes and beliefs to fit with the decision he has made.

Measuring Attitudes

Psychologists have developed many scales, constructed much like personality questionnaires, for measuring a great number of attitudes. Each scale consists of a group of statements related to a particular attitude. Some scales ask the person to respond by indicating whether he agrees or disagrees with each statement. Then, because the statements have been previously calibrated, a certain number of points can be assigned to each, and a score can be calculated (see Table 12.1). Other scales ask the person to specify the *degree* of his agreement with a statement. Say, he might be asked to assign the value 7 to a statement he completely agrees with or 1 to a statement he totally disagrees with. A value of 4, then, would mean that he partly disagrees and partly agrees, or that he has no strong feelings one way or the other.

Scales and norms have been developed for measuring attitudes toward such things as family, education, religion, sex, health, politics,

Table 12.1
Statements from a scale for measuring attitudes toward war.
The person indicates whether he agrees or disagrees with each
statement, which has a scale value that is used to arrive at his
total score. Low scale values represent prowar statements; high
scale values antiwar statements.

Scale value	Statement
1.3	1. A country cannot amount to much without a national honor, and war is the only means of preserving it.
2.5	2. When war is declared, we must enlist.
5.2	3. Wars are justifiable only when waged in defense of weaker nations.
5.6	4. The most that we can hope to accomplish is the partial elimination of war.
8.4	5. The disrespect for human life and rights involved in a war is a cause of crime waves.
10.6	6. All nations should disarm immediately.

Source: Droba, 1930.

law, ethnic groups, and international affairs (Shaw and Wright, 1967). More general scales, combining items for several attitudes, have been constructed to yield scores on a dimension often called "conservatism versus liberalism." All these scales are used in psychological research to correlate attitudes with other personality variables or study factors in attitude change.

To measure the attitudes of consumers or voters, a different approach is used—the so-called public opinion poll. Here a large number of people are asked only a question or two, because they do not have the time to respond to many items. The questions are chosen so that a person's attitude toward an issue or political candidate can be quickly classified as favorable, unfavorable, or undecided.

There are two major problems in public opinion polling. One is the wording of questions; slight differences in wording often make a large difference in the results. To assess the effects of wording, polling agencies frequently pretest different forms of their questions on small samples of people before deciding on the wording to use in the full-fledged poll.

The second important problem is that of sampling. A poll attempts to measure the attitudes of the population at large by taking a small sample, usually a few hundred to a couple of thousand people. For the poll to be "accurate," the sample must be *representative*. Several differ-ent methods can be used to ensure representative sampling, the most efficient of which is *stratified*. In this approach, the polling agencies set quotas for certain categories of people based on census data. The most common categories are age, sex, socioeconomic status, and geographical region, all of which are known to influence opinions. By seeing to it that the quotas in the sample are in proportion to the categories in the general population, the sample is made more representative.

Even so, polls are only moderately accurate. Pollsters usually estimate that there is a leeway of about 6 percent in their forecasts. When elections are closer than that, as they frequently are, polls are not good predictors. Moreover, when there is a large group of voters who remain undecided up to the last minute, the polls may be very wrong. This was the case in the Dewey-Truman Presidential race of 1948 in the United States and in the Conservative-Labor contest in England in 1970. In both instances most of the undecided votes swung one way instead of splitting down the middle, as the polls had assumed. Good as they are, the polls can't win them all.

DEVELOPMENT OF ATTITUDES

How do attitudes develop from birth to adulthood? To give you an answer, this section will sometimes refer to specific attitudes and often discuss the general dimension of *conservative-liberal* attitudes. A word of warning about this dimension: Attitudes, like the personality characteristics of which they are a part, are not global; they are specific to certain objects and situations. A person can be very conservative in some respects, very liberal in others. His particular pattern of attitudes will depend on his previous learning experiences. Thus to classify him along a single dimension of conservative to liberal is really to average his many different attitudes. Conservative-liberal scales are used in research not to give an exact profile of a person's opinions, but as a simple convenience in obtaining some overall measure of social attitudes (Shaw and Wright, 1967).

With this qualification in mind, let us look at some of the components that go into a scale of conservative-to-liberal attitudes. Here is a list of conservative attitudes: In family matters, the conservative emphasizes strong family ties, with dominant parents and obedient children. In education, he favors practical training against theory. In economic matters, he is for making each person "earn his own way" and tends to favor businessmen over labor leaders. In politics, he opposes big spending by government, objects to programs of public welfare, and favors as little intervention by government as possible. He tends to be nationalistic and objects to international involvements except to fight Communism. He is for strict law enforcement and for severe punishment of criminals. Finally, he tends to be socially prejudiced, or racist, and status-conscious, feeling that his own kind of people are "better" than others.

To define liberal attitudes, it is enough to say that they are the opposite of these conservative attitudes. But remember that each person possesses some mixture of attitudes on the various issues included in a conservative-liberal scale.

Parental Influences

From birth to puberty a child's attitudes are shaped primarily by his parents. When they are interviewed, grammar school children frequently quote their mothers and fathers. They will say things like "Mama tells me not to play with colored children," or "Daddy says black people are lazy."

Studies that compare the attitudes of children and their parents always show a sizable correlation between the two, especially in political and religious attitudes. The following study investigated religious and political affiliations (Jennings and Niemi, 1968).

> A national cross section of 1,669 high school seniors was interviewed. Separately, 1,992 of their parents were surveyed as a check on what the seniors had reported. Some of the questions concerned the religious and political affiliations of the children and of the parents. As in previous studies, the greatest agreement was on religious affiliation: 74 percent of the seniors had the same affiliation (Protestant, Catholic, or Jewish) as their parents. A negligible percentage had shifted to another religion. A similar, but not so strong, agreement was found in political-party affiliation: 60 percent of the students who named a party chose the same one as their parents. Some had shifted to independent status, but less than 10 percent had defected to the other party. Moving back a whole generation, very similar results were obtained for the parents' agreement with their own parents.

Although agreement in such studies is high on religion and political party, it is not so close on specific issues. A child of a Protestant may remain a Protestant, but he is likely to be less fervent or less conservative than his parent. The son of a Republican may remain a Republican, but his attitudes on particular political issues are likely to be more liberal than those of this parents. Even so, there is more overall similarity than dissimilarity between children's and parents' attitudes. Hence children's attitudes show long-lasting effects of parental influence.

Critical Period in Attitude Formation

Parental influences wane as children grow older, and other social influences become increasingly important with the beginning of adolescence. During the period from 12 to 30, most of a person's attitudes take final form and thereafter change rather little. This has been called the *critical period* (Sears, 1969)—the period during which attitudes crystallize. During the critical period three main factors are at work: peer influences, information from news media and other sources, and education.

Peer influence Your peers are the people of the same general age and educational level with whom you associate. What peers think begins to have an effect on attitudes during adolescence, when the individual begins to spend less time at home, less time with his parents, and more time with friends and acquaintances. Peers become powerful influences because we most readily accept as "authorities" the people whom we like and find it easy to talk to.

Information A factor in modern life that has weakened parental influences is the greater availability of information, especially in the form of television. Television vividly portrays events that the adolescent would be only vaguely aware of if he had to depend on newspapers or his parents' conversation. Today young people know more than they used to about what is going on in the world.

Education Of all the factors involved in attitude formation, education consistently stands out. It has as strong an influence on the individual as parental political orientation and religious affiliations. Its importance, of course, depends on how far a person goes in school—but children increasingly go farther than their parents did.

Study after study shows that the more education people have, the more liberal they are. In one recent analysis, 66 percent of college graduates but only 16 percent of grade school graduates held liberal views on civil liberties (Sears, 1969).

Liberalism also correlates with socioeconomic status (Harding et al., 1969). Socioeconomic status, however, is itself a mixture of three variables: income, education, and occupation. The most important of these is education: People high in economic status but low in education tend to be conservative, especially in economic matters. On the other hand, those with high status and high education tend to be liberal.

Adolescence and Young Adulthood

The critical period from 12 to 30 in attitude formation can be divided into two parts: adolescence (12 to 21) and young adulthood (21 to 30). During adolescence, attitudes are being shaped; during young adulthood, they are being crystallized or "frozen." This sequence comes about in the following way.

Commitment An adolescent's attitudes vary quite a bit, and they are not yet strongly held. As a person moves into the twenties, however, he begins to *commit* himself in various ways. He votes in elections, he marries, he finishes his education and chooses a line of work. These commitments, made on the basis of the attitudes he holds at the time, tend to "freeze" the attitudes so that they do not change much afterwards.

Another way of explaining the crystallization of attitudes that occurs in the period of young adulthood is through the concept of cognitive dissonance. As a person learns more and more, he has more information that affects his attitudes. Some of this information is inconsistent. As he commits himself, he arrives at "final" attitudes that are in keeping with his decisions. Thus he reduces his cognitive dissonance.

Conservative drift The permanence of attitudes from the early twenties on throughout life is striking. In one experiment, the attitudes of Bennington college students were surveyed in the late 1930s. Twenty years later, the investigator located most of the women and assessed their attitudes again (Newcomb, 1963). On most issues on the conservative-liberal dimension, he found that they held almost exactly the same views as they had earlier. The only change was that they were slightly more conservative than they had been upon graduating from college. This small drift toward conservatism, which many older people see in themselves, is about the only thing that happens to attitudes once they are crystallized in the twenties.

Generation Changes

Is there really a "generation gap"—a discontinuity between the attitudes and thinking of the younger and older generations—or is it imagined?

Many studies bear on this question. They show that there are indeed differences in the attitudes of the two generations, especially in two general areas. One is that of prejudice: young people are less prejudiced about ethnic groups, such as Negroes and Jews, than their parents are or were at their age. In general, prejudice is on the way down in the United States, especially among the more educated (Harding et al., 1969).

An example is seen in a 30-year study of Princeton students (Karlins et al., 1969). Some of the results are given in Table 12.2. Actually, three different studies were made: one in 1932 (Katz and Braly, 1933); another in 1950 (Gilbert, 1951); and a third in 1967 (Karlins et al., 1969). In each case a representative sample of about 200 white Gentiles was used as subjects. Approximately 80 adjectives (or phrases) were presented to the students, who were asked to select the 5 that they thought best described ten different ethnic groups. Table 12.2 gives the results for five of the groups. It shows that prejudiced attitudes have largely faded out in

Table 12.2
The fading of prejudiced attitudes in Princeton students.

| Group trait | | Students attributing trait to group, % | | |
		1932	1950	1967
Americans:	Industrious	48	30	23
	Intelligent	47	32	20
	Materialistic	33	37	67
	Ambitious	33	21	42
	Pleasure loving	26	27	28
Germans:	Scientifically minded	78	62	47
	Industrious	65	50	59
	Stolid	44	10	9
	Intelligent	32	32	19
	Extremely nationalistic	24	50	43
Japanese:	Intelligent	45	11	20
	Industrious	43	12	57
	Progressive	24	2	17
	Sly	20	21	3
	Imitative	17	24	22
Jews:	Shrewd	79	47	30
	Mercenary	49	28	15
	Industrious	48	29	33
	Grasping	34	17	17
	Ambitious	21	28	48
Negroes:	Superstitious	84	41	13
	Lazy	75	31	26
	Happy-go-lucky	38	17	27
	Ignorant	38	24	11
	Musical	26	33	47

Source: Karlins et al., 1969.

Princeton students. No longer are two or three largely derogatory descriptions applied to a group. Thus on the whole, the students have come to regard different ethnic groups as being made up of people possessing many different traits.

The second general area is in political attitudes, where young people are more liberal than their parents. This conclusion comes out of a large study conducted in the early sixties (Middleton and Putney, 1964). Of nearly 1,500 college students questioned across the country, 33 percent saw themselves as being to the left of their parents, and only 8 percent to the right. About 60 percent called themselves socialists or liberals as compared with 30 percent of their parents. On the other hand, 32 percent considered themselves mildly or strongly conservative, in contrast to 49 percent of their parents. Differences of this sort reflect a clear trend toward liberalism, which for some combinations of parents and children could be called a "gap."

Besides the generation gap there is always talk about students being in rebellion against parental attitudes and restraints. This is sometimes given as the explanation of student activism. To look at the question, surveys were made of the leaders of right- and left-wing organizations at a time when student activism was at its peak (Braungart, 1966).

> The subjects were a sample of 180 students attending a convention of Students for a Democratic Society (left wing) and a sample of 155 attending a convention of Young Americans for Freedom (right wing). The right-wing students, the survey showed, were predominantly Protestant, churchgoers, and middle-class (Braungart, 1966). Their parents most often worked in administrative or clerical jobs and were Republicans or political conservatives. Most of these parents had not graduated from college. In contrast, the left-wing activists were predominantly Jewish or nonreligious, usually were not churchgoers, and came mostly from the upper and upper-middle classes. More often than not, their parents were college graduates in executive and professional occupations. The parents usually belonged to the Democratic party or a liberal party.

Other studies show that student activists on the left have parents who are considerably more liberal than the liberalism found in typical upper-class educated parents (see Flacks, 1967). The "rebellion" of these leftist activists, then, consists of being somewhat more liberal than their parents. And the rightists are being active about the same conservative views held by their parents.

ATTITUDE CHANGE

Although their general attitudes may be well formed, adults are continually acquiring new attitudes, or changing their attitudes, toward specific people and objects. When a new political candidate runs for office, we need to form some attitude toward him. We may simply transfer to him the attitude we have toward his party, but if he is in the "right" party, we must decide between him and another candidate for nomination. Similarly, new issues are always arising in the world, and we must form attitudes about them and the people who are concerned with them.

The attitudes we form are important to other people, especially businessmen and politicians, because our attitudes determine what we buy and how we vote. Many individuals and organizations are busy trying to shape our attitudes in ways favorable to them. Through advertising, political speeches and campaigns, and many other means, a great barrage of "messages" is directed at us day in and day out to change our attitudes. There are three principal aspects of any situation in which attitude change is attempted: (1) the *source* of the message, that is, the person or group trying to work a change, (2) the *message* itself, meaning the statement or appeal used to produce the change, and (3) the characteristics of the person who receives the message—the *recipient.* (These characteristics include his existing attitudes.)

Source of the Message

Three characteristics of the source that strongly affect our response are its credibility, attractiveness, and power.

Credibility   The more reason we have to believe the person sending a message, the more likely he is to persuade us. And if we think he is not telling the truth, he has little chance of changing our attitudes.

What makes somebody credible? One factor is prestige. If a person is a well-known authority on some topic, we are more apt to believe him than if he is just another face in the crowd. Another factor, which becomes important after we have had a chance to check on a person, is whether he has told the truth in the past. If so, we are apt to believe him this time. If we have caught him in the wrong, we are not likely to believe him again. This was the trouble in the 1960s when the Johnson administration was said to have a "credibility gap." Some of the statements made by the administration turned out, for whatever reason, to be wrong. After that, statements by the administration become less credible. In the 1972 Presidential campaign, the McGovern forces made an issue of the credibility of the Nixon administration.

Attractiveness   People who are attractive to us are more likely to sway us than those who are not. Just as attractiveness influences the groups we join (more on this in Chapter 13), so it influences the attitudes we form. The factor of attractiveness can be broken down into three related components: similarity, friendship, and liking.

The more *similar* two people perceive themselves to be, the more inclined they are to believe each other. Women can persuade other women more easily than they can men. A student is more likely to be swayed by another student than by anyone else, including a professor. A workingman is more apt to be persuaded by fellow workingmen than by college professors. Other factors being equal, we tend to be influenced most by people we feel are just like us.

Friendship is also a potent factor in attitude change. We tend, of course, to become friends with people we agree with. Still, the fact that people are our friends makes us want to agree with them and believe what they say. Studies show that this desire is often involved in voting behavior. During the course of a campaign, if a person changes his mind about his vote, it is often in the direction of agreeing with his friends (Kitt and Gleicher, 1950).

Friendships are formed, of course, by mutual *liking*, or attraction but liking is important outside of friendship, too. Dwight Eisenhower was a war hero, but more than that, he was a very likable man. He swept to victory as President on a slogan of "I like Ike," even though he was a member of the minority party. His likableness persuaded many people to vote for him who normally voted Democratic. Experimental studies in which the likableness of the persuader is deliberately varied show the same thing: Attitude changes depend in part on how well we like the person who is trying to persuade us.

Power and prestige   A person in a position of power or prestige is more likely to persuade us than one who is not. Here, however, we must distinguish between private acceptance and superficial compliance (page 319). A powerful or prestige-laden person may get us to go along with him publicly when privately we stick to our own opinion. This was the case with attempts to indoctrinate—"brainwash"— American prisoners during the Korean War. The purpose of brainwashing was to give prisoners favorable attitudes toward Communism. Although many professed to be convinced, most showed no permanent attitude change when they were released. On the other hand, a few soldiers did refuse repatriation. There were also signs of some other attitude changes in some of the prisoners (Schein et al., 1961).

The Message

Persuaders of all sorts work tirelessly on their messages to make them successful in changing attitudes. What can be done to messages to increase their effectiveness?

Suggestion   Advertisers and propagandists often rely on suggestion, or the *uncritical acceptance of a statement.* They design the message in hopes that the person will accept a belief, form an attitude, or be incited to action by someone else's say-so, without requiring facts.

The most common form of suggestion is *prestige suggestion*, in which the message appeals to people's regard for authority or prestige. Advertisers often boast that some famous person uses their product. (This is usually partly true because they pay him to use it.) Politicans frequently refer to Abraham Lincoln, John F. Kennedy, and other respected leaders to promote their ideas. You can see countless examples of prestige suggestion by watching TV for a few hours or by looking at billboards along the highway.

Appeals to fear Another method of persuading people is to try to scare them. Political candidates may claim that if the other side wins, we will have higher taxes, poorer services, inflation, or war. In the 1972 Presidential campaign, for example, Republicans put out estimates that McGovern's proposals would cost an enormous amount of money. Whether true or not, this message certainly scared many voters into believing that a McGovern victory would mean higher taxes. The slogan "Speed kills," seen along many highways, is an attempt to scare people into observing speed limits. (The same slogan is also used to warn people against misusing amphetamine drugs.)

Are scare tactics effective in changing attitudes? The evidence is mixed. Up to a point they tend to work. Fear of injury has induced many people to wear seat belts in American automobiles. Fear of disease frequently impels people to get inoculations. Strong appeals to fear, however, are likely to backlash, since people respond to them with a reaction called *defensive avoidance.* This means that they avoid information put out by the communicator, or they refuse to accept the communicator's conclusions. There is the story of the cigarette smoker who was so upset by newspaper accounts of smoking and lung cancer that he stopped reading the papers.

Loaded words The stock-in-trade of the propagandist is loaded words—words that evoke strong emotional reactions, usually negative. An unfavorable attitude can be created in people by calling an opponent a "Communist," "dictator," "militant," or "revolutionary." In the early 1950s, Senator Joseph McCarthy succeeded in casting suspicion on reputable citizens by calling them Communists. George Wallace, in his campaign for reelection as governor of Alabama in 1970, subtly evoked prejudice by campaigning against the "bloc" vote. And some anti-Nixon politicians in the 1972 campaign called him a "dictator."

Loaded words, of course, are not loaded in themselves. They become loaded when they are used in a certain context, like a political campaign, to arouse unjustified negative feelings. If we happen to agree with the people using them, we may not even notice them. We may simply accept them as good descriptions of the "other side." If we disagree with the people using them, we are more apt to spot them as

Figure 12.1 *(Opposite page) Prestige suggestion (top) and an appeal to fear. (General Motors Corp.; Metropolitan Life.)*

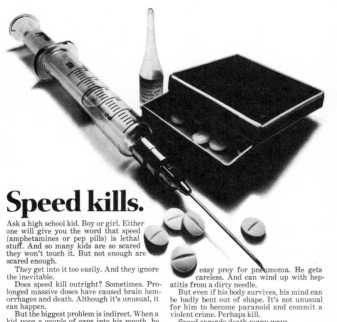

Speed kills.

Ask a high school kid. Boy or girl. Either one will give you the word that speed (amphetamines or pep pills) is lethal stuff. And so many kids are so scared they won't touch it. But not enough are scared enough.

They get into it too easily. And they ignore the inevitable.

Does speed kill outright? Sometimes. Prolonged massive doses have caused brain hemorrhages and death. Although it's unusual, it can happen.

But the biggest problem is indirect. When a kid pops a couple of caps into his mouth, he experiences a real high. When he comes down, he's so low he's tempted to start another run.

And that's the start of real trouble. Speed isn't addictive, but the body builds up a tolerance. So he has to take more to get the same jolt. And more. And more. He often ends up shooting massive doses into his veins.

He has an abnormal feeling of power. Superiority. He can easily become violent and aggressive. If he gets in a car, look out.

In his confused state, he ignores his body's normal need for food, drink and sleep. So he's easy prey for pneumonia. He gets careless. And can wind up with hepatitis from a dirty needle.

But even if his body survives, his mind can be badly bent out of shape. It's not unusual for him to become paranoid and commit a violent crime. Perhaps kill.

Speed spreads death many ways.

If you know anyone who's thinking of experimenting with this stuff, we urge you to have a talk with him. If he's been on it a while, get him to a doctor.

You could save his life.

 Metropolitan Life

Reprints available in limited quantities. Write Metropolitan, Dept. O-99, One Madison Ave., New York, N.Y. 10010.

distortions of the facts. But the person who has no strong attitudes or beliefs on the subject of the message may easily be taken in.

One-sided versus two-sided messages   If you want to convince people of your point of view, is it better to present only one side of the issue or both sides? A lot of research has been done on this question (McGuire, 1968), and the results are not simple. Much depends on the attitudes you are trying to change. A general rule, however, fairly well summarizes the findings: A one-sided approach is effective when people are either neutral or already favorable to the message. A two-sided approach is more likely to win converts from an opposing point of view.

Receiver of the Message

Now we come to the characteristics of the person on the receiving end of the message. What in him creates a tendency for attitude change?

Influenceability   Most personality traits do not correlate with a propensity for attitude change. In other words, we cannot tell from a personality profile whether or not a person would be easily persuaded. We do know, however, that some people are more easily influenced than others. In fact, some people are downright gullible. Bombarded with conflicting viewpoints, they believe the one they have heard most recently. As might be expected, there are group differences in this trait. Women are more easily influenced than men, children more than adults, and poorly educated people more than well-educated ones (McGuire, 1968).

Needs and goals   How well a message gets through to a person depends on his needs. If he has no needs that are related to the message, it will leave little impression on him. But if the message does appeal to his needs, and makes him think he can satisfy one or more of his goals, he is more likely to believe it. In one study, for example (Carlson, 1956), college students changed their unfavorable attitudes toward racially desegregated housing after they were persuaded that it would contribute to certain goals (improving American prestige abroad) and would not interfere with other goals (maintaining property values). In another study (DiVesta and Merwin, 1960), attitudes toward teaching as a career became more favorable in subjects with high achievement motivation when speeches showed the possibilities for achievement in teaching. (In neither study, however, do we know how long the changes lasted.)

Selective interpretation   Whether or not a message influences the recipient also depends on his selective interpretation. In selectively interpreting what we hear, we pay attention to the points that fit with our attitudes and ignore those that do not. This tendency makes us resist changes in attitude. In fact, it is this tendency that helps freeze attitudes early in life. The bigot who thinks that Negroes are dirty notices a black man coming home in dirty work clothes. This confirms his prejudice. A white man in the same state either does not catch his attention or looks to him like a breadwinner coming home after a hard day's work. Suppose a newspaper headline reads: "Congress Appropriates $80 Billion for Armed Forces." If a person is opposed to big government spending, he sees this as more money down the drain. But if he favors a strong national defense, the message he gets is that Congress is providing for his safety. In almost all messages several "facts" are presented; typically we perceive only those that fit in with existing attitudes.

Avoidance of information   In some instances the tendency toward selective interpretation goes even further—the person actively avoids information that disagrees with his attitudes. This is the extreme of defensive avoidance. A confirmed liberal may refuse to read conservative magazines or newspapers. The anti-Semite may avoid virtually all contact with Jews, thus giving himself no chance to acquire information that might change his mind. People in general tend to expose themselves only to the viewpoints they agree with, thereby strengthening the attitudes and beliefs they already hold.

Immunization   In medical practice, a person can be immunized to certain diseases by inoculating him with small doses of them. If we apply this notion to attitudes, can we say that mild exposure to an attitude opposed to his own will immunize a person against stronger attacks on his position? There is some evidence that this takes place. If a person resists mild arguments against his point of view, he is given strength to stand up against strong arguments. If he is not exposed to the mild arguments first, he is more easily shaken by the strong arguments. Thus immunization is one more factor that tends to freeze attitudes, once they are formed. Evidence for immunization comes from studies like this (McGuire, 1961):

> Changes in attitudes toward four commonsense health propositions were measured. (They were propositions most people view favorably, such as "Everyone should get a medical checkup once a year.") Five groups of subjects were used as shown in Figure 12.2. All of them at certain points in the experiment rated their attitudes toward the health propositions on a 15-point scale. Four of the groups were exposed to arguments *against* the health propositions. Of these, three were inoculated by exposure to mild

arguments which they could easily combat. At the end, before the ratings made in Figure 12.2, the four groups were given strong arguments against the propositions. As you can see, the inoculated groups were less swayed by the strong arguments; in fact, they remained about as favorable as the control group, which was given no arguments. The uninoculated group, by contrast, showed a marked shift in attitude in the unfavorable direction.

PREJUDICE AND SOCIAL CONFLICT

Social conflict, as the term is used here, refers to any situation in which two groups or segments of society are emotionally opposed to each other. Usually one group is strong enough in numbers, education, and/or economic position to dominate or oppress the other. The conflict comes out into the open with demonstrations and violence when the oppressed group attempts to change its oppressed condition.

The most common forms of conflict are racial conflicts, as seen in

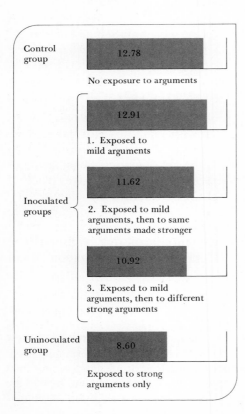

Control group
12.78
No exposure to arguments

Inoculated groups
12.91
1. Exposed to mild arguments

11.62
2. Exposed to mild arguments, then to same arguments made stronger

10.92
3. Exposed to mild arguments, then to different strong arguments

Uninoculated group
8.60
Exposed to strong arguments only

Figure 12.2 *People can be "im-munized" against strong attacks on their attitudes. Each bar represents a group's average attitude (on a 15-point scale) toward four common-sense health propositions. The three inoculated groups, who were given practice in refuting mild attacks on their position, showed considerable resistance to strong attacks. (Adapted from McGuire, 1961.)*

Africa and in the United States in recent years. Religious differences, especially when they are coupled with economic differences, are also the basis of social conflict; witness in Northern Ireland. And economic differences alone can trigger social conflict, as seen in labor-management strife. Whatever the source of the conflict, it is always marked by strong prejudices, for prejudice and social conflict go hand in hand. Most of the examples in this section will come from anti-Negro prejudice, since it is so often encountered in the United States that it has been thoroughly studied. But the same principles apply to all types of social conflict.

Acquiring Prejudices

The word *prejudice* was defined earlier in the chapter as an unjustified prejudgment. In principle, prejudices can be favorable or unfavorable. In practice, the ones of greatest concern to statesmen and social scientists alike are unfavorable, hostile attitudes toward a racial, religious, or economic group.

Prejudices, like other attitudes, obey the principles of attitude formation and maintenance that have already been discussed. In particular, prejudices are learned. People acquire them (1) from contact with others who have the prejudice, and (2) from contact with the object of the prejudice.

Contact with prejudiced people Most prejudices are learned from people who already have them, starting with parents. There is a high correlation between the prejudices of parents and those of their children, because parents often consciously or unconsciously (through modeling) train their children to be prejudiced.

But parents are not the only teachers of prejudice; school friends, teachers, and the communication media are often responsible, though the media in recent years have been doing a better job of counteracting prejudice. In addition, many of the people the individual meets throughout his life are prejudiced, and he picks up their prejudice through conforming behavior.

Contact with the objects of prejudice It is rare that prejudice grows out of personal experience with its object. In fact, direct contact and shared experiences are frequently, but not always, a cure for prejudice. Since the United States Army has integrated its fighting units, prejudice against blacks has gone down considerably. It is not uncommon for white soldiers to become "color blind" after they have fought side by side with a black buddy. Similarly, studies of biracial housing projects find that prejudice usually decreases (Figure 12.3). White housewives who formerly held strongly unfavorable attitudes

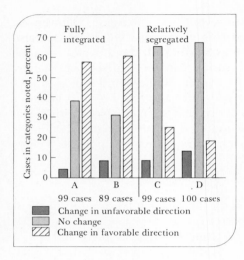

Figure 12.3 *Direct contact and shared experience often cure prejudice. Changes in attitudes toward Negroes held by white housewives in integrated and in relatively segregated housing projects. (From Newcomb et al., 1965; adapted from Deutsch and Collins, 1951.)*

toward blacks become less prejudiced after they have had opportunities for contact and friendship with blacks in integrated housing.

But sharing experiences through integration does not always alleviate prejudice. The U.S. military services, for example, have had several outbreaks of racial violence. Where racial prejudice is widespread, as anti-Negro prejudice has traditionally been in the United States, there is no simple cure. Too many psychological factors keep supporting it.

Supports for Prejudice

Once prejudices are acquired, they are not easily abandoned. In fact, the remarkable thing about prejudice is that it can last for years without the person's having much experience with the objects of prejudice. Why is this?

Needs For one reason, prejudice tends to remain strong because it can satisfy needs in those who have it. The need best served by prejudice is the need for a feeling of superiority or status. "Racism" creates a social hierarchy in which the prejudiced person has a superior status because he perceives someone else to be inferior to him. The poorest, least-educated white in a backwoods Southern town—or for that matter, Northern town—can feel superior because he "knows" he is mentally, morally, and socially superior to blacks.

Racism also serves a need to express aggression. As Chapter 3 said, aggression itself is probably not a need, but it often results from the frustration of other needs. Most people suffer some frustration and thus have reason to be angry or aggressive. Yet as Chapter 4 emphasized, frequently they cannot vent their aggression on the real source of frustration but must express it against some convenient, even if innocent, object.

Scapegoating When aggression is displaced toward a minority group, it is called scapegoating. The prejudiced person who suffers economic, social, or political frustrations displaces his aggression to a convenient object, and this is often a group toward which he already has a prejudice. An infamous example is Hitler's persecution of the Jews in the 1930s and 1940s. During the 20 years before that, the German people had suffered a military defeat in World War I followed by depression, inflation, and a host of social ills. Most Germans already held a prejudice against Jews, as did most of the Gentiles in the Western world. It was easy, then, for Hilter to convince his countrymen that the Jews were responsible for their economic and social problems. At times Jews have also been scapegoats in the United States, as well as in other nations around the world.

Perception To summarize, prejudice is supported by needs—especially the need to feel superior and the need to vent aggression on some convenient object. But prejudice is also supported by distortions in perception. Earlier, the chapter pointed out that strong attitudes make a person *selectively perceive* situations so that his perception fits with his attitude. Prejudice is just another instance of the same thing. A racist sees only what he wants to see. If a person feels that Jews are "pushy," he takes special note of instances in which Jews may be pushy. In similar instances involving Gentiles, he pays little attention, or he interprets the behavior differently. With practice we all become skilled at perceiving only things that are consistent with our prejudices.

Social handicaps Another strong support of racism is the social consequences of prejudice itself; that is, prejudice in social affairs produces a world which is close to what the prejudiced person expects it to be. People with racist attitudes believe that blacks are inferior to whites. Believing this, they prevent blacks from getting adequate schooling, library facilities, housing, and other social advantages. The result is a social handicap for blacks that keeps them from being as well educated as whites. Thus a vicious circle is set up in which the effects of prejudice help to maintain prejudice by providing a real basis for it.

Social Effects of Prejudice

Another effect as well as cause of prejudice—in fact, the means through which social handicaps are created—is segregation. Wherever racism has been strong and widespread—against Jews in the Middle

Ages (and much later, in some countries), against blacks in South Africa, and against similar groups in the United States—the oppressed group has been segregated in schools, in housing, and in jobs. Segregation is a means of depriving the oppressed of the opportunities enjoyed by the oppressors. Any attempt to combat prejudice must begin with efforts to abolish segregation. The Supreme Court recognized this in its landmark decision of 1954, and civil rights legislation of the 1960s has attempted to implement that decision. But removing all forced segregation in education, housing, and employment will be a long, uphill battle. Even tougher is the struggle to break down the de facto segregation that is widespread in the Northern cities of the United States. Racist practices in buying, selling, and renting houses are hard to combat by legal methods, yet they maintain segregation.

Still another social effect of racism is the fact that the oppressed come to hate their oppressors. So long as the oppressed are thoroughly cowed, the hate may not be seen openly. In the days of complete segregation (slavery) in the South, for example, there were relatively few civil disturbances. When the restraints were later removed, and the oppressed had some hope of attaining equality, the hatred erupted in violence and race riots.

To sum up, the psychological forces for maintaining prejudice are powerful and their effects oppressive. Hence prejudice produces the most disruptive tensions to be dealt with in a society. Fortunately, many white Americans are becoming less prejudiced, a trend that is most pronounced in the young and better educated. They are leading the movement to erase prejudice and its oppressive effects. But it will be a long time, and there will be more racial conflict, before it finally succeeds.

SUMMARY

An attitude is a tendency to respond to some person, object, or situation in a positive or negative way. It usually has an emotional component and a belief component. A belief is the acceptance of a statement. A belief supports the emotional component of the attitude, and vice versa.

The different attitudes we may have concerning a particular object, based on different pieces of information, tend to average into one general attitude that lies somewhere on a scale of favorable-unfavorable. But when there is a large discrepancy in information and we must commit ourselves in one way or another, we tend to reduce "cognitive dissonance" by altering our beliefs and attitudes to fit our behavior.

Many attitude scales have been developed for measuring a person's attitudes. These are most useful in research. To measure quickly the attitudes of many people on political matters, the public opinion poll is used.

Early in life, a child's attitudes are shaped primarily by his parents. During the period between ages 12 and 30—the critical period—most of a person's attitudes take final form. The major influences at work during this period are a person's peers, the information he receives through various media, and education. After 30, general attitudes usually change very little, except that there is a tendency to become more conservative. In general, today's children are more liberal than their parents.

Changes in attitudes on specific issues depend on the characteristics of the source, the characteristics of the message, and the characteristics of the recipient of the message. The important characteristics of the source are credibility, attractiveness, and power and prestige. The characteristics of the message that can help to change attitudes are suggestion, appeals to fear, loaded words, and the extent to which both sides of an issue are presented. Characteristics of the receiver that influence attitude change are his influenceability, his needs and goals, selective interpretation, avoidance of information, and prior inoculation.

Prejudice is acquired primarily from other people. Once established, prejudices are hard to dislodge because they are strongly supported by other psychological factors, such as a person's needs, the tendency to find scapegoats, the selective perception of information, and social handicaps created by prejudice. The principal effect of racial prejudice is segregation, both legal and de facto. As a result of that, the racially oppressed come to hate their oppressors and often express this hatred in violence.

SUGGESTIONS FOR FURTHER READING

Allport, G. W. *The nature of prejudice*. Reading, Mass.: Addison-Wesley, 1954. *A readable summary and analysis of the literature on group prejudice.*

Brown, J. A. C. *Techniques of persuasion: From propaganda to brainwashing*. Baltimore: Penguin, 1963. (Paperback.) *Attitude formation and change are the focus of this survey of various kinds of persuasion, including advertising, political propaganda, and psychological warfare.*

Kiesler, C. A., Collins, B. E., and Miller, N. *Attitude change*. New York: Wiley, 1969. *A compact, balanced text covering theory and facts of attitude change.*

McGrath, J. E. *Social psychology: A brief introduction*. New York: Holt, 1964. (Paperback.) *An overview of the major concepts of social psychology.*

McGuire, W. J. *Attitudes and attitude change*, in G. Lindzey and E. Aronson (Eds.), *Handbook of social psychology*. (2d ed.) Reading, Mass.: Addison-Wesley, 1968. *A comprehensive summary of research on the factors influencing attitude change.*

Shaw, M. E., and Wright, J. M. *Scales for the measurement of attitudes*. New York: McGraw-Hill, 1967. *A reference work covering methods of constructing attitude scales that are useful in research.*

13

Social Groups

LEARNING OBJECTIVES

Main objective
After studying this chapter you should be able to analyze the reasons for conforming in most cultures.

Other major objectives
You should be able to
Explain how social structures arise in a culture.
Explain how people in crowds sometimes behave as if they were "not themselves."
Name five factors that determine whether one person is attracted to another.

Minor objectives
Describe the conditions for effective leadership.
Explain why people living in large cities sometimes seem callous.

From the moment you are born you come under the influence of other people. At first it is your mother and your family group. Later it is schoolteachers and peer groups—other children your age. And throughout life you are under the influence of the groups you belong to and the groups you come in contact with: schools, employers and fellow employees, churches, friends, neighbors, policemen, politicians, and society in general.

Groups influence your behavior in many ways. First, they all have a structure into which you must fit—or stay out of the group. The study of *social structure* is primarily the business of the sociologist, but psychologists also need to understand the nature of groups. Second, groups exert a conforming influence: they exact *conforming behavior*. Third, you always find that you like some people and dislike others, and these likes or dislikes affect the way you get along in a group. They may also determine which groups you choose to join—if you have a choice. The structure of groups, the conforming behavior they exact, and the psychological factors that determine attraction or dislike will be the subjects of this chapter.

CULTURE AND SOCIAL STRUCTURE

Each society as a whole has a culture which is shared by the various groups and subgroups within it. Culture, used in a scientific sense, means the customs and traditions of a people and the attitudes and beliefs they have about important aspects of their life. Put another way, culture refers to learned ways of behaving that are shared and transmitted by the members of a particular society. Each cultural group has worked out certain ways of handling various universal problems, such as feeding and sheltering themselves, caring for and training their children, and so on. Successful practices are adopted and passed on to future generations.

Socialization
The social learning process through which the infant is trained in the attitudes, beliefs, and behaviors appropriate to his culture is called *socialization*. This process ensures that new members of a society—the young and developing children—learn what the society has to say about getting along in the world and with other people. In a word, they learn the culture of the society into which they are born.

The socialization process of learning culture follows the same principles of learning that have already been described. Through classical conditioning, the society teaches an individual to give emotional reactions to some situations and not to others. Through operant conditioning, it reinforces some behaviors and extinguishes others. What it does not teach directly through classical or operant conditioning it teaches with models through observational learning. By seeing how other individuals behave in various situations, the child learns how he is expected to behave.

Social Structure
Each society has not only a culture but also a social *structure*. Because of its structure, each individual in the society occupies certain statuses and is expected to play certain roles. (These terms will be defined below.)

Much of the structuring of society arises from differences among people in the goods and services they produce. One person makes trinkets, another makes shoes, and another controls the production of an entire factory. In more informal groups, one person may supply ideas and leadership while others are workers carrying out the ideas. The general point is that the dependence of people on each other is not equally distributed, and differences in dependence give rise to social structure. Once established, however, a social structure may not accurately reflect differences in dependence. For example, a person or family that has acquired status and wealth may continue to hold them long after he or it has stopped doing anything useful in society.

Status and Role

The term *status* is used in different senses. In one, it refers to a person's position on some social or economic scale. For example, he may be a high-ranking official in a bank, be wealthy, be well educated, and have a good reputation in the community. Or he may be poorly educated, work as a window washer, and belong to a low-income group. Statuses of this type are frequently lumped together to assign the person one status on a socioeconomic scale.

Status in another sense refers to the position occupied by a person at a particular time. In this sense he has many statuses that may change from time to time: age status (teenager, adult), occupational status (worker, foreman), social status (member of the Elks Club, member of Rolling Green Country Club), or family status (bachelor, husband). Some statuses are inherited: for example, sex status or, in some societies, social status. Other statuses are acquired. In any case, a person has many statuses at different times of the day, week, year, or lifetime.

Along with each status goes a *role*. This is the kind of behavior a person is supposed to exhibit in a certain status. At a very early age, for example, boys and girls learn that different behaviors are expected of them. A man in his status as father and head of a household has a role, or mode of behavior, which he is expected to act out in his status. So does a person in the role of mother, teacher, or employer. Status and role are key concepts in understanding social structure, and they must be clearly distinguished. Status applies to a *position* in the structure; role to the *behavior* that goes with the status.

Statuses are so arranged in a social structure that a person can be categorized in many ways: head of a household, teacher, employee, church member. For some part of his daily life he occupies one status; for other parts, other statuses. Since a different role goes along with each status, a person finds himself in multiple statuses and multiple roles.

For most people most of the time, their multiple statuses and roles cause no trouble. They usually perceive only the status that is most appropriate to the situation they are in at the moment. Usually an unscrupulous businessman sees no conflict between his business behavior and the beliefs he professes on Sunday in church. As a businessman he does not think of his status as churchgoer; as a churchgoer he does not think of his business behavior. By such compartmentalized thinking he escapes any conflict.

But for some people some of the time roles do come into conflict, causing strain and anxiety. The women's liberation movement focuses on just such a conflict. When an intelligent, educated woman marries and has children, she finds herself cast in the roles of maid, baby-sitter, chauffeur, cook, handyman, and companion. These roles are different from the ones she played before marriage, and are in conflict with other possible roles such as employer or employee, teacher, lawyer, or doctor.

Another time when roles may conflict is the occasion of a person's shift from one status to another. The foreman who drives his men hard may find his behavior inappropriate when he is promoted to executive status. The class president in a small-town high school may be a "fish-out-of-water" when he becomes just another freshman in a large university. The professor used to the manners and talk of his fellow professors may find himself uncomfortable in a gathering of the poor. In all such cases, the conflict between the behavior learned in one status and that required in another may cause the person anxiety and frustration. Indeed, it may lead to a serious problem of adjustment (McGrath, 1964).

Social Classes

Most societies arrange their statuses on a *scale of prestige*, because people in the society regard certain statuses as more important or more desirable than others. The awards that the community has to distribute, such as wealth, power, respect, and honors, are parceled out according to the prestige scale. Naturally there is no one-to-one correlation between, say, wealth and prestige. Nevertheless, people of all ages in a society agree fairly consistently when they rank occupations according to status. These rankings may shift over a period of time, but they are surprisingly stable.

The prestige scale becomes the basis for forming social classes. People high on it are largely in one class, those low on it in another class. In a number of societies, particularly ancient and undeveloped ones, the class system is rigid: it restricts the occupations a person may enter and the way he must behave with members of other classes. Western society, on the other hand, is not so rigid; it permits a lot of "mobility"; but it does have classes, and will continue to have them for the foreseeable future.

The social class in which a person is reared is likely to affect his behavior in several ways. In our society, people in the lower classes have lower educational and occupational goals than those in the upper. More specifically, our social classes differ in *achievement motivation.* Children from the higher classes more often have high standards of performance. They are more likely to believe that it is possible for a person to improve his status in life. And they think it worthwhile to postpone present pleasures for future goals. These attitudes and beliefs, which together produce high achievement motivation, are much less common in the lower classes. The class difference in achievement motivation is one of the strongest arguments for integrated schools—to expose minority groups to a model of achievement motivation presented by middle- and upper-class youngsters (Coleman, 1966).

Communication

So far this discussion of social structure has dealt mainly with society as a whole. Now it will treat smaller groups of the kind people find themselves in at work, school, and elsewhere in their daily lives. All such groups, whether they are student activist organizations or corporate boards of directors, have two important characteristics. One is that people in the group communicate with each other. Indeed, it is through such communication that social influences are felt. The other characteristic is that the groups have leaders, either formal or informal.

As for communication, in most groups it is regulated in some way. Perhaps a chairman decides who will speak and what topics are in order. Or in a business or military organization there are rules about "lines of communication." In either case communication has some pattern or structure. Of the many structures that are possible, several have been studied in psychological experiments. The two extremes diagrammed in Figure 13.1 show what is meant by communication structure and how it affects people. The structure at left is an "open" one; any person can talk to any other person in the group. This structure simulates an informal study group, or a work situation in which a person communicates with anybody he needs to in order to get his work done. The structure at right is called a "star" pattern because all messages must be sent through a central person, who decides whether to forward them or forget them. The star structure represents a military organization or a business in which a person is supposed to follow a "chain of command."

Is one of these structures better than another? Generally speaking,

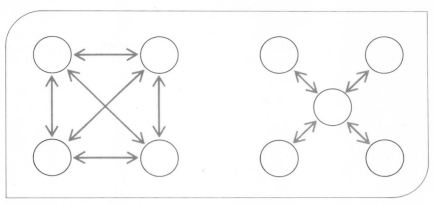

Figure 13.1 *Two types of communication structure. Left, a completely connected "open pattern" in which each person may communicate with everyone else. Right, the "star" pattern in which group members may communicate only with a central person.*

the star pattern is better for getting things done, especially if the central person is the most competent in the group. But a lot depends on the complexity of the problem to be solved and the work load given to each group member. On the other hand, people definitely like the open structure better than they do the star, because the open pattern gives them more freedom and independence. Communication patterns that thwart the desire to communicate freely make people dissatisfied. Hence most groups use some combination of a star and an open structure: they have leaders who coordinate communication, but at times they allow people to communicate freely with each other (Shaw, 1955).

Leadership

A leader is a person who influences or directs a group to follow a course of action that he advocates. He is thus the group's major influence in the achievement of certain goals. In work situations these goals are usually the manufacture of a product or the performance of a service desired by management. In political or social organizations the leader helps the group realize the goals that people joined the group to achieve.

Leaders may be either formal or informal. A formal leader influences his group largely because he occupies a formally recognized status: he is the president, chairman, or king. In this role it is his job to lead and the job of his followers to follow. In this role too, he can influence his followers because he has authority over them; he dispenses rewards and punishments. A great deal of political and military leadership falls into the formal category. In such situations people know clearly who is boss, and leadership can be effective.

In most situations, however, a leader is most effective when his followers accept his ideas because they truly believe in them. If he leads in this sense, he is both a formal and an informal leader.

An informal leader derives his influence not from an explicit position of authority, but because his personal qualities convince the followers that he can help them satisfy their needs. They have certain goals, often involving social changes, that they want to achieve, and they cannot attain these goals as individuals. They turn to a leader to help them organize their efforts to reach their goals.

What qualities should a leader possess? The many books that have been written about leadership often stress such personality traits as proficiency, popularity, and assertiveness. But a great deal of research over the past twenty years has discredited this trait approach to leadership, just as the concept of the personality trait has proved ineffective in predicting behavior in specific situations (page 240). Instead, the study of many groups and their competence has led to a *contingency model* of leadership (Fiedler, 1967).

According to the contingency model, the success of a leader depends upon an interaction between (1) his power, (2) his orientation, and (3) the tasks to be performed. The power of a formal leader is relatively great, that of an informal leader rather weak. Other things being equal, the greater his power, the more effective he will be. But leaders also vary in their orientation. At one extreme is the "task-oriented" leader who is simply interested in getting the job done. At the other extreme is the "affective" leader—the socially oriented person who tries to be liked and to improve social relationships (that is, to decrease tensions). Finally, some tasks have solutions that are easily seen by both the leader and the group; other tasks are more difficult.

In analyzing the interaction of power, orientation, and tasks, the contingency model of leadership says that the task-oriented leader is most effective when he has power and when tasks are either very difficult or very easy to perform. A socially oriented leader, on the other hand, is most effective when the task is of moderate difficulty and when he has limited power. In such a case he leads the group by friendly persuasion, not by formal direction.

Research leading to the contingency model is based on the study of more than 800 groups (Fiedler, 1967). The model gives us a general idea of the factors involved in leadership, but does not make specific predictions. A person who is a leader in one situation may be ineffective in another. For example, a man may be a good business manager but a failure as president of a university or a country club.

Social scientists still have much to learn about the roles that effective leaders play in different situations.

CONFORMING BEHAVIOR

One of the outstanding features of a person's behavior in a social group is his *conformity* to the group. Conformity is a general term that implies going along with the behaviors, attitudes, and beliefs of the group (Chapter 12 provided information on attitudes and beliefs). For the most part, we conform to groups we are in because we are convinced of the group's "rightness." In this case the term *private acceptance* is applied to our conformity, meaning that we have accepted privately what we publicly profess. But sometimes we go along with the group although our private attitudes and beliefs are different, and then the term *compliance* is more appropriate. There is an element of both in most conformity behavior, so that it is seldom possible to disentangle private acceptance from compliance. The difference between compliance and acceptance is illustrated by the following studies.

In one experiment (Asch, 1956) subjects were asked to make estimates of the length of lines. Actually, there was only one real subject in each experimental session; unknown to him, the rest of his group had been coached to make erroneous judgments. So it often happened that his eyes told him one thing while his group agreed that something else was correct. Some of the actual subjects consistently yielded to the erroneous group opinion (Figure 13.2). When interviewed later, these conformists usually stated that they thought something was wrong with their eyesight. They accepted the erroneous judgments because they believed that the group must be right.

Another experiment was essentially the same *except* that the actual subjects were permitted to express their opinions anonymously after hearing the group's judgment (Deutsch and Gerard, 1955). Under this condition, subjects yielded much less often to the erroneous majority than the subjects did in the "nonanonymous" condition. But even so, a few of the "anonymous" subjects conformed to the group. Thus most of the subjects who expressed the majority opinion apparently did so in order not to appear different—they complied—rather than because they believed the majority to be correct.

Conformity and Group Norms

What do we conform to? The answer is *group norms.* A norm is a standard of behavior that is *expected* of us in each of our statuses and roles. As members of many groups—family, university, community, church, commune, and so on—we have many roles to play. We must somehow conform to the expectations of the group, or else! These

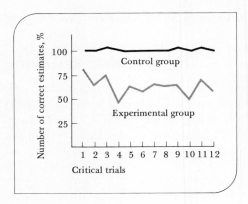

Figure 13.2 *Group pressures may make us conform: In this experiment, the task was to estimate the length of various lines. Each control-group subject was alone when he judged the lengths of the lines. But each experimental subject was with a group of people who all agreed on an incorrect answer. (After Asch, 1956.)*

expectations constitute group norms. Defined more formally, group norms are widely shared expectations among most members of a group, class, or culture.

Group norms seem to emerge, like statuses and social structure, whenever a group is formed. In more formal groups, people consciously strive to reach agreements with each other on how they are to live together. They establish rules about who will do what, how it is to be done, how the results are to be shared, and so on. These rules are really group norms. In informal groups, norms arise simply through the interaction of the members. "Interaction" means any conversation, exchange of goods and services, or joint efforts that give group members any kind of status. The longer people interact and the more they interact, the more they tend to adopt common ways of perceiving the world. From shared perceptions, it is only a short step to shared rules or norms—expectations—governing the behavior of group members in each status. The expectations then take on a demand quality. Not only do people tend to see the world and act the way other group members do, but they *must* do so. A group norm has been established.

Reasons for Conforming Behavior
Why do people usually conform to the group norms imposed on them? The reasons are not as simple as they may seem. A number of forces are at work to produce conforming behavior.

Reward and punishment The strongest reason for conformity is the fact that many of a person's rewards and punishments are dished out by the groups he belongs to. The strongest of all group norms—those with the highest demand quality—are the laws of a society. These tell a person what he must do or else be punished with fines or jail sentences. Fear of such punishment clearly motivates most people to abide by the laws.

Even when no laws are involved, groups have powerful means of reinforcement. When children are young they mind their parents—conform to the norms—because parents provide the satisfaction of their various needs. Later other groups take over to satisfy needs—for companionship, recognition, achievement, and so on. In fact, there is hardly anything we want that does not require us to interact with somebody else in some kind of group, small or large. Because groups dispense the things we want, and help us avoid the things we want to avoid, we learn to conform to group expectations. This learning is not necessarily conscious; often it is not. The anthropologist who asks a native in a primitive society why things are done in certain ways is likely to get the answer, "That's just the way things are done." If he presses with a further "Why?" the answer, after some pondering, is usually "Because that's the way it's always done."

Need for liking and social approval Closely related to reward and punishment is the desire most people have to be liked and approved by the group. A teenager wants to be accepted by his peers and may find it hard to resist group pressures to conform. To accept him, a group may require him to wear certain clothes, adopt certain hair styles, know the latest dances, and own a car. In other groups, conformity behavior may involve drinking, shoplifting, sex exploration, and experimentation with drugs. Fear of disapproval by his peers can provide strong motivation to conform—at least to comply if not to privately accept.

The desire for social acceptance produces a certain sameness among the members of a group. Even the extreme "nonconformists" who exist on the fringes of many university communities have identifiable habits and modes of dress that are norms in their own groups. Though they wish to be considered nonconformists, they often conform slavishly to the behaviors expected by their friends.

One reason we conform, then, is to be accepted by others. Similarly, we may use conformity as a technique to make other people like us. Indeed, conformity is a common "tactic of ingratiation . . . a means of currying favor with a more powerful individual" (Jones, 1965). By subtly agreeing with the opinions of a more powerful or more important person, we may make him like us more.

Attractiveness of the group The more strongly a person is attracted to a group, either because he likes it or because he somehow sees it as meeting his needs, the readier he is to conform to its expectations. And of course the greater the attraction, the more he wants to belong to the group and the more he is inclined to agree with the opinions of its members. One factor in this willingness to agree is certainly fear of disapproval. But in addition, Chapter 12 has already shown that we have a higher regard for the opinions of the people we like than for those we don't. This leads us to "go along" with their opinions, especially when we have no objective way of deciding whether the opinions are correct.

Consensus versus dissonance Conformity breeds more conformity through the consensus it produces. People in a group with established group norms tend to have similar opinions, and when an individual comes up against them, he is inclined to go along on the assumption that the group must be right. The greater the consensus in the group, the more his tendency is to conform. If there is some disagreement among members, the individual feels freer to stray from group opinions (Asch, 1958). Strong agreement in a group apparently carries with it a greater threat of disapproval of nonconformists.

Consensus induces conformity in another way—through cognitive dissonance (page 291). If a person is inclined to hold an opinion different from the group's, he suffers cognitive dissonance. He is motivated to reconcile the difference in the "facts," and the simplest way of reducing his cognitive dissonance is to conform to the consensus of opinion.

Gradual Conformity Induction

Of course, there are many situations in which most people feel no need to conform, as when a salesman tries to peddle his product at the front door. In these situations, however, a person can cometimes be trapped into conforming by a technique known as *gradual conformity induction.* It might also be called the foot-in-the-door technique. The trick is to get the person to comply with some small, rather trivial request, because the compliance itself makes him more willing to yield to more demanding requests. This technique was used in the brainwashing of Korean War prisoners. The Communists first tried to persuade the prisoners to sign some mild, rather meaningless confession, and frequently those who did so could later be induced to sign more incriminating documents. Another example of gradual conformity induction is seen in the following experiment (Freedman and Fraser, 1966).

> The experimenters employed four different conditions, but we will consider only two: a performance condition and a control condition. In the performance condition the experimenters, posing as researchers for

Guide, a bogus consumer magazine, telephoned housewives, talked to them about *Guide,* and made a small request. They asked the women to answer some questions about the kind of household soap they were using. Women in the control condition were not contacted at this time.

Several days later, the experimenters telephoned the women in both the performance and control conditions and asked them to allow several men from *Guide* to spend several hours in their homes to inventory all their household products. The men were to be free to rummage through the cupboards and cabinets looking for products—an outrageous request! Yet of the housewives in the performance group, 53 percent agreed to let the men snoop around their houses, while only 22 percent of the control subjects agreed to it. The first small request had considerably increased the conformity of the women in the performance condition.

Crowd Behavior

Conforming behavior is prominent in a special way in mobs or crowds, where people often do things they would never think of doing otherwise. Here are some of the reasons for their different behavior.

First, certain behaviors are appropriate in a crowd that are not appropriate elsewhere. If I jump up at my desk and let out rhythmic yells when I am alone, I am acting peculiarly. But if I jump up and cheer at the top of my lungs in a crowd at a basketball game, I am acting as I should. The crowd, therefore, provides a setting in which different behaviors are appropriate.

Another factor in crowd behavior is modeling (page 249). As explained earlier, a person learns many ways of behaving by watching the behavior of other people in similar situations. The tendency to model is especially strong in a crowd, when the individual sees a great many people all doing the same thing. If the crowd is behaving violently and emotionally, he tends to act the same way; consequently, crowds that start out with peaceful intentions frequently become progressively aroused and wind up rioting or panicking.

A third factor in crowd behavior is anonymity, or *deindividuation* (Zimbardo, 1970). People in a crowd have lost their individual identities, and their feeling of anonymity tends to free them from the usual social constraints. Put another way, they no longer feel individually responsible for their actions. Hence they go along—conform to—the behavior of the crowd, even though that behavior violates other social norms (see Figure 13.3).

City Living

People who live in small towns are usually shocked when they visit a large city by what they see as the pushiness, discourtesy, and callousness of city dwellers. Of course this description does not apply to

Figure 13.3 *Crowd behavior can be ugly and violent. These youths are threatening a motorist during a night of rioting in response to an 8 P.M. city-park curfew imposed by the local police. Anonymity, or deindividuation, is one important factor in the behavior of rioters. (UPI.)*

everybody in all large cities, but by and large it is true. What factors are involved in "callous" city behavior?

One, *anonymity,* was mentioned above. People in large cities tend to lose their individuality when they are acting as members of a city crowd. This makes them feel less responsible in their relations with other anonymous individuals.

Another fact about large cities with their masses of people is that responsibility is diffused. As a consequence, a person can become confused about what he should be doing. A famous example is the story of Kitty Genovese, who was murdered on a residential street in New York City while 38 people living in the apartments on all sides heard her screams and did nothing to help. When interviewed later, many of the observers said they did nothing because they thought that somebody else would call the police. Taking their cue from this case, two psychologists conducted the following experiment on "helping behavior" (Darley and Latané, 1968).

The hypothesis of the study was that the more people there are in an emergency situation, the less likely any one of them is to help. In each experimental session one real subject talked over an intercom to various numbers of people, varying from one to five. An emergency situation was created by having one of the other people cry for help after first talking about having epileptic seizures, making choking noises, and finally lapsing into silence. The experimenter stood outside the real subject's room to see whether he would come out to offer help.

The results corroborated the hypothesis. If a subject thought that only he was present besides the victim, 85 percent of the subjects came out to help. If a subject thought that another person was present besides himself and the victim, 62 percent offered to help. The percentage dropped to 31 when the subject thought that there were three other people present. Such results offer strong support for the idea that the presence of a number of people diffuses responsibility among members of a group.

A third feature of living in large groups has been called *cognitive overload.* The word "overload," has been borrowed from communications engineering, where it means that a channel is given more information than it can handle. If this happens, priority must be assigned to some messages and others must be rerouted or not sent at all. By analogy, people exposed to more information than they can digest must give priority to certain perceptions and block out others.

In large urban areas, the amount of information impinging on a person is staggering. When he rides to work on a subway, his senses are bombarded with data. He can respond only to a limited amount of sensory input and must disregard the rest. This is adaptive behavior, for otherwise he would be swamped. So what looks like callousness, indifference, or irritability may be just an expression of adaptive overload that enables a person to function in crowded city life. After all, if you were to greet everybody you met on the street in New York City, you would never stop waving, smiling, and talking (and everybody would think you a bit strange). Figure 13.4, showing the hectic rush of city life, indicates how cognitive overload occurs.

These points about social factors in city crowds are not meant to imply that city living is all bad. Some people like the anonymity of the large city, for it permits them to "do their own thing," whereas they would be miserable in a small town under the watchful eye of neighbors and friends. Large cities also offer many cultural, educational, and recreational opportunities often lacking in smaller communities.

INTERPERSONAL ATTRACTION

Your likes and dislikes where people are concerned account for a good deal of your social behavior. You try to pick a roommate whom you like; you choose friends by deciding which people you like; you join groups largely on the basis of your liking for their members. What

Figure 13.4 *The bustle of the city, where selective "tuning out" is necessary if one is to cope with it all. (Gabriele Wunderlich.)*

governs your liking for people—or more generally, what factors determine interpersonal attraction?

Social Contact

One important factor in attraction is simply the amount of *social contact* that exists between people. Research shows that the more they see of each other, the friendlier they usually feel, and friendliness is an expression of liking. Social statistics reveal that people tend to marry people who live near them. As the saying goes, "Marriages are made on the block, not in heaven." Careful studies of friendships between people living in housing projects and apartments confirm the importance of propinquity (Festinger et al., 1950): On the whole, people were most friendly with those who lived near them, and the people who had no near neighbors had the fewest friends.

But social contact is a coin with two sides, for when other factors cause us to dislike a person, frequent social contact can increase our dislike. Then social contact breeds enemies—and in fact, most assaults and murders are committed by people who know each other, not by strangers. If you are going to be knifed, bashed, shot at, or raped, it will most likely be by someone you know well. This is why the police often suspect family members or close acquaintances first in assault cases.

Physical Attractiveness

Another factor in our liking for people is their physical attractiveness. One study of a social "mixer" for college freshmen found that attractiveness correlated significantly with liking (Walster et al., 1966). Partners for the mixer were selected by a computer—or so the subjects were told. During an intermission, they filled out questionnaires which were presumably related to computer selection. These showed that both men and women felt the most liking for the partners who were the "prettiest" or "best looking."

This finding, however, is not universal; it probably applies best to young people meeting others of the opposite sex. Older people do not seem to put so much emphasis on physical attractiveness. Moreover, the importance of physical attractiveness fades as people come to know each other better. Other factors then make more difference to the relationship.

Satisfaction of Needs

One of the reasons why we like particular people is that they satisfy our needs—perhaps by comforting us, enhancing our self-esteem, or reducing our anxieties. The power of reward is operating here. Put another way, we are attracted to certain people—they become positive learned goals (see Chapter 5)—because they supply us with reinforcements of various kinds.

A special version of this principle, known as *need complementarity*, says that people who are attracted to each other tend to fit each other's needs. A nonassertive person may be attracted to an assertive one; a person with a need to dominate may be attracted to a person who needs to be dominated. This idea comes close to the common notion that "opposites attract." But just being opposites is not enough; in fact, there is little evidence that people with generally opposite traits do attract each other. Such a conclusion comes out of the following study (Kerckhoff and Davis, 1962).

College couples who were seriously contemplating marriage were interviewed and given personality tests in order to collect data on similarities of social class, religion, and attitudes. Some of the information also concerned complementarity of needs.

The importance of the various factors in the selection of a "mate" was found to depend on the length of the engagement. For couples who had been engaged a short time—less than 18 months—similarities of social class, religion, and attitudes were the main factors in the relationship. Couples with long engagements—more than 18 months—indicated that need complementarity also played a role. They had come to depend on each other for the satisfaction of some of their needs.

Similarity of Attitudes

Attitudes, as Chapter 12 showed, are closely related to needs and need satisfaction. We tend to have favorable attitudes toward things and people who satisfy our needs. And of course, we have a favorable attitude toward our own attitudes, and toward people who share them. This, in fact, is one of the most important elements in our liking for people, as illustrated by the following experiment (Byrne, 1969).

> The subjects were college students whose attitudes on several topics were measured by appropriate scales. Each subject was then given a description of the attitudes of a stranger. The experimenter deliberately "matched" attitudes of the subject and stranger so that they varied from complete agreement to complete disagreement. The subjects were asked how they thought they would like the stranger if they knew him. The straightforward result was that the greater the similarity in attitudes, the greater the liking for the stranger (see Figure 13.5).

Reciprocity

The outcome of the experiment described above has more than one interpretation. As just mentioned, finding attitudes in others that are similar to our own is rewarding and therefore represents a kind of need satisfaction. Another possible interpretation is that we expect other people with similar attitudes to like us. This notion has been called *reciprocity.*

Whether or not reciprocity explains the effect of similarity of attitudes, it is certainly a factor in attraction. "Be a friend to others, and they will be friends to you" is the theme of many books on how to be popular. Experimental evidence demonstrates that there is some truth in the idea (Backman and Secord, 1959).

> Ten college students took a personality test and then met each other for the first time. Each subject had been privately told that according to the personality test results, he would be liked by three particular members of the group. After the group had met, ratings of liking were made. The

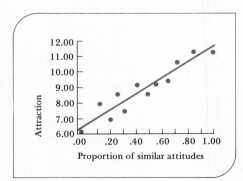

Figure 13.5 *Like likes like. College students were given a description of the attitudes of a stranger and were asked whether they thought they would like him. The closer his attitudes were to their own, the more they thought they would like him. (After Byrne, 1969.)*

ratings showed that the subjects most liked the group members who supposedly liked them—a reciprocity effect.

In subsequent meetings, however, this effect did not last; the persons whom the subjects had initially liked were no longer especially liked. In these meetings the subjects had a chance to find out about the attitudes and beliefs of the other people, and the factor of attitude similarity, as well as other factors in attractiveness, seemed to cancel out the reciprocity effect.

In passing, it should be noted that two other factors affect liking and interpersonal attraction. One is obvious: We like people who say and do nice things. The other factor is ability: In general, we like people who are intelligent, able, competent, and talented (Aronson, 1970).

Disliking People

We all know people whom we neither like nor dislike very much. This happens when the factors which cause liking are weak. Beyond that, we know some people whom we do not like at all. Our dislike may stem from dissimilarity of attitudes or from their physical unattractiveness. The biggest factor in causing us to dislike others, however, is frustration—people who block our motives are people whom we strongly dislike (Berkowitz, 1968).

Frustration produces dislike because it arouses anger (page 77). A person is quick to anger when he is frustrated, and he tends to get angry with people who do the frustrating. His frustration may merely be perceived rather than actual, but in this case perceiving makes it so. Moreover, frustration is most likely to produce anger when it is perceived as a deliberate act by the frustrator. Whether or not frustration will lead to expressed anger and aggression depends on the circumstances. We may not express our anger because we fear the other person's retaliation, but whether we show it or not we will certainly dislike him.

SUMMARY

Socialization is the process of learning one's culture—learning the shared attitudes, beliefs, and ways of behaving that are characteristic of the culture. Cultures have a social structure that arises from the various statuses occupied and the roles played by people in the culture. Statuses and roles usually become arranged into social classes. Groups and organizations within a culture have different communication patterns, varying from open communication among the members to a star pattern in which all messages must go through one person. The effectiveness of a leader depends on the interaction of his power, his orientation toward work and the group, and the nature of the tasks to be performed.

The interaction of people in groups leads to the development of group norms which demand a certain amount of conformity. Conforming behavior has several causes: (1) Rewards are given for it, and punishment is often applied for not conforming. (2) People conform because they want to be liked and want the approval of the group. (3) The more attractive a group is to a person, the more likely he is to conform to its norms. (4) Disagreeing with the consensus of the group causes dissonance, which can be reduced by conforming. Conforming behavior can also be induced by the "foot-in-the-door technique."

People in crowds tend to do things they would not do alone because they conform to the crowd's behavior, do not feel individually responsible for their acts, and tend to model their behavior after others. Certain factors influence the behavior of people living in large cities: anonymity or deindividuation, diffusion of responsibility, and cognitive overload of information.

We like and dislike people for a number of reasons. In general, the more social contact we have with a person, the more we like him. We also like people whom we find physically attractive. We like people who help us satisfy our needs, people who have attitudes similar to our own, and finally, people who like us—a reciprocity effect. We dislike people who frustrate us and thereby make us angry.

SUGGESTIONS FOR FURTHER READING

Benedict, R. *Patterns of culture.* (2d ed.) Boston: Houghton Mifflin, 1959. (Paperback available.) *A classical description, written by a social anthropologist, of patterns of culture in primitive societies.*

Berkowitz, L. *Roots of aggression: A re-examination of the frustration-aggression hypothesis.* New York: Atherton, 1969. (Paperback.) *An analysis of the causes of human aggression.*

Berscheid, E., and Walster, E. H. *Interpersonal attraction.* Reading, Mass.: Addison-Wesley, 1969. (Paperback.) *A summary of the social psychology of people's likes and dislikes.*

Kiesler, C. A., and Kiesler, S. B. *Conformity.* Reading, Mass.: Addison-Wesley, 1969. (Paperback.) *Major theories of social conformity are discussed.*

Wrightsman, L. S. *Social psychology in the seventies.* Monterey, Calif.: Brooks/Cole, 1972. *An up-to-date textbook of social psychology.*

PART IV

Biology of Behavior

To many students, the study of personality, abnormal behavior, and social behavior is the most interesting part of a psychology course. Certainly these topics have the most relevance to our everyday lives. Those of a philosophical or scientific bent, however, may like to know what goes on inside the head when we experience, or behave in, different situations. This is the area we examine in the last two chapters.

Chapter 14 covers the processes taking place in sensory experience. It begins with the operation of sense organs in general, then goes on to consider each of the senses. The greatest emphasis is on vision and hearing, for these are the senses we use the most in perception and learning, but other senses will also be briefly considered.

Chapter 15 explains how messages are carried in the nervous system. Next it sketches the structure of the nervous system with emphasis on the brain. It then explains how the brain works in sensory experience, skilled movements, motivation, emotion, learning, and memory.

14

Sensory Processes

LEARNING OBJECTIVES

Main objective

After studying this chapter you should be able to describe the mechanism for our having different qualities of experience in the different senses.

Other major objectives

You should be able to

Describe the physiological mechanism by which we see color.

Explain how tones have different perceived pitches.

Indicate the four primary qualities of taste.

Minor objectives

Name ten distinct senses in man.

Distinguish between absolute and differential thresholds.

Compare the nature and causes of two different kinds of deafness.

Describe the proprioceptive senses.

People have been taught from time immemorial—actually, from the Greeks on—that they have five senses. But the fact is that man really has ten senses, and these are the subjects here. Chapters 12 and 13 dealt with the social aspects of psychology—the way people interact with each other. Now the last two chapters of the book turn to the physiological aspects of psychology. This chapter covers various forms of sensory experience and the sensory processes that underlie them. Chapter 15 will show how events in the nervous system are involved in behavior.

When people talk about man's five senses, they mean vision, hearing, taste, smell, and a skin sense which they call the sense of touch. But the last is not just one sense; it is four. Scientists have identified distinctly different receptors for touch, cold, warmth, and pain. Furthermore, there are two other senses which were not included at all in the traditional five. These are the kinesthetic sense and the vestibular sense (together, called the proprioceptive senses). The kinesthetic sense organs are receptors in your muscles, tendons, and joints that give you information about the position of your limbs and tensions in your muscles. The vestibular sense is a key sense in maintaining balance; it gives you information about the movement and position of your head. These are the ten senses of man.

SENSORY MECHANISMS

Although by and large the operations of the ten senses are quite different from one another, they have some mechanisms which are common to all. This section presents a general view of the mechanisms of sensory experience, while the following sections take up the senses one by one.

Receptors

The important element in each sense is a set of receptor cells— sometimes just called receptors. These cells have become specialized so that they are very sensitive to different forms of energy in the environment. In the case of smell and vision, the receptors are neurons (nerve cells) which migrated out from the brain when it was forming in the embryo. In the case of taste, hearing, the vestibular sense, and some of the skin receptors, the cells are derived from cells of the skin.

Each receptor responds to a different form of energy. Visual receptors respond to certain wavelengths of light, smell receptors to chemicals in gas form, taste receptors to chemicals in solution, temperature receptors to changes in skin temperature, and the other receptors—for hearing, the vestibular and kinesthetic senses, and touch and pain—to mechanical stimuli of one sort of another.

Connecting with each receptor cell is the fiber of a nerve cell (to see generally what a nerve cell looks like, turn to Figure 15.1 on page 356 in Chapter 15). Very frequently this nerve fiber serves more than one receptor cell. Usually the fiber runs directly into the nervous system before making any more connections. But in the case of smell and vision, whose receptors are really a part of the brain, connections are made with other nerve cells in the sense organ before the fibers relay impulses to the brain.

When a receptor is stimulated, two events take place in rapid succession. (1) The stimulating energy is *transduced* into electrical energy called the *generator potential.* (Whenever energy is changed from one form to another, say, from sound to electrical energy, the process is called *transduction.*) This generator potential is proportional in size to the intensity of the stimulus. (2) If the generator potential in the receptor cell is large enough, it sets off a *nerve impulse* in the nerve fiber connected with the nerve cell. This nerve impulse is called the *spike potential* by physiologists because it is relatively large, yet very brief (Figure 15.2 on page 358 of the next chapter has a diagram of a spike potential). It travels down the fiber toward the nervous system and, after being relayed through several nerve cells, reaches the cerebral cortex of the brain.

Sensory Codes
The transduction that takes place in receptors means that you do not experience the world directly. What you experience is the events taking place in your receptors. And the *kind* of experience you have—of light, color, pitch, or pain—depends on which receptors are stimulated. Each type of receptor maintains its own separate connections in the nerve cells carrying information to the brain. For example, by placing electrodes on cells in a subject's brain, the experimenter can tell which receptor in a sense organ has been stimulated. If he places the electrodes in the visual system of the brain, he finds that one set of cells responds when the system is stimulated by a green light and that another set of cells responds when the light is blue. If he inserts the electrodes in the brain's auditory system, one set of cells responds when the pitch of a tone is high, another when it is low. And so on in all the senses.

The general point is that the *quality* of your experiences depends on which receptors and their connecting nerve cells are in action. To put it another way, the sensory code through which you experience different sensations is determined by *which* receptors and their connecting fibers are more active. To demonstrate this point, you might put your finger in your eye. If you do you will see light, because pressure on the eyeball stimulates light receptors. Yet the stimulus is pressure, not light. It was the sense organ you excited, not the particular stimulus you used, that made you see light.

Thresholds
The generator potential, as said earlier, is proportional to stimulus intensity. But this is not true of nerve impulses: they have an absolute threshold, and whenever the generator potential reaches a certain size,

they are tripped off. Generator potentials die down slowly, however, and if they are relatively large, they will trip off a whole series of nerve impulses. As a result, the more intense a stimulus, the larger the generator potential and the greater the number of impulses traveling into the brain. This relationship explains how people experience the *intensity* of a stimulus. They feel one stimulus as more intense than another because it causes more impulses to be sent to the brain. However, there is a limit to the number of impulses people can discriminate, and consequently a limit to the differences in intensity they can discriminate. This limit is known as the *differential threshold.*

An interesting fact about the differential threshold is that it is not constant. Rather, it depends on the intensity of the stimulus we use to measure it. In general, the more intense the stimulus, the larger the differential threshold. If you turn on a 25-watt lamp in a room where only one other 25-watt lamp is burning, you easily perceive the increase; the difference is far above the differential threshold. But if you add a 25-watt light to a room that is already illuminated with a thousand 25-watt bulbs, you will not be able to tell the difference. At this high level of intensity, the additional light is less than the differential threshold.

This example has been stated in *absolute* terms: the differential threshold, measured as the smallest difference a person can perceive, grows larger as the stimulus is more intense. If the relationship is stated in *relative* terms, it goes the other way: if you consider the *ratio* of the differential threshold to the intensity of a stimulus, you find that the ratio decreases as the stimulus is made more intense. In other words, a person's *relative* sensitivity to changes in stimulus intensities in the environment becomes better the stronger the stimulus.

Adaptation

People's ability to discriminate differences in intensity also depends on another factor, *adaptation.* The various receptors adapt in varying degrees to the intensity of stimulation. The eye, for example, adapts over an enormous range of intensities. As you go from bright sunlight into the darkness of a movie theater, you can see very little at first; but soon the eye adapts—it becomes more sensitive—to light. And when you come out of the theater into sunlight, it is blindingly bright for an instant before the visual receptors adapt. Some receptors, like those for hearing, adapt very little; but on the whole receptors adapt a great deal to the intensity of steady stimulation. With this adaptation go changes in the absolute threshold, the differential threshold, and the perceived intensity of the stimulus.

The notion that *adaptation level* determines the perception of differences in stimulation goes far beyond the physical intensity of a stimulus. It applies to all sorts of perceptual situations, including social situations (Helson, 1964). Suppose that you have been looking at a number of squares differing in size, but all relatively large. If you are then shown a small square, it will look smaller than it would if you had been looking at small squares. You have become "adapted" to large squares. The general principle is that the kinds of stimuli you have been looking at form a context—adaptation level—that affects your perception of other stimuli.

VISION

The general mechanics of how we see are fairly simple. Certain electromagnetic waves in the visible spectrum are focused by a lens in the eye onto the receptors of the retina. There the light breaks down a photosensitive pigment. The decomposition of the pigment produces a generator potential which in turn sets up nerve impulses. These travel out of the eye along the optic nerve and into the brain. Now let us consider each of these events in more detail.

The Light Stimulus

The light that serves as a stimulus in vision is just a portion of a vast spectrum of *electromagnetic radiation.* This radiation can be thought of as particles moving through space, oscillating in waves as they go. It is the length of the wave, measured from one peak to the next, that places any particular radiation at a point in the electromagnetic spectrum. Some waves are as short as a few trillionths of a meter (gamma waves). Some are as long as many thousands of meters (radio waves). In between are waves with lengths somewhat less than a millionth of a meter. These are the ones we can see. Actually, scientists measure them in units called nanometers, or billionths of a meter. The particular range of wavelengths humans can see is from about 380 to 760 nanometers. Wavelengths around 380 look violet in color, those around 760 look red, and in between, going from 380 to 760, people see blue, green, and yellow.

The Eye

A diagram of the eye is shown in Figure 14.1. In front is the cornea, through which light enters the eye. Behind that is a set of muscles, the iris, that form a pupil, an opening whose size regulates the amount of light admitted. Behind the iris is a lens which helps focus light on the retina, where the photosensitive receptors are located.

The whole arrangement is somewhat like a camera. As in a

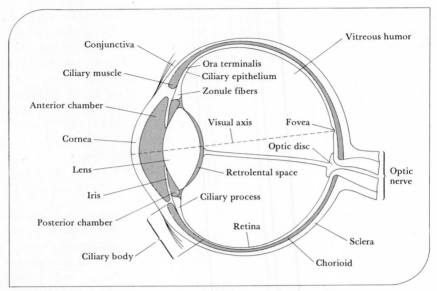

Figure 14.1 *The eye and some of its principal parts. (Based on Walls, 1942.)*

camera, the eye has a lens for focusing light on a photosensitive surface. On the other hand, it differs from a camera in several ways. The chief difference is that the eye focuses light by changing the *shape* of the lens, whereas a camera is focused by changing the *distance* of the lens from the film.

Day and Night Vision

When light passes through the cornea, lens, and the transparent fluid (vitreous humor) within the eye, it strikes the receptor cells of the retina. These are of two general types: *rods* and *cones,* which contain somewhat different photosensitive pigments, and in different amounts. The rods have much more pigment than the cones and because of this are much more sensitive. All rods contain the same pigment, *rhodopsin.* Cones, on the other hand, possess at least three different pigments, which are responsible for our color vision.

The difference in the *amount* of pigment in the rods and cones permits them to function at two different levels of adaptation. You can see this in the dark-adaptation curve shown in Figure 14.2. The curve is obtained by measuring a person's absolute threshold—the least light he can see—as he adapts in a pitch-black room after being in very bright light. The curve has two limbs: the first shows the adaptation of the cones, the second the adaptation of rods. Thus you can see that the receptors being used in bright light (day vision) are the cones, whereas the rods take over in dim light (night vision).

The difference in the *kind* of photosensitive substances in the rods and cones determines which wavelengths people see most easily. The difference consists of a slight variation in chemical structure. Because of it the pigment of the rods absorbs the most light in the blue-green region of the spectrum, around 500 nanometers. This means that at night we see the wavelengths of that part of the spectrum best. In contrast, pigments of the cones, taken together, absorb best in the yellow-green part of the spectrum, around 550 nanometers. Hence in daylight vision, our absolute thresholds for seeing are best in that region.

Taken separately, the three different pigments in the cones absorb light differently. One absorbs best in the blue region of the spectrum, around 450 nanometers. Another has its peak of absorption in the green near 530 nanometers, and a third absorbs best in the orange region at 600 nanometers. These three pigments are found in different cones: one kind of cone contains one pigment and another another. It is these differences in cone pigments that endow us with color vision.

Color Vision

Most of the facts of color vision are best explained by a scheme in which there are four basic hues. (Hue is the term used for a color as it is *perceived* by human beings, not as it is on the physical spectrum.) These are blue, green, yellow, and red. The two most compelling arguments for such a four-color scheme are supplied by the facts of *complementary colors* and of *color blindness*.

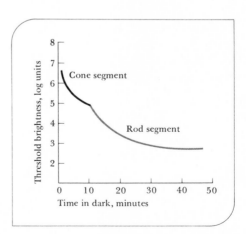

Figure 14.2 In the dark, the eye becomes thousands of times more sensitive. The graph shows a typical curve of dark adaptation. Notice the two segments of the curve; after 7 or 8 minutes the rods, which are re-sponsible for our dim-light vision, take over from the cones, which function in bright light.

Complementary colors Suppose that an experimenter has the gadgetry for producing single hues of any wavelength. Say that he has two such gadgets, and he can mix the output of the two by superimposing them on a screen. Thus he can present all possible combinations of wavelengths and ask a subject what he sees. The subject need merely describe the color he perceives as greenish-blue, yellow, orange, and so on.

An experiment of this sort illustrates the important phenomenon of complementary colors. Here complementary means that certain pairs of hues cancel each other, leaving the perception of gray or white. Red and green, for example, are complementary, and so are blue and yellow. In fact, for every color we can see, there is a complementary color. All the pairs of hues that are complementary can be represented on a diagram called a color circle. Any line drawn from one point on the circle through its center to the other side of the circle connects two complementary colors. (For a further explanation of the color circle, see Figure 14.3.)

Research workers have recorded from individual nerve cells in the brain and find that these behave exactly as one would expect from the color circle (de Valois et al., 1966). For example, a nerve cell that responds most vigorously to a green stimulus is inhibited—its activity is canceled—by the complementary red stimulus. Other cells behave in a similar way to yellow and blue. Hence the color mechanism of the brain consists of cells that respond positively to certain stimuli and negatively to their complementary colors.

Color blindness The facts of color blindness also fit the scheme of the four basic hues which can be divided into two complementary pairs of colors. In most cases, what is called color blindness is not a complete lack of color vision. In fact, completely color-blind persons are so rare that only a handful have been found. The color blindness that is common—1 out of 15 men have it, although less than 1 out of 100 women do—is two-color vision. The person can see one pair of colors, but not the other pair seen by normal people. And the two-color blindness that is most common is red-green blindness, where the person sees all hues of the spectrum as either blue or yellow. For him, all reds are tints of yellow, and all greens, with one exception, are tints of either yellow or blue. The exception is a wavelength between yellow and blue that people with normal vision see as fairly pure green. To the red-green color-blind person, however, this green appears white, and thus has no hue at all!

Visual Acuity
The fineness of detail that an individual can perceive in his visual environment is called visual acuity. It can be measured in the laborato-

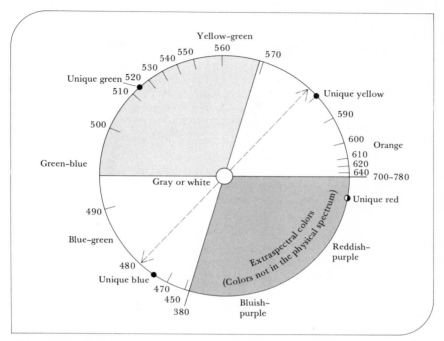

Figure 14.3 *The color circle, showing colors as perceived by humans. The hues opposite each other on the circle are complementary. This means that in human vision their wavelengths cancel each other out when mixed together so that we see only gray or white. The numbers are wavelengths given in nanometers. Unique colors are wavelengths that seem "pure" to humans: thus a unique yellow is a hue that seems to be untinged with green or red. The darkly shaded wedge of the circle stands for extraspectral hues, meaning colors that we perceive but not color as it exists in the physical spectrum. For example, unique red is in the extraspectral part of the circle. This is because the reddest red in the physical spectrum is still not red enough for us to perceive it as "pure"; a little blue from the other end of the physical spectrum must be mixed with it before we call it pure red. The colors on the lightly shaded wedge of the circle have no complementary wavelengths in the physical spectrum. They are formed out of mixtures of the red and the blue ends of the spectrum. But for human vision, any straight line drawn from one point on the circle through the center to the other side of the circle connects two complementary colors. (Note that the rules for mixing wavelengths are not the same as those for mixing paints. Paints do not emit light; they reflect or absorb it in varying degrees. The color circle refers only to wavelengths of light.)*

ry, but for most purposes the eye chart used by physicians and optometrists will do. This tests the smallest letters a person can read at a standard distance of 20 feet. If he is normal, he is said to have 20/20 vision. By contrast, a person who must be as close as 20 feet to see what a normal person sees at 50 feet is said to have 20/50 vision. Simply as a matter of convenience, the eye chart varies the *size* rather than the *distance* of letters.

Visual acuity depends on how well the eye can focus objects on the retina. This in turn depends on the cornea and the accommodation of the lens. The cornea helps the lens by slightly bending the light that strikes it. To do the job correctly, it must have the same curvature in all directions—up, down, and sideways. If the curvature is not the same in all directions, the person is said to have astigmatism. For this condition the doctor prescribes a corrective lens—eyeglasses—whose curvature compensates for the irregularity of the cornea.

The task of accommodating to the distance of objects is performed by the lens of the eye. How well it does the job depends on two things: the length of the eyeball, and the hardness of the lens. Some people's eyeballs are too long—so long that the lens cannot flatten enough to focus on distant objects. These people are nearsighted and need eyeglasses to correct the defect. Other people have eyeballs that are too short, so that the lens cannot bulge enough to focus on near objects. They too need corrective glasses; they are farsighted. Another cause of farsightedness is the hardening of the lens with age, a process which goes faster and further in some people than in others. As the lens hardens, it is less and less able to bulge and so less able to focus on near objects. This is why most people become farsighted as they grow older, and increasingly so in their later years.

HEARING

In hearing, the general sequence of events is the same as it is in vision, but the details differ considerably. Instead of electromagnetic radiation, the stimulus is an acoustic wave, or sound wave. In hearing there is no chemical step, as there is in vision; rather, the mechanical vibration causes some hair cells in the ear to generate a potential which in turn trips off nerve impulses.

The Ear
As shown in Figure 14.4, the ear has three main parts: the external ear, middle ear, and inner ear.

1 *External ear.* This area consists of the fleshy part that we commonly call the ear, a canal, and at the end of it a membrane named the *tympanic membrane* or eardrum. A pressure wave in the air strikes this drum, causing it to vibrate.

2 *Middle ear.* Located on the other side of the tympanic membrane, the middle ear is connected to the mouth by the Eustachian tube. Normally, pressure on the two sides of the eardrum is kept equal

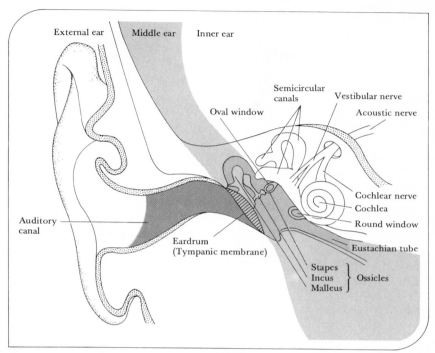

Figure 14.4 *The human ear and its three major parts—external ear, middle ear, and inner ear. The cochlea in the inner ear is the true organ of hearing. (Based on a modification from M. Brodel in E. Gardner,* Fundamentals of Neurology, *5th ed., Philadelphia, Saunders, 1968.)*

by air entering or leaving through this tube. When the tube is sucked shut by lowered pressure in the middle ear, as it often is when we are in a descending airplane, we may have to increase the pressure in the mouth to blow out the middle ear. The main feature of the middle ear is a series of three small bones (see the ossicles in Figure 14.4) that conduct vibration from the eardrum to another membrane, the oval window, which lies at the entrance to the inner ear.

3 *Inner ear.*   Two structures occupy the inner ear: the cochlea, which is the true organ of hearing, and the vestibular organs, which are involved in the sense of balance. At the moment we are concerned only with the cochlea. As shown in Figure 14.4, it is a bony coil—in Latin cochlea means snail shell. Inside it (not shown in the drawing) are three canals separated from each other by membranes. On one canal's membrane—called the basilar membrane—is the all-important organ of Corti. This tiny structure contains the receptors for hearing, which are cells with hairs embedded in a membrane hanging just above them.

When the basilar membrane vibrates, the hairs are stimulated. That activity sets up a generator potential—called the microphonic potential—which in turn stimulates nerve fibers connected to the base of hair cells. Over these fibers nerve impulses travel to the brain.

Sound Stimuli

Acoustic waves, which are the stimulus for hearing, consist of alternations in air pressure that travel through air. An object produces acoustic waves by vibrating in some fashion. (A bomb blast or pistol shot may produce only one vibration.) As the object vibrates, it first pushes air molecules together, increasing the pressure, then sucks them back, decreasing it. The alternating series of high- and low-pressure pulses of moving air constitute the pressure wave, which is conventionally but loosely called the "sound wave." The physicist can get a precise picture of any sound by setting up a microphone that transduces sound into electrical energy, then running the electrical signal through an amplifier onto a cathode ray screen, which is an instrument of the same general type as a television screen.

The simplest and purest of sounds is known as a *sine wave*. Figure 14.5 shows, at left, sine waves being produced by a sound source; at bottom left, waves plotted as a graph; and right, ordinary graphs of three sine waves. Notice on the graphs at right that the scales for plotting a sine wave are pressure and time. The greater the pressure, the more intense (louder) the sound. To measure loudness scientists use a unit called the *decibel*, which is a ratio of the pressure of a given sound to the absolute threshold of hearing. Thus 20 decibels represents a ratio of 10 times the slightest sound a "perfect" ear can hear, 40 decibels a ratio of 100 times, 60 decibels a ratio of 1,000 times, and so on up to 120 decibels, which represents a ratio of 1 million times the absolute threshold of hearing.

The time scale of a sine wave is related to its frequency. If one complete wave occupies one thousandth of a second, the wave will occur 1,000 times a second. This is its frequency. Cycles per second are called *hertz* (Hz). So, in this case, the sound would have a frequency of 1,000 Hz, like two of the sine waves at the right of Figure 14.5. Sound waves can have any frequency up to thousands of Hz, but the ones we hear run from about 20 Hz to 20,000 Hz. Frequencies above that are called *ultrasonic* frequencies. (The term *supersonic*, on the other hand, refers to traveling at a speed faster than sound, which is about 760 miles an hour at sea level.)

Sine waves are heard only in the laboratory, where electronic equipment can produce tones of one frequency. The sounds heard in everyday life are always mixtures of several, sometimes hundreds, of

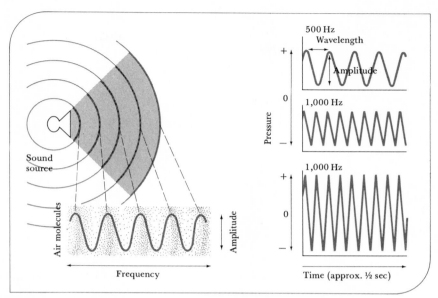

Figure 14.5 *Left, a pressure wave generated by a sound source. Bottom left, a sound wave corresponding to a given pressure wave can be represented graphically. The sound wave's amplitude is the strength of the pressure wave—the difference in pressure between its densest and most rarified points. The sound wave's frequency is the number of pressure waves generated per second. Right, three sine waves, or simple sound waves, with different amplitudes and frequencies. The upper and middle sine waves have the same amplitude, or pressure, but the middle one has a frequency twice that of the upper one. The middle and lower sine waves have the same frequency, but the lower one has an amplitude twice that of the middle one.*

sine waves, although the tone of the tuning fork often used to tune up musical instruments is nearly pure. Musical instruments produce a dominant sine-wave sound, called the fundamental, mixed with some components called overtones which are multiples of the fundamental frequency. Noises like the hiss of escaping steam contain many different frequencies in no particular relation to each other. When a noise includes nearly all possible frequencies in the audible range, it is called *white noise*. The parallel here is that people normally see white when light contains many frequencies of the spectrum.

Frequency and Pitch

Frequency, we have just seen, is a physical aspect of the sound stimulus. The term *pitch*, in contrast, refers to the psychological attribute of tones. It is what we perceive. Pitch and frequency change in the same direction; when one goes up, so does the other; but they do not change in a one-to-one fashion. This can be demonstrated by constructing a pitch scale, then relating it to frequency.

A pitch scale can be obtained in the hearing laboratory by giving a subject headphones and presenting him with a pure tone chosen by the experimenter. This is the standard tone. The subject is also given a dial with which he can select a tone of any frequency. He is instructed to find one that seems to him just twice as high as the standard tone. He uses a switch to change back and forth from one to the other so he can compare the two. When he feels that he has chosen the correct frequency, the experimenter records it and then gives him another standard tone, for which he is supposed to find another tone just twice as high in pitch.

The scale can be constructed by taking as a standard tone for the base of each "step" the last tone judged to be twice as high. As you can see in Figure 14.6, a subject chooses a tone of about 1,000 Hz as being twice the pitch of 400 Hz. He chooses another at 3,500 Hz as being twice the 1,000-Hz tone. And so on. Clearly, pitch and frequency are not the same thing; a twofold increase in frequency falls short of producing a similar increase in pitch.

How do we hear pitch? According to modern research, the answer lies in the basilar membrane. When a sound enters the inner ear, it travels down the canals of the cochlea, making the cochlea bulge. The basilar membrane varies in width and stiffness, the first part of it being narrower and stiffer than the far end. This affects how easily it bulges for tones of different frequencies. It bulges more at the first part when the frequency is high, and more at the far end when the frequency is low. Hence tones of different frequencies stimulate the basilar membrane at different places. This pattern of activity is maintained throughout the auditory system up through the brain. Consequently

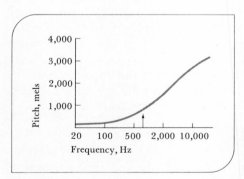

Figure 14.6 *This pitch scale helps make the point that pitch is a psychological experience, whereas frequency is a physical dimension. Units of pitch are called "mels."*

our ability to hear pitch, like our perception of hue, depends on *which* nerve fibers are stimulated.

Intensity and Loudness
As mentioned earlier, the range of frequencies heard by people is roughly 20 to 20,000 Hz. Besides having upper and lower limits, a person's audible range has a central portion of greatest sensitivity— usually from about 1,000 to about 4,000 Hz. In this range of frequencies we hear best. The consonants of speech, which are most important for speech intelligibility, fall largely in the central range.

Tones presented at increasing intensity above the lower limit, of course, sound louder and louder. Figure 14.7 shows the intensity in decibels of some familiar sounds. But again, intensity is a physical attribute that is not the same as loudness, which is a psychological attribute. Loudness grows rather slowly in the middle part of the spectrum where hearing is most sensitive. On the other hand, it grows quite rapidly, for a given decibel increase in intensity, at the two ends of the spectrum where hearing of low intensities is poor. Experiments done by physiologists show further that loudness is correlated with the number of impulses traveling in the auditory pathways. This fact is comparable to the fact that in vision, the brightness of a light is determined by the number of impulses.

Deafness
In the common sensory defect of deafness, the person's absolute threshold for sound is raised above normal. For example, if it is elevated an average of 50 decibels, we say he has a hearing loss of 50 decibels.

There are two kinds of deafness: conduction deafness and nerve deafness. *Conduction deafness* occurs when the conduction of sound through the middle ear is blocked in some way. A broken eardrum can do it. Or the middle ear bones may be "frozen" by diseases of the middle ear so that they do not properly transmit vibrations to the inner ear. In conduction deafness, the person's hearing for both low and high tones is impaired.

The second kind of deafness, *nerve deafness*, is so named because it is thought to be caused by degeneration of nerve fibers serving the cochlea. This kind of deafness has a hereditary basis, for it runs in families. However, almost everyone suffers some degree of nerve deafness as he grows older, just as most people become more farsighted. In most people the loss is not severe enough to harm speech perception, but in some the impairment can be profound.

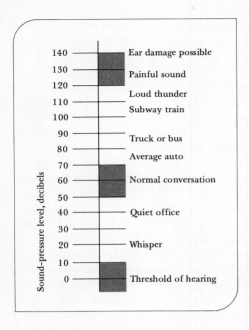

Figure 14.7 *The intensity of familiar sounds, in decibels. Normal conversation is about 60 decibels above the threshold of hearing; loud thunder is about 120 decibels above.*

What makes nerve deafness different from conduction deafness is the loss of high-tone hearing. The patient's first losses are in the high frequencies which people use very little. As his deafness progresses, his hearing in the middle frequencies becomes impaired. This is a real handicap, because the consonant sounds necessary for understanding speech have frequencies in the middle range. As the impairment invades lower and lower frequencies, the patient has increasing difficulty in hearing what people are saying. Even then, his hearing of very low frequencies may be intact, and with these he can listen to music. He will not hear everything the normal person does, but he can follow the drums and the notes made by the lower-pitched instruments.

THE CHEMICAL SENSES

The senses other than vision and hearing are sometimes called the lower senses. Certainly they are much less important to us than vision and hearing. Taste and smell are often classed as the *chemical senses* because they are stimulated by chemical substances. In taste, the chemicals are in watery solutions bathing the tongue and surfaces of the mouth. In smell, they are in gases that can be absorbed by the receptor cells of the nose.

Taste

The receptors for taste consist of cells with hairs on them. They are located in pits and supported by other cells, and the whole structure forms a *taste bud*. Chemical substances seeping into the buds produce generator potentials in the taste cells. These in turn trigger impulses in the nerve fibers connected to the base of the cells.

Research indicates that there are four primary taste qualities in man: sweet, sour, salt, and bitter. By mapping the tongue using an appropriate stimulus for each, physiologists have found that the qualities are differently distributed: some areas have more sweet spots than sour spots, and so on. As seen throughout this chapter, studies of nerve fibers present the same general picture: some fibers respond predominantly to one kind of stimulus, other fibers to other stimuli. So again in this case, as in the sensory mechanisms of vision and hearing, different receptors give rise to different experiences.

Researchers who try to find out what chemical differences in stimuli are responsible for these different experiences achieve only partial success. Salts, like common table salt, are the main stimuli for the taste of salt. Acids, like citric acid, are the main ones for the taste of sour. Various sugars give rise to a sweet taste. But the experience of bitterness is aroused by many different stimuli, the most potent of which is quinine. Moreover, the relationships for the first three are only approximate. Some salts also taste sweet, and acids may taste salty. Therefore scientists do not yet know what features of chemical substances give rise to the various taste experiences.

Smell

Smell is the most enigmatic of the senses. It is exquisitely sensitive, for it sometimes requires only a few molecules of a gas to be detected. This is the case with musk (from a gland of the musk deer) and with the odor of a skunk. On the other hand, physiologists still have no good idea of how many basic qualities of smell there are. Some schemes propose six, others nine; but no one is satisfied with any of them. So there is little that we can say positively about smell.

One interesting point is that many of the things we eat or drink both taste and smell, so that the two senses are stimulated at the same time. For that reason we tend to confuse flavors and odors, and often think that we are tasting what we are actually smelling. You can make your own experiment by asking a friend to hold his nose while you place familiar foods on his tongue. If you give him a drop of lemon juice, the chances are that he will only be able to say it is something sour. If you drop a little Coke on his tongue, he may know only that it is something bittersweet. If you give him a piece of potato, he may be unable to distinguish its taste from that of an apple. Now repeat the experiment when he can smell too, and he will immediately identify the substance.

SKIN SENSES

Scientists have known for nearly a century that there are four distinct skin senses. This fact can be proved in several ways. One of the simplest is to perform the following experiment:

A grid is stamped on the undersurface of a subject's forearm. The experimenter has a corresponding grid printed on paper so that he can plot the results of the experiment. Using a fine hair that exerts a constant pressure when applied to the skin, he touches first one square, then another. When the subject says he feels it, the point is recorded on the experimenter's chart. After plotting all the points at which the subject feels the hair, the experimenter now turns to mapping cold spots. He takes a metal rod, kept at a temperature of 28°C (somewhat below skin temperature) and touches each square of the grid, asking the subject to report "cold." Next he does the same thing to map "warm" spots, using a metal rod kept at 35°C (slightly above skin temperature) while the subject reports whenever he feels warmth. Finally the experimenter maps the grid a fourth time, using a fine needle to produce pain.

The results of such an experiment are shown in Figure 14.8. Notice two features: First, any one of the different sensations is felt at certain

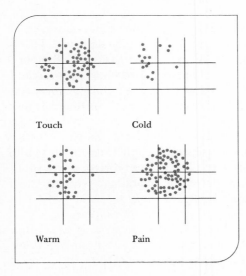

Touch   Cold

Warm   Pain

Figure 14.8 *Mapping the sensitivity of the skin. By marking a grid on an area of the skin and then systematically stimulating different spots, we can construct a map of the sensitive spots. Maps for touch, cold, warmth, and pain stimuli are usually different, indicating that there are four distinct skin senses. (Diagram from Gerard, 1941.)*

points on the skin and not at others. This phenomenon is known as *punctate sensitivity*. What it means is that the skin is more sensitive to a particular kind of stimulus at some points than at others. Secondly, no two maps are the same. The points at which a person feels "cold" are not the same as those at which he feels "warmth." This indicates that there are two distinct temperature senses. Neither are the touch and pain maps the same, which proves that pain is a separate sense from the others.

Touch or pressure   The sensation of touch or pressure is aroused, as in the experiment above, whenever the skin is touched. What causes the sensation is a depression of the skin. The same sensation is experienced when one of the hairs on the body is bent—in this case because stress is placed on the root of the hair, stimulating cells around the root which in turn activate a nerve fiber ending on them. In the case of depression of the skin, there are sometimes special structures, called *encapsulated end organs*, that serve as the receptors. Free nerve endings, terminating in the skin but not in any special structure, can also act as receptors.

Cold and warmth   If a physiologist digs out the skin under a cold or a warm spot—does a *biopsy*—and looks at it under a microscope, sometimes he finds encapsulated end organs and sometimes he does not. So the only really essential is a nerve ending that is responsive to cold or to warmth. Hence unspecialized (free) nerve endings serve as receptors for all the skin senses. Nevertheless, these nerve endings must be specialized in ways that scientists cannot see, because different endings respond to different kinds of stimuli.

Warmth fibers respond when the skin is warmed above its normal "physiological zero" of 32–33°C. Cold fibers respond when the skin is cooled below that point. Curiously, though, cold fibers also respond when the skin is warmed above 45°C. This means that as the skin is warmed (say, by increasingly warm or hot water), the warmth receptors are activitated first, but at a higher temperature, both cold and warmth receptors are stimulated. It is then that the sensation changes from warm to hot. "Hot," therefore, is the sensation of both warmth and cold. Of course, if a stimulus is very hot we experience pain. Such a stimulus evokes impulses in three kinds of receptors at the same time—cold, warmth, and pain.

Pain   Besides heat, many other stimuli produce pain—a needle prick, a hard blow to the skin, or strong acid. One of the most precise ways to elicit pain in the laboratory is with radiant heat. By regulating the temperature of the heater, the experimenter can measure the threshold for pain—which turns out to be very close to the point at which tissues begin to break down. Thus pain is in effect a warning of impending injury.

Various experiments indicate that the receptors for pain are almost surely unspecialized free nerve endings. A liberal supply of these is found in most parts of the skin, particularly where sensitivity to pain is greatest. Though unspecialized in appearance, the free nerve endings for pain are specialized in their sensitivity: they respond to injurious stimuli but not to temperature and pressure. Of course, since the things that cause pain also touch the skin and sometimes also are warm or cold, people normally do not experience pain without experiencing one or more of the other skin sensations as well.

PROPRIOCEPTIVE SENSES

Proprioception, the general term for our sense of body position, is two senses. One is the kinesthetic sense, whose receptors are in our muscles, tendons, and joints. The other, the vestibular sense, is located in the part of the ear which is not concerned with hearing.

Kinesthetic Sense
Kinesthetic sense organs tell us the posture of the body and the position of our arms and legs, even when we cannot see them or they are not in contact with anything else. The receptors that supply the information are located in three distinct places: (1) One is a structure known as a muscle spindle found in skeletal muscles. The receptors in this spindle signal the *stretch* of the muscle. (2) Another is in the tendons that connect muscles to bones. The receptors in these tendons signal pull or *tension.* (3) Finally, in the linings of our joints are the receptors that indicate the *position* of the joint.

Vestibular Sense
The vestibular receptors are found in the same bone of the skull which contains the cochlea. They consist of three *semicircular canals* (shown in the diagram of the ear, Figure 14.4) and two *otolith organs.* The canals are arranged so that each one is at right angles to the other two. Fluid in one or more of them is displaced whenever the head is rotated in any direction, and the displaced fluid causes hair cells to be stimulated. The canals are therefore organs for sensing head movement.

The otolith organs also contain hair cells as receptors. The cells are so arranged that certain ones are stimulated according to the position of the head. The otolith organs are therefore position receptors.

The vestibular sense is unique in supplying information that is not directly experienced. When you move your head, you do not experience the input from the vestibular receptors. Instead you experience kinesthetic information coming from tendons connected with various muscles of the head. All the other senses except the vestibular sense provide conscious sensations.

Vestibular information is useful because it evokes reflex reactions of the body and limbs to keep us upright. Such *righting actions,* as they are called, can be seen when a cat is dropped. Even if the cat begins to fall with its back toward the ground, it will land on its feet because of reflex responses to position information coming from the otolith organs. The dizziness we feel when we spin rapidly is due to the unnatural sloshing around of the fluid in the semicircular canals. The motion sickness which makes so many people miserable when they are in boats or cars is also caused by impulses from the vestibular organs.

SUMMARY

Man has ten distinct senses: vision, hearing, taste, smell, touch, cold, warmth, pain, kinesthesis, and a vestibular sense. Each sense has a certain kind of receptor cell that is specialized to respond to a particular form of energy. Each kind of receptor has a sensory code that determines the quality of experience resulting from activation of the receptor. Receptors have absolute and differential thresholds. All receptors undergo adaptation, some much more than others.

The eye generally functions like a camera. It has two kinds of receptors: rods for night vision, cones for day vision. Only the cones see color. Different cones respond to different wavelengths of light, so that we experience four primary colors divided into two complementary pairs of colors. The most common form of color blindness is red-green blindness. Visual acuity depends mainly on how well the lens of the eye can focus.

The stimulus for hearing is pressure changes in the air. Vibrations are transmitted through the middle-ear bones to the cochlea, where a traveling bulge stimulates hair cells of the basilar membrane. The purest sound is a sine wave. We can hear sine waves with frequencies between about 20 Hz and 20,000 Hz. Pitch is the subjective experience that is related, but not in a one-to-one fashion, to the frequency of a tone. There are two varieties of deafness: conduction deafness and nerve deafness. In conduction deafness the hearing of both low and high tones is impaired; in nerve deafness the hearing of high tones is lost.

In taste, one of the chemical senses, there are four primary qualities: sweet, sour, salt, and bitter. No satisfactory classification of smells exists. There are four distinct skin senses: touch or pressure, cold, warmth, and pain. Of the proprioceptive senses, kinesthesis, which has receptors in the muscles, tendons, and joints, provides information about movement. The vestibular sense, which has receptors in the inner ear, supplies information about balance and the movement of the head.

SUGGESTIONS FOR FURTHER READING

Alpern, M., Lawrence, M., and Wolsk, D. *Sensory processes.* Monterey, Calif.: Brooks/Cole, 1967. (Paperback.) *A short textbook on sensory mechanisms, with emphasis on peripheral receptor processes.*

Bergeijk, W. A. van, Pierce, J. R., and David, E. E., Jr. *Waves and the ear.* Garden City, N. Y.: Doubleday, 1960. (Paperback.) *A popular and interesting account of many aspects of hearing and speech sounds.*

Geldard, F. A. *The human senses.* (2d ed.) New York: Wiley, 1972. *A well-written standard textbook on the senses.*

Gregory, R. L. *Eye and brain: The psychology of seeing.* New York: McGraw-Hill, 1966. *An interesting and colorful account of visual sensation and perception.*

Lowenstein, O. *The senses.* Baltimore: Penguin, 1966. (Paperback.) *A survey of sensory mechanisms with special attention to the sensory capacities of lower animals.*

15

The Nervous System and Behavior

LEARNING OBJECTIVES

Main objective
After studying this chapter you should be able to outline the functions of the parts of the brain that are most involved in behavior.

Other major objectives
You should be able to
Diagram the way in which neurons are joined in synapses to form reflex arcs.
Draw and label the principal parts of the nervous system.
Indicate the role of the hypothalamus in motivation and emotion.
Discuss localization of function in the cerebral cortex.

Minor objectives
Describe the transmissions of neural messages in fibers and across synapses.
Account for the length(s) of human reaction time.
Outline the pathways in the nervous system of the various senses.
Describe the role of the limbic system and hypothalamus in emotion.

The nervous system is *the* organ of behavior. Everything you sense, perceive, learn, think, and do is the outcome of activities within it. Knowing something about these activities will help you to understand behavior better.

NEURONS AND SYNAPSES

Every individual begins life as a single cell, which divides and multiplies over and over again until the various organs of the body take form. In the multiplication, cells *differentiate*—specialize in form and function—so that each comes to play a particular role in the body's activities. Although every organ of the body eventually consists of many kinds of cells, one kind usually serves the organ's principal function. In the case of the nervous system this cell is the *neuron*, and its function is to conduct nerve impulses.

Neurons

Neurons vary a great deal in size and shape. The one sketched in Figure 15.1 was chosen to bring out the essential features of all. There you can see that neurons have two general parts: a *cell body* and *fibers*. The cell body contains structures that keep the neuron alive and functioning normally. Fibers are of two types: *dendrites*, which are stimulated by neighboring neurons or by physical stimuli, and *axons*, which deliver nerve impulses to adjacent neurons or to an *effector*, such as a muscle.

Dendrites and axons may be relatively long or very short, depending on the cells they connect with. Many of the neurons within the brain are closely packed, and some have very short fibers less than a millimeter in length. The sensory neurons serving the skin of the arms

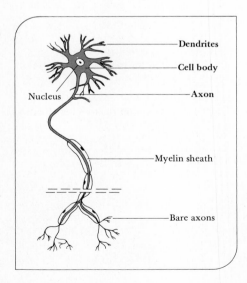

Figure 15.1 *Diagram of a neuron, the basic unit of the nervous system. Essentially it consists of a cell body and two kinds of fibers: dendrites and axons. The neuron's main function is to conduct nerve impulses. (Modified from Brazier, 1968.)*

and legs have dendrites as long as 3 feet and rather short axons. On the other hand, motor neurons, which serve the distant muscles of the body, have axons as long as 3 feet and short dendrites.

Nerve Impulses

The neuron's chief function is to conduct nerve impulses. These are very brief electrical changes traveling along the fiber at speeds of 1 to 100 meters a second. Figure 15.2 shows a record of a nerve impulse, or spike potential, as it moves along the nerve fiber toward the nervous system. The spike takes about a thousandth of a second, more or less, to pass any particular point on the fiber.

What sets off a nervous impulse is a *graded potential* in the dendrite of a neuron. If the neuron is sensory, this potential is the *generator potential* caused by an external stimulus (already described on page 335). In neurons further "upstream" (closer to the nervous system), the graded potential is aroused by a neurotransmitter secreted by the adjacent neuron (a process described in the next section). In either case, the graded potential is proportional in size to the stimulus that arouses it.

Not so with the nervous impulse. When the generator or graded potential reaches some threshold size, the nervous impulse it trips off follows an *all-or-none law*: The impulse either appears at its maximum size or does not occur at all. It goes off much like the shot of a gun. When it occurs, it travels down the dendrite, through the membrane of the cell body, and then down the axon to its very end (look again at Figure 15.1). This is unlike the generator or graded potential that builds up locally without traveling away from its point of origin. The graded potential serves only as the link between a stimulus and a nerve impulse.

For a brief moment—a thousandth of a second or so—during the spike, the fiber cannot respond to further stimulation. It is said to be in an *absolute refractory period*. After this, however, it begins to recover its sensitivity. During the period of recovery, called the *relative refractory period*, a stimulus can produce another impulse, but the stimulus must be more intense than is necessary for a fully rested fiber.

The length of the refractory period, especially the absolute refractory period, limits the rate of firing of a neuron. Just as the rifleman who can reload his gun faster can fire more often, so the neuron that recovers more quickly than another can deliver impulses at a more rapid rate. The larger fibers recover in about one millisecond; hence they can fire as often as 1,000 times a second. Some of the smaller fibers can deliver impulses at the rate of only a few a second.

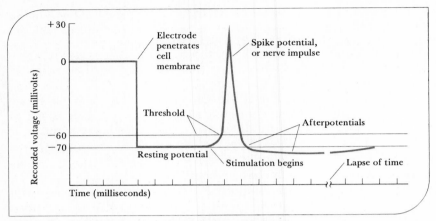

Figure 15.2 *A schematic record of the voltage changes inside a nerve cell during an experiment in which the cell is stimulated. At first, the elctrode is outside the cell and the recorded voltage is zero. When the electrode penetrates the cell membrane, the voltage drops suddenly to the resting potential, which is −70 millivolts in this experiment.*
Next, stimulation begins, and at first the change of voltage is slow. When the threshold is reached, sodium ions rush into the cell and the change of voltage is very rapid. The inside of the cell becomes positive, about +30 millivolts, for a brief period during the spike. Then the voltage declines and, after going through a period when afterpotentials appear, finally comes to the resting potential again. (Modified from Ruch and Patton, 1965.)

Synaptic Connections

Neurons that serve as receptors or are connected to receptors are called *sensory neurons.* As a nervous impulse comes to the end of a sensory neuron—in fact, any neuron—there is a gap between that neuron and the next one. This gap is known as a *synapse.* Nervous impulses cannot cross synapses. Instead, something else happens to bridge the gap.

This something else is the secretion of a chemical transmitter, otherwise known as a neurotransmitter. The transmitter is secreted by the axon and stored in sacs in the foot of the axon. When an impulse reaches this point, it causes some transmitter to be squirted out into the synaptic gap. There the transmitter excites the membrane of the dendrite across the gap, arousing in it a graded potential—in this case, the *postsynaptic potential.* This, like the generator potential or any graded potential, serves to get another impulse started in its neuron.

Most sensory neurons extend all the way from a sense organ—no matter how far away it may be—to the central nervous system. This is the part of the nervous system contained in the bony case of the skull and spinal column. There the sensory neurons make their first synapses with adjacent neurons. In some instances—for example, in the eye—there are several synapses within the sense organ itself, so that the neuron which enters the central nervous system is the third or fourth in a chain.

Reflexes

Within the central nervous system, several arrangements of neurons are possible. Fixed arrangements connecting sense organs with muscles are called *reflex arcs* (Figure 15.3). Some of these involve only one or two synapses in the spinal cord. The reflexes executed by such arcs can be classified into two general groups: flexion reflexes and extension reflexes. Most of us have observed our own flexion reflexes when we have touched a hot stove or stepped on a sharp object. In each case we react by quickly flexing (bending) the limb concerned to withdraw it rapidly from the stimulus.

Extension reflexes are even more common than flexion reflexes, but we are less aware of them. Each time we put a foot down in walking, for example, pressure on the bottom of the foot causes the leg to stiffen to support our weight. And when we lift a foot off the ground, the opposite leg reflexly stiffens to support the body. The reflex in this case has its stimulus in the kinesthetic receptors of the flexed leg. Extension reflexes aid us in standing, walking, and running, and they occur so regularly that we seldom notice them.

Other sets of reflexes are executed through the brain and involve several synapses. Examples are the blink of the eyelid when the cornea of the eye is touched, the contraction of the pupil in bright light, salivation when food is placed in the mouth, the pricking of a dog's ears when it hears an unfamiliar sound, and the turning of a cat's head toward the ground when it is held upside down.

More complex reflexes may involve several neurons whose fibers extend some distance in the nervous system. One example is the scratch reflex seen in our household pets or occasionally in ourselves. The scratch reflex is a nicely timed alternation of flexion and extension reflexes.

Inhibition

The timing and smoothness of reflex action depend not only on impulses traveling through reflex pathways but also on the *inhibition* of some impulses. Inhibition works like this: The muscles of the body, and particularly those of the limbs, are arranged in *antagonistic* pairs. One set of muscles extends the limb; another set, the antagonistic set, flexes it. The two sets of antagonistic muscles, however, seldom contract at

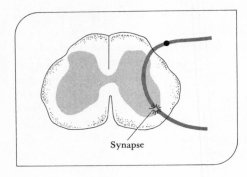

Figure 15.3 *The simplest reflex arc. This is a cross section of the spinal cord showing two fibers and the synapse between them. Such arcs can produce flexion and extension reflexes.*

Synapse

the same time. When the extensor muscles contract, the flexor muscles are relaxed because they are inhibited, and vice versa. Thus through the inhibition of some muscles, antagonistic muscles are kept from working against each other, and only one reflex is dominant at a time.

The inhibition of reflexes is just one case of inhibition, which is a general phenomenon of synaptic function. An inhibitory impulse causes a neuron to be less excitable and so not to respond to impulses from another source. Inhibitory impulses can come from the muscles (kinesthetic receptors) involved in a reflex and from various other pathways in the nervous system. Inhibition, in fact, is prominent in most of the sensory pathways.

Reaction Time

Every reaction to a stimulus requires a finite amount of time. This time between presentation of a stimulus and reaction to it is called *reaction time.* For simple reflexes, it is on the order of $1/10$ second, though it varies with the reflex. For simple voluntary reactions, such as pushing a key when a light is flashed or a bell is sounded, the reaction time is roughly $2/10$ second. For more complex reactions, like pushing the brake pedal of an automobile, reaction time is closer to 1 second.

From studies of nerve activity, scientists know that reaction time depends mostly on the number of synapses involved. Although it takes time for nerve impulses to travel along nerve fibers, their speed is very fast. Reaction times would be much shorter than they actually are if nothing besides nerve impulses were involved. It is the secretion of neurotransmitters at synapses that is the slow event in the chain. This causes a delay of several milliseconds at each synapse, so that the more synapses, the more delay. Thus synaptic transmission accounts for relatively long reaction times, especially in responses that involve many neurons and synapses of the nervous system.

THE NERVOUS SYSTEM

The parts of the nervous system can be classified in several ways. Each method of classification has its use. One general approach is to distinguish between the *central nervous system* and the *peripheral nervous system*. The central nervous system is the part of the system that lies inside the bony case formed by the skull and spine. The neurons, or parts of neurons, together with supporting tissues, enclosed within this bony case make up the central nervous system. Those that lie outside the bony case constitute the peripheral nervous system. Other methods of classification will be given later.

Peripheral Nervous System

In large part, the peripheral nervous system consists of fibers of sensory and motor neurons. These fibers are always collected together in bundles called *nerves*. For most of the journey to and from the central nervous system the nerves contain both sensory and motor fibers, although some of the nerves entering and leaving the skull are only sensory or only motor. Just outside the central nervous system, most nerves divide into two roots: a sensory root and a motor root. They do this because they have different points of origin and departure in the central nervous system.

What has just been said applies to *fibers* of the peripheral nervous system. Taking the system as a whole, it has two parts: the autonomic and the somatic systems. The *autonomic system* was briefly discussed in connection with emotion (Chapter 4). It serves blood vessels, the heart, glands, and other internal organs of the body. It is stirred up in emotion. The *somatic system* serves the ten senses and the skeletal muscles of the body that are involved in standing, walking, writing, and other forms of activity.

Central Nervous System

The neurons within the central nervous system are more or less segregated into centers and pathways. The centers are made up of cell bodies; the pathways consist of bundles of fibers. Frequently, however, the cell bodies in a center have very short fibers that synapse with neighboring neurons within the same center. Fibers in the pathways also usually synapse with other neurons in these centers. The center is therefore something of a mixture of cell bodies and fibers.

Centers have special names depending on where they are and how they are arranged. Sometimes they are called *nuclei*, in other cases *ganglia*, and in still others simply *areas*. Whenever one of these terms is used, it refers to collections of cell bodies where synaptic connections are made.

White and gray matter   A coincidence of nature makes it easy to tell pathways and centers apart. The normal color of a neuron is gray. But the color of the fatty sheath—the myelin sheath, shown in Figure 15.1—that clothes most fibers of the central nervous system is white. Cell bodies do not have this sheath and so appear gray. For this reason, when you look at tissues from the central nervous system either with the naked eye or under the microscope, pathways are white and centers gray. For this reason too, pathways are often spoken of as *white matter* and centers as *gray matter*.

The spinal cord   The central nervous system is housed in two places: the spinal cord enclosed by the backbone, and the brain within the skull. The center of the spinal cord is gray and its outside is white—meaning that the central gray consists of cell bodies of neurons, while the conducting pathways are in the outside white. In general, the pathways in the back are sensory pathways, and those in the front, that is, toward the abdomen, are motor fibers.

The spinal cord has two general functions: as a conduction path to and from the brain, and as an organ for producing reflex action. Most reflexes are affected by impulses descending from the brain, yet when the brain is disconnected from the cord in experimental animals, many reflexes can operate as purely spinal affairs. In fact the extension, flexion, and scratch reflexes mentioned earlier, as well as the basic pattern of alternating steps in walking, are organized at the spinal level.

The Brain

Of the two principal parts of the central nervous system, the spinal cord and the brain, the brain is naturally the most interesting. It plays the central role in all complex activities: learning, thinking, perception, and so on. The brain's role in these processes will be the subject of the following sections. In order to understand it, however, you must first take time to look at its general structure. The relation of the brain and spinal cord to the head is shown in Figure 15.4; the principal divisions of the brain are diagrammed and labeled in Figure 15.5. They may be considered in three main groups: the hindbrain, the midbrain, and the forebrain.

1   Within the *hindbrain* are the cerebellum and the medulla. The *medulla* contains vital centers for breathing and heart rate. It also includes centers that relay sensory impulses to the midbrain and forebrain. The *cerebellum* is a center (but not the only center) for motor coordination; it helps make our movements smooth and accurate. By utilizing vestibular and kinesthetic information, it is also an essential organ in maintaining posture and balance.

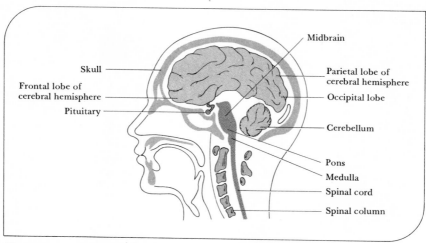

Figure 15.4   *The relationship of the brain and spinal cord to the bony skull and spinal column. (Modifed from Ranson and Clark, 1959.)*

2   The *midbrain* is a sort of bridge connecting the forebrain and hindbrain. It contains a number of pathways conveying impulses upward and downward. It also has centers that are important for vision and hearing.

3   The *forebrain* is the "highest" part of the brain. Though it was slow to develop in animal evolution, it eventually became the most highly developed part of the brain in man and the higher animals. Its mass is considerably greater than that of either the midbrain or the hindbrain.

Many parts of the forebrain are known to take part in complex behavior. Those of greatest interest to the psychologist fall into four main groups: the cerebral cortex, the thalamus, the reticular activating system, and the limbic system. (Actually, only part of the reticular activating system is in the forebrain; the rest stretches down through the midbrain and hindbrain. But its function is so closely tied to the cerebral cortex that we should consider it along with the forebrain.)

Cerebral cortex   A photograph of the outside of the human brain is really a picture of the cerebral cortex. This is because the cerebral cortex encloses almost all of the forebrain and midbrain (see Figure 15.6). The cortex looks rather like a rumpled piece of cloth that has many ridges and valleys. Anatomists call a ridge a *gyrus* (plural, gyri), and a valley or crevice sometimes a *sulcus* (plural, sulci) and sometimes a *fissure*.

The large sulci or fissures can be used to mark off the cerebral

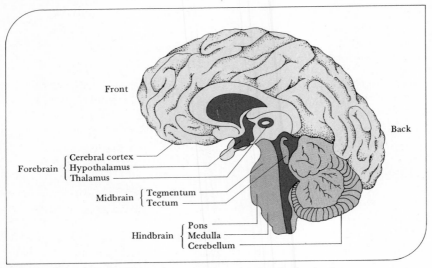

Figure 15.5   *Cross section of the human brain showing the forebrain, midbrain, and hindbrain.*

cortex. Along the midline of the brain (looking down on it from the top of the head) is a deep fissure that divides the cortex, and the parts underlying it, into two symmetrical halves: the *cerebral hemispheres.* Running across the top of the brain and down the sides of the two hemispheres (see Figure 15.6) is the central sulcus, which sets off the *frontal lobes* in front of it from the rest of the cortex. These lobes of the cortex are *expressive* in function, since they contain motor centers for controlling movements and actions. Just behind the central sulcus is a *somatosensory area* of the cortex. Impulses from the kinesthetic and skin senses project to this area. Along the side of each hemisphere is a lateral sulcus. Below it and to the side of it is the *temporal lobe,* which functions in hearing.

There are still two other lobes of the cortex, making four lobes in all. These are not clearly marked by any crevices. In the very back of the hemispheres is the *occipital lobe,* an important center for vision. In front of it, and running forward to the central sulcus, is the *parietal lobe.* This is concerned not only with somatosensory activities but with the integration of complex sensory activities.

Thalamus   The thalamus lies just above the midbrain, well enveloped by the cerebral cortex and other forebrain structures (Figure 15.7). It is best thought of as a *relay station,* although some of its parts have other functions. Sensory impulses coming into the spinal cord, hindbrain, and midbrain make their way, after intervening synapses, to centers in the thalamus. In the case of vision, the sensory nerve goes directly into the thalamus. Other sensory pathways are longer and involve several synapses. In all cases, however, thalamic centers relay impulses from below to various parts of the cortex.

Reticular activating system (RAS) The reticular activating system, as shown in Figure 15.6, runs from the hindbrain through the midbrain into the thalamus. Its function is parallel to that of the thalamus, for it is also a relay station for sensory impulses. The thalamus, however, is a direct relay to the cortex, and its projection is quite specific. Visual impulses, for example, arrive at a visual center in the thalamus and are relayed to the visual area of the cortex (in the occipital lobe). Hearing and other senses similarly have their own thalamic centers and their own areas of projection to the cerebral cortex.

The projection of the RAS to the cortex is much more diffuse. It receives impulses from sensory systems "on the side" as sensory fibers ascend to the thalamus (Figure 15.8). It also relays impulses to the cerebral cortex, but to a relatively large part of it. Although it may relay more visual impulses to the visual area of the cortex than to other areas, the RAS does not keep different impulses entirely separate from each other. Rather, it is a general activating system for the cerebral cortex; hence its name.

Figure 15.6 *This side view of the brain is dominated by the cerebral cortex. Note the many sulci, or fissures, and gyri, or ridges.*

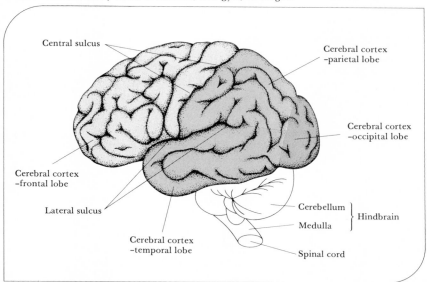

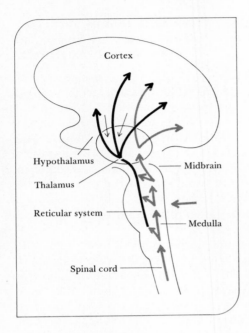

Figure 15.7 *Thalamus and reticular activating system. The RAS (black region) is an indirect sensory pathway (black arrows) to several areas of the cortex. It receives "side" branches from the direct sensory pathway (gray arrows) which goes to the thalamus. Pathways also lead back (black arrows) from the cortex to the reticular system, thus forming a loop.*

Not only does the RAS send impulses to the cortex, but the cortex sends impulses back to the RAS. Thus the RAS and cerebral cortex form a closed loop. In the loop the RAS arouses the cortex, and the cortex arouses the RAS. Later we shall see the part played by this loop in sleep and arousal.

Limbic system   The limbic system contains a number of centers and pathways. To keep your life simple, concentrate on these three: the hypothalamus, the septum, and the amygdala. They are the important structures in motivation and emotion.

The general size and location of the *hypothalamus* can be seen in Figure 15.8. As its name suggests, it lies underneath the thalamus in a nook in the floor of the skull. (A surgeon reaches it most easily through the roof of the mouth.) It is hardly larger than a peanut, yet it is the key center in a number of important functions.

The *septum*, which is also rather small, lies in front of and above the hypothalamus (Figure 15.7). The two are joined by a large bundle of fibers. The *amygdala* lies behind and somewhat to the side of the hypothalamus, with which it too is connected. The septum and the amygdala act in opposing ways on the hypothalamus; the septum is inhibitory, the amygdala excitatory. You will see later how the two regulate the expression of emotion.

SENSORY AND MOTOR MECHANISMS

To give you a background for understanding how the brain controls behavior, this chapter has sketched the structure of the nervous system and described the way neurons conduct impulses in it. Now it will show you how psychological functions are related to activities in the nervous system.

Skilled Movements

Two areas of the cerebral cortex are especially important in movement and motor functions. These are the motor area and premotor area, both lying in front of the central sulcus in the frontal lobe.

Experiments show that the *motor area* is the "executive" area of the cortex. Through it, a person can execute different patterns of movement. In this area are neurons that send fibers downward to the motor neurons of the hindbrain and spinal cord. Those neurons in turn activate skeletal muscles. Thus there is a direct, two-neuron link between the motor areas and the muscles. This link is essential for the performance of coordinated movements.

An electrical stimulus applied to the motor cortex in a conscious human being evokes movement somewhere in the body. The kind of

Figure 15.8   *The limbic system, which is important in the expression of emotion. (Modified from MacLean, 1949.)*

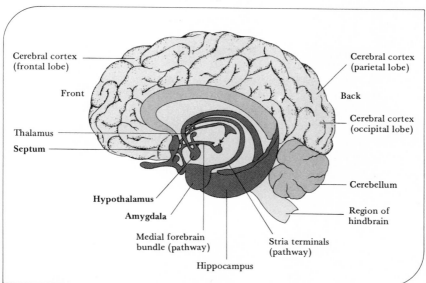

movement and the place where it occurs depend on the point stimulated. At the top of the motor area, a stimulus produces movements of the leg. A little to the side, it elicits movements of the trunk. More to the side is a region where stimulation causes movements of the hand and arm. Still further to the side is an area for movements of the face and mouth. By plotting each point on the cortex that evokes a movement, scientists have constructed a map of the motor cortex. The map shows that the areas concerned with trunk and leg movements are relatively small; those for the hand are somewhat larger, and those for the face and mouth are, by comparison, enormous. Such differences in size correlate with the precision of movements in various parts of the body. For example, our control of the movements of mouth, tongue, and eyes is meticulous. So is our control of finger movements. By contrast, the movement of the trunk, arms, and legs is coarse.

When tissue in the motor cortex is destroyed through surgery, through a cerebral hemorrhage (stroke), or by some other injury, paralysis results. If the entire motor area is destroyed, a whole side of the body will be paralyzed. (The paralysis occurs on the opposite side of the body from the injury, because fibers from the motor area cross over as they descend.) If only a part of the motor area is destroyed, a partial paralysis of the corresponding part of the body will follow.

Premotor area of the cortex is part of a complex system involving subcortical centers and the cerebellum. The system regulates posture and tension in different parts of the body. Thus it provides the "ground" on which the "figure" of a specific movement occurs. If a person's premotor area is removed or damaged, his movements become awkward. He seems to know what he wants to do, but he has trouble doing it well. Continuous tension in his muscles prevents him from making smooth, accurate movements.

The system regulating posture and muscular tension, of which the premotor area is a part, also contains a collection of cell bodies called the basal ganglia. These lie below the cortex. At birth, the cortex is relatively immature and immune to damage, but the basal ganglia are not. If a person is brain-injured in the process of birth, the basal ganglia are likely to be damaged. In that case he displays tense, awkward movements much like those which result in later life from damage to the premotor area. Children afflicted in this way are said to have cerebral palsy.

Sensory Centers and Pathways

The senses of vision, hearing, taste, smell, and balance are all located in the head. Hence the nerves for these senses enter the head, and all their centers and pathways are in the brain. But the four skin senses and the kinesthetic sense, which can be grouped together and called the *somesthetic senses*, are located all over the body. Many of the nerves from them enter the spinal cord and, as described earlier in this chapter, are involved in spinal reflexes. Through relays, pathways for these senses also extend to the brain and there join the incoming somesthetic pathways for the head and face. Coming directly into the brain are the nerves from the head serving vision, hearing, balance, taste, and smell.

After relaying at various points in the brain, pathways for all the senses lead to the cerebral cortex. Smell pathways go to the "old" cortex at the base of the brain ("old" because this cortex is present in animals like the fish and frog), where there are several areas concerned with smell. The other sensory pathways end in the "new" cortex that develops in birds and mammals and makes up nearly all of the human cerebral cortex. In the case of vision, the cortical area concerned is located at the back in the occipital lobe (look again at Figure 15.6). For hearing, the cortical area is at the side in the temporal lobe. The sensory pathways for taste and for the somesthetic senses end in the cortex immediately behind the central sulcus.

Topographical Arrangement

An interesting feature of all the sensory pathways, except those for smell, is their *topographical arrangement.* At various points along these pathways, including the sections which are in the cortex, neurons are arranged in a map that represents the sense organs on the surface of the body. In vision, for example, both the thalamic center and the primary cortical area are patterned so that different points on them represent different points on the retina. This can be demonstrated by recording with electrodes while stimulating different points on the retina. Often the map arrangement is spoken of as *point-to-point projection.*

There is a similar, though perhaps not so accurate, projection in hearing and somesthesis. As Chapter 14 explained, different frequencies of sound waves stimulate different places in the cochlea (page 342). This organization is preserved in the auditory system and thus is found in the auditory cortex. A similar order prevails in the somesthetic cortex, where parts of the body are topographically represented. In fact, one can draw a map of the somesthetic cortex that is very much like the map for the motor cortex. In summary, all the senses except smell are represented in the thalamus and cortex in a topographical way.

Sensory Experience

How do the centers and pathways of the various senses participate in sensory experience? To study this question the scientist has two general methods: stimulation and destruction. In the first he excites different centers; in the second he removes them.

The method of *stimulation* has been used with human subjects whose brains have been exposed under local anesthesia. While an electrical stimulus is applied, the person is asked to report whatever he experiences (Penfield and Rasmussen, 1950). He describes sensations of warmth or pressure when his somesthetic cortex is stimulated, visual experiences when his visual cortex is stimulated, and various sounds when his auditory cortex is the site of stimulation. (He never reports pain, however.) But an electrical stimulus is not actually a good duplication of the impulses normally coming to the cortex, so that the experiences reported by subjects are usually bizarre ones, such as flashing lights, buzzing sounds, or tingling sensations.

The method of *destruction*, of course, is seldom used in human cases. When it is, the surgeon is more interested in removing a cancerous tissue or a blood clot than in studying sensory functions. Most of the data obtained by this method come from animals. Many animal experiments have contributed to one general conclusion: The cerebral cortex is mainly concerned with the *spatial* aspects of experience. Subcortical centers, on the other hand, are mainly concerned with the *intensity* of experience.

Another general conclusion is that the cortex is more important in man then it is in animals. If the visual cortex of the monkey is removed, the animal still sees light. Its ability to discriminate objects and patterns (the spatial aspect) is gone, but it can discriminate differences in the intensity of light—though not as well as before surgery. A man, it seems, is entirely blind after removal of the visual cortex (although this point has not been proved conclusively). In other senses as well, evidence indicates that functions carried out below the cortex in lower animals are performed by the cortex in higher animals and in man.

MOTIVATION AND EMOTION

This section takes another look at topics already covered in Chapters 3 and 4 on motivation and emotion. But here, you will see what the underlying physiological mechanisms are.

Sleep and Arousal
Chapter 4 discussed the physiological arousal that takes place in emotion and stressed the autonomic components of arousal. The term *arousal*, however, can be used in a more general sense to refer to the state of being awake and alert in contrast to being asleep.

Stages in sleep and arousal   Think of a continuum from deep sleep to high arousal. From everyday experience we can divide the continuum into five steps: (1) alert wakefulness, (2) relaxed wakefulness, (3) drowsiness, (4) light sleep, and (5) deep sleep. It happens that there are changes in the electroencephalogram (EEG), or brain waves recorded from the human skull that correspond to each of these five steps. They are shown in Figure 15.9.

To study the state of *relaxed* wakefulness, a subject is seated in a laboratory with electrodes attached to his skull. He is told to sit quietly, close his eyes, and think about nothing in particular. In this state a characteristic rhythm, the *alpha rhythm*, usually appears in the EEG record. It is a rhythm of 8 to 12 Hz (cycles per second), averaging around 10. Suppose now that he is startled by a loud sound, or he opens his eyes and looks around, or something else happens to make him alert. In this state of *alert* wakefulness the alpha rhythm will disappear. In its place fast, irregular waves of frequencies higher than alpha will be seen. Their pattern in the EEG is known as the *activation pattern*, or arousal pattern.

Now suppose that a subject goes from relaxed wakefulness to *sleep*. As he becomes drowsy his alpha rhythm begins to disappear, giving way to a mixture of slow waves (slower than alpha) and fast waves (faster than alpha). As he goes into light sleep the slow waves become slower, but they are interrupted by bursts of fast waves, called *sleep spindles*, that can be seen in Figure 15.9. The presence of these spindles is a good indication that he has gone to sleep. Finally, when the subject is in deep sleep, the sleep spindles disappear and leave only very slow waves, between 1 and 4 Hz.

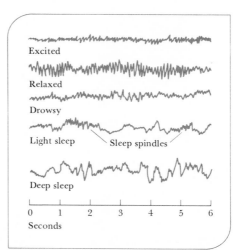

Figure 15.9 *Electrical activity of the human brain ("brain waves") typical of various states of alertness. (After Jasper, 1941.)*

For a long time the EEG signs just described were taken to be the whole story of brain waves in sleep, but then another pattern was discovered (Dement and Kleitman, 1957). It was called *paradoxical sleep* because the subject appears to be in deep sleep, yet his EEG record has changed to the activation pattern seen in alert wakefulness. Once this stage of sleep had been discovered, an observer could tell from the EEG record whether a person was in normal sleep or in paradoxical sleep.

A careful study of paradoxical sleep revealed that it is accompanied by rapid eye movements (REM for short), and now this stage of sleep is called REM sleep more often than paradoxical sleep. Researchers also found that a lot of dreaming takes place in it. In fact, most dreaming (but not all) occurs in the REM stage of sleep. This has made it much easier to study dreaming, since the experimenter need only watch a subject's EEG and wake him up whenever it shows an activation pattern. REM sleep occurs in fairly regular cycles of 1 to 2 hours throughout the night, but there is more REM sleep later in the night than in the early part of it. This correlates with the fact that people do more dreaming toward the end of a night's sleep than toward the beginning.

No one is sure where EEG rhythms originate in the brain. What we do know is that alpha waves are most prominent in the occipital areas near the visual projection area, that the slower waves are characteristic of the deeper parts of the brain, and that the activation pattern is produced by the reticular activating system.

RAS in sleep and waking   As noted earlier, the reticular activating system extends through most of the hindbrain. It receives branches of fibers from all the sensory pathways to the cortex. It in turn sends fibers to the cerebral cortex, and these can activate the cortex. In relaxed waking, some nerve impulses from the RAS continually ascend to the cortex and help keep us awake, although they are not numerous enough to disturb the alpha rhythm. But when a novel stimulus alerts us, many more nerve impulses go from the RAS to the cortex and so produce the activation pattern.

When we are asleep the RAS is largely "shut down." In fact, it is this state of the RAS which is responsible for sleep. When a large part of the RAS is surgically removed, an animal stays asleep most of the time and may have to be tube-fed to be kept alive. As shown back in Figure 15.7, the reticular activation system not only sends impulses to the cortex but receives them from the cortex, so that the RAS and the cortex form a loop. Thus the RAS is affected not only by incoming sensory impulses but also by cortical activity. A consequence of this loop is that we can be kept awake both by sensory stimuli and by cortical activities such as thinking. To go to sleep, therefore, we need to reduce sensory stimulation as much as possible and also to "get things off our mind."

Emotion

In that peanut-sized structure, the hypothalamus, located at the base of the brain and connected with the limbic system, are the centers for emotion, hunger, thirst, and sexual drive. The role of the hypothalamus in emotion was established a long time ago by some simple experiments (Cannon, 1927; Bard, 1928).

> Using cats as their experimental animals, the investigators made a series of cuts through the forebrain. Cat by cat they sliced off a little more until in the last cat, they severed the entire forebrain from its connections with the midbrain and hindbrain. Before and after the operation each cat was tested for angry behavior by pinching its tail, confronting it with a dog, or blowing a bugle. The characteristic pattern for angry behavior in cats includes growling, hissing, spitting, biting, tail lashing, fur standing up, forelegs thrashing, claws unsheathing, urinating, and rapid breathing. The researchers found that this pattern of behavior was always present as long as the hypothalamus was intact. When the hypothalamus was cut away by the operation, leaving only the midbrain and hindbrain, the pattern of angry response was broken up. The subjects might show some fragments of emotion, but not the entire gamut.

The experimenters concluded that the hypothalamus is the "seat" of emotion. Later work has largely confirmed their conclusion. If points in the hypothalamus are stimulated, patterns of emotion can be elicited. Stimulating certain places produces rage; stimulating others, fear. From this kind of evidence as well as from the earlier work, scientists are sure that the hypothalamus is an important center in emotion.

It is not, however, the only center. There are a number of places in the brain which elicit some kind of emotional behavior when they are stimulated. Most (but not all) are in the limbic system; in fact, physiologists have come to regard the limbic system, together with the hypothalamus, as *the* system for emotion.

The two most important centers of the limbic system are the septum and the amygdala. These exert opposing influences on the hypothalamus (Thompson, 1967), as can be demonstrated in two ways. One is to make lesions in the amygdala, whereupon a ferocious animal will turn into a docile, tame one. The other is to stimulate the amygdala, thereby producing rage reactions very much like those seen in hypothalamic stimulation. The septum, on the other hand, normally inhibits the hypothalamus, the amygdala, or both. At least, it seems so because lesions of the septum make an animal very emotional; it will readily attack with little provocation and becomes dangerous to handle.

To summarize, the main structures involved in emotion are those of the hypothalamus and limbic system, in which the septum and amygdala exert opposing influences on the hypothalamus.

Brain Stimulation

The septum is not only an inhibitory center in the emotional system, but a "pleasure center" as well. This fact was discovered in 1954 when two experimenters (Olds and Milner) implanted electrodes in rats for the purpose of administering electrical stimulation. They found that the stimulation could serve as a reward for teaching a rat just about anything that it would learn with conventional rewards. Nowadays, the simple way of studying the rewarding effects of brain stimulation is to put the rat in an operant chamber arranged as shown in the drawing at right in Figure 15.10. Then the animal just pushes a bar to obtain brain stimulation. Similar arrangements have been used with other animals, including cats and monkeys—all of which typically push the bar two or three times a minute to receive brief stimulation.

Many electrode positions in the brain are rewarding positions. Some are in unexpected places, but most are in the hypothalamus and limbic system. Besides the septum and its connecting pathway to the hypothalamus, a good spot is the lateral hypothalamus (which is a

Figure 15.10 *Electrical stimulation at various points in the brain is pleasurable for animals. Left, an x-ray photograph of an electrode permanently implanted in the brain of a rat. Right, the electrode is in a self-stimulating circuit, and the rat is pushing a bar to stimulate his brain. (Olds, 1956; University of Michigan.)*

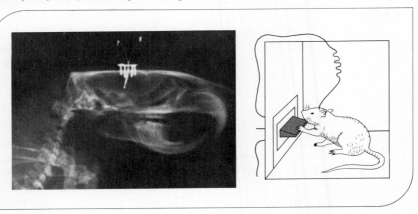

center otherwise involved in hunger, as the following section will explain). Scientists do not know why certain centers are "good" placement and others are not. All they know is that with good electrode placements, the animal will work to obtain stimulation and thus apparently "likes" it.

Naturally, medical ethics do not normally permit the implanting of electrodes in human brains. It has, however, been tried in a few cases with hopeless schizophrenics (Heath and Mickle, 1960; Sem-Jacobsen and Torkildson, 1960). But severe schizophrenics, being so withdrawn, do not make good experimental subjects. Their vague reports indicate only that people, like animals, find brain stimulation in certain spots to be pleasurable.

Drives

Besides being involved in emotion, the limbic system also plays a part in the major physiological drives. Stimulating it at several points can produce eating and drinking. The main centers for these drives, however, seem to be in the hypothalamus.

Hunger   Two centers form a regulating system for hunger. One center, along the midline of the cerebral cortex, is called a *satiety center* (Teitelbaum, 1961). Stimulating it causes an animal to stop eating, if it is eating. But making a lesion in the satiety center destroys the animal's control of eating, so that it eats two or three times as much as normal at each meal. Naturally it gains weight and eventually becomes a "butterball" at two or three times its normal weight. The abnormal appetite caused by lesions to the satiety center is known as *hypothalamic hyperphagia*, because "hyperphagia" means overeating.

A little to the side of the satiety center is the *feeding center*, which has an opposing function. Here lesions cause an animal to lose its appetite—it becomes *aphagic*, and will starve to death if not maintained by tube feeding. In time, however, the animal gradually recovers its appetite and can maintain normal weight. Scientists believe this is because some cells in the center are always left after the operation, and they gradually take over the functions of the cells that were destroyed.

The two opposing centers involved in hunger have sometimes been given other names that indicate their normal functions. The feeding center is called the "start" center, for it seems to start the process of eating. The satiety center is called the "stop" center, because it regulates the length of a meal by "telling" the animal when to stop eating.

What do these animal experiments have to do with human hunger and eating? Physiologists are fairly sure that the "start" and "stop" mechanisms are the same in man as they are in the rat. In both, the two centers are controlled by some chemical substance (as yet unidentified) circulating in the blood, as well as by sensory stimuli related to food and eating. Some cases of human obesity may be due to a derangement of the "stop" center, for tumors in the hypothalamus have occasionally been found. But most human obesity has psychological causes, perhaps reinforced by a genetic predisposition to overeating. Studies of obese people, however, do show a striking similarity between their eating habits and those of rats with lesions in the satiety center (Schachter, 1971).

Drinking The "start" center for eating in the hypothalamus is also a "drinking" center. Making a lesion in it not only causes an animal to stop eating, but also destroys its thirst. In fact, the loss of thirst is even more dramatic than the loss of hunger. And in recovering from the lesion, the animal takes longer to resume drinking than eating. In the tube feeding required to keep the animal alive, it must still be tube-fed water for a while after its appetite for solid food has returned to normal. So far, scientists have not found a "satiety" center for drinking behavior, and they are beginning to believe that it does not exist. The "stop" factor in this case may be a change in the makeup of blood that affects the "drinking" center.

Sex The hypothalamus also contains a center or centers for sexual drive, because lesions at certain places reduce sexual drive and at other places occasionally increase it. Also, sexual drive can be increased by either electrical or chemical stimulation of a certain spot toward the front of the hypothalamus. The experiments with chemical stimulation are probably the most dramatic (Fisher, 1956). In these, estrogen (the female sexual hormone that brings a female animal into "heat") was implanted in the hypothalamus of female rats through a tube. The estrogen was in crystalline form so that it took weeks to be fully absorbed, and all during this time the rats were in heat and readily copulating with available males. Normally a rat is in heat only a few hours in a cycle that lasts 4 to 5 days.

This experiment illustrates the general conception of modern theorists about what goes on in physiological motivation. Drives are produced, they believe, by conditions in the blood that stimulate appropriate centers in the hypothalamus. In the case of sexual drive, a sex hormone like estrogen arouses certain cells in the hypothalamus that are especially sensitive to it. Researchers are sure that thirst is produced by dehydration of cells in the "drinking" area of the hypothalamus. Hunger appears to be induced by some chemical condition in the blood that varies with weight.

These are the conditions, scientists think, that "start" drives. The mechanisms that "stop" them are somewhat more complicated. Briefly, the physical act of eating, drinking, or copulation is a "stop" factor; after the organism performs the act for a certain time, the drive is reduced. In the case of hunger and thirst, having food or water in the stomach for a brief period of time is a "stop" factor. But exactly how these conditions reduce drive is not clear. Probably sensory impulses to the brain and changes in blood conditions are both involved.

LEARNING AND MEMORY

What happens in the brain when we learn? This section will summarize current knowledge of the brain's general function in learning and memory, and recent research on local areas of the cortex that specialize in certain kinds of learning.

Equipotentiality

Research on the role of the brain, especially the cerebral cortex, got well underway in the 1920s. The principal investigator was Karl Lashley (1890–1958). Lashley, like most psychologists of the time, was much influenced by the ideas of Pavlov and Watson, who thought that conditioning was the fundamental element in all learning. Pavlov and Watson also regarded complex learning as being made up of many conditioned responses. If this was the case, Lashley reasoned, different conditioned responses ought to be "wired" into the brain in different places. Therefore he set out to trace some localization of function: to find certain habits localized in one place, others in others.

Lashley began making lesions of different sizes and in different places in the central cortexes of rats. He taught them various habits before each lesion, then tested them on the habits after a suitable time for recovery from the operation. But as his research continued, he gradually came to realize that his original idea was wrong. He could find localization only of simple sensory and motor functions such as the ones described earlier in this chapter. Otherwise he could find no localization of habits in the cortex. Thus his research led him to believe that most of the cerebral cortex is *equipotential* in learning and memory. That is to say, whatever change in nervous tissue takes place in learning, it is reduplicated in several parts of the brain, including the cortex.

Since then, experimenters have found that things are not quite as extreme as Lashley thought: there is some localization, as we shall see. But in general, Lashley was right.

Limbic System and Avoidance Learning

Among the instances of learning in which, despite Lashley, there is some localization of function is the relation between the limbic system and avoidance learning. This chapter has emphasized that the limbic system is involved in emotion, and Chapter 3 showed that avoidance learning depends on the conditioning of fear. In learning to avoid shock by responding to a signal, a subject first acquires a fear elicited by the signal, and then reduces this fear by learning an avoidance response (page 109). We might expect that the limbic system and the learning of avoidance responses would be related, and they are. Time after time researchers find that lesions in parts of the limbic system affect avoidance learning. Since septal lesions increase emotion, they can speed the learning of avoidance responses. And conversely, the calming effect on emotion of amygdaloid lesions retards avoidance learning.

Temporal Cortex and Visual Associations

Many years ago, almost by accident, an *association* area was discovered in the temporal cortex (Kluver and Bucy, 1937). (Association area is the term for an area which has neither sensory nor motor functions and is presumed to be concerned in some kind of learning.) The area lies on the tip of the temporal lobe (which is shown in Figure 15.6). In the original experiment, the investigators removed this area on both sides in some monkeys. After the operation they noticed that the monkeys seemed to have "object blindness." The animals did poorly on visual discrimination problems—for example, differentiating between a piece of food and a piece of wood.

Following this lead, experimenters have since studied the function of the temporal area systematically (Pribram, 1969). They gave all sorts of learning problems to monkeys before and after removing the area and found that its role is strictly visual, for the monkeys have trouble only on visual problems. Yet the animals' vision is not impaired: they can pull in fine strings attached to food, and they show in other ways that they can see perfectly well. What the monkeys forget, if they have learned a problem before the operation, or what they have trouble learning, if they are operated before training, are visual discriminations of *form* and *objects*. Human patients who have had operations involving the temporal lobes show similar deficits. For example, they may see a spoon perfectly well but not remember what it used for. Thus in the temporal lobe there is a localized area concerned with visual associations.

Prefrontal Cortex and Delayed Responses

In the frontal lobe of the cortex (Figure 15.6) are the *frontal association areas*. Removal of these areas slightly impairs the learning of avoidance problems and some visual discrimination problems. The greatest effect, however, is on one particular kind of learning called *delayed response* learning (Mishkin and Pribram, 1956).

A delayed response problem requires a visual discrimination, but after a delay. For example, a monkey is presented with two stimulus objects and is shown which one is correct—say, the experimenter places food in front of the correct object. Then a curtain is pulled down between the monkey and the objects for a given period—say, one minute. After that the curtain is raised, and the monkey can now reach for the object previously shown to be correct.

Normal monkeys have no trouble mastering this problem when the delay is several minutes, but a monkey with its frontal cortex removed cannot do so after a delay of even a few seconds. Many experiments have been carried out to analyze exactly what is wrong with such monkeys. The results indicate that several things are amiss; among them, a lack of attentiveness and a tendency to *perseverate* (to repeat the same response over and over). These combine to prevent the monkey from noting what was correct in the first place and from keeping its "mind" on it during the delay interval. Human patients with prefrontal lesions, unlike monkeys, are able to solve delayed response problems; but like monkeys, they tend to perseverate. They cannot shift as readily as normal people from one mode of attack to another (Milner, 1964).

Parietal Cortex and Touch Associations
Data on the effects of lesions in both men and monkeys have demonstrated that a part of the parietal lobe is an association area for recognizing objects by touch (Teuber et al., 1960). A chimpanzee given lesions in this area has a great deal of trouble discriminating objects by touch alone. It learns to solve simple touch discrimination problems only after prolonged training, and it never masters tough problems, like discriminating a cone from a pyramid. Similarly, a patient with injuries in this association area may not be able to identify a pair of scissors, a knife, a ball, or other objects when he feels them—although he can easily recognize them visually.

Speech Areas
In human beings a fairly large area extending along the side of the parietal cortex forward into the frontal lobe is involved in speech. Different parts of the area are concerned in different ways, so we speak of *speech areas.* They are found on only one side of the brain—almost always on the left, but on the right in a few cases.

In a particular patient, the side on which speech is localized can be determined in two ways. If he has a speech disorder due to brain injury, the side of the brain that was damaged is the side containing the speech areas. In cases of cerebral hemorrhage (stroke), for example, if the stroke impairs speech, speech function is localized on the side of the stroke. In a healthy person a sedative can be injected into the carotid artery on one side of the brain while he talks. If his speech is impaired while the sedative takes effect, speech is located on the side of the injection; if not, it is on the other side.

Within the speech areas there is some division of function. Neurologists do not agree on just how much there is, but certainly a twofold division exists. The forward part of the areas is concerned in the *production* of speech; stimulation of this part evokes involuntary speech sounds. When the area is damaged by a stroke or by surgery, the person may know what he wants to say but be unable to say it. Yet he can write it down if his arm is not paralyzed.

The part of the speech area in the parietal lobe is concerned with language formulation and recognition. Injuries in this area knock out linguistic memories, so that the person cannot think of the word he wants to say. If the injury is severe, he may not even be able to recognize the word he wants.

SUMMARY

The basic unit of the nervous system is the neuron. It consists of one or more dendrites, a cell body, and an axon. The neuron's chief function is to conduct nerve impulses, which are all-or-none electrical changes in the membrane. Conduction at synapses, the junctions between neurons, occurs when a neurotransmitter, secreted by an axon, stimulates the neighboring dendrite. Reflexes are made possible by the joining of sensory neurons to motor neurons through intervening neurons in a reflex arc. A person's reaction time—the time required to react to a stimulus as rapidly as possible—is determined more by the slow rate of transmission at the synapse than by the conduction time of impulses.

The nervous system is divided into a central nervous system inside the bony case of the skull and backbone, and a peripheral nervous system lying outside this case. The peripheral nervous system may in turn be divided into a somatic system serving skeletal muscles and the external senses, and an autonomic system serving the internal organs. The central nervous system consists of the brain and spinal cord. The brain has three main parts: the hindbrain, containing the medulla and cerebellum; the midbrain; and the forebrain. The most important structures in the forebrain are the cerebral cortex, the thalamus, the reticular activating system, the limbic system, and the hypothalamus.

Skilled movements involve the motor and premotor areas of the frontal lobe. All the senses except the sense of smell relay in the thalamus, then project to the cortex. In this projection, the topographical arrangement of the senses is preserved.

The important structures in motivation and emotion are located subcortically in the limbic and reticular activating systems. Sleep and arousal are regulated by a loop formed by the cerebral cortex and the reticular activating system. Emotional expression is mainly organized in the hypothalamus. The septum normally inhibits the hypothalamus; the amygdala excites it. There are many points in the brain where electrical stimulation is rewarding. The hypothalamus is the seat of the major physiological drives. In the hypothalamus is a satiety center and a feeding center. The latter is also a drinking center. Centers for sexual drive also are in the hypothalamus.

To a large extent, areas of the cerebral cortex are equipotential (potentially interchangeable) in learning and memory. However, there is some localization of function. The limbic system, being concerned in emotion, is important in avoidance learning. The temporal lobe contains an area that is important in visual recognition of objects. The prefrontal cortex is especially concerned with attention. The posterior part of the parietal lobe is involved in the recognition of objects by touch. Speech areas are localized on one side of the cerebral cortex, usually on the left.

SUGGESTIONS FOR FURTHER READING

Butter, C. M. *Neuropsychology: The study of brain and behavior.* Monterey, Calif.: Brooks/Cole, 1968. (Paperback.) *An introductory treatment of physiological mechanisms of behavior.*

McGaugh, J. L., et al. (Eds.) *Psychobiology: The biological bases of behavior.* San Francisco: Freeman, 1966. (Paperback.) *A collection of interesting reprints from* Scientific American.

Morgan, C. T. *Physiological psychology.* (3d ed.) New York: McGraw-Hill, 1965. *One of the standard texts on physiological mechanisms of behavior.*

Teitelbaum, P. *Physiological psychology.* Englewood Cliffs, N.J.: Prentice-Hall, 1966. (Paperback.) *A short, readable introduction to the topic.*

Thompson, R. F. *Foundations of physiological psychology.* New York: Harper & Row, 1967. *A standard text intended for somewhat advanced students.*

Wooldridge, D. E. *The machinery of the brain.* New York: McGraw-Hill, 1963. (Paperback.) *A popularly written book explaining things in nontechnical terms.*

Glossary

ability A general term referring to the potential for the acquisition of a skill or to an already acquired skill. Cf. *aptitude.*

abscissa The horizontal axis of a graph; measures of the independent variable (q.v.) are usually plotted on this axis.

absolute refractory period A brief period during the discharge of a nerve impulse when the neuron cannot be fired again. Cf. *relative refractory period.*

absolute threshold The smallest amount of a stimulus that can be perceived. Cf. *differential threshold.*

abstraction A learning process in which an individual learns to disregard some properties of objects and to respond only to certain properties that the objects have in common. It is the process through which concepts (q.v.) are formed.

accommodation A change in the shape of the lens of the eye that focuses the image of an object on the retina. It compensates for the distance of the object from the observer.

achievement need A need to succeed and to strive against standards of excellence; it serves to motivate an individual to do well.

achievement test Any test used to measure present knowledge or skills—especially knowledge or skills developed through specific training.

activation pattern An EEG pattern accompanying arousal in which fast, irregular waves appear.

activity A general term covering restlessness, exploration, and miscellaneous responses to environmental stimuli; considered to be a general unlearned drive.

adaptation A change in the sensitivity of a sense organ due to stimulation or lack of stimulation. In general, all senses become less sensitive as they are stimulated and more sensitive in the absence of stimulation.

adaptation level A theory of context effects which holds that background acts to set a standard against which events or objects are perceived.

addictions States of periodic or chronic intoxication produced by a drug, with an overpowering desire for the drug, a tendency to increase the dose, and a physical and a psychological dependence on the drug. Cf. *habituation.*

adjustment The relationship that exists between an individual and his environment, especially his social environment, in the satisfaction of his motives.

adrenal glands A pair of endocrine glands located on the top of the kidneys. They secrete the hormones epinephrine (q.v.), nonepinephrine, and cortin.

adrenaline See *epinephrine.*

affectional drive A general unlearned drive to have contact with and be close to another organism.

affectional motive See *affectional drive.*

affective reactions Psychotic reactions marked by extremes of mood, e.g., depression or manic elation.

affiliation (affiliative) need The need to associate with or belong with other people.

aggression A general term applying to feelings of anger or hostility. Aggression functions as a motive, often in response to threats, insults, or frustrations.

all-or-none law The principle that a nerve impulse (q.v.) is either evoked at full strength or not evoked at all. See *threshold*.

alpha rhythm One of the named rhythms of the EEG (q.v.); has a frequency of 8–12 Hz and a voltage of about $50\,\mu$ V as measured at the surface of the skull.

amnesia Generally any loss of memory; specifically, a neurotic reaction in which a person forgets his own identity and is unable to recognize familiar people and situations. See also *dissociative reaction*.

amplitude The intensity at any given instant of energy, e.g., acoustic or electric energy.

amygdala A structure of the forebrain connected with the hypothalamus and concerned in emotion.

antisocial reaction Little or no concern for other people and little feeling of right and wrong. See *sociopathic personality*.

anxiety A vague, or objectless, fear.

anxiety attack See *anxiety reaction*.

anxiety reaction One of the major classes of psychoneurosis, characterized by anxiety.

aphasia A language defect ordinarily due to damage or disease of the brain. It may be a sensory disorder consisting of some impairment in reading or understanding of speech, or it may be a motor disorder consisting of an impairment in the writing or speaking of language.

apparent motion Perceived motion in which no actual movement of the stimulus pattern over the receptor occurs.

approach-approach conflict Conflict in which a person is motivated to approach two different goals that are incompatible.

approach-avoidance conflict Conflict in which a person is both attracted and repelled by the same goal.

aptitude Ability to profit by training. See also *scholastic aptitude, vocational aptitude*.

arousal An increase in alertness and muscular tension.

art A skill or knack for doing something that is acquired by study, practice, and special experience. Cf. *science*.

association A general term referring to any connection formed through learning.

"association" cortex A general term for areas of the cortex outside the primary sensory and motor areas.

association neuron A neuron, usually within the central nervous system, which occupies a position between sensory and motor neurons.

associative meaning The meaning of a word or concept measured by the number of associations it evokes.

astigmatism Irregularities in the shape of the cornea or other structures of the eye transmitting light to the retina; these cause parts of an image projected on the retina to be out of focus.

atmosphere effect Distortion of reasoning due to the way in which the premises of a syllogism (q.v.) are worded. Cf. *opinion effect*.

attention Focusing on certain aspects of current experience and neglecting others. Attention has a focus in which events are clearly perceived and a margin in which they are less clearly perceived.

attitude A tendency to respond either positively or negatively to certain persons, objects, or situations. See also *set*.

attitude scale A method of measuring attitudes which typically consists of a set of items, each having a preestablished scale value, to be checked with favor or disfavor by the examinee.

attribute The perceived quality or aspect of a stimulus or person; a psychological dimension of sensory experience.

audiogram A graph representing the absolute threshold of hearing at different frequencies.

audiometer A device for obtaining an audiogram, used to detect deafness.

autonomic changes Changes in heart rate, blood pressure, and so forth, controlled by impulses in the autonomic system.

autonomic conditioning The conditioning of responses controlled by the autonomic nervous system, e.g. salivation, heart rate, dilation or constriction of blood vessels, intestinal contraction or relaxation.

autonomic system A division of the nervous system serving certain endocrine glands and the smooth muscles. It controls internal changes in the body during emotion as well as other functions that are essential to homeostasis. See also *parasympathetic and sympathetic systems*.

aversion therapy A form of behavior modification (q.v.) in which the stimuli eliciting the behavior to be eliminated are paired with unpleasant states of affairs; in time, these stimuli tend to be avoided.

avoidance-avoidance conflict Conflict in which a person is caught between two negative goals. As he tries to avoid one goal, he is brought closer to the other, and vice versa.

avoidance conditioning (or learning) Learning to avoid a noxious stimulus, e.g., shock, by responding appropriately to a warning signal.

axon A nerve fiber transmitting impulses from the cell body to an adjacent neuron or to an effector.

baseline A stable and reliable level of performance that can be used as a basis for assessing changes in behavior caused by the introduction of independent variables (q.v.).

basilar membrane The membrane in the cochlea on which the organ of Corti is located. Its motion is important in hearing.

behavior Any observable action of a person or animal.

behavior disorder A general term referring to psychoneurotic reactions, psychotic reaction (q.v.), personality disorder (q.v.), and chronic brain syndrome (q.v.). Means about the same thing as "mental disorder" or "mental illness."

behavior modification A form of psychotherapy which focuses on changing the behavioral problem by using techniques of classical conditioning (q.v.), operant conditioning (q.v.), and perceptual learning (q.v.). See *desensitization, counter-conditioning, reciprocal inhibition, aversion therapy.*

behavior therapy See *behavior modification.*

behavioral sciences The sciences most concerned with human and animal behavior. The principal behavioral sciences are psychology, sociology, and social anthropology, but they also include certain aspects of history, economics, political science, and zoology.

behaviorism A viewpoint held early in the twentieth century by some experimental psychologists who were opposed to the method of introspection and proposed that psychology be limited to the study of observable behavior.

belief The acceptance of a statement or proposition. It does not necessarily involve an attitude (q.v.), although it may.

binocular Pertaining to the simultaneous use of the two eyes.

bipolar cell A neuron (q.v.) with a single axon and a single dendrite; in the eye, a cell connecting the rods and cones (q.v.), with ganglion cells (q.v.).

blind spot The region of the retina where fibers leave the eyeball to form the optic nerve. There are no photosensitive receptors at this point.

brain The part of the nervous system cased in the skull. It is the site of centers for sensory experience, motivation, learning, and thinking.

brainwashing Systematic attempts to change attitudes, especially political attitudes.

brain waves Electrical fluctuations in brain activity recorded from the skull. See also *electroencephalogram.*

brightness A dimension of color that refers to the relative degree of whiteness, grayness, or blackness of the color, as distinguished from hue and saturation (q.v.). The term is also used to refer to the perceived intensity of a light.

brightness constancy A phenomenon of perception in which a person perceives an object as having the same brightness despite marked differences in the physical energy stimulating the eye.

CA See *chronological age.*

catatonic type A kind of schizophrenia (q.v.) characterized by negativism and a state of muscular rigidity.

central nervous system The part of the nervous system enclosed in the bony case of the skull and backbone. Cf. *peripheral nervous system.*

central stimulation Electrical or chemical stimulation of some region of the brain, usually in the waking animal, by means of a permanently implanted electrode or pipette.

central sulcus A groove in the cerebral cortex dividing the frontal lobe from the parietal lobe.

CER See *conditioned emotional response.*

cerebellum A structure in the hindbrain concerned with the coordination of movements and balance.

cerebral cortex The gray matter covering the cerebrum.

cerebrum The largest structure of the forebrain consisting of white matter (fiber tracts), deeper structures, and covered by the cerebral cortex (q.v.).

chemical senses The senses of taste and smell.

chemotherapy The treatment of a psychoneurotic or a psychotic reaction with a drug or chemical substance, e.g., with a tranquilizer (q.v.).

choroid layer The middle layer of the wall of the eyeball, dark in color and opaque. See *retina and sclera.*

chromosome A long chain-like structure in the nuclei of body and germ cells containing genes.

chronic brain syndrome Behavior disorders produced by long-lasting disturbances in brain function.

chronological age (CA) Age in years. Cf. *mental age.*

ciliary muscle A muscle attached to the lens of the eye which thickens the lens when it contracts, and flattens the lens when it relaxes. It controls accommodation.

cingulate gyrus A cortical portion of the limbic system (q.v.) which lies in the longitudinal fissure above the corpus callosum (q.v.).

class See *social class.*

classical conditioning Learning that takes place when a conditioned stimulus is paired with an unconditioned stimulus.

client-centered therapy A non-directive therapy developed by Carl Rogers which typically is not so intensive or prolonged as psychoanalysis.

clinical methods Methods of collecting data in which information is obtained about people who come to physicians and psychologists for assistance.

clinical psychology A branch of psychology concerned with psychological methods of recognizing and treating behavior disorders, and research into their causes.

closure The tendency for gaps to be perceived as filled in.

clustering The tendency in free recall (q.v.) for items to be recalled in groups that are similar in meaningfulness, hierarchy, or conceptual category.

cochlea A bony cavity, coiled like a snail shell, containing receptor organs for hearing. It contains three canals: vestibular, tympanic, and cochlear.

cochlear duct One of the canals in the cochlea.

cochlear microphonic potential A fluctuating voltage, or potential (q.v.), recorded from the inner ear that follows the stimulating energy very closely.

coefficient of correlation A number between +1.00 and −1.00 expressing the degree of relationship between two sets of measurements arranged in pairs. A coefficient of +1.00 (or −1.00) represents perfect correlation, and a coefficient of .00 represents no correlation at all.

cognition A thought or idea.

cognitive dissonance A motivational state produced by inconsistencies between simultaneously held cognitions (q.v.), or between a cognition and behavior.

cognitive overload A state in which there is more information directed at a person than he can process in thought at a particular time. See *cognition*.

color blindness A defect that makes a person unable to tell the difference between two or more colors that most other people can easily distinguish.

color circle An arrangement of colors in which hues are spokes of a wheel and saturation is represented by radial distance on the spokes.

color constancy The tendency to perceive colors as unvarying despite changes in the sensory input.

communication structure The pattern of closed and open channels of communication within a group of individuals.

comparative psychology The branch of psychology that compares the behaviors of one species with those of others.

compensation A defense mechanism in which an individual substitutes one activity for another in an attempt to satisfy frustrated motives. It usually implies failure or loss of self-esteem in one activity and the compensation of this loss by efforts in some other realm of endeavor.

competence motivation The motive to develop skills which make possible effective interaction with the environment; also, to exercise one's potentialities.

complementary colors Pairs of hues that, when mixed in proper proportions, are seen as gray.

compliance Behavior in accordance with group pressures without accepting the values and norms (q.v.) of the group as our own. Cf. *private acceptance*.

compulsion An irrational act that constantly intrudes into a person's behavior. See *obsessive-compulsive reaction*.

compulsive personality Personality pattern disturbance characterized by rigidity of habits and excessive conscientiousness.

compulsive reaction Behavior disorder in which a person finds ambiguity and uncertainty extremely uncomfortable. Extreme emphasis is put on "doing things the right way."

concept An internal process representing a common property of objects or events, usually represented by a word or name.

conjunctive concept A concept defined by the joint presence of several characteristics. See *concept;* cf. *disjunctive concept, relational concept*.

conditioned emotional response (CER) Fear conditioned to stimuli associated with noxious events; often investigated by using a baseline technique in a Skinner box (q.v.)

conditioned reinforcement See *secondary reinforcement*.

conditioned response A response produced by a conditioned stimulus after learning.

conditioned stimulus The stimulus that is originally ineffective but that, after pairing with an unconditioned stimulus, evokes the conditioned response. See also *classical conditioning*.

conditioning A general term referring to the learning of some particular response. See also *classical conditioning*.

conduction deafness Deafness due to an impairment of the conduction of energy to the cochlea. Cf. *nerve deafness*.

cone A photosensitive receptor in the retina and most sensitive under daytime conditions of seeing. Cones are closely packed in the fovea and are the receptors in color vision. cf. *rod*.

conflict See *approach-avoidance conflict, approach-approach conflict, avoidance-avoidance conflict, motivational conflict*.

conflict of motives See *motivational conflict.*

conformity The tendency to be influenced by group pressure and to acquiesce to group norms (q.v.) See *private acceptance, compliance.*

consistency theory A theory of attitudes (q.v.) which states that attitudes provide consistency for cognitions (q.v.) and tendencies to respond that otherwise would be discrepant, incongruous, or dissonant.

constancy See *perceptual constancy.*

constitution The genetic (q.v.) makeup of an individual.

consummatory response A response that tends to satisfy a primary drive, e.g. eating, drinking, copulation.

context Surroundings, background, or environment.

contiguity, law of The principle that two events must occur close together in time and space to be associated in learning.

contingency Generally, the state of affairs that exists when one thing depends upon another. More specifically, reinforcement is said to be contingent upon certain responses in operant conditioning (q.v.).

continuation The tendency to perceive objects as forming a line, curve, or other continuous pattern. See also *grouping.*

continuity theory A theory which holds that learning occurs by a gradual strengthening of S-R bonds.

continuous reinforcement Reinforcement of all correct responses.

control Used in two senses: (1) The group or condition in an experiment that is similar in all respects to the experimental group or condition except that it does not include the independent variable. (2) Any stick, switch, wheel, or other device used by an individual to operate a device or machine.

convergence Turning the eyes inward toward the nose as objects are brought closer to the eyes.

conversion reaction A psychoneurotic reaction in which motivational conflict has been converted into physical symptoms, so that the person appears to have various ailments that have no physical basis.

coping behavior Behavior used to reduce anxiety caused by frustration over motivational conflict. See also *defense mechanism.*

cornea The outermost, transparent layer of the front of the eye.

corpus callosum A band of fibers connecting the two cerebral hemispheres.

correlation Generally, the relationship between any two events. See *coefficient of correlation.*

correlation coefficient See *coefficient of correlation; correlation.*

cortex A rind or covering. See also *cerebral cortex.*

cortical Pertaining to a cortex; usually refers to the cerebral cortex, but can also refer to the cortex of other structures, e.g., the adrenal gland.

counseling See *counseling psychology.*

counseling psychology The branch of psychology stressing the giving of advice and assistance to individuals with vocational or personal problems. See *clinical psychology.*

counterconditioning The weakening of a conditioned response (q.v.) by conditioning the stimuli that elicit the response to other responses which are incompatible with the response to be eliminated. See *behavior modification.*

CR See *conditioned response.*

cranial nerves The nerves serving the brain. There are 12 cranial nerves, some sensory, some motor, and some of mixed function.

criterion In the evaluation of tests, the job or performance that a test is supposed to predict; in learning, the level of performance considered to represent relatively complete learning.

critical period A period of time in which an organism is most ready for the acquisition of certain responses.

CS See *conditioned stimulus.*

cue-producing response A response which serves as a kinesthetic stimulus for another response. It may be either an observable response or an implicit response.

culture The customs, habits, traditions, and artifacts that characterize a people or a social group. It includes the attitudes (q.v.) and beliefs (q.v.) that the group has about important aspects of its life.

culture pattern Widely shared ways of behaving in a society together with the beliefs that accompany them.

curiosity A tendency to prefer or to respond to novel stimulation; considered to be a general unlearned drive (q.v.) See also *exploratory drive.*

decibel The unit of measurement used to express the intensity of a sound. It is essentially the logarithm of a ratio of pressures or energies; usually expressed by the formula

$$\text{db} = 20 \log \frac{P_1}{P_2}$$

A reference must be given. In hearing, the reference level is a pressure of 0.0002 dyne per square centimeter.

defense mechanism A reaction to frustration that defends the person against anxiety and serves to disguise his motives, so that he deceives himself about his real motives and goals. Defense mechanisms also enhance self-esteem. For examples, see *displacement, reaction formation, repression.*

deindividuation Anonymity; not knowing the names and personal characteristics of other people in a social situation. Cf. *individuation.*

delayed reaction A type of experiment in which a subject is shown the correct stimulus, usually along with incorrect stimuli, but must wait for an interval before having an opportunity to make the correct choice.

delta rhythm One of the named rhythms of the EEG (q.v.); has a frequency of about 1–3 Hz and its voltage is relatively great, about 150μ V as measured at the surface of the skull. Characteristic of deep sleep.

delusion A groundless, irrational belief or thought, usually of grandeur or of persecution. It is characteristic of paranoid reactions (q.v.)

dendrite A nerve fiber that normally is stimulated by an external physical stimulus or by the impulse brought to it by an axon (q.v.).

dependency need The need to depend on other people for advice, counsel, and moral support.

dependent variable The variable that changes as a result of changes in the independent variable (q.v.).

depolarization A decrease in the internal negativity of a nerve cell, especially when stimulated. If depolarization goes to threshold (q.v.), the cell will fire.

depressive disorder A mental disorder, characterized by anxiety, guilt feelings, self-depreciation, or suicidal tendencies.

depressive reaction Psychoneurotic reaction characterized by severe depression; often a reaction to a severe loss.

depth perception Perception of the relative distance of objects from the observer.

descriptive statistics Statistical measures that summarize the characteristics of a frequency distribution, or the relationship between two or more distributions. Cf. *inferential statistics.*

desensitization Generally, a weakening of a response, usually an emotional response, with repeated exposure to a situation; more specifically, a method used in psychotherapy to enable a person to be comfortable in situations in which he was previously highly anxious. See *behavior modification.*

developmental psychology The branch of psychology studying changes in behavior (q.v.) that occur with changes in age.

deviation IQ An intelligence quotient (q.v.) based on standard scores, so that IQs more nearly compare in meaning from one age to another.

deviation score The difference between the score obtained and the mean of the distribution that includes the obtained score. Symbol: *x.*

differential psychology The study and comparison of the differences between groups of people, e.g. men and women.

differential reinforcement Reinforcement of the response to one stimulus but not to another. Such reinforcement is used experimentally to establish a discrimination.

differential threshold The smallest difference in a stimulus that can be perceived. See also *absolute threshold.*

discrimination learning Learning in which the subject learns to choose one stimulus and not another. Usually responses to one stimulus, the positive one, are reinforced, while responses to the other stimulus are extinguished. See *simultaneous discrimination.*

disjunctive concept A concept that contains at least one element from a larger class of elements. Something is a member of the concept class if it contains at least one of a particular pool of elements, e.g. a strike in baseball is defined in different ways. See *concept;* cf. relational concept.

displacement The disguising of the goal of a motive by substituting another in place of it.

dissociative reaction A neurotic reaction involving repression (q.v.) in which certain aspects of personality and memory are compartmentalized and function more or less independently, e.g., amnesia and multiple personality (q.v.).

distributed practice Periods of practice interspersed with periods of rest, often permitting more efficient learning than continuous practice.

dizygotic (DZ) twins See *fraternal twins.*

dream analysis The analysis of the dream content to obtain information about the source of a person's emotional problems; sometimes used in psychoanalysis.

drive A term implying an impetus to behavior or active striving; often used synonymously with motive or need (q.v.).

eardrum A thin membrane which separates the outer ear from the middle ear and which vibrates when sound waves reach it.

educational psychology A field of specialization concerned with psychological aspects of teaching and the formal learning processes in school.

Edwards Personal Preference Schedule (EPPS) A test which purports to measure the major personal, or social, motives of individuals.

EEG See *electroencephalogram.*

effectors Organs of response (q.v.), muscles and glands.

efferent fibers Nerve fibers which carry impulses from the central nervous system to the organs of response.

eidetic imagery Extremely detailed imagery; a sort of projection of an image on a mental screen. See *image.*

electroconvulsive shock therapy (EST) A form of therapy used primarily with depressed patients; consists of administering electrical shocks to the brain sufficient to produce convulsions and to render the patient unconscious.

electroencephalogram (EEG) A record of electrical fluctuations in the brain (brain waves), usually obtained by placing electrodes on the skull. See *alpha rhythm,* and *delta rhythm.*

embryo A young organism in the early stages of development. In man, it refers to the period from shortly after conception until 2 months later. Cf. *fetus.*

emotion Affective states, often accompanied by facial and bodily expression, and have arousing and motivating properties.

empirical Founded on experiments, surveys, and proven facts, as distinguished from that which is asserted by argument, reasoning, or opinion.

empiricist One who argues that behavior tendencies, especially perceptual organizing tendencies, depend upon learning and past experience (q.v.). Cf. *nativist.*

encounter group One form of group therapy in which group members talk about their problems.

equipotentiality The idea that capacity for learning is not narrowly localized in the brain.

escape learning Learning to escape from a noxious or unpleasant situation by making an appropriate response.

esteem needs Needs for prestige, success, and self-respect.

ethology The study of behavior, especially the instinctive behavior, of animals.

evoked potential The electrical activity recorded from the nervous system that is produced by a stimulus.

excitation (1) Arousal (q.v.); (2) increased tendency to respond; (3) depolarization (q.v.) or firing of nerve cells. Cf. *inhibition.*

exorcism The attempt to cast out demons or evil spirits by such acts as prayer, religious rites, medicines, or whipping.

experience (1) Refers to the past history of the organism; (2) the immediate perception (q.v.) of the present situation or the present content of consciousness.

experimental method A scientific method in which conditions that are likely to affect a result are controlled by the experimenter. It involves dependent and independent variables. Cf. *method of systematic observation.*

experimental psychology A subfield of psychology which seeks to learn more about the fundamental causes of behavior by investigating problems in the areas of sensation and perception, learning and memory, motivation, and the physiological basis of behavior. Cf. *clinical psychology.*

exploratory drive A tendency to explore a novel environment; is considered a general unlearned drive (q.v.) not clearly distinguishable from curiosity or manipulative drive (q.v.).

extinction The procedure of presenting the conditioned stimulus without reinforcement to an organism previously conditioned; also the diminution of a conditioned response resulting from this procedure.

extinction curve A graph of the diminution of previously learned responses during the course of extinction (q.v.).

extrasensory perception (ESP) The perception of information without the use of sensory cues.

face validity The appearance of validity (q.v.) in a test because of the similarity of the test to the job to be performed. Face validity is not, however, necessarily true validity. Tests should always be examined with validating procedures to determine whether they are, in fact, valid.

factor analysis A general statistical method, involving coefficients of correlation, that isolates a few common factors in a large number of tests, ratings, or other measurements.

fantasy Daydreaming and imagining a world of one's own, often used as a defense mechanism (q.v.).

father figure An instance of transference (q.v.) in which a person is regarded as though he were a father.

feedback The situation in which some aspect of the output regulates the state of the system.

fetus A young organism in the later stages of prenatal development. In man, it refers to the period from 2 months after conception until birth. Cf. *embryo.*

fiber See *nerve fiber.*

field theory A type of psychological theory that stresses the importance of interactions between events in the person's environment.

figure-ground perception Perception of objects or events as standing out clearly from a background.

firing Electrical activity of single nerve cells. See *nerve impulse.*

fissure A relatively deep crevice in the cerebral cortex. Cf. *sulcus.* See also lateral fissure.

fixation A rigid habit developed by repeated reinforcement or as a consequence of frustration.

fixed-interval schedule A schedule of partial reinforcement (q.v.) in which a response made after a certain interval of time is reinforced.

fixed-ratio schedule A schedule of partial reinforcement (q.v.) in which every nth response is reinforced.

flexion reflex A reflex in which a limb is bent.

forebrain The most forward of three divisions of the brain. It includes the **cerebrum, thalamus, and hypothalamus.** See also *hindbrain, midbrain.*

forgetting A partial or total loss of retention of material previously learned.

formal group A social group that has a relatively permanent structure of positions, jobs, and roles.

fovea A central region of the retina where cones are closely packed together and visual acuity is at its best.

fraternal twins Twins who develop from two different fertilized eggs (ova), and who consequently may be as different in hereditary characteristics as ordinary brothers and sisters. Also called dizygotic (DZ) twins. Cf. *identical twins.*

free association The technique of requiring a patient in psychotherapy to say whatever comes to his mind, regardless of how irrelevant or objectionable it may seem.

free nerve endings Nerve endings that are not associated with any special receptive structures. They are found in the skin, blood vessels, and many parts of the body. They are regarded as sense organs for pain and probably also for touch and temperature.

free recall Learning a series of words, syllables, or other material without regard to order. Subjects may recall the material in any order it occurs to them.

free-response method A method of measuring the meaning of concepts in which a person is asked to describe or define a concept.

frequency One of the dimensions of vibrational stimuli, such as light or sound. It is most often used with sound and is stated in number of cycles per second, or hertz (q.v.), which is the number of alternations in air pressure per second.

frontal association area The nonmotor areas of the frontal lobes said to be involved in certain complex behavioral functions.

frontal lobe The lobe of the cerebrum (q.v.) which lies in front of the central sulcus (q.v.). See *frontal association areas.*

frustration The thwarting of motivated behavior directed at a goal.

functional autonomy The ability of certain motives to continue functioning without further reinforcement of the conditions under which they were learned. See also *learned goal.*

functional fixedness A special type of set (q.v.) in which individuals cannot use objects in novel ways. It may hinder problem solving.

functionalism A viewpoint taking the middle course among structuralism (q.v.), behaviorism (q.v.), and gestalt psychology (q.v.). Functionalists proposed that all activities serving some adaptive function, including both behavior and experience, be studied by psychologists.

galvanic skin response (GSR) A change in the electrical resistance of the skin, occurring in emotion and in certain other conditions.

ganglion A collection of the cell bodies of neurons.

ganglion cell In the eye, the cells of the third cell layer of the retina. Fibers of the retinal ganglion cells make up the optic nerve.

gene The essential element in the transmission of hereditary characteristics, carried in chromosomes.

generalization The phenomenon of an organism's responding to situations similar to the one to which it has been conditioned. See also *stimulus generalization.*

generator potential The voltage change that occurs in receptor cells when acted upon by physical energy. Generator potentials trigger nerve impulses from the receptor organ.

genetic See *gene.*

germ cell An egg or sperm cell.

gestalt psychology A viewpoint, developed by German psychologists, that considered introspection (q.v.) and behaviorism (q.v.) too atomistic and emphasized the importance of configuration in perception (q.v.) and insight (q.v.) in learning.

gland An organ that secretes. There are two general types, endocrine glands and exocrine glands.

goal The place, condition, or object that satisfies a motive.

Golgi tendon organs Receptors located in tendons that are activated when the muscle to which the tendon is attached contracts putting tension on the tendon. See *kinesthetic receptors.*

gonads The sex glands, which are the testicles in the male and the ovaries in the female. They determine secondary sex characteristics such as growth of the breasts, beginning of menstruation, growth of the beard, and change of the voice and also influence sexual motivation.

gradient of texture One of the principal monocular cues for depth perception. Consists of a gradation in the fineness of detail which can be seen at increasing distances from a person.

grammar The study of the rules for combining words into meaningful sentences.

gray matter Collections of cell bodies in the nervous system. Cf. *white matter.*

group See *social group.*

group norm A widely shared expectation or standard of behavior among most members of a group, class, or culture (q.v.).

group test A test that may be administered to a group of people at one time.

group therapy A specialized technique of psychotherapy, consisting of a group of patients discussing their personal problems under the guidance of a therapist.

grouping The tendency to perceive objects in groups rather than as isolated elements. Grouping is determined by such factors as nearness, similarity, symmetry, and continuation of objects.

GSR See *galvanic skin response.*

gyrus A ridge in the cerebral cortex of the brain. Cf. *sulcus.*

habit A learned response.

habituation The tendency of a response to weaken with repeated presentation of a stimulus; similar to desensitization (q.v.).

hair cell Pressure sensitive cells located in the organ of Corti (q.v.) which convert pressure waves to nerve impulses.

hallucination Sensory experience in the absence of stimulation of receptors. Hallucinations are present in certain behavior disorders such as schizophrenia (q.v.).

hebephrenic type A variety of schizophrenia (q.v.) characterized by childishness and regressive behavior.

hertz (Hz) One cycle per second; e.g., the alpha rhythm (q.v.) has a frequency of XX 8–12 Hz.

higher order conditioning Conditioning of a response to a stimulus by pairing the stimulus with another stimulus to which the response has previously been conditioned.

hindbrain The third of three divisions of the brain. It includes the medulla, cerebellum, and pons. See also *forebrain, midbrain.*

hippocampus An important structure in the limbic system (q.v.).

hostility See *aggression.*

hue The aspect of a color that is largely determined by wavelength and that enables us to discriminate blue from red, red from yellow, and so on, as distinguished from brightness and saturation (q.v.).

hunger A drive stemming from a physiological need for food.

hyperphagia Eating abnormally large quantities of food; associated with injuries in certain regions of the hypothalamus.

hypnosis A state in which a person is extremely susceptible to the suggestion of the hypnotist.

hypnotherapy The use of hypnosis as an aid in therapy; especially useful in the temporary alleviation of certain symptoms and in the temporary lifting of repression (q.v.).

hypochondriasis A neurotic reaction (q.v.) in which a person is excessively concerned with his physical welfare or constantly complaining of minor ailments; seen in anxiety reactions.

hypothalamus A region of the forebrain which contains centers for the regulation of sleep, temperature, thirst, sex, hunger, and emotion.

hysteria Cf. *conversion reaction.*

Hz See *hertz.*

iconic imagery Fleeting images that may represent persistent activity in sensory channels after exposure to stimulation. See *image.*

identical twins Twins who develop from the same fertilized egg (ovum). They have exactly the same kinds of chromosomes and genes and hence the same hereditary characteristics. Also called monozygotic (MZ) twins. Cf. *fraternal twins.*

identification The tendency of children to model their behavior after that of appropriate adults; a defense mechanism (q.v.) in which one thinks himself to be like someone else.

illusion A perception that does not agree with other, more trustworthy perceptions.

image A representation in the brain of sensory experience. Images may be involved in some thinking (q.v.).

imageless thought Thought occurring without the presence of images. The phrase refers particularly to a theory of the nature of thinking entertained by a group of German psychologists about 1900.

imitation Copying the behavior of another.

immunization The hardening of a person's attitude on a particular subject by giving him a mild exposure to an opposing attitude. This exposure hardens the originally held attitude so that it is resistant to change by further facts or arguments, no matter how strong.

implicit response A minute muscle movement ordinarily detectable only by special electrical or mechanical recording methods. Implicit responses, miniatures of large, observable movements, are acquired in previous learning and may be involved in thinking (q.v.).

imprinting The very rapid development of response to a stimulus at some critical period of development. Particularly characteristic of some species of birds.

impulse (1) Sometimes used in psychoanalysis to refer to motive (q.v.). (2) The spike potential—the nerve impulse.

incentive A term approximately synonymous with goal, but implying the manipulation of a goal to motivate the individual.

Money, for example, is used as an incentive to motivate people to work.

incidental learning In animal learning, learning without incentive or reinforcement. In human learning, learning without intending to learn. See *latent learning*.

incubation A stage in creative thinking during which the problem is put aside and unconscious factors are permitted to work.

independent variable The variable that may be selected or changed by the experimenter and is responsible for changes in the dependent variable (q.v.).

individual test A test that can be given to only one individual at a time, e.g., the Stanford-Binet Intelligence Scale (q.v.).

individuation In social situations, the condition in which individual persons in a group are known personally by name and characteristics. Cf. *deindividuation*.

induced movement Movement of a stationary spot perceived when the background of the spot moves. The moon "racing" through the clouds is an example.

induction The logical process by which principles or rules are derived from observed facts.

industrial psychology A field of specialization concerned with methods of selecting, training, counseling, and supervising personnel in business and industry. It sometimes includes problems of increasing efficiency in work and of redesigning machines to suit better the capacities of the worker.

inferential statistics The statistical methods for inferring population values from obtained sample values. See *statistical decisions*.

inhibition (1) A decreasing tendency to respond with repetition of a response. (2) Hyperpolarization of a nerve cell making it less responsive to stimulation.

inner ear See *cochlea, vestibular sense*.

insight (1) In learning and problem solving, the relatively sudden solution of a problem. (2) In psychotherapy, the understanding of one's own motives and their origins.

insight therapy Treatment of a personality disorder by attempting to uncover the deep causes of the patient's difficulty and to help him rid himself of his defense mechanisms.

instinctive behavior A complex, unlearned, pattern of behavior which persists beyond the duration of the stimulus instigating it.

instrumental behavior Behavior that typically accomplishes a purpose, usually the satisfaction of a need, e.g., working for a living.

instrumental conditioning Learning situations in which the responses of the subject are instrumental in producing reinforcement. Sometimes known as instrumental learning. See also *operant conditioning*.

intelligence A general term covering a person's abilities on a wide range of tasks involving vocabulary, numbers, problem solving, concepts, and so on. As measured by a standardized intelligence test, it generally involves several specific abilities, with special emphasis on verbal abilities.

intelligence quotient (IQ) Classically, a number obtained by dividing chronological age into mental age and multiplying by 100. Now other methods are used to compute the intelligence quotient. See *deviation IQ*.

intensity A general term referring to the amount of physical energy stimulating a sense organ. It is expressed in physical units appropriate to the kind of energy involved.

interference A factor in learning and forgetting; the incompatibility of two learned associations.

interference theory A theory of extinction which holds that nonreinforced responses decline in strength because other incompatible responses are learned during the extinction period.

internal environment The environment of the bodily organs, including the temperature of the body, oxygen, food supplies, minerals, hormones, and related substances.

interpersonal attraction The study of the reasons why people like (or dislike) each other.

interposition A cue in depth perception (q.v.) in which near objects block off portions of faraway objects.

intoxication psychosis (alcohol) A psychosis developing as a result of prolonged alcoholism. It is characterized by defects of memory, disorientation, delusions, and other symptoms similar to those seen in senile psychosis (q.v.).

introspection A method of psychological experimentation in which a subject is presented with some stimulus, such as a colored light, and asked to give a detailed report of his sensations.

introspectionism A viewpoint held early in the twentieth century by one group of experimental psychologists who employed the method of introspection. It regarded sensation as the important psychological element in consciousness and attempted to analyze mental content.

inventory A detailed questionnaire that provides specific information about a person's likes, dislikes, habits, preferences, and so on. It usually refers to a personality or interest test.

involutional reactions Agitated depression or paranoid reactions (q.v.) in women at menopause and in men at slightly older ages. Perhaps a physical brain disorder is responsible, but the most prevalent idea of causation emphasizes the psychological stress of approaching old age.

IQ See *intelligence quotient.*

iris The set of muscles, controlled by the autonomic system, that varies the amount of light admitted to the eye by narrowing or enlarging the pupil. It gives the eye its distinctive color, such as blue or brown.

kinesthesis See *kinesthetic receptors.*

kinesthetic receptors Sense organs located in the muscles, tendons, and joints that provide information about the position of the limbs and body in space.

knowledge of results A person's knowledge of how he is progressing in training or in the performance of his job. It is usually necessary for the most rapid learning and for the best performance of the job.

language A set of symbols used for communication and in thinking.

latent learning Learning that becomes evident only when the occasion arises for using it. See *incidental learning.*

lateral fissure A deep cleft in the cerebral cortex dividing the temporal lobe from the frontal and parietal lobes.

learned goal A goal that has been acquired through learning, as distinguished from a physiological goal.

learning A general term referring to a relatively permanent change in behavior that is the result of past experience or practice. It includes classical conditioning, operant conditioning, and perceptual learning.

learning curve Any graphical representation of progress in learning. Usually a curve in which performance is plotted on the ordinate (q.v.) and trials or time are plotted on the abscissa (q.v.).

learning set A kind of transfer of training (q.v.) in which a subject becomes increasingly adept at learning problems of the same general type.

lens The adjustable refractive element of the eye.

lesion Any damage or change in a tissue due to injury or disease.

lie detector A popular name for a device designed to detect emotional responses when a person lies. It usually involves measures of breathing, heart rate, blood pressure, and galvanic skin response.

light The visible spectrum (q.v.) of electromagnetic radiation. It may be specified by wavelength and intensity.

limbic system A series of related structures in the core of the brain concerned with emotion and motivation. The septal area (q.v.), hypothalamus (q.v.), amygdala (q.v.), and cingulate gyrus (q.v.) are important limbic system structures.

linear perspective The perception of far-away objects as close together and of nearby objects as far apart. It is an important factor in depth perception.

linguistics The study of languages as systems of rules.

loaded words Words having an emotional tone, used by propagandists and advertisers for creating and maintaining attitudes.

logical thinking Reasoning carried out according to the formal rules of logic; not very common in human thinking.

loudness A psychological attribute of tones, related to intensity but not directly proportional to it.

luminosity The perceived brightness of a visual stimulus. See also *luminosity curve.*

luminosity curve A curve depicting the visual threshold at different wavelengths. The luminosity curve for daylight vision has its greatest sensitivity at about 555 millimicrons; the comparable curve for night vision has its greatest sensitivity at about 505 millimicrons. See also *cone, rod.*

MA See *mental age.*

maladjustment A broad term covering not only the psychoneurotic and psychotic but also mild disturbances in which a person is anxious or behaves peculiarly.

manic-depressive psychosis See *affective reactions.*

maternal behavior Behavior concerned with giving birth to young, nursing them, and caring for them.

maturation The completion of developmental processes in the body. Maturation is governed both by heredity and by environmental conditions. Growth; changes of behavior through growth of the body.

maze A device used in animal and human learning experiments that has blind alleys and a correct path. It presents the subject with the task of taking a path through it without entering any blind alleys.

mechanical-ability test A vocational-aptitude test for predicting success in jobs requiring mechanical ability.

median The middle score in a frequency distribution when all scores are ranked from highest to lowest (or lowest to highest). It is one measure of central tendency (q.v.).

mediating process An associative process connecting previously learned processes and responses. See *thinking.*

medical therapy The treatment of an illness by using medicines, drugs, or surgery. Cf. *psychotherapy.*

medulla The lowest division of the brain stem; contains several kinds of nuclei, especially those concerned with the vital functions of breathing and cardiovascular regulation.

memory See *retention.*

memory drum Apparatus used to present verbal material in studies of verbal learning.

mental age (MA) A type or norm. Gives the relative degree of mental development of a child by stating the age level at which the child is performing. For example, if a five-year-old child does as well as an intelligence test as the average child of seven, his mental age is 7. See also *intelligence quotient.*

mental deficiency Often synonomous with mental retardation (q.v.), but more often used for mental retardation caused specifically by injury or disease.

mental disease See *behavior disorder.*

mental disorder See *behavior disorder.*

mental illness See *behavior disorder.*

mental retardation A condition marked by a deficiency in general intellectual ability. Usually an IQ below 70. See also *intelligence quotient.* See *mental deficiency.*

meter A unit of length in the metric system; 39.37 inches.

method of rating A method that requires a person to assign comparative adjectives or numbers on a scale to indicate preferences, judgments, or opinions. See also *rating.*

method of systematic observation Scientific study of a natural situation or problem, under controlled conditions, without any experimental manipulation of the variables involved. Cf. *experimental method.*

microelectrode An electrode so small that it can provide a record of electrical activity in a single neuron or sensory cell.

midbrain The middle of three divisions of the brain. It contains reflex centers for hearing and vision, pathways to and from the forebrain, and several other centers. See also *forebrain, hindbrain.*

middle ear A bony cavity containing ossicles which link the eardrum to the cochlea.

mild retardation A degree of mental retardation characterized by an IQ of from 69 to 53.

millilambert A physical unit of reflected light energy.

millimicron A nanometer (q.v.).

mind Conscious experience as reported by an individual.

Minnesota Multiphasic Personality Inventory (MMPI) A widely used pencil-and-paper personality questionnaire. An important feature is its empirical validity (q.v.).

MMPI See *Minnesota Multiphasic Personality Inventory.*

modeling Learning by observing the behavior of another person. Also a technique of behavior modification (q.v.). See also *observational learning, socialization.*

moderate retardation A degree of mental retardation characterized by an IQ of from 52 to 36.

Mongolism A mild to moderate form of mental retardation in which the facial features resemble somewhat those of Mongoloid people.

Mongoloid See *Mongolism.*

monocular Pertaining to the use of only one eye. Cf. *binocular.*

monozygotic (MZ) twins See *identical twins.*

motivated forgetting Forgetting due to active forces relating to a person's needs. Repression (q.v.) and forgetting due to weakening of tension systems are two examples.

motivation A general term referring to behavior instigated by needs and directed toward goals (q.v.).

motivational conflict A conflict between two or more motives resulting in the frustration of a motive. Most motivational conflict involves acquired motives. See *approach-approach conflict, avoidance-avoidance conflict, and approach-avoidance conflict.*

motive A term implying a need and the direction of behavior toward a goal; often used synonymously with need or drive (q.v.).

motor area An area of the cerebral cortex lying around the central fissure. Movements can be elicited by stimulation of this region. The threshold for movement is least for the portion just in front of the central fissure.

motor learning The learning of a skill such as driving, typewriting, or playing a musical instrument.

multiple personality A dissociative reaction (q.v.) in which a person displays two or more relatively distinct personalities, each with its own set of memories. See also *amnesia, dissociative reaction.*

muscle spindle Receptors in muscles that signal stretch of the muscle. See *kinesthetic receptors.*

mutation A change in a gene and, hence, in the characteristic it determines.

nanometer (nm) A billionth of a meter; 10^{-9} meters.

nativist One who argues that behavioral tendencies, especially perceptual organizing tendencies, are inborn, or innate. Cf. *empiricist.*

natural observation The observation of events as they occur in nature or in the course of human affairs without exercising experimental controls and without using methods of systematic sampling. Cf *method of systematic observation.*

nature The genetic factors contributing to behavior. Cf. *nurture.*

need Any lack or deficit within the individual, either acquired or physiological; often used synonymously with drive or motive (q.v.). See also *social needs.*

need complementarity The idea that people with different needs like each other because they provide mutual satisfaction of opposed needs.

negative acceleration The characteristic of a curve that is steep at its beginning but becomes increasingly flat as it approaches its end. Learning curves are typically of this shape.

negative reinforcement A reinforcement is a stimulus or event that strengthens a response when it follows the response; *negative* means that reinforcement occurs when the learner escapes from or avoids a noxious, or unpleasant, stimulus. Cf. *positive reinforcement.*

negative transfer The harmful effect on learning in one situation because of previous learning in another situation. It is due to incompatible responses being required in the two situations. Cf. *positive transfer.*

neocortex The six-layered covering of the cerebrum. See *gray matter, cerebral cortex.*

nerve A bundle of nerve fibers.

nerve deafness Deafness due to an impairment of the sense organs or of the nerves concerned in hearing. It is also called perception deafness or perceptual deafness. Cf. *conduction deafness.*

nerve fiber An axon or a dendrite of a neuron. It conducts nerve impulses.

nerve impulse An electrical change in the membrane of a nerve fiber, propagated along the length of the fiber. It is the basic message unit of the nervous system and obeys an all-or-none law (q.v.).

nervous system The brain, spinal cord, and nerves serving the various sense organs, endocrine glands, and muscles of the body.

neurasthenia Type of anxiety reaction (q.v.) in which the person complains of general nervousness, fatigue, and insomnia; often accompanied by depression, feelings of inadequacy, and inability to work.

neuron The cell that is the basic unit of the nervous system. It conducts nerve impulses and consists of dendrite(s) (q.v.), cell body, and axon (q.v.).

neurosis or neurotic reaction See *psychoneurotic reaction.*

nondirective therapy Psychotherapy in which the patient is dominant and given the greatest possible opportunity to express himself. The method is based on the principle that the patient must learn how to solve his own problems and cannot have them solved for him by the therapist. See *client-centered therapy.*

nonsense syllable A syllable, usually of three letters, constructed so as to resemble meaningful English as little as possible. Nonsense syllables are used in learning experiments as new or unfamiliar material.

normal curve A bell-shaped frequency distribution, also called the normal-probability curve, which is an ideal approximated by many distributions obtained in psychology and biological sciences. It can be derived mathematically from the laws of chance.

norms An average or standard, or a distribution of measurements, obtained from a large number of people. It permits the comparison of an individual score with the scores of comparable individuals.

nucleus A collection of cell bodies of neurons within the central nervous system; also a structure within cells containing chromosomes. Plural: nuclei.

nurture The learned factors contributing to behavior; the factors that depend upon experience. Cf. *nature.*

observational learning A form of perceptual learning (q.v.) in which the person learns by observing the behavior of another person. See also *modeling.*

obsession A seemingly groundless idea that constantly intrudes into a person's thoughts; seen in obsessive-compulsive reactions. Cf. *compulsion.*

obsessive-compulsive personality A behavior pattern characterized by excessive conformity and adherence to standards of conscience; not as severe as the obsessive-compulsive reaction (q.v.).

obsessive-compulsive reaction A psychoneurotic reaction characterized by obsessions and/or compulsions (q.v.).

obstruction method A method for measuring the strength of a motive by seeing how much noxious stimulation an organism will tolerate in order to satisfy the motive.

occipital lobe The part of the cerebral cortex lying at the back of the head. It contains the primary sensory areas for vision.

oldsightedness Farsightedness characteristic of old age and typically increasing beyond the age of forty.

olfaction, olfactory sense Smell.

operant conditioning Learning to make a particular response to secure positive reinforcement (q.v.) or to escape or avoid negative reinforcement (q.v.). See *instrumental conditioning.*

opinion Acceptance of a statement accompanied by an attitude of pro or con.

opinion effect Distortion of reasoning due to the emotional connotations of the premises of syllogisms. Cf. *atmosphere effect.*

opponent process theory The theory that

human color vision depends on three pairs of opposing processes: white-black, yellow-blue, and red-green.

optic nerve The nerve formed by axons of the ganglion cells of the retina. It leaves the eye at the blind spot and ends in relay centers of the thalamus.

ordinate The vertical axis of a graph; values of the dependent variable (q.v.) are usually plotted on this axis.

organ of Corti The organ containing receptors for hearing, located on the basilar membrane which separates the vestibular canal and tympanic ducts of the cochlea.

orienting reaction A reaction to a novel stimulus in which muscles are tensed and the position of the body is changed to maximize effectiveness in reacting to the stimulus.

oscilloscope An electronic voltage recording device. In psychology, used especially in studies of audition and neural activity. It typically records changes of voltage over time.

ossicles Three bones in the middle ear through which sound is conducted from the eardrum to the oval window of the cochlea.

otolith organs Sense organs found in chambers near the cochlea. They are sensitive to gravity and to the position of the head; they are part of the vestibular sense (q.v.).

oval window The entrance to the cochlea through which sound vibrations pass from the ossicles of the middle ear to the canals of the cochlea.

ovum The cell formed in the ovary of the female which, when fertilized by the sperm of the male, may develop into a new individual. Plural: ova.

pacinian corpuscle A specialized structure serving as a receptor for pressure, located below the skin, in joints, and other deep parts of the body. See *kinesthetic receptor.*

paired-associate learning Learning in which the subject must respond with one word or syllable when presented with another word or syllable.

papillae Bumps on the tongue that are heavily populated with taste buds.

paradoxical sleep A state of sleep in which it is difficult to wake a person, yet his EEG (q.v.) pattern is like that in light sleep. It is accompanied by rapid eye movements, and is therefore also known as REM sleep. Most dreaming occurs in this stage of sleep.

paranoid reactions Behavior disorders marked by extreme suspiciousness of the motives of others, often taking the form of elaborate beliefs that they are plotting against the person. In the paranoid reactions the delusions (q.v.) of persecution are usually systematized. See also *projection.*

paranoid type A kind of schizophrenia (q.v.) characterized by delusions (q.v.), often of persecution. Different from the paranoid reaction (q.v.) in that the delusions are less systematic in the paranoid type of schizophrenia.

parasympathetic system A subdivision of the autonomic system arising in the cranial and sacral portions of the central nervous system. Tends to be active during quiescent states of organism. Cf. *sympathetic system.*

parietal lobe The part of the cerebral cortex lying immediately behind the central fissure. It contains areas involved in somesthesis and somesthetic discrimination learning.

part learning Learning, usually in the sense of memorizing, in which the task is divided into smaller units and each unit is separately learned. Cf. *whole learning.*

partial reinforcement Reinforcement of some proportion of unconditioned responses (in classical conditioning), or of some proportion of instrumental responses (in operant learning). See *schedule of reinforcement.*

passive-aggressive personality A person who expresses hostility by excessive aggression, stubborn pouting, or extreme dependence.

peer An equal in a given respect, an associate at roughly the same level.

perception A general term referring to the awareness of objects, qualities, or events stimulating the sense organs; also refers to a person's experience of the world. See *experience.*

perception deafness See *nerve deafness.*

perceptual constancy A general term referring to the tendency of objects to be perceived in the same way despite wide variations in the energies impinging upon the receptors. See also *brightness constancy, shape constancy.*

perceptual learning Used in two senses. (1) the influence of learning on perceptual organization; (2) learning to associate stimulus events with each other. See also *observational learning.*

performance (1) Observed behavior; as distinct from hypothetical internal states of an organism. See *latent learning.* (2) Nonlinguistic ability; performance tests are so constructed that they do not handicap a person who speaks no English or who has verbal deficiences.

performance test Tests which measure nonverbal activity or performance.

peripheral nervous system The part of the nervous system lying outside the skull and the backbone. Cf. *central nervous system.*

personality The traits, modes of adjustment, defense mechanisms, and ways of behaving that characterize the individual and his relation to others in his environment.

personnel psychology Concerns the applications of psychology to the selection, training, and supervision of people in business and industrial settings; also concerned with improving communications, counseling employees, and attempting to solve industrial strife. See *industrial psychology.*

personality disorders Characterized by developmental defects or pathological trends in the personality structure, with minimal accompanying anxiety.

personality structure In general, the unique organization of traits, motives, and ways of behaving that characterizes a particular person.

phobia An intense, irrational fear. See *phobic reaction.*

phobic reaction A psychoneurotic reaction (q.v.) characterized by intense irrational fear.

photosensitive substances Chemical substances in the rods and cones of the retina that are decomposed by light and initiate the visual process.

physiological motive A motive (q.v.) arising from some lack or deficit, from hormones, or other conditions within the body.

physiological psychology The branch of psychology which deals with the physiological mechanisms of behavior.

pitch A psychological attribute of tones, related to frequency but not directly proportional to it.

pitch scale A curve depicting the relationship between physical frequency and perceived pitch.

place theory A theory of pitch, widely accepted, that assumes different places on the basilar membrane (q.v.) are activated by different frequencies of a sound stimulus.

polarized membrane The inside of a nerve cell is negatively charged with respect to the outside. See *depolarization.*

pons A region of the brain stem above the medulla (q.v.) which contains ascending and descending pathways, fibers connecting the lobes of the cerebellum (q.v.), and many nuclei.

population The group of individuals on which measurements are made. The total population consists of all possible individuals on which measurements might be made, e.g., all voters. A sample population is a smaller group drawn from the total population so as to be representative of it. See *sampling.*

positive reinforcement A reinforcement is a stimulus or event that strengthens a response when it follows the response; *positive* means that the reinforcement is something that the learner approaches. Cf. *negative reinforcement.*

positive transfer More rapid learning in one situation because of previous learning in another situation. It is due to a similarity of the stimuli and/or responses required in the two situations. Cf. *negative transfer.*

posthypnotic suggestion Suggestion made by the hypnotist while a person is in a hypnotic state but carried out after the hypnosis has been terminated. See *hypnotherapy.*

potential (1) Generally an aptitude (q.v.), or a psychological capacity that requires training for its realization; (2) a voltage difference.

predisposition In the study of personal adjustment, a tendency that is inherited and gives a biological basis for the development of certain temperamental and personality characteristics.

prefrontal areas See *frontal association area.*

prehension The grasping of objects with the hands, the fingers, or (in the case of some monkeys) the tail.

prejudice Literally, a prejudgment; more generally, an emotionally toned attitude (q.v.) for or against an object, person, or group of persons. Typically, it is a hostile attitude that places a person or group at a disadvantage.

prenatal Before birth.

prestige The feeling of being better than other persons with whom one compares oneself. The prestige need is a social need to achieve prestige. The need is frequently exploited with propaganda and social techniques.

primary goal The goal of a physiological or unlearned motive. Cf. *secondary goal.*

primary group A small group with which a person has frequent informal contacts, such as family, friends, associates.

primary reinforcement In classical conditioning (q.v.), the presentation of the unconditioned stimulus immediately following the conditioned stimulus; in operant conditioning (q.v.), the presentation of an incentive immediately following the operant response.

primary sensory area An area of the cerebral cortex to which fibers transmit impulses from the receptors of a particular sense. There are primary sensory areas for each of the senses except pain, the vestibular sense, and smell.

private acceptance A type of conformity (q.v.) in which we make the norms and values of a group our own. Cf. *compliance.*

proactive inhibition See *negative transfer.*

probability The relative frequency of occurrence of an event expected over the long run.

process schizophrenia The type of schizophrenia (q.v.) in which there is a slow, insidious onset and in which the person's adjustment before hospitalization is poor. Cf. *reactive schizophrenia.*

product-moment correlation A widely used coefficient of correlation (q.v.) devised by the British mathematician Karl Pearson. Used for interval and ratio measurements. Symbol: *r*.

profound retardation A degree of mental retardation characterized by an IQ of 20 or below.

programmed learning Self-instruction by means of carefully designed questions or items which, through immediate reinforcement, motivate and enhance the learning process. See *teaching machine.*

projection The disguising of a source of conflict by ascribing one's own motives to someone else; prominent in paranoid reactions (q.v.).

projective methods Methods used in the study of personality, in which a subject is presented with a relatively ambiguous stimulus and asked to describe it in a meaningful way or to tell a story about it. See *Thematic Apperception Test, Rorschach test.*

propaganda The deliberate attempt to influence attitudes (q.v.) and beliefs (q.v.).

proprioception See proprioceptive sense.

proprioceptive sense The sensory input arising from the kinesthetic (q.v.) and vestibular receptors within the body.

psychiatry A branch of medicine specializing in the diagnosis and treatment of behavior disorders.

psychoanalysis Primarily a method of psychotherapy developed by Sigmund Freud, but also a theory of the development and structure of personality. As a psychotherapy, it emphasizes the techniques of free association (q.v.) and the phenomenon of transference.

psycholinguistics The branch of psychology concerned with the ways in which people generate and comprehend language.

psychology The science that studies the behavior of animals and human beings.

psychometric psychology The branch of psychology concerned with the development of tests, research on the usefulness of tests, and, in general, ways of measuring behavior.

psychometrist A psychologist primarily concerned with the giving and scoring of tests (q.v.).

psychomotor test A test involving movement and coordination; usually a vocational-aptitude test.

psychoneurosis See *psychoneurotic reaction.*

psychoneurotic reaction A behavior disorder, less severe than a psychotic reaction (q.v.), in which a person is unusually anxious, miserable, troubled, or incapacitated in his work and his relations with other people. He often attempts to ward off anxiety by using exaggerated defense mechanisms. Also called a neurosis or psychoneurosis.

psychosomatic illness A bodily disorder precipitated or aggravated by emotional disturbance.

psychotherapy The treatment of behavior disorders and mild adjustment problems by means of psychological techniques. Cf. *medical therapy.*

psychotic reaction A behavior disorder more severe than a psychoneurotic reaction (q.v.) and often requiring custodial care. See *affective reactions, paranoid reactions, schizophrenic reactions, involutional reactions.*

public-opinion poll A method of surveying opinions on certain issues by selecting a sample of the population and interviewing each member of the sample.

punctate sensitivity In the study of the skin senses, greater sensitivity in certain spots of the skin than in others. It is a phenomenon that allows us to distinguish four primary senses among the skin senses.

punishment The application of an unpleasant stimulus for the purpose of eliminating undesirable behavior.

pupil The aperture through which light is admitted to the eye; altered in size by the action of the iris muscles.

pure tone One resulting from simple sine-wave (q.v.) energy.

RAS See *recticular activating system.*

rating A general term for the method in which a judge or observer rates the amount of aptitude, interest, ability, or other characteristic that an individual is considered to have.

rationalization The interpretation of one's own behavior so as to conceal the motive it expresses and to assign the behavior to some other motive.

reaction formation The disguising of a motive so completely that it is expressed in a form that is directly opposite to its original intent.

reaction time The time from the onset of a stimulus until the organism responds.

reactive schizophrenia The type of schizophrenia (q.v.) in which the person's adjustment before the disorder is fairly good and in which the onset of the disorder is rapid. Cf. *process schizophrenia.*

readiness The point in maturation (q.v.) when a behavior can emerge with training; before this point, the behavior is not possible, no matter how intense or sophisticated the training.

reasoning Thinking (q.v.) in which one attempts to solve a problem by combining two or more elements from past experience.

recall A method of measuring retension (q.v.) in which the subject reproduces with a minimum of cues something that he has previously learned.

receptor The structures at which transduction (q.v.) takes place in the sensory systems. Each receptor is most sensitive to a particular kind of energy; it is through the action of the receptors that we know about events in the world around us.

recessive gene A gene whose hereditary characteristics are not expressed when it is paired with a dominant gene.

reciprocal inhibition (1) The relaxation of a muscle simultaneously with the contraction of its antagonist. (2) A form of behavior modification (q.v.) in which classical conditioning (q.v.) is used to condition responses incompatible with the response to be eliminated. See *counterconditioning, behavior modification.*

recognition A method of measuring retention in which the subject is required only to recognize the correct answer when it is presented to him along with incorrect answers, e.g., in a true-false or multiple-choice examination.

reflex A relatively rapid and consistent unlearned response to a stimulus. It is ordinarily not conscious or subject to voluntary control. It lasts only so long as the stimulus is present. Cf. *instinctive behavior, taxis.*

refractory period See *absolute refractory period, relative refractory period.*

regression A retreat to earlier or more primitive forms of behavior, frequently encountered in children and adults faced with frustration.

reinforcement See *primary reinforcement, secondary reinforcement.*

relational concept Defined in terms of relationships between elements rather than in terms of the absolute properties of the elements. See *concept*; cf. *disjunctive concept.*

relative refractory period A brief period after the discharge of a nerve impulse when the neuron can only be fired by a stimulus that is much stronger than normal. Cf. *absolute refractory period.*

releasing stimuli Stimuli which are thought to release the fixed action patterns from inhibition so that they can be expressed.

reliability The self-consistency of a method of measurement, or the degree to which separate, independent measurements of the same thing agree with each other. Reliability is usually expressed by a coefficient of correlation (q.v.) representing the relationship between two sets of measurements of the same thing. See also *validity.*

REM sleep See *paradoxical sleep.*

representative sampling Sampling (q.v.) so as to obtain a fair cross section of a population without introducing biases that make the sample unrepresentative. See also *stratified sampling.*

repression A psychological process in which memories and motives are not permitted to enter consciousness but are operative at an unconscious level. Repression is one of several reactions to frustration and anxiety.

resistance A phenomenon observed in psychotherapy, exhibited as an inability to remember important events in one's past or to talk about certain anxiety-charged subjects. Resistance may be indicated by a blocking of free associations or by a person's steering away from certain subjects during free association (q.v.).

response Generally, any behavior of an organism. See *behavior.*

resting potential A voltage difference, found in the inactive nerve fiber between the outside and the inside of the polarized membrane (q.v.). The inside is negative with respect to the outside.

retention The amount correctly remembered. The principal methods of measuring retention are savings, recognition, and recall.

reticular activating system (RAS) A network of cell bodies and fibers extending through the medulla, midbrain, hypothalamus, and thalamus forming an indirect sensory pathway to the cerebral cortex.

retina The photosensitive layer of the eye on which images of objects are projected. It contains receptors, known as rods (q.v.) and cones (q.v.), and nerve cells that convey impulses to the brain.

retinal disparity A slight difference in the images of an object projected on the retinas (q.v.) of the two eyes. It arises from the fact that the two eyes view the object from slightly different angles.

retroactive inhibition The harmful effect of learning or activity on the retention of previous learning.

reward (1) Loosely equivalent to reinforcement (q.v.). (2) In social psychology, pleasures or satisfactions occurring as a result of behaviors chosen.

rod A photosensitive receptor in the retina, long and cylindrical, like a rod, and most sensitive in nighttime conditions of seeing. Cf. *cone.*

role A pattern of behavior that a person in a particular social status (q.v.) is expected to exhibit.

Rorschach test A projective method (q.v.) using inkblots as stimuli.

rotary pursuitmeter A device used in human learning experiments that requires the subject to keep a stylus on a moving spot while the spot rotates on a circular platform.

sampling The process of selecting a set of individuals or measurements from a large population (q.v.) of possible individuals or measurements. See also *stratified sampling*.

sampling error The error due to chance differences in selecting a sample from a population.

saturation A dimension of color that refers to the amount or richness of a hue, as distinguished from brightness or hue (q.v.); e.g., a red that is barely distinguishable from a gray is low in saturation.

savings A method of measuring retention (q.v.) in which the subject learns again what he previously learned. Savings are measured by the difference between the number of trials or errors originally required to learn and the number required in relearning.

scapegoating The displacement of aggression to a convenient group or class.

scatter diagram (scattergram) A plot of the scores made by the same individuals on two different variables providing a visual picture of the degree of correlation between the variables.

schedule of reinforcement Some specified sequence of partial reinforcement (q.v.) such as a ratio schedule or an interval schedule. See also *partial reinforcement, fixed-internal schedule, fixed-ratio schedule, variable-internal schedule, variable-ratio schedule*.

schizoid personality A personality disorder characterized by withdrawal from other people and eccentric thinking; not psychotic. Cf. *schizophrenic reactions*.

schizophrenia See *schizophrenic reactions*.

schizophrenic reactions One of the psychotic reactions, characterized by fantasy, regression, hallucinations (q.v.), delusions (q.v.), and general withdrawal from contact with the person's environment. Also called schizophrenia.

scholastic aptitude Ability to succeed in some specified type of formal schooling. For example, college aptitude refers to aptitude for doing college work.

school of psychology See *structuralism, functionalism, behaviorism, or gestalt psychology*.

school psychology Counseling psychology (q.v.) in the schools. See *educational psychology*.

science A body of systematized knowledge gathered by carefully observing and measuring events. See *empirical*.

sclera layer The white outermost coat of the eyeball. In the front of the eye, it becomes the transparent cornea. See *choroid and retina*.

secondary goal A goal learned through association with a primary goal. Cf. *secondary reinforcement*.

secondary reinforcement The reinforcing effect of a stimulus that has been paired with a primary reinforcement (q.v.). See *conditioned reinforcement*.

self-stimulation Central stimulation, usually electrical, of the brain which is administered by the animal's pressing a bar or switch.

semantic differential A method of measuring the connotative meaning (q.v.) of a concept (q.v.) in which the person rates the concept on several bipolar scales.

semantics The study of the meaning of words and sounds.

semicircular canals Three canals found near the cochlea (q.v.) in each ear. They are sensitive to rotation and to changes in the position of the head. See *vestibular sense*.

senile psychosis A psychotic reaction that tends to appear in some individuals with advancing age; characterized by defects of memory, general disorientation, and delusions. See also *intoxication psychosis (alcohol)*.

sensation A general term for the sensitivity of an organism to external and internal stimulus (q.v.) events. See *receptor*.

sensitivity groups See *encounter groups*.

sensory area An area of the brain concerned in sensory functions. It is usually an area of the cerebral cortex. See also *primary sensory area*.

sensory code The means by which we experience different sensations. It is determined by which receptors (q.v.) and their connecting fibers are most active.

sensory deprivation Experimental restriction of sensory input; used in the study of perceptual organization.

sensory neuron A neuron that conveys nerve impulses away from sense organs into the central nervous system.

septal area One of the structures in the limbic system (q.v.) of the forebrain containing complex connections with other parts of the brain; seems involved in emotional expression.

set A readiness to react in a certain way when confronted with a problem or stimulus situation.

severe retardation A degree of mental retardation characterized by an IQ of from 35 to 20.

sex hormones Hormones secreted by the gonads and responsible for the development of secondary sex characteristics such as the male's beard and the female's breasts. They are involved in sexual motivation.

sex-linked characteristic A hereditary characteristic controlled by a gene carried on the chromosomes that determine sex; for example, color blindness (q.v.).

sex typing Learning the roles (q.v.) appropriate to the status (q.v.) of being a woman or a man. See *socialization*.

shape constancy The tendency to perceive the "true" shape of an object even when the image on the retina is distorted. For example, a circle is seen as a circle even when viewed at an angle.

shaping Teaching a desired response through a series of successive steps which lead the learner to the final response. Each small step leading to the final response is reinforced. See also *successive approximations.*

shock therapy The treatment of behavior disorders by some agent causing convulsion and/or coma. Such agents include insulin, metrazol, and electric shock to the brain. See *electroconvulsive shock therapy* (EST).

sibling A brother or sister.

signal A stimulus used to indicate the time and place for something to happen is at hand.

significance A probability statement of the likelihood of obtaining a given difference or correlation between two sets of measurements by chance. Often stated by giving P values, e.g., $P < .001$.

simple type A kind of schizophrenia (q.v.) characterized by apathy, indifference, and mental deterioration.

sine wave A particular type of energy wave. In audition, the simplest kind of sound wave, generated by a vibrating object moving back and forth freely like a pendulum.

single-blind technique An experimental method in drug studies in which the subjects of the experiment do not know whether or not they have received the drug.

situational test A test in which a person is observed in some real-life situation, e.g., in managing a group of men in the building of a small bridge.

skin conductance See *galvanic skin response.*

skin senses The senses of pain, warmth, cold, and pressure located in the skin.

Skinner box A simple box with a device at one end, which, if operated, will produce reinforcement; used to study operant conditioning. Also called a standard operant chamber.

sleep spindles Bursts of relative high-voltage 12–14 Hz waves on a relatively low-voltage background. Characteristic of the early stages of falling asleep.

smooth muscle Muscle that under the microscope exhibits no stripes. It is found in blood vessels, intestines, and certain other organs. Cf. *striped muscle.*

social class A grouping of people on a scale of prestige in a society according to their social status. It is determined by many factors, such as nature of occupation, kind of income, moral standing, family genealogy, social relationships and organizations, and area of residence.

social group Any group of people, formal or informal, assembled or dispersed, who are related to each other by some common interest or attachment.

social motives Motives (q.v.), usually learned, that require the presence or reaction of other people for their satisfaction. In human motivation, *need* and *motive* are used synonymously. See also *achievement motive, affiliative need.*

social needs See *social motives.*

social prejudice A hostile attitude toward some social group. See *prejudice.*

social psychology A field of specialization concerned with the effects of group membership upon the behavior, attitudes, and beliefs of an individual.

social structure A general term referring to the fact that each society typically assigns ranks to its members, expects them to do certain kinds of work and to have certain attitudes (q.v.) and beliefs (q.v.).

social worker A person with advanced training in sociology who investigates the family and social background of persons with personality problems and who assists the psychotherapist by maintaining contact with a patient and his family. The social worker is often a member of a psychiatric team consisting also of psychiatrists and clinical psychologists.

socialization Learning to behave in a manner prescribed by one's family and culture (q.v.) and to adjust in relationships with other people.

society A group of individuals, as large as several countries or as small as a portion of a community, that have a distinguishable culture.

sociopathic personality A type of behavior disorder characterized by little anxiety. May take several forms: antisocial reaction (q.v.), sexual deviation, or an addiction (q.v.).

somatic system The part of the nervous system serving the sense organs and the skeletal muscles.

somesthesis The senses of the skin and of kinesthesis (q.v.)—the body sense.

somnolence A tendency to sleep all the time.

sound wave Alternating increases and decreases in pressure propagated through a medium, usually air. It may be regarded as a vibration having a certain frequency (or wavelength) and a certain intensity.

species-specific behavior Behavior (q.v.) characteristic of one species of animal, but not another. See *instinctive behavior.*

spike See *nerve impulse.*

spinal cord The part of the nervous system encased in the backbone. It is a reflex center and a pathway for impulses to and from the brain (q.v.).

spontaneous recovery An increase in the strength of an extinguished (q.v.) conditioned response after the passage of an interval of time.

standardization The establishment of uniform conditions for administering a test and interpreting test results. A large number of individuals are tested in the same way to provide norms (q.v.) with which to compare any particular test score.

standardization group The group of people on which a test is standardized. To interpret individual scores on a test, one should know the characteristics of the standardization group.

Stanford-Binet Intelligence Scale An individual test designed by L. M. Terman, based on the early work of Binet, for children and young adolescents; predicts achievement in grammar and high school.

startle pattern An extremely rapid reaction to a sudden, unexpected stimulus (e.g., a gunshot), relatively consistent from person to person. It consists, in part, of a closing of the eyes, a widening of the mouth, and a thrusting forward of the head and neck.

static senses The part of the vestibular senses responding to gravity and to position of the head. See *otolith organs.*

statistical decisions Ways of deciding whether obtained differences between experimental groups, or in correlations, are real or due to chance sampling errors. See *inferential statistics, sampling error.*

statistics A collection of techniques used in the quantitative analysis of data, and used to facilitate evaluation of the data. Also, numbers used to describe distributions and to estimate errors of measurement.

status In motivation (q.v.), a social motive; in a social structure (q.v.), a position representing differences that are important in the exchange of goods and services and in the satisfaction of needs in a society. Cf. *role.*

status needs Needs to achieve a status with respect to other people in a group. They include more specific needs, such as needs for prestige, power, and security.

stereotype A fixed set of greatly oversimplified beliefs (q.v.) that are held generally by members of a group.

stimulus Any object, energy, or energy change in the physical environment that excites a sense organ. See *sensation.*

stimulus generalization The tendency to react to stimuli that are different from, but somewhat similar to, the stimulus used as a conditioned stimulus.

stratified sampling Polling a set quota of people in categories based on census data; the most common categories are age, sex, socioeconomic status, and geographical region.

striped muscle Muscle that, under the microscope, appears to be striped. It is found in the muscles of the skeleton, such as those that move the trunk and limbs. Cf. *smooth muscle.*

structuralism An early school of psychological thought which held that all mental contents could be analyzed into mental elements through the experimental method of introspection (q.v.). Cf. *functionalism, gestalt psychology, behaviorism.*

subcortical centers Centers of the brain below the cerebral cortex.

sublimation The use of a substitute activity to gratify a frustrated motive. Freud believed, for example, that a frustrated sex drive could be partially gratified by channeling it into some aesthetic activity.

subliminal perception Perception of a stimulus or some feature of a stimulus, as measured by a response, without conscious awareness of the perception.

subvocal speech Talking that is inaudible to others, but sufficiently stimulating (kinesthetically) to oneself to permit an internal conversation. It may be one kind of implicit response involved in thinking.

successive approximations Reinforcing components of the final complex response in an effort to lead the learner to this final response. See also *shaping.*

suggestion The uncritical acceptance of an idea. Suggestion is used in psychotherapy (q.v.) to effect temporary relief of neurotic symptoms, particularly hysterical symptoms. It is also used by propagandists and advertisers to change or maintain attitudes and beliefs.

sulcus A relatively shallow crevice in the cerebral cortex. Cf. *fissure.*

survey methods Methods of collecting data by sampling a cross section of people, e.g., questioning a large number of married couples about factors in marital happiness, or conducting a public-opinion poll. Sometimes used as a rough synonym for the method of systematic observation (q.v.).

syllogism A logical form containing two premises and a conclusion. See *reasoning.*

symbol A stimulus that represents something else by reason of relationship, association, convention, etc. A symbol may be an external stimulus, e.g., a spoken word, or an internal process, e.g., an image involved in thinking. The latter may also be called a symbolic process (q.v.).

symbolic process A representative process standing for previous experience; essential in thinking.

sympathetic system A subdivision of the autonomic system (q.v.) arising in the thoracic and lumbar portions of the spinal cord. Most active in aroused states of the organism. Cf. *parasympathetic system.*

synapse The gap between two neurons.

TAT See *Thematic Apperception Test.*

taxis Innate tendencies to orient the body toward certain stimuli.

teaching machine A mechanical or electronic device which presents programmed material. See also *programmed learning.*

temperament The aspects of personality pertaining to mood, activity, general level of energy, and tempo.

temporal lobe The part of the cerebral cortex lying on the side of the head beneath the lateral fissure.

test A standardized sample of the performance of a person on a task or set of tasks.

thalamus An area in the forebrain concerned with relaying nerve impulses to the cerebral cortex.

Thematic Apperception Test (TAT) A frequently used projective method (q.v.) consisting of pictures about which a person tells stories.

theory In science, a principle or set of principles that explains a number of facts and predicts future events and outcomes of experiments.

therapy The treatment of an illness. See also *medical therapy, psychotherapy.*

theta rhythm One of the named rhythms of the EEG (q.v.); has a frequency of about 4–7 Hz and somewhat greater voltage than the alpha rhythm (q.v.).

thinking Processes that are representative of previous experience; consisting of images, minute muscle movements, language and other activities in the central nervous system. See also *image, implicit response, cognition.*

thirst A drive stemming from a physiological need for water.

thought experiment A type of experiment employed by early experimental psychologists in an attempt to discover the nature of thought. See also *imageless thought.*

threshold Generally, the level of stimulus energy which must be exceeded before a response occurs.

token economy The use of secondary reinforcers (q.v.)—money-like tokens—to reinforce behaviors in the quasi-social setting of the hospital ward. By the use of these tokens, desirable behaviors which aid therapy can be shaped (see *shaping*) and maintained. See *behavior modification.*

topographic projection (arrangement) An orderly mapping, on the brain, of the sensory, or receptor (q.v.), surface. See *point-to-point projection.*

trait An aspect of personality that is reasonably characteristic of a person and distinguishes him in some way from many other people.

transduction The process of converting one kind of energy into another kind. In sensation (q.v.), the conversion of physical energy into nerve impulses. See *generator potential.*

transfer of training More rapid learning in one situation because of previous learning in another situation (positive transfer, q.v.), or slower learning in one situation because of previous learning in another situation (negative transfer, q.v.). See also *stimulus generalization.*

transference In psychotherapy and especially psychoanalysis, the reenactment of previous relationships with people and principally of the parent-child relationship. In psychoanalysis, the therapist becomes the object of transference; the transference aids in the analysis because it permits the patient to express toward the therapist attitudes and feelings he has held toward other people.

transmitter A substance released from the presynaptic element which depolarizes (q.v.) or hyperpolarizes (q.v.) the postsynaptic element.

T score A derived standard score, obtained by multiplying the z score (q.v.) by 10 or 100 and adding 50 or 500 to the result. See also *standard score.*

T (training) groups See *encounter groups.*

two-factor theory A theory which postulates that both classical and instrumental conditioning are involved in avoidance learning (q.v.).

tympanic membrance Another name for eardrum (q.v.).

unconditioned response (UR) The response elicited by the unconditioned stimulus (US) (q.v.).

unconditioned stimulus (US) A stimulus which consistently elicits a response. See also *classical conditioning.*

unconscious motivation Motivation that can be inferred from a person's behavior, but the person does not realize the presence of the motive.

unconscious processes Psychological processes or events of which a person is unaware.

unique color A pure color judged not to be tinged with any other hue.

UR See *unconditioned response.*

US See *unconditioned stimulus.*

validity The extent to which a method of measurement measures what it is supposed to measure. Validity is expressed in terms of a coefficient of correlation (q.v.) representing the relationship of a set of measurements to some criterion.

variable One of the conditions measured or controlled in an experiment. See also *dependent variable, independent variable.*

variable-interval schedule A program used in instrumental learning experiments in which subjects are reinforced after an interval of time which varies around a specified average.

variable-ratio schedule A program used in instrumental learning experiments in which subjects are reinforced after a number of responses which varies around a specified average.

verbal learning Learning that involves words either as stimuli or as responses.

vestibular sense The sense of balance and movement, consisting of two groups of sense organs: the semicircular canals and the otolith organs (q.v.).

visible spectrum Those electromagnetic radiations that are visible, extending from about 380 to 780 nanometers (q.v.).

visual acuity Ability to discriminate fine differences in visual detail. It may be measured with the physician's eye chart or by more precise tests, such as the Landoit ring (q.v.) or parallel bars.

visual cliff An apparatus for measuring depth perception (q.v.) in animals and young children. Consists of two areas, a "deep" area and a "shallow" area, covered by glass. Subjects with depth perception avoid crawling out on the glass over the "deep" area.

vocational aptitude Aptitude for learning a specific vocation. For example, clerical aptitude is the ability to learn a clerical vocation.

Wechsler Adult Intelligence Scale An individual intelligence test for adults, with eleven subtests.

Wechsler Intelligence Scale for Children (WISC) An individual intelligence test for children, with several subtests.

white matter Nerve fibers covered with a white myelin sheath. The peripheral part of the spinal cord is white matter; so are several different regions of the brain. Its presence indicates tracts of nerve fibers, as distinguished from cell bodies. Cf. *gray matter*.

whole learning Learning, usually in the sense of memorizing, in which the entire learning material is studied before going through it again. Cf. *part learning*.

WISC See *Wechsler Intelligence Scale for Children*.

word association A method of testing or measuring in which a person is given a stimulus word and asked to respond with a word he associates with it.

zygote The product of the union of a sperm cell from the father and an egg cell from the mother.

Acknowledgments

In addition to the acknowledgments given in the text and the references, credit is also gratefully given to the following:

Table 1.1. Data from Cates, J. Psychology's manpower: Report on the 1968 National Register of Scientific and Technical Personnel. *American Psychologist*, 1970, 25, 254–263. Copyright 1970 by the American Psychological Association, and reproduced by permission.

Figure 1.3. From Weil, A. T., Zinberg, N. E., and Nelsen, J. M. Clinical and psychological effects of marihuana in man. *Science*, 1968, 162, 1234–1242. Copyright 1968 by the American Association for the Advancement of Science. This figure originally appeared in Mirsky, A. F., and Kornetsky, C. On the dissimilar effects of drugs on the digit symbol substitution and continuous performance tests. *Psychopharmacologia*, 1964, 5, 161-177. Copyright 1964 by Springer-Verlag. Reproduced by permission.

Figure 2.1. Modified from Tinbergen, N. *The study of instinct.* Oxford: The Clarendon Press, 1951. Reproduced by permission.

Figure 2.5. Based on data from Erlenmeyer-Kimling, L., and Jarvik, L. F. Genetics and intelligence: A review. *Science*, 1963, 142, 1477–1479.

Figure 3.6. Modified from Atkinson, J. W., and Litwin, G. H. Achievement motive and test anxiety conceived as motive to avoid failure. *Journal of Abnormal and Social Psychology*, 1960, 60, 52–63. Copyright 1960 by the American Psychological Association, and reproduced by permission.

Figure 4.2. From: Hess, E. H. Attitude and pupil size. *Scientific American*, 1965, 212(4), 46–54. Reproduced by permission.

Figure 4.6. Modified from Schlosberg, H. Three dimensions of emotion. *Psychological Review*, 1954, 61, 81–88. Copyright 1954 by the American Psychological Association, and reproduced by permission.

Figure 5.7. From Solomon, R. L., and Wynne, L. C. Traumatic avoidance learning: Acquisition in normal dogs. *Psychological Monographs*, 1953, 1–67 (whole no. 354). Copyright 1953 by the American Psychological Association, and reproduced by permission.

Figure 6.2 From Spielberger, C. D. The effects of manifest anxiety on the academic achievement of college students. *Mental Hygiene*, 1962, 46, 420–426. Copyright 1962 by the National Association for Mental Health.

Figure 6.5. From Bower, G., Clark, M. C., Lesgold, A. M., and Winzenz, D. Hierarchical retrieval schemes in recall of categorized word lists. *Journal of Verbal Learning and Verbal Behavior*, 1969, 8, 232–243. Copyright 1969 by Academic Press.

Figure 6.7. Modified from Underwood, B. J. Interference and forgetting. *Psychological Review*, 1957, 64, 49–60. Copyright 1957 by the American Psychological Association, and reproduced by permission.

Figure 7.1. Modified from Sperling, G. The information available in brief visual presentations. *Psychological Monographs*, 1960, 74 (whole no. 498). Copyright 1960 by the American Psychological Association, and reproduced by permission.

Table 7.1. From: Luchins, A. S. Classroom

experiments in mental set. *American Journal of Psychology*, 1946, 59, 295–298.

Figure 7.3. Modified from Bruner, J. S., Goodnow, J. J., and Austin, G. A. *A study of thinking.* New York: Wiley, 1956.

Figure 7.5. From Carroll, J. B. *Language and thought.* Englewood Cliffs, N.J.: Prentice-Hall.

Figure 8.7. From Gibson, E. J., and Walk, R. D. The "visual cliff." *Scientific American*, 1960, 202, 64–71.

Table 9.1. From Terman, L. M., and Merrill, M. A. *Stanford-Binet Intelligence Scale: Manual for the Third Revision,* Form L-M. Boston: Houghton Mifflin, 1960. Reproduced by permission of the Houghton Mifflin Company.

Table 10.1. Adapted from Norman, W. T. Toward an adequate taxonomy of personality attributes: Replicated factor structures in peer nomination personality ratings. *Journal of Abnormal and Social Psychology*, 1963, 66, 574–583. Copyright 1963 by the American Psychological Association, and reproduced by permission.

Table 10.3. Based on Heston, L. L. The genetics of schizophrenic schizoid disease. *Science*, 1970, 167, 249–255. Copyright 1970 by the American Association for the Advancement of Science.

Page 264. Quotation from Kutash, S. B. Pychoneuroses. In B. B. Wolman (Ed.), *Handbook of clinical psychology.* New York: McGraw-Hill, 1965. Reprinted by permission.

Page 267. Quotation from p. 33 of *Diagnostic and Statistical Manual of Mental Disorders.* Washington, D.C.: American Psychiatric Association, 1968.

Table 11.1. Modified from Jones, K. L., Shainberg, L. W., and Byer, C. O. *Drugs and alcohol.* New York: Harper & Row, 1969.

Figure 11.5. Modified from Ayllon, T., and Azrin, N. H. The measurement and reinforcement of behavior of psychotics. *Journal of the Experimental Analysis of Behavior*, 1965, 8, 357–383. Copyright 1965

by the Society for the Experimental Analysis of Behavior, Inc.

Table 12.2. Extracted from Karlins, S. M., Coffman, T. L., and Walters, G. On the fading of social stereotypes: Studies in three generations of college students. *Journal of Personality and Social Psychology*, 1969, 13, 1–16. Copyright 1969 by the American Psychological Association, and reproduced by permission.

Figure 12.2. Adapted from McGuire, W. J. Resistance to persuasion conferred by active and passive prior refutation of the same and alternative counterarguments. *Journal of Abnormal and Social Psychology*, 1961, 63, 326–332. Copyright 1961 by the American Psychological Association, and reproduced by permission.

Figure 12.3. From Newcomb, T. M., Turner, R. H., and Converse, P. E. *Social psychology: The study of human interaction.* New York: Holt, Rinehart, & Winston, 1965.

Figure 13.2. Adapted from Asch, S. E. Studies of independence and conformity: I. A minority of one against a unanimous majority. *Psychological Monographs*, 1956 (whole no. 416).

Figure 13.6. After Byrne, D., and Nelson, D. Attraction as a linear function of proportion of positive reinforcements. *Journal of Personality and Social Psychology*, 1965, 1, 659–663. Copyright 1965 by the American Psychological Association, and reproduced by permission.

Figure 14.4. Modified from M. Brodel in E. Gardner. *Fundamentals of Neurology*, 5th ed. Philadelphia: Saunders, 1968.

Figure 15.2. Modified from Patton, H. D. Spinal reflexes and synaptic transmission. In T. C. Ruch and H. D. Patton (Eds.), *Physiology and biophysics* (19th ed.). Philadelphia: Saunders, 1965.

Figure 15.8. Modified from MacLean, P. D. Psychosomatic disease and the "visceral brain." Recent developments bearing on the Papez theory of emotion. *Psychosomatic Medicine*, 1949, 11, 338–353.

Author Index and References

The numbers in parentheses at the end of each reference indicate the pages of this text where the works are cited. When a person is the subject of discussion in the text, his name will be found in the Subject Index.

Adamson, R. E. (1952). Functional fixedness as related to problem solving: A repetition of three experiments. *J. exp. Psychol.*, 44, 288–291. (181)

Allport, G. W. (1937). *Personality.* New York: Holt, Rinehart and Winston. (59)

Allport, G. W., and Odbert, H. S. (1936). Trait names, a psycholexical study. *Psychol. Monogr.*, 47 (whole no. 211). (237)

American Psychiatric Association (1968). *Diagnostic and statistical manual of mental disorders* (2d ed.). Washington, D.C.: Amer. Psychiat. Assn. (259, 267, 268)

Anastasi, A. (1968). *Psychological testing* (3d ed.) New York: Macmillan. (216)

Anderson, N. H. (1968). A simple model for information integration. In R. P. Abelson, E. Aronson, W. J. McGuire, T. M. Newcomb, M. J. Rosenberg, and P. H. Tannenbaum (Eds.) *Theories of cognitive consistency.* Chicago: Rand McNally. (291).

Aronson, E. (1970). Some antecedents of interpersonal attraction. In *Nebraska Symposium on motivation.* W. J. Arnold, D. Levine (Eds.) Lincoln: University of Nebraska Press. (329)

Asch, S. E. Studies of independence and conformity: A minority of one against a unanimous majority. *Psychol. Monogr.*, 70 (whole no. 416). (319, 320)

Asch, S. E. Effects of group pressure upon the modification and distortion of judgments. In E. E. Maccoby, T. M. Newcomb, and E. L. Hartley (Eds.) *Readings in social psychology* (3d ed.). New York: Holt, Rinehart and Winston. (322)

Atkinson, J. W., and Litwin, G. H. (1960). Achievement motive and test anxiety conceived as motive to approach and motive to avoid failure. *J. abnor. soc., Psychol.*, 60, 52–63. (75)

Atkinson, J. W., and Feather, N. T. (Eds.) (1966). *A theory of achievement motivation.* New York: Wiley. (74–77)

Ayllon, T. (1963) Intensive treatment of psychotic behaviour by stimulus satiation and food reinforcement. *Behav. Res. Ther.*, 1, 53–61. (281)

Ayllon, T., and Azrin, N. H. (1965). The measurement and reinforcement of behavior of psychotics. *J. exp. anal. Behav.*, 8, 357–383. (284)

Backman, C. W., and Secord, P. F. (1959). The effect of perceived liking on interpersonal attraction. *Human Relations*, 12, 379–384. (328)

Baker, C. H., and Young, P. (1960). Feedback during training and retention of motor skills. *Canad. J. Psychol.*, 14, 257–264. (143)

Bandura, A. (1969). *Principles of behavior modification.* New York: Holt, Rinehart and Winston. (262, 279)

Bandura, A., Grusec, J. E., Menlove, F. L. Vicarious extinction of avoidance behavior. *J. Pers. soc. Psychol.*, 5, 16–23. (282)

Bandura, A., Ross, D., and Ross, S. A. (1963). Imitation of film-mediated aggressive models. *J. abnor. soc. Psychol.*, 66, 3–11. (78, 249)

Bard, P. (1928). A diencephalic mechanism for the expression of rage with special reference to the sympathetic nervous system. *Amer. J. Physiol.*, 84, 490–515. (373)

Barker, R. G., and Wright, H. F. (1951). *One boy's day.* New York: Harper & Row. (19)

Bennett, E. M., and Cohen, L. R. (1959). Men and women: Personality patterns and contrasts. *Genet. Psychol. Monogr.*, 59, 101–155. (19)

Bennett, G. K., Seashore, H. G., and Wesman, A. G. (1951). *Counseling from profiles: A casebook for the Differential Aptitude Tests.* New York: Psychol. Corp. (223)

Berkowitz, L. (1968). *Roots of aggression: A re-examination of the frustration-aggression hypothesis.* New York: Atherton. (77)

Bexton, W. H., Heron, W., and Scott, T. H. (1954). Effects of decreased variation in the sensory environment. *Canad. J. Psychol.*, 8, 70–76. (67)

Bower, G., Clark, M. C., Lesgold, A. M., and Winzenz, D. (1960). Hierarchical retrieval schemes in recall of categorized word lists. *J. verb. Learn. verb. Behav.*, 8, 323–343. (152)

Braungart, R. G. (1966). SDS and YAF: Backgrounds of student political activists. Paper presented at meeting of the American Sociological Association, Miami. (299)

Brazier, M. A. B. (1959). The historical development of neurophysiology. In J. Field (Ed.), *Neurophysiology.* vol. L. Washington, D.C.: American Physiological Society. (356)

Brehm, J. W., and Cohen, A. R., (1962). *Explorations in cognitive dissonance.* New York: Wiley. (292)

Bruce, R. W. (1933). Conditions of transfer of training. *J. exp. Psychol.*, 16, 343–361. (137, 138)

Bruner, J. S., Goodnow, J. J., and Austin, G. A. (1956). *A study of thinking.* New York: Wiley. (170, 171)

Burt, C., and Howard, M. (1956). The multiple factorial theory of inheritance and its application to intelligence. *Brit. J. Statist. Psychol.*, 9, 95–131. (46)

Butler, R. A. (1954). Incentive conditions which influence visual exploration. *J. exp. Psychol.*, 48, 19–23. (67)

Byrne, D. (1969). Attitudes and attraction. In L. Berkowitz (Ed.), *Advances in experimental social psychology.*, vol. r. New York: Academic Press. (328)

Cabak, V., and Najdanvic, R. (1965). Effect of undernutrition in early life on physical and mental development. *Arch. Dis. Childhood*, 40, 532–534. (33)

Cannon, W. B. (1927). The James-Lange theory of emotions: A critical examination and an alternative theory. *Amer. J. Psychol.*, 39, 106–124. (373)

Carlson, E. R. (1956). Attitude change and attitude structure. *J. abnorm. soc. Psychol.*, 52, 256–261. (304)

Carroll, J. B. (1964). *Language and thought.*

Englewood Cliffs, N.J.: Prentice-Hall. (178)

Cates, J. (1970). Psychology's manpower: Report on the 1968 national register of scientific and technical personnel. *Amer. Psychologist*, 25, 254–263. (7)

Cofer, C. N., and Appley, M. H. (1964). *Motivation: Theory and research.* New York: Wiley. (63, 74)

Coleman, J. C. (1964). *Abnormal psychology and modern life* (3d ed.). Chicago: Scott, Foresman. (260)

Coleman, J. C. (1966). *Equality of educational opportunity.* Washington, D.C.: Government Printing Office. (316)

Corbit, J. D. (1969). Osmotic thirst: Theoretical and experimental analysis. *J. comp. physiol. Psychol.*, 67, 3–14. (65)

Cronbach, L. J. (1970). *Essentials of psychological testing* (3d ed). New York: Harper & Row. (229)

Crowne, D. P., and Marlow, D. (1964). *The approval motive: Studies in evaluative dependence.* New York: Wiley. (73)

Darley, J. M., and Latané, B. (1968). Bystander intervention in emergencies: Diffusion of responsibility. *J. Pers. soc. Psychol.*, 8, 377–383. (324)

Davis, F. C. (1932). The functional significance of imagery differences. *J. exp. Psychol.*, 15, 630–661. (168)

Davis, K. (1947). Final note on a case of extreme isolation. *Amer. J. Sociol.*, 52, 432–437. (40)

Deese, J., and Hulse, S. H. (1967). *The psychology of learning* (3d ed.). New York: McGraw-Hill. (107, 137, 145)

Dember, W. N., and Jenkins, J. J. (1970). *General psychology.* Englewood Cliffs, N.J.: Prentice-Hall. (69)

Dement, W., and Kleitman, N. (1957). Cyclic variations in EEG during sleep and their relation to eye movements, body motility, and dreaming. *EEG clin. Neurophysiol.*, 9, 673–690. (372)

Deutsch, M., and Collins, M. E. (1951). *Interracial housing: A psychological evaluation of a social experiment.* Minneapolis, Minn.: Univ. Minnesota Press. (308)

Deutsch, M., and Gerard, H. (1955). A study of normative and informational social influences upon individual judgment. *J. abnor. soc. Psychol.*, 51, 629–636. (319)

DeValois, R. L., Abramov, I., and Jacobs, G. H. (1966). Analysis of response patterns of LGN cells. *J. Opt. Soc. Amer.*, 7, 966–977. (340)

DiVesta, F. J., and Merwin, J. C. (1960). The effects of need-oriented communications on attitude change. *J. abnor. soc. Psychol.*, 60, 80–85. (304)

Dollard, J., Doob, L., Miller, N., Mowrer, O. H., and Sears, R. (1939). Frustration and aggression. New Haven, Conn.: Yale Univ. Press. (78)

Dollard, J., and Miller, N. E. (1950). *Personality and psychotherapy.* New York: McGraw-Hill. (17, 278)

Droba, D. D. (1930). *A scale for measuring attitude toward war.* Chicago: Univ. Chicago Press. (293)

Engen, T., Levy, N., and Schlosberg, H. (1958). The dimensional analysis of a new series of facial expressions. *J. exp. Psychol.*, 55, 455–458. (95)

Erlenmeyer-Kimling, L., and Jarvik, L. F. (1963). Genetics and intelligence: A review. *Science*, 142, 1477–1479. (49)

Ferster, C. B., and Skinner, B. F. (1957). *Schedules of reinforcement.* New York: Appleton-Century-Crofts. (118)

Festinger, L. *A theory of cognitive dissonance.* New York: Harper & Row. (291)

Festinger, L., Riecken, H. W., and Schachter, S. (1956). *When prophecy fails.* Minneapolis: Univ. Minnesota Press. (19)

Festinger, L., Schachter, S., and Back, K. (1950). *Social pressures in informal groups: A study of human factors in housing.* New York: Harper & Row. (326)

Fiedler, F. E. (1967). *A theory of leadership effectiveness.* New York: McGraw-Hill. (318)

Fishbein, M., and Ajzen, I. (1972) Attitudes and opinions. In P. H. Mussen and M. R. Rosenzweig (Eds.), *Annual Review of Psychology*, vol. 23. Palo Alto, Calif.: Annual Reviews. (290, 291)

Fisher, A. E. (1956). Maternal and sexual behavior induced by intracranial chemical stimulation. *Science*, 124, 228–229. (376)

Flacks, R. (1967). The liberated generation: An explanation of the roots of protest. *J. soc. Issues*, 23, 52–75. (299)

Freedman, J. L., and Fraser, S. C. (1966). Compliance without pressure: The foot-in-the-door technique. *J. Pers. soc. Psychol.*, 4, 195–202. (322)

Gardner, E. (1968). *Fundamentals of neurology* (5th ed.). Philadelphia: Saunders. (343)

Gardner, R. A., and Gardner, B. T. (1969). Teaching sign language to a chimpanzee. *Science*, 165, 664–672. (40)

Gerard, R. W. (1941). *The body functions.* New York: Wiley. (350)

Gesell, A., and Thompson, H. (1929). Learning and growth in identical infant twins: An experimental study by the method of co-twin control. *Genet. Psychol. Monogr.*, 6, 1–124. (38)

Getzels, J. W., and Jackson, P. W. (1962). *Creativity and intelligence.* New York: Wiley. (224)

Gibson, E. J., and Walk, R. D. (1960). The "visual cliff." *Sci. Amer.*, 202(4), 64–71. (202)

Gilbert, G. M. (1951). Stereotype persistence and change among college studies. *J. abnor. soc. Psychol.*, 46, 245–254. (297)

Glaser, R. (1971). *The nature of reinforcement.* New York: Academic Press. (123)

Haber, R. N. (1969). Eidetic images. *Sci. Amer.*, 220(4), 36–44. (167)

Hall, C. S. (1938). The inheritance of emotionality. *Sigma Xi Quart.*, 26, 17–27. (47)

Harding, J., Proshansky, H., Kutner, B., and Chein, I. (1969). Prejudice and ethnic relations. In G. Lindzey and E. Aronson (Eds.), *Handbook of social psychology* (2d ed.), vol. VII. Reading, Mass.: Addison-Wesley. (296)

Harlow, H. F. (1949). The formation of learning sets. *Psychol. Rev.*, 56, 61–65.

Harlow, H. F. (1958). The nature of love. *Amer. Psychol.*, 13, 673–685. (70, 71)

Harlow, H. F. (1962). The heterosexual affectional system in monkeys. *Amer. Psychol.*, 17, 1–9. (51)

Harlow, H. F., and McClearn, G. E. (1954). Object discrimination learned by monkeys on the basis of manipulation motives. *J. comp. physiol. Psychol.*, 47, 73–76. (69)

Hartshorne, H., and May, M. A. (1928). *Studies in the nature of character.* Vol. I. *Studies in deceit.* New York: Macmillan. (240)

Hayes, K. H., and Hayes, C. (1951). The intellectual development of a home-raised chimpanzee. *Proc. Amer. phil. Soc.*, 95, 105–109. (39)

Heath, R. G., and Mickle, W. A. (1960). Evaluation of seven years' experience with depth electrode studies in human patients. In E. R. Ramey and D. S. O'Doherty (Eds.), *Electrical studies on the unanesthetized brain.* New York: Paul B. Hoeber. (375)

Hebb, D. O. (1955). Drives and the C. N. S. (Conceptual nervous system). *Psychol. Rev.*, 62, 243–254. (87)

Helson, H. (1964). Current trends and issues in *adaptation-level* theory. *Amer. Psychol.*, 19, 26–38. (337)

Heron, W., Doane, B. K., and Scott, T. H. (1956). Visual disturbance after prolonged perceptual isolation. *Cand. J. Psychol.*, 10, 13–16. (200)

Hess, E. H. (1965). Attitude and pupil size. *Sci. Amer.*, 212(4), 46–54. (84)

Hess, E. H., and Polt, J. M. (1960). Pupil size as related to interest value of visual stimuli. *Science*, 132, 349–350. (84)

Heston, L. L. (1970). The genetics of schizophrenic and schizoid disease. *Science*, 167, 249–256. (245)

Hill, W. F. (1956). Activity as an autonomous drive. *J. comp. physiol. Psychol.*, 49, 15–19. (68)

Hovland, C. I. (1938). Experimental studies in rote-learning theory. III. Distribution of practice with varying speeds of syllable presentation. *J. exp. Psychol.*, 23, 172–190. (142)

Hovland, C. I. (1951). Human learning and retention. In S. S. Stevens (Ed.), *Handbook of experimental psychology.* New York: Wiley. (158)

Hull, C. L. (1920). Quantitative aspects of the evolution of concepts. *Psychol. Monogr.*, 28 (whole no. 123). (174)

Humphreys, L. G. (1971). Theory of intelligence. In R. Cancro (Ed.), *Intelligence: Genetic and environmental influences.* New York: Grune & Stratton.

Hunt, J. McV. (1969). Has compensatory education failed? Has it been attempted? *Harvard Educ. Rev.*, 39, 278–300.

Hunt, J. McV., and Kirk, G. E. (1971). Social aspects of intelligence: Evidence and issues. In R. Cancro (Ed.), *Intelligence: Genetic and environmental influences.* New York: Grune & Stratton. (50)

Jacobson, L. E. (1932). The electrophysiology of mental activities. *Amer. J. Psychol.*, 44, 677–694. (168)

Jasper, H. H. (1941). Electroencephalography. In W. Penfield and T. Erickson (Eds.), *Epilepsy and cerebral localization.* Springfield, Ill.: Charles C Thomas. (371)

Jenkins, J. G., and Dallenbach, K. M. (1924). Oblivescence during sleep and waking. *Amer. J. Psychol.*, 35, 605–612. (161)

Jenkins, J. J., Russell, W. A., and Suci, G. J. (1958). An Atlas of semantic profiles for 360 words. *Amer. J. Psychol.*, 35, 605–612. (178)

Jennings, M. K., and Niemi, R. G. (1968). The transmission of political values from parent to child. *Amer. polit. Sci. Rev.*, 62, 169–184. (295)

Jensen, A. R. (1969) How much can we boost IQ and scholastic achievement? *Harvard Educ. Rev.*, 39, 1–123. (52)

Jersild, A. T., Markey, F. V., and Jersild, C. L. (1933). Children's fears, dreams, wishes, daydreams, likes, dislikes, pleasant and unpleasant memories. *Child Develop. Monogr.*, no. 12. (89)

Jones, K. L., Shainberg, L. W., and Byer, C. O. (1969). *Drugs and alcohol.* New York: Harper & Row. (274)

Jost, H., and Sontag, L. W. (1944). The genetic factor in autonomic nervous system function. *Psychosom. Med.*, 6, 308–310. (48)

Kagan, J. (1969). Inadequate evidence and illogical conclusions. *Harvard Educ. Rev.*, 39, 274–277. (52)

Kagan, J., and Berkun, M. (1954). The reward value of running activity. *J. comp. physiol. Psychol.*, 47, 108. (68)

Kallmann, F. J. (1951). Twin studies in relation to adjustive problems of man.

Trans. N. Y. Acad. Sci., 13, 270–275. (266)

Karlins, M., Coffman, T. L., and Walters, G. (1969). On the fading of social stereotypes: Studies in three generations of college students. *J. Pers. soc. Psychol.*, 13, 1–16. (297, 298)

Katz, D., and Braly, K. (1933). Racial stereotypes of one hundred college students. *J. abnorm. soc. Psychol.*, 28, 280–290. (297)

Kellogg, W. N., and Kellogg, .L. A. (1933). *The ape and the child.* New York: McGraw-Hill. (39)

Kennedy, J. L. (1939). A methodological review of extrasensory perception. *Psychol. Bull.*, 36, 59–103. (204)

Kerckhoff, A. C., and Davis, K. E. (1962). Value consensus and need complementarity in mate selection. *Amer. sociol. Rev.*, 27, 295–303. (327)

Kimble, G. A., and Garmezy, N. (1968). *Principles of general psychology* (3d ed.). New York: Ronald. (102)

King, F. A. (1958). Effects of septal and amygdaloid lesions on emotional behavior and conditioned emotional responses in the rat. *J. nerv. ment. Dis.*, 126, 57–63. (52)

Kisker, G. W. (1964). *The disorganized personality.* New York: McGraw-Hill. (273)

Kitt, A., and Gleicher, D. B. (1950). Determinants of voting behavior: A progress report on the Elmira election study. *Publ. Opin. Quart.*, 14, 393–412. (301)

Kline, L. W., and Johannsen, D. E. (1935). Comparative role of the face and of the face-body-hands as aids in identifying emotions. *J. abnorm. soc. Psychol.*, 29, 415–426. (96)

Klüver, H., and Bucy, P. C. (1937). "Psychic blindness" and other symptoms following bilateral temporal lobectomy in rhesus monkeys. *Amer. J. Physiol.*, 119, 352–353. (378)

Kohler, I. (1964). The formation and transformation of the perceptual world (trans. H. Fiss). *Psychological Issues*, 3, monograph 12. (200)

Krech, D., Crutchfield, R. S., and Livson, N. (1969). *Elements of psychology* (2d ed.). New York: Knopf.

Krueger, W. C. F. (1929). The effect of overlearning on retention. *J. exp. Psychol.*, 12, 71–78. (158)

Kutash, S. B. (1965). Psychoneuroses. In B. B. Wolman (Ed.), *Handbook of clinical psychology.* New York: McGraw-Hill. (264)

Lambert, W. W., Solomon, R. L., and Watson, P. D. (1949). Reinforcement and extinction as factors in size estimation. *J. exp. Psychol.*, 39, 637–641. (201)

Leonard, W. E. (1927). *The locomotive god.* New York: Appleton-Century-Crofts. (103, 261)

Lowell, E. L. (1952). The effect of need for achievement on learning and speed of performance. *J. Psychol.*, 33, 31–40. (74)

Luchins, A. S. (1946). Classroom experiments on mental set. *Amer. J. Psychol.*, 59, 295–298. (181)

McCarthy, D. A. (1946). Language development in children. In L. Carmichael (Ed.), *Manual of child psychology.* New York: Wiley. (130)

McConnell, R. A. (1966). ESP research at three levels of method. *J. Parapsychol.*, 30, 195–207. (204)

McGeoch, J. A., and Irion, A. L. (1952). *The psychology of human learning* (2d ed.) New York: Longmans. (102, 159)

McGrath, J. E. (1964). *Social psychology: A brief introduction.* New York: Holt, Rinehart and Winston. (315)

McGuire, W. J. (1961). Resistance to persuasion conferred by active and passive prior refutation of the same and alternative counterarguments. *J. abnorm. soc. Psychol.*, 63, 325–332. (305, 306)

McGuire, W. J. (1968). The nature of attitudes and attitude change. In. G. Lindzey and E. Aronson (Eds.), *The handbook of social psychology.* (2d ed.), vol. III. Reading, Mass.: Addison-Wesley. (304, 305)

McNemar, Q. (1942). *The revision of the Stanford-Binet scale.* Boston: Houghton Mifflin. (46)

MacLean, P. D. (1949). Psychosomatic disease and the "visceral brain." Recent development bearing on the Papez theory of emotion. *Psychosom. Med.*, 11, 338–353. (367)

Mandler, G. (1967). Organization and memory. In K. W. Spence and J. T. Spence (Eds.), *The psychology of learning and motivation.* New York: Academic. (150)

Maslow, A. H. (1968). *Toward a psychology of being* (2d ed.) Princeton, N.J.: Van Nostrand. (69)

Masserman, J. H. (1961). *Principles of dynamic psychiatry.* (2d ed.) Philadelphia: Saunders. (262)

Max, L. W. (1937). Experimental study of the motor theory of consciousness. IV. Action-current responses in the deaf during awakening, kinesthetic imagery and abstract thinking. *J. comp. Psychol.*, 24, 301–344. (168)

Middleton, R., and Putney, S. (1964). Influences on the political beliefs of American college students: A study of self-appraisals. *Il Politico*, 29, 484–492. (298)

Miller, G. A. (1956). Human memory and the storage of information. *IRE Trans. Inform. Theory*, IT-2, 129–137. (160)

Miller, N. E. (1948). Studies of fear as an acquirable drive. I. Fear as motivation and fear-reduction as reinforcement in the learning of new responses. *J. exp. Psychol.*, 38, 89–101. (58)

Milner, B. (1964). Some effects of frontal lobectomy in man. In J. M. Warren and K. Akert (Eds.), *The frontal granular cortex and behavior.* New York: McGraw-Hill. (379)

Mischel, W. (1968). *Personality and assessment.* New York: Wiley. (238, 239, 243, 259, 276)

Mishkin, M., and Pribram, K. H. (1956) Analysis of the effects of frontal lesions in monkey: II. Variations of delayed response. *J. comp. physiol. Psychol.*, 49, 36–40. (379)

Morgan, C. T. (1965). *Physiological psychology* (3d ed.). New York: McGraw-Hill. (64)

Morgan, C. T., and Deese, J. (1969). *How to study* (rev. ed.), New York: McGraw-Hill. (141, 144)

Morphett, M. V., and Washburn, C. (1931). When should children begin to read? *Elem. Sch. J.*, 31, 496–503. (2, 20, 40)

Murphy, G. (1967). Introductory aspects of modern parapsychological research. *Trans. N.Y. Acad. Sci.*, 30, 256–260. (204)

Murray, H. A. (1938). *Explorations in personality.* New York: Oxford University Press. (233, 241, 242)

Murray, H. A. (1943). *Thematic apperception test.* Cambridge, Mass.: Harvard Univ. Press. (234)

Newcomb, T. M. (1963). Persistence and regression of changed attitudes: Long-range studies. *J. soc. issues*, 19, 3–14. (297)

Newman, H. H., Freeman, F. N., and Holzinger, K. J. (1937). *Twins: A study of heredity and environment.* Chicago: Univer. Chicago Press. (46)

Noble, C.E. (1952) An analysis of meaning. *Psychol. Rev.*, 59, 421–430(a). (149)

Noble, C.E. (1952). The role of stimulus meaning (*m*) in serial verbal learning. *J. exp. Psychol.*, 43, 437–466(b). (149)

Norman, W. T. (1963) Toward an adequate taxonomy of personality attributes: Replicated factor structures in peer nomination personality ratings. *J. abnor. soc. Psychol.*, 66, 574–583. (239)

Olds, J. and Milner, P. (1954). Positive reinforcement produced by electrical stimulation of septal area and other regions of rat brain. *J. comp. physiol. Psychol.*, 47, 419–427. (374)

Osgood, C. E., Suci, G. J., and Tannenbaum, P. H. (1957). *The measurement of meaning.* Urbana, Ill.: Univer. Illinois Press. (177)

Passini, F. T., and Norman, W. T. (1966). A universal conception of structure? *J. Pers. soc. Psychol.*, 4, 44–49. (239)

Pavlov, I. P. *Conditioned reflexes* (trans. G. V. Anrep). London: Oxford Univer. Press. (60, 101).

Pavlov, I. P. *Lectures on conditioned reflexes*

(trans. W. H. Gantt). New York: International. (101)

Pavlov, I. P. (1960). *Conditioned reflexes.* New York: Dover. A reprint of Pavlov, I. P., *Conditioned reflexes* (trans. G. V. Anrep). London: Oxford Univer. Press, 1927. (101)

Penfield, W., and Rasmussen, T. (1950). *The cerebral cortex of man.* New York: Macmillan. (370)

Postman, L. (1962). Retention as a function of degree of overlearning. *Science*, 135, 666–667. (158)

Premack, D. (1970). The education of S*A*R*A*H. *Psychology Today*, 4, 54–58. (40)

Pribram, K. H. (1969). The amnestic syndromes: Disturbances in coding? In G. A. Talland and N. C. Waugh (Eds.), *The pathology of memory.* New York: Academic. Pp. 127–157. (378)

Rabinovitch,, M. S., and Rosvold, H. E. (1951). A closed-field intelligence test for rats. *Cand. J. Psychol.*, 5, 122–128. (45)

Ranson, S. W., and Clark, S. L. (1959). *The anatomy of the nervous system: Its development and function* (10th ed.). Philadelphia: Saunders. (363)

Raymond, M. J. (1956). Case of fetishism treated by aversion therapy. *Brit. med. J.*, 2, 854–857. (280)

Roethlisberger, F. J., and Dickson, W. J. (1939) *Management and the worker.* Cambridge, Mass.: Harvard Univer. Press. (25)

Rogers, C. R. (1951) *On becoming a person: A therapist's view of psychotherapy.* Boston: Houghton Mifflin. (279)

Rosenblatt, J. S. (1967). Nonhormonal basis of maternal behavior in the rat. *Science*, 156, 1512–1514. (66)

Rosenthal, D., and Kety, S. S. (Eds.) (1968). *The transmission of schizophrenia.* New York: Pergamon. (246)

Rosenthal, R. (1964). Experimenter outcome-orientation and the results of the psychological experiment. *Psychol. Bull.*, 61, 405–412. (26)

Rozin, P. (1967). Specific aversions as a component of specific hunger. *J. comp. physiol. Psychol.*, 64, 237–242. (64)

Ruch, T. C., and Patton, H. D. (Eds.) (1965). *Physiology and biophysics* (19th ed.) Philadelphia: Saunders. (358)

Sawrey, W., and Weiss, J. D. (1956). An experimental method of producing gastric ulcers. *J. comp. physiol. Psychol.*, 49, 269–270. (85)

Schachter, S. (1959). *The psychology of affiliation: Experimental studies of the sources of gregariousness.* Stanford, Calif.: Stanford Univer. Press. (72)

Schachter, S. (1971). *Emotion, obesity, and crime.* New York: Academic. (65, 93, 376)

Schachter, S., and Singer J. (1962) Cognitive, social and physiological determinants of emotional state. *Psych. Rev.*, 69, 379–399. (93)

Schein, E. H., with Schnier, I. and Barker, G. H. (1961). *Coercive persuasion: A sociopsychological analysis of the "brainwashing" of American prisoners by the Chinese communists.* New York: Norton. (301)

Schlosberg, H. (1954). Three dimensions of emotion. *Psychol. Rev.*, 61, 81–88. (86, 95)

Sears, D. O. (1969). Political behavior. In G. Lindzey and E. Aronson (Eds.) *Handbook of social psychology* (2d ed.), vol. VII. Reading, Mass.: Addison-Wesley. (296)

Seevers, M. H. (1962). Medical perspectives on habituation and addiction. *J. Amer. med. Assoc.*, 181, no. 2, 92–98. (274)

Sells, S. B. (1936). The atmosphere effect: An experimental study of reasoning. *Arch Psychol.*, 29 (whole no. 200). (185)

Sem-Jacobsen, C. G., and Torkildsen, A. (1960). In E. R. Ramy and D. S. O'Doherty (Eds.), *Electrical studies on the unanaesthetized brain.* New York: Hoeber-Harper. (375)

Shaw, M. E. (1955). A comparison of two types of leadership in various communication nets. *J. abnorm soc. Psychol.*, 50, 127–134. (317)

Shaw, M. E., and Wright, J. M. (1967). *Scales for the measurement of attitudes.* New York: McGraw-Hill. (293, 294)

Shirley, M. M. (1931). *The first two years: A study of twenty-five babies.* Vol. 1. *Postural and locomotor development.* Minneapolis: Univer. Minnesota Press. (38)

Skinner, B. F. (1938) *The behavior of organisms.* New York: Appleton-Century-Crofts. (107)

Skodak, M., and Skeels, H. M. (1949). A final follow-up of one hundred adopted children. *J. genet. Psychol.*, 75, 3–19. (299)

Smith, S. M., Brown, H. D., Toman, J. E. P., and Goodman, L. S. (1947). The lack of cerebral effects of d-tubocurarine. *Anasthesiol.*, 8, 1014. (168)

Solomon, R. L. (1964). Punishment. *Amer. Psychol.*, 19, 239–253. (111, 123, 126)

Solomon, R. L., and Wynne, L. C. (1953). Traumatic avoidance learning: Acquisition in normal dogs. *Psychol. Monogr.* 67 (whole no. 354). (109, 110)

Sperling, G. (1960). The information available in brief visual presentations. *Psychol. Monogr.* 74, (whole no. 498). (166)

Spielberger, C. D. (1962) The effects of manifest anxiety on the academic achievement of college students. *Ment. Hyg.*, 46, 420–426. (136)

Stone, C. P. (1932) Wildness and savageness in rats of different strains. In K. S. Lashley (Ed.), *Studies in the dynamics of behavior.* Chicago: Univ. Chicago Press. Pp. 3–55. (47)

Stratton, G. M. (1897). Vision without inversion of the retinal image. *Psychol. Rev.*, 4, 341–360; 463–481. (199)

Teitelbaum, P. (1961) Disturbances in feeding and drinking behavior after hypothalamic lesions. In M. R. Jones (Ed.), *Nebraska Symposium on motivation.* Lincoln, Neb.: Univer. of Nebraska Press. (375)

Teitelbaum, P., and Epstein, A. N. (1962). The lateral hypothalamic syndrome: Recovery of feeding and drinking after later hypothalamic lesions. Psychol. Rev., 69, 74–90. (64)

Telford, C. W., and Sawry, J. M. (1967). *The exceptional individual: Psychological and educational aspects.* Englewood Cliffs, N.J.: Prentice-Hall. (32)

Terman, L. M., and Merrill, M. A. (1960). *Stanford-Binet intelligence scale: Manual for the third revision form.* Boston: Houghton Mifflin. (217)

Terman, L. M., and Oden, M. H. (1959). *Genetic studies of genius.* Vol. V. *The gifted group at midlife.* Stanford, Calif.: Stanford Univer. Press. (226, 246)

Teuber, H.-L. Perception. In J. Field, et al. (Eds.), *Handbook of physiology.* Vol. 3. Washington, D.C.: Americal Physiological Society. Pp. 1595–1668. (196)

Teuber, H.-L., Battersby, W. S., and Bender, M. D. (1960). *Visual field defects after penetrating missile wounds of the brain.* Cambridge, Mass.: Harvard Univer. Press. (379)

Thigpen, C. H., and Cleckley, H. M. (1957). *The three faces of Eve.* New York: McGraw-Hill. (264)

Thompson, R. F. *Foundations of physiological psychology.* New York: Harper & Row. (373)

Thompson, W. R. (1954). The inheritance and development of intelligence. *Proc. Assoc. Res. nerv. ment. Dis.*, 33, 209–231. (44)

Thompson, W. R., and Melzack, R. (1956). Early development. *Sci. Amer.*, 194(1), 38–42. (51)

Thurstone, L. L., and Thurstone, T. G. (1941). Factorial studies of intelligence. *Psychometr. Monogr.*, (whole no. 2). (223)

Tinbergen, N. (1951) *The study of instinct.* Oxford: Clarendon Press. (37)

Traux, C. B., and Carkhuff, R. R. (1965). Experimental manipulation of therapeutic conditions. *J. consult. Psychol.*, 29, 119–124. (279)

Underwood, B. J. (1957). Interference and forgetting. *Psychol. Rev.*, 64, 49–60. (151, 160, 162)

Underwood, B. J. (1961). Ten years of massed practice on distributed practice. *Psychol. Rev.*, 68, 229–247. (142)

Underwood, B. J. (1964). The representativeness of rote verbal learning. In A. W. Melton (Ed.), *Categories of human learning.* New York: Academic. Pp. 48–78. (a) (150, 151)

Underwood, B. J. (1964). Forgetting. *Sci. Amer.*, 210(3), 91–99. (b) (157)

Wallach, H. (1963). The perception of neutral colors. *Sci. Amer.*, 208(1), 107–118. (192)

Wallas, G. (1926). *The art of thought.* New York: Harcourt, Brace & World. (179)

Walls, G. L. (1942). *The vertebrate eye.* Bloomfield Hills, Mich.: Cranbrook Institute of Science. (338)

Walster, E. (1966). Assignment of responsibility for an accident. *J. of Pers. soc. Psychol.*, 3, 73–79. (327)

Warden, C. J. (1931). *Animal motivation studies. The albino rat.* New York: Columbia Univer. Press. (62)

Watson, J. B., and Rayner, R. (1920). Conditioned emotional reactions. *J. Exp. Psychol.*, 3, 1–14. (103, 104)

Wechsler, D. (1958). *Measurement and appraisal of adult intelligence* (4th ed.). Baltimore: Williams & Wilkins. (219)

Weil, A. T., Zinberg, N. E., and Nelson, J. M. (1968). Clinical and psychological effects of marihuana in man. *Science*, 162, 1234–1242. (23)

Werner, H., and Kaplan, E. (1950). Development of word meaning through verbal context: An experimental study. *J. Psychol.*, 29, 251–257. (173)

White, R. W. (1959). Motivation reconsidered: The concept of competence. *Psychol. Rev.*, 66, 297–333. (69)

White, R. W. (1964). *The abnormal personality.* (3d ed.) New York: Ronald. (266)

Wilkins, L., and Richter, C. P. (1940). A great craving for salt by a child with cortico-adrenal insufficiency. *J. Amer. med.Assoc.*, 114, 866–868. (56)

Wolfe, J. B. (1936). Effectiveness of token rewards for chimpanzees. *Comp. Psychol. Monogr.*, 12 (whole no. 60). (58)

Wolman, B. B. (Ed.) (1965). *Handbook of clinical psychology.* New York: McGraw-Hill. (268)

Wolpe, J., and Lazarus, A. A. (1966). *Behavior therapy techniques: A guide to the treatment of neuroses.* Oxford: Pergamon Press. (28).

Zimbardo, P. G. (1970). The human choice: Individuation, reason, and order versus deindividuation. In W. J. Arnold and D. Levine (Eds.), *Nebraska symposium on motivation.* Lincoln, Nebr.: Univer. of Nebraska Press. (323)

Zubek, J. P. (1969). *Sensory deprivation: Fifteen years of research.* New York: Appleton-Century-Crofts. (200)

412

Subject Index